THE GREAT HISTORIES

A series under the general editorship of

Hugh R. Trevor-Roper,

REGIUS PROFESSOR OF MODERN HISTORY, OXFORD UNIVERSITY

THE CONQUEST OF MEXICO
THE CONQUEST OF PERU
and
Other Selections

THE GREAT HISTORIES *Series*

HERODOTUS, *edited by W. G. Forrest.*

THUCYDIDES, *edited by P. A. Brunt.*

POLYBIUS, *edited by E. Badian.*

JOSEPHUS, *edited by Moses I. Finley.*

TACITUS, *edited by Hugh Lloyd-Jones.*

PROCOPIUS, *edited by Mrs. Averil Cameron.*

BEDE, *edited by James Campbell.*

AMMIANUS MARCELLINUS, *edited by Geoffrey de Ste. Croix.*

MACHIAVELLI, *edited by Myron P. Gilmore.*

GUICCIARDINI, *edited by J. R. Hale.*

SARPI, *edited by Peter Burke.*

VOLTAIRE, *edited by J. H. Brumfitt.*

GIBBON, *edited by Hugh R. Trevor-Roper.*

PRESCOTT, *edited by Roger Howell.*

MACAULAY, *edited by Hugh R. Trevor-Roper.*

BURCKHARDT, *edited by Alexander Dru.*

HENRY ADAMS, *edited by E. N. Saveth.*

PRESCOTT

THE CONQUEST OF MEXICO
THE CONQUEST OF PERU
and Other Selections

Edited, Abridged, and with an Introduction by

ROGER HOWELL

Assistant Professor of History
Bowdoin College

TWAYNE PUBLISHERS, INC.
31 Union Square, N. Y. 3

 This Twayne Publishers edition
is published by special arrangement with
Washington Square Press, Inc.

Library of Congress Catalog Card Number: 66-12300

Grateful acknowledgment is made to the following publishers for permission to include certain maps which appear in this volume:

"Spain in the 15th Century" is reprinted by permission of the publishers, Houghton Mifflin Company, from *European Civilization* by Ferguson and Brunn.

"The March to Mexico, 1519" is reprinted by permission of Cooper Square Publishers from *The Rise of the Spanish Empire* by Roger Merriman.

"Inca Empire" is modified from a map which appeared in Urteaga: *El Fin de un Imperio*, and reprinted by permission of Longmans, Green & Co., Ltd. from *The Last of the Incas* by Hyams and Ordish.

Contents

Introduction

[a] AMERICAN HISTORY IN THE EARLY NINETEENTH CENTURY

In 1774 Horace Walpole wrote to Sir Horace Mann that the next Augustan Age would dawn on the American side of the Atlantic and that perhaps there would be "a Thucydides at Boston." Less than one hundred years later, another Englishman could write, "Twenty years ago we were not accustomed, as we are now, to look across the Atlantic for regular contributions of the highest class to every department of literature." In the field of historical writing, the work of William Hickling Prescott, the first American historian to win European-wide acclaim, had done as much as any other single factor to cause this reversal in judgment. Prescott may not have been exactly the American Thucydides about whom Walpole had written; nonetheless, he was widely recognized as being one of the foremost practitioners of the historical art in the nineteenth century and played a crucial role in raising international respect for American historical writing.

Serious historical study in the United States can be said to have begun with the work of Jared Sparks, whose collections of the writings of George Washington are the first major historical product of the new country. Not surprisingly, much of the significant historical work in the young republic was concerned with essentially American themes. The work of Sparks himself was typical of this concern; in addition to the volumes on Washington, he produced twelve volumes of documents illustrating the diplomatic history of the American Revolution, collected the writings of Franklin and Gouverneur Morris, and was a guiding spirit behind the *Library of American Biography.* which contained some sixty lives of persons active in the history of North

America. This sort of nationally oriented history came to maturity in the writings of Prescott's contemporary George Bancroft (1800-1891), who wrote a long, detailed account of the emergence of the United States, and in the work of John G. Palfrey. The latter wrote a *History of New England* up to the time of the Revolution, but his enthusiasm for the colonists led him to be something less than critical.

At the same time that Bancroft was turning his attention to American history, some pioneer American historians began to deal with European subjects other than the English background to American history. Washington Irving is not now thought of primarily as a historian but as a man of letters, yet his contribution to historical writing in the United States was of great significance. The distinction between the man of letters and the historian is, moreover, for the early nineteenth century, a misleading one. Each of the four great American romantic historians who were to emerge in this period (Prescott, Bancroft, Motley, Parkman) could easily be classed as a man of letters as well and would have welcomed the appellation, for to all of them the writing of history was closely involved with the narrative and literary art.

The contribution of Irving to the widening of the historical perspective of American writers is especially interesting in connection with Prescott, since Irving began the exploration of the Spanish theme to which Prescott was to devote his scholarly life. It should not be thought that this widening of interest on the part of Irving and other Americans was an isolated phenomenon; it was part of the general growth of interest in historical studies characteristic of the whole Western world in this period. Yet the early nineteenth century was peculiarly ripe for the opening of Spanish studies. When, in the eighteenth century, the Scottish historian Robertson had written on Charles V and other aspects of Spanish history, he had been denied access to important documentary collections; now, in the nineteenth century, Spain was becoming aware of the historical significance of its manuscript treasures. At the Royal

Academy of History in Madrid were collected the documentary materials of the cosmographer of the Indies, Juan Bautista Muñoz, and the president of the Academy, Martin Fernández de Navarrete, had been drawing together and editing the records of Spanish overseas discovery. Within Prescott's own lifetime, the archives of Simancas would be opened, a storehouse of information which Prescott was able to use with great profit as the result of the labors of a friend, the Spanish scholar Pascual de Gayangos.

Moreover, the temper of the times leaned toward an interest in Spain. This was true not only in the sphere of politics, where Wellington's campaigns in the Peninsular had forced the area into public notice, but also in the realm of letters, where the English poets (notably Southey, who published a translation of the sixteenth-century Spanish romance of chivalry, *Amadis of Gaul*) had displayed interest. It was equally true in the field of scholarship. In the last category lies the closest and most crucial tie to Prescott himself. One of his closest friends from his school days on had been George Ticknor. Ticknor, like many young American intellectuals, had migrated to Germany to complete his studies and at Göttingen had been plunged into an active center of Spanish studies. Following this, he had been tutored at Madrid by the noted Spanish scholar Conde, author of a history of the Arabs in Spain. Ticknor had returned to Harvard to take a position there as the foremost scholar in the New World on the subject of Spanish literature.

It was thus into a well-prepared and receptive world that Irving launched his *Life of Columbus* in 1826. Based closely on the collections made by Navarrete, supplemented by original research in sources at Madrid and Seville, it was the first modern account of Columbus which could be called scholarly, and despite its shortcomings it marked a crucial stage in the development of American historical writing. The next year, Irving followed this account with a *Chronicle of the Conquest of Granada*. Irving regarded this as his best work, yet in a historical sense it represented something of a retreat since it contained deliberately imaginative elements much as his history of the Dutch in America had done. But the rich pattern of Spanish history was being presented to a wider and wider public. Irving will never be classed as a great historian; in terms of historical writing it is probably fortunate that he abandoned his plans to write on the conquest of Mexico in favor of Prescott, for he never had the rigorous and scholarly application to research which would be necessary if American historical writing was to be able to stand securely on its own feet. But he opened a field, and Prescott himself acknowledged the respect due him when he commented in a letter to Irving, "There are few persons among us who have paid much attention to these studies, and no one here or elsewhere is familiar as yourself with the track of Spanish adventure in the New World and so well qualified to give advice to a comparatively raw hand." The respect may seem even greater when one remembers that the "comparatively raw hand" of Prescott had already published *Ferdinand and Isabella* when he wrote those words.

Several factors, then, were crucial to the emergence of Prescott as the first American historian to gain international recognition and respect. American historical writing was already working toward significant results and competent scholarship in the person of Bancroft. The romantic movement was to offer it a vital leaven. The opening of interest in Spain and the consequent opening of Spanish sources to the inquiring historian had begun. In Ticknor, Prescott had as his closest friend the most notable Hispanic scholar in North America. One further feature of the scene needs, however, to be noted. That is the active intellectual life of Boston and Cambridge, the broadening scholarly and literary interests of the community which surrounded Prescott.

How should one identify the spirit of that community and that age? It is not an easy question to answer. The formative middle years, as they have often been called, were a period marked by ferment. It is an age which can be and has been described in a multitude of catchphrases. It is the age of rising American nationalism, of the flowering of New England, of awkward adolescence. Whatever the spirit of the age was, it encompassed growth and change; it was an exuberant blossoming. America was moving, developing, coming into its own. Of this fact, the inhabitants of Boston and Cambridge were sure, and they were sure too that they were the center of it. Dr. Bowditch was confidently to proclaim, "We are living in the best days of the Republic." Rather more arrogantly, Emerson was to suggest a parallel between the Boston of his own age and the Florence of the Renaissance:

> What Vasari said, three hundred years ago, of the republican city of Florence might be said of Boston: "that the desire for glory and honour is powerfully generated by the air of that place, in the men of every profession; whereby all who possess talent are impelled to struggle that they may not remain in the same grade with those whom they perceive to be only men like themselves, even though they may acknowledge such indeed to be masters, but all labour by every means to be foremost."

A more apt comparison than Florence was, however, even closer to hand, as Van Wyck Brooks has suggested; that was Edinburgh, the Edinburgh of the *Review* and the Waverly Novels. For Boston too was to develop its own review, *The North American Review,* imitative of the great British periodicals yet distinctively a product of New England. And Boston was to have its enthusiasm for Scott. This ardent following of the Scottish novelist was of extreme importance to the developing art of historical writing in the United States. Prescott was to trace his own historical origins in writers other than Scott, but he and the rest of the romantic historians were never backward in expressing their debt to him. They would all have agreed with Carlyle that Scott had taught the historian "that bygone ages of the world were actually filled with living men, not by protocols, state-papers, controversies, and abstractions of men." The advance of historical writing in this period was not simply a question of taking up the technique and theories of the professionals; it was also very much involved with breathing into the past the lively narrative characteristic of Scott's historical novels. The contrast between Sparks and the later writers is suggestive on this point; Sparks compiled an edition of letters as his first great contribution to historical writing. It was Prescott, Bancroft, Motley, and Parkman who were to give their writings the sense of local color and the atmosphere of the times in which they were dealing.

Boston, then, became the Edinburgh of the United States for at least a generation. The intellectual life became the fashion, and the impulse was there to make it an individual and independent intellectual life. Boston's ties with Europe were never broken; Henry Adams was later to comment on the propensity of the true Bostonian to kneel "in self-abasement before the majesty of English standards." The Boston intellectuals (and the historians among them) desired, indeed courted, the respect of their European counterparts—of Humboldt, Madame de Staël, above all of the British critical reviews. But they wanted that respect to come on the basis of a distinctive American contribution. They wanted to show that Boston's intellectual contributions could be weighed in the European balance and not be found wanting. In many respects it was in historical writing that they first achieved this recognition, and it was the appearance of Prescott's *Ferdinand and Isabella* that signalized it. An ironic aspect of this situation is that Prescott had not originally intended to be a professional historian, nor, in a strict sense, did he ever become one. Prescott was an enlightened amateur, a scholar without institutional affiliations, and, in his own view, no less a contributor to literature than he was to history as an academic subject.

[b] PRESCOTT'S LIFE

Prescott's own life is perhaps more admirable than exciting; it was a life whose chief feature was an unending and courageous battle against the limitations imposed by damaged eyesight. This was a battle in which Prescott had, admittedly, great personal aids. He was a member of one of the most distinguished families in Boston society. He was independently wealthy and this enabled him to hire secretaries and collect books and manuscripts on a scale which would have been beyond the reach of most. He had, moreover, received a sound although not exceptional schooling. Between 1803 and 1808 he attended school in Salem, Massachusetts; in 1808, after his family had moved to Boston, he began to attend Dr. Gardiner's school. Gardiner, the rector of Trinity Church, had been educated in England and was a sound scholar; his example was fundamental in forming the mind of the young Prescott. As Prescott's first biographer, his close friend Ticknor, commented, Prescott early displayed a fondness for books of "the higher sort." These, and indeed books of any description, were difficult to come by in the period of Prescott's youth because of commercial restrictions which had been imposed preceding the War of 1812. Prescott was fortunate enough to gain permission to read in the library of the Athenaeum, and there he spent many of his play hours in wide albeit somewhat idle reading. There can be little doubt that this reading, which probably did little to nourish his mind, contributed materially to forming his literary tastes and tendencies. Among the books which had a notable effect on him was Southey's translation of *Amadis of Gaul.* It was a work which was to plant the seeds of his interest in Spain and the *conquistadores* and their romantic, chivalric world; one might remember that it had been one of the most popular books among the Spanish soldiery of whom he was later to write. Prescott was far from being a scholar at this point; he was no infant prodigy. As Ticknor summed him up at this age, there was little to distinguish him from his contemporaries: "He was, in short, neither more nor less than a thoroughly natural, bright boy, who loved play better than work, but who could work well under sufficient inducements and penalties."

In August, 1811, Prescott was admitted to the sophomore class at Harvard. In his collegiate career, he portrayed a strange mixture of puritanical devotion to work (embodied in a set of rules drawn up to regulate his hours of study) and a taste for the high living that went with his social position. More significantly, it was at Harvard that he suffered the unfortunate accident which was to shape his life. In his junior year, he was hit directly in the left eye by a hard piece of bread thrown in the course of an undergraduate frolic in the Hall. The accident was nearly fatal; even when he recovered his strength, the eye was permanently damaged.

After leaving Harvard, Prescott commenced a career in the law as a student in his father's office. In January, 1815, he developed trouble in his other eye, and late in the year, he left Boston on a voyage of recuperation to visit his grandfather in the Azores. Recovery was far from quick; indeed, there was never to be a complete recovery. From November until February, he was forced to spend his time in a dark room in order to avoid strain on his weakened eye. In April, he went to England to take medical advice on his situation; the results were discouraging, for no solutions were found. Prescott's personal state at this time is well illustrated in a letter he wrote in that year from London. "As to the future," he said, "it is too evident I shall never be able to pursue a profession. God knows how poorly I am qualified, and how little inclined, to be a merchant. Indeed, I am sadly puzzled to think how I shall succeed even in this without eyes, and I am afraid I shall never be able to draw upon my mind to any large extent."

Yet on his return to Boston, Prescott did not become an idle parasite. His intellectual interests, never at any time neglected or negligible, began to occupy more and more of his time, and despite his fears that he would not be able to draw upon his mind, he was soon on the way to becoming a cultivated, if amateur, man of letters. As early as the winter of 1817-1818, he had submitted his first review anonymously to *The North American Review;* it had been rejected. In June of 1818, he began to attend meetings of a literary group called simply the Club; in 1820, the Club published four issues of its own journal to which Prescott contributed several relatively undistinguished pieces. But by 1820, Prescott had firmly decided on a literary career. For several years, he pursued studies in the literature of France, England, Italy, and Germany. In 1824, under the directing influence of George Ticknor, he took the crucial decision of turning to Spanish as a substitute for German. Increasingly in this period, his interests gravitated toward history, although he never abandoned his interest in literature and, in fact, at a later stage in his career contemplated writing a life of Molière. By 1826, he had resolved to write a detailed review of the history of the reigns of the Catholic rulers, Ferdinand and Isabella. In his journal for 19 January, 1826, he noted, "I subscribe to the history of the reign of Ferdinand and Isabella"; twenty-one years later he was to write against this entry a further note, "A fortunate choice."

Something of the determination with which Prescott approached the new task is indicated in a letter to Alexander Everett, the American minister in Madrid to whom Prescott wrote for aid in procuring books: "Johnson says, in his life of Milton, that no man can compile a history who is blind. But although I should lose the use of my vision altogether (an evil not in the least degree probable) by the blessing of God, if my ears are spared me, I will disprove the assertion, and my chronicle, whatever other demerits it may have, shall not be wanting in accuracy and research."

Further indications of his determination are to be found in his methods of work. Physically incapacitated as he was, Prescott had to rely much on the aid of others. Using his wealth to advantage, he built up a significant personal library; in it were included not only printed works but also transcripts of manuscript sources from a number of European archives. To amass this collection, he called on the aid of an ever-widening circle of friends and interested scholars. Acquaintances in the diplomatic service proved invaluable, and in this respect, the social position of the Prescott family was a distinct advantage. Among those who were called on to provide aid were Arthur Middleton, a classmate at Harvard who was Secretary of Legation in Madrid; Alexander Everett; Washington Irving; Edward Everett in England; G. W. Greene in Italy; Henry Wheaton in Berlin. Personal friends like Ticknor and Fanny Inglis Calderon de la Barca who had visited the locale of his histories contributed to his labors. Foreign booksellers sought out his needs; particularly helpful in this respect was Obadiah Rich. Added to this already impressive list were a number of internationally famous scholars who, appreciating the significance of his work, came to his assistance: in Spain, Fernández de Navarrete himself; in Germany, Alexander von Humboldt and Ranke; in Italy, another blind historian, the Marquis Gino Capponi; in France, Count Adolphe de Circourt; in England, Sir Thomas Phillipps and Richard Ford. Above all there was Pascual de Gayangos, a young Spanish scholar living in England, a man who has been called with justification "Prescott's most indispensable aide."

These were Prescott's foreign assistants. At home he was forced to rely on a series of secretaries who aided him in the reading and copying of materials. Composition was a physical strain to Prescott because of his weakened eyes; early in his career he began to use a noctograph, a device to enable the blind to write. Increasingly, he developed an ability to compose and retain material in his mind, to digest and alter his text mentally over a period of several days. Ticknor claimed that Prescott could keep about sixty pages in his memory for several days at a time, by this method thinking over and improving his text before he committed it to paper. In his working habits, he attempted to establish a regular pattern. He was an early riser, although this was a great effort for him. He took large amounts of physical exercise. At ten o'clock, his reader came and they worked together for three hours. At one, he took a two-mile walk. Later in the afternoon, he had his reader back with him for an additional two hours. Prescott constantly fought off temptations to idleness, often by somewhat bizarre methods such as the posting of a bond of $1,000 with his secretary James English to finish a certain portion of *Ferdinand and Isabella* within a specified time.

Despite the thoroughness with which he approached his study, Prescott kept the secret of his writing close; only a week before the appearance of *Ferdinand and Isabella* catapulted him to fame, Prescott was criticized by an elderly relative for wasting his time away and was told that it was about time he amounted to something. On Christmas, 1837, he answered that rebuke by delivering his first work to the public. When published, it excited an interest that had not been foreseen by anyone, Prescott included. As Ticknor recorded, "It was read by great numbers who seldom looked into anything so solid and serious; it was talked of by all who ever talked of books."

Prescott became a famous historian overnight. The foreign press was, on the whole, as enthusiastic as the American reviews. The one dark note was some plainly snobbish criticism on the part of Richard Ford in the *Quarterly Review;* among the "serious" objections raised by Ford was what he felt was a "tendency to sneer at monarchies, courts, chivalry, and all those nobler institutions, the lack of which . . . forms the present weakness and will eventually decide the problem of democracy now pending in the United States." Prescott was much perturbed by this since he desperately wanted to please the English reviewers. It was, however, a last expression of English criticism of American historical work as unworthy. Elsewhere, the trend of the criticism was clear; as Gayangos had put it in the *Edinburgh Review,* "Mr. Prescott's work is one of the most successful historical productions of our time." American historical writing was gaining significant respect, despite European intellectual pride.

Following the completion of *Ferdinand and Isabella,*

Prescott turned to Mexico and the conquests of Cortes. An exchange of letters with Washington Irving, who might be thought to have had prior claims on the field, cleared the way. Prescott found the composition of his new work difficult. Determined to present a picture of the Aztec civilization on the eve of the conquest, he delved into what he called the "moonshine" period of pre-Columbian history. He confided in his journal that he found Mexican antiquity "an appalling subject." He spent far more time over this portion of the work than he had wanted to, yet the final result was well worth the effort; in these introductory pages, Prescott presented the fullest account of Mexican antiquities yet to appear in English. The chief merits of the work, however, lay in its account of Cortes, and when the volume was published in 1843, it elicited praise from every quarter. Still considered his masterpiece, *The Conquest of Mexico* displayed Prescott at the height of his dramatic art. Even the *Quarterly Review* was enthusiastic this time. Prescott expressed his gratitude for this English recognition in a letter to the Rev. H. H. Milman: "I assure you the American scholar, next to his own country, looks for sympathy and countenance to his fatherland more than any other country in the world. And when he receives the expression of it from those he has been accustomed to reverence, he has obtained one of his highest rewards."

A year after the completion of *The Conquest of Mexico,* Prescott began his account of the Pizarros and Peru. Before it had appeared, he had also put together a volume of his articles from *The North American Review* under the title of *Miscellanies.* Prescott had written reviews on a regular basis for the journal (an "annual peppercorn," he termed them) as a means of forming and testing his style. He himself tended to be rather scoffing about the value of these writings: "It is impossible for one who has done that sort of work himself to have any respect for it; how can one critic look another in the face without laughing?" Nonetheless, the essays are not without interest; this is particularly true of the reviews of Irving and Bancroft, both of which contain valuable commentary on Prescott's own view of history. The year following *Miscellanies, The Conquest of Peru* came from the press, accompanied by the now usual critical acclaim.

In 1849 he began the composition of his last work, a study of the Spanish king Philip II. This work was frequently interrupted. A major break occurred when Prescott left the United States for a visit to Europe in 1850. The details of the visit need not be lingered on. Ticknor summed it up well: "His table was covered with cards and invitations. . . . He was invited everywhere. He was the lion of the season. . . . [It was] the most brilliant visit ever made to England by an American citizen not clothed with the prestige of official station." The significance of the visit for Prescott's work and for American historical writing in general was that it constituted an open recognition that both had come of age. International acclaim was heaped on Prescott as the most distinguished American contributor to the field of history: a doctorate from Oxford, membership in the French Institute as a corresponding member of the Academy of Moral and Political Science, membership in the Royal Society of Berlin. By 1857 Prescott had received four honorary degrees and had been elected to twenty-seven historical and philosophical societies.

On his return to the United States, Prescott found it difficult to resume work. Trouble with his eyes increased. But by the winter of 1852-1853 he felt once again that he was making good progress, and in 1855 the first two volumes of his *Philip II* appeared. Once again, he turned temporarily aside from his work, this time to prepare a new conclusion to Robertson's study of Charles V; Prescott's addition was to be based on materials recently uncovered in Spain. He had no wish to compete with the older work, and his attitude toward it is well shown in the letter he wrote to Ticknor when the volume appeared in 1856:

> My Charles the Fifth or rather Robertson's with my continuation, made his bow to the public today, like a strapping giant with a little urchin

> holding on to the tail of his coat. I can't say I expect much from it, as the best and biggest part is somewhat of the oldest. But people who like a complete series will need it to fill up the gap betwixt Ferdinand and Philip.

Prescott had, however, only two years to live and there were to be large gaps in *Philip II* as well. A third volume of the work did appear, but in February, 1858, Prescott suffered his first stroke of apoplexy. In January, 1859, he died. His last request was characteristic, for in imitation of the great Spanish scholar Navarrete, who had paved the way for him, he asked to be taken into his library to bid farewell to the books and manuscripts which had been his lifelong companions. It was a sentimental and very nineteenth-century sort of gesture, yet it seems oddly appropriate. Ticknor described the scene in flowery but touching terms: "There he lay in unmoved, inaccessible peace, and the lettered dead of all ages and climes and countries collected there seemed to look down upon him in their earthly immortality and claim that his name should hereafter be imperishably associated with theirs."

[c] PRESCOTT'S VIEW OF HISTORY

To Prescott, the ideal historian needed many qualifications. Impartiality was far from the least of these, yet Prescott felt that the true historian must have much more. He needed a deep understanding of the people about whom he was writing—a familiarity "not merely with their laws, constitutions, and general resources and all the other more visible parts of the machinery of government, but with the nicer moral and social relations, the informing spirit which gives life to the whole, but escapes the eye of a vulgar observer." The ideal historian, in his mind, should be able to transport himself into the past about which he was writing, "expatriating himself, as it were, from his own [time] in order to get the very form and pressure of the times he is delineating." He must be scrupulous in his attention to factual detail, yet he must also be able to mix in with these "drier details" the narrative powers of the novelist or the dramatist, outlining and boldly sketching his characters, arousing interest by dramatic contrast. Yet, as Prescott admitted, there was no such "monster" as the perfect historian.

How then did Prescott see himself in relation to this ideal? Some idea of his approach to history is revealed by what he considered to be the crucial steps in the evolution of historical writing. Prescott, it should be remembered, was not only a student of Spain and her overseas empire; the reading programs which at various points he set for himself exposed him to much of the standard and great historical writing of the past. He owed much to the reading of Greek and Roman historians: Herodotus, Thucydides, Livy, Tacitus. He was able, and willing, to use material from their works to illustrate generalizations made in connection with Spain and the New World. But he was also acutely aware that history in their time was in its formative stages. There was, he argued, a wide difference between the complexion given to history in their hands and that which it assumed in his own. What he identified as the element of poetry was to him both the special charm and the fatal flaw of ancient historical writing. The maturing of reason (which Prescott took to be an unassailable fact) had changed all, and with the development of the more modern ages, a wider scope for the historian had been opened. Scholarship in the sense of rigorous research in documentary materials now became more of a necessity; as Prescott viewed it, the historian was to become both critic and antiquarian, and he was to become even more, for with these qualities "the modern historian was to combine that of the philosopher, deducing from his mass of facts general theorems and giving to them their most extended application."

Despite the obvious attention and respect which Prescott gave to the ancients, he could assert bluntly that "the peculiar forms of historic writing, as it exists with the moderns, were not fully developed until the last century." Renaissance historiography had been, to him, a halfway point which had combined some elements of the generalizing and reflecting spirit or philosophy of the moderns with traces of the poetry of the ancients. Of the Italian historians of the period, Prescott felt that Machiavelli was the best, yet he could still be very critical of the historical writing of the Renaissance, especially of the Spaniards; and he dismissed the highly regarded Jesuit historian of Spain, Juan de Mariana, as a monk, "one of a community who have formed the most copious but in many respects the most incompetent chroniclers in the world."

The writer whom Prescott saw as the inaugurator of modern historical writing was Voltaire. Not only in the spirit of history through his "baleful, withering skepticism" but also in the matter of arrangement of materials were his effects felt. Prescott drew attention to the fact that Voltaire had arranged his material by subject rather than by strict chronology, and, although admitting that this arrangement was open to abuse, he argued that "it enabled the reader to arrive more expeditiously at the results, for which alone history is valuable, while, at the same time, it put it in the power of the writer to convey with more certainty and facility his own impressions."

The growth of philosophical history was to Prescott's mind nowhere more marked than in Great Britain. He noted in that nation's writings after the middle of the eighteenth century a combination of qualities: "erudition, critical penetration, powers of generalization and a political sagacity unrivalled in any other age or country." As keenly aware as some modern writers of the abuses that history is prone to, Prescott did recognize that unfortunately the spirit of the new forms of historical composition was too frequently made subservient to party and sectarian prejudices. He felt strongly that the historian should not pervert history to prove cases, should not act as a skillful lawyer defending a client:

> History seems to be conducted on the principles of a judicial process, in which the writer, assum-

ing the functions of an advocate, studiously suppresses whatever may make against his own side, supports himself by the strongest array of evidence which he can muster, discredits, as far as possible, that of the opposite party, and by dexterous interpretation and ingenious inference, makes out the most plausible argument for his client that the case will admit.

These, however, are only the abuses of philosophic history and do not discredit the whole product. History, although it had lost much of the simplicity and graphic vivacity of the ancients by his own time, had, according to Prescott, gained much more in the amount of useful knowledge and sound philosophy which it could inculcate. No writer exhibited more distinctly the full development of the principles of modern history to Prescott than did Gibbon. Yet even in Gibbon's work Prescott found something with which to quibble. He felt that Gibbon displayed "a bloated dignity of expression and an ostentation of ornament." But even more than this, he drew attention to a quality in both Gibbon and Voltaire which perhaps says more about Prescott himself than it does about either of his predecessors. This was the quality of skepticism, and, as he put it, "it is a consequence of this skepticism in Gibbon, as with Voltaire, that his writings are nowhere warmed with a generous moral sentiment."

Prescott's admiration for Gibbon was great, but the most influential historical writer on his intellectual growth was not Gibbon but the Frenchman the Abbé de Mably, whose *Etude de l'Histoire* Prescott claimed to have read ten times. He was, as Prescott noted, a severe, shrewd, and sensible writer. Prescott was attracted particularly by Mably's insistence that historical writing should tend to some obvious point or moral. He saw his own history of Ferdinand and Isabella in this light. It was to be the portrayal of a glorious epoch lying between anarchy and despotism, an epoch during which the Spanish nation reached a high degree of prosperity and yet one containing the seeds of future destruction.

His treatment of the Inquisition is relevant to this point and shows the extent to which he would implant a moral. The religious bigotry of that body he saw as one of the seeds of the disaster which would eventually overcome Spain, and the implication he drew was that bigotry was inevitably destructive of a nation.

Yet Prescott had doubts about his own ability to write philosophic history. At one point he confessed that he felt unable to make his history profound and (in an excess of modesty) suggested that he had neither the talent nor the knowledge for this. What he would do, he said, was to make his history entertaining. This eagerness to write lively, engaging, narrative history often, in fact, buried the first desire to write philosophic history and draw morals, although Prescott was always careful to see that it did not lead to the falsification of events for the sake of novelty.

The background, then, of Prescott's historical writing was the school of philosophical history and especially the dictates of Mably. Of what elements did Prescott compose his own writing? They would seem to be a concentration on dramatic narrative involving considerable care in the application of style, a great concern for both accuracy and impartiality using the best available documentary sources, and a biographical framework.

Prescott is best known as a dramatic, narrative historian, and as such he has had few peers. Here very clearly is revealed his concern to be a literary man as well as a historian. All of his works from first to last display this ability to construct a telling narrative, and even though modern historians may be critical of the narrative approach and tend themselves more to analytical history, telling a story remains an important element of historical writing. For Prescott this was not just a question of constructing isolated though brilliant set pieces like the description of the Battle of Lepanto. He was concerned to arrange a whole book in dramatic form. *The Conquest of Mexico,* generally acknowledged to be his masterpiece, reveals this clearly. It has been pointed out by several writers that the structure of the book is very like that of a play. The sketch of Aztec civilization forms a prologue to the whole; at the other end, Book VII with its commentary on the later career of Cortes stands as an epilogue. In between there is a neatly balanced dramatic structure. In Books I and II the reader is presented with the drama of conquest and the initial success of the Spaniards. In Book IV the fortunes of the conquerors take a decided turn for the worse, while in Book V and VI the Spaniards recoup their losses and the narrative hastens toward the spectacular climax of the siege of Tenochtitlan and the eventual Spanish triumph.

Other factors besides arrangement contribute much to the dramatic structure. Cortes bestrides the book like an epic hero, and one of the major reasons why *The Conquest of Mexico* is a more successful literary product than Prescott's other works is that it is the one with something resembling a genuine chivalric hero. There is much use made of contrasting characters: the Spaniards set against the Indians, Cortes against Montezuma. Each person of importance in the work is given a brief character sketch, and these are integrated in such a way as to make more meaningful the character of Cortes himself. Moreover, there is skillful use of suspense; the most successful case of this is the description of the *Noche Triste,* when Prescott presents much of the early scene through the eyes of the Spanish themselves and then, drawing away from them, reveals to the reader the watching and waiting Indians.

It is very important to remember, however, that Prescott did not subordinate history to art or the facts to romance. Cortes may be the epic hero, but Prescott provides commentary on his dark as well as his good side. There is nothing included in the text which Prescott could not document from his researches as having a sound basis in fact. A major part of his achievement as a historical writer was his ability to incorporate this material into the text in such a way that it added to the artistic force of the whole. A striking contribution to Prescott's success here was his style. As a literary man, Prescott was keenly aware of the importance of style and was able to develop a distinctive and successful writing technique of his own. It has been at times fashionable to deride Prescott's style for its excesses, and there are no doubt examples of overwriting, particularly when he is dealing with the gory part of his battle scenes. But the over-all impact is impressive. Indeed, it could be argued that Prescott's style should not be subjected to the critical canons of modern writing. The great and overwhelming proof of the success of his style is the continued popularity which his writings have had; the pundits may shake their heads, but the public has approved, and, as Prescott himself was wont to admit, it is the public which is the final arbiter in this matter.

Prescott took great pains over style. His journals are full of comments on the importance of it and on the necessity of originality of style. He stressed that any form of writing must maintain unity, proportion, and interest. The last of these could be sustained with the aid of the other two, but it was important to keep it constantly in mind. Several times in his journals he returned to this point in connection with the volumes on Mexico and Peru. In both he feared that the introduction would not maintain the readers' interest; because of this, he suggested, the rest of the work must be more enjoyable for both author and reader. Style had to be above all a personal matter, and Prescott was much concerned to develop his own distinctive one. He felt that imitation was futile; good imitations, he said, were bad enough, but bad ones were indescribable.

With all this emphasis on style, Prescott was careful not to neglect accuracy. Although he cautioned himself at one time not to aim at research, there can be little doubt that Prescott was, in fact, a conscientious and careful researcher. He was one of the first historians to use extensively the Spanish manuscript sources relating to his subject. The case of *The Conquest of Peru* is a clear example. Other writers had written on the conquest, but none had delved so deeply into the sources. The Peruvian section of Robertson's *History of America* relied on nine authorities; when this is compared with a list ot Prescott's sources, the contrast is striking, for it took a modern scholar nineteen pages to list Prescott's sources on Peru. One should not think that he uncovered every useful source; some of what he consulted was in incorrect, partial, or altered form and some sources (such as the *Relacion* of Cristobal de Molina and the *Nueva Coronica* of Poma de Ayala) were totally unknown to him. But even with these qualifications, the difference in approach between Prescott and his predecessors is obvious. Prescott was fully convinced that the historian must return to the basic sources and from these he must construct his story. Manuscript, as he once observed, was the only staple for the historic web.

But what sort of manuscript sources were the most useful? Here, perhaps, the modern historian would quibble with Prescott. Prescott's interest in administrative history was not great, and because of this, he found official documents to be of limited use. State papers were useful on many counts, but, he complained, they contained no private relations. "A good gossiping chronicle" was to him a far better source. His reliance on this sort of evidence is seen, for example, in the extensive use of Bernal Diaz's account of the conquest of Mexico. Yet for all his fondness for this type of source, he used it carefully. A major feature of all his works was critical appendices assessing the merits and demerits of the chroniclers whom he used. In some of his later writing, Prescott apparently began to rely increasingly on correspondence rather than on chronicles. As he related it to Gayangos in letters in 1852 and 1853 concerning his work on Philip II, he was taking the story out of the letters of the actors far more than from chronicles or history; this, he felt, would give it greater vitality and authenticity.

Closely coupled with Prescott's insistence on documentary research was a passion to be impartial, to immerse himself in the standards of the time and judge by them rather than by modern standards and prejudices. Prescott was, admittedly, not entirely consistent on this point—he tended to judge non-Christians by Christian standards—but on the whole, his work is remarkably free from prejudice of this sort. Many would feel that John Quincy Adams's verdict on Prescott was close to the truth; the remark was recorded by Edmund Otis who served four years as Prescott's secretary:

> Mr. Adams said that Mr. Prescott possessed the two great qualifications of an historian, who should be apparently without country and without religion. This he explained by saying that the history should not show the political or religious bias of the historian. It would be difficult, Mr. Adams thought, to tell whether Mr. Prescott were a Protestant or a Catholic, a monarchist or a republican.

This is not to deny that Prescott had some fixed social, political, and religious attitudes; he certainly did, and his letters and journals reveal these clearly. What it does stress is that he was remarkably capable of keeping them out of his work.

Prescott constantly gave expression in his journals and letters to his concern over the historian's judgment on his characters. He stressed that the historian should deal candidly with his subjects, but he also stressed that there was no place in historical writing for name-calling. This was the very fault of writers like Southey; it was, to Prescott's view, unhistorical, unphilosophical, and ungentlemanly. Prescott nowhere better summed up his own position on the matter than in a letter to John C. Hamilton in 1844:

> The immorality of the act and of the actor seem to me two very different things; and while we judge the one by the immutable principles of right and wrong, we must try the other by the fluctuating standard of the age. The real question is, whether a man was sincere and acted according to the light of his age. We cannot fairly demand of a man to be in advance of his generation, and where a generation goes wrong, we may be sure that it is an error of the head, not of the heart.

To the very end, this problem would concern Prescott. It is apparent that he thought of it closely in respect to his last subject, Philip II. As he commented in a letter to Lady Lyell in 1855, "there is one [of the Spaniards—Philip II] that I am sure will owe me a grudge, and that is the very man I have been making two big volumes upon; with all my good nature, I can't wash him even into the darkest French gray. He is black and all black."

One reason why this question of judgment on his characters should form such a prominent place in Prescott's approach to history was his concern with writing biographical history. Prescott was plainly more concerned with people than he was with things. He felt strongly that the human character was the most interesting subject to every reader, and in his journals he commented on Irving's *Columbus* precisely along these lines, arguing that where Irving developed the character of Columbus he displayed far greater success than when he dealt with lifeless details. Elsewhere, he wrote that the historian must approach as near to biographical interest as possible. In this respect, the comment of Carlyle on Scott that he made history out of people rather than out of protocols and treaties could be applied to Prescott as well, and it shows the extent to which the American historian had absorbed the lessons of the Scottish novelist.

[d] THE ASSESSMENT OF PRESCOTT

How are we to rank Prescott as a historian? There are a number of ways to approach an answer to this question. One has already been indicated in the comment that Prescott has had few peers in the writing of narrative history. That his accounts of the conquests of Mexico and Peru should still be usable over a hundred years after they were written is a tribute to the skill with which they were originally conceived. Few would deny that they need to be supplemented; on some points of detail they are in error, and on some matters of interpretation (especially the relations between Cortes and Montezuma) they are confusing. But as a narrative account of the history of conquest, they are still standard, and thus Prescott can stand comfortably beside Gibbon as a historian who is still read not only for his style but also for his content.

A further way to assess Prescott would be to compare his work with that of his notable American contemporaries. It has already been suggested that he was on a level not attained by either Irving, who wrote in Prescott's own field of Spanish history, or by Bancroft, who wrote the history of his own country. Two other men are often suggested as the equals of Prescott: Motley, whose work on the revolt of the Netherlands overlapped Prescott's *Philip II,* and Parkman, whose volumes on France in the New World treated an imperial theme as sweeping as that of Prescott and who, like Prescott, triumphed over physical disabilities.

Motley and Prescott were similar in some notable respects. Both were keen and penetrating researchers. Motley's efforts carried him into the Continental archives which Prescott was forced to use in transcript. Motley had the advantages of living in and visiting the places about which he wrote. He also had a more impressive academic background, including work at two German universities (Berlin and Göttingen), and thus direct exposure to the stimulating influence which German scholarship had on nineteenth-century historical writing. Although there are faults to be found in Motley's over-all interpretation, his scholarship was admittedly as impressive as that of Prescott. In addition, there can be little doubt that Motley was a skillful stylist. He has been called, with some justice, the most literary of all the so-called literary historians, and his narrative exudes the passion with which he wrote. He was skillful too in the portrayal of character, and at times he does seem to push somewhat further below the surface of events than Prescott did and thus uncovers factors which Prescott tended to overlook.

Yet, when all this is admitted, Motley is still not Prescott's equal as a historian. Motley was very openly too partisan to be a great historian if one takes impartiality to be a test of that greatness. Motley was a great pleader for a case, the case of Protestant liberty, and he allowed his feelings to intervene in his work in a way in which the more judicious Prescott, who also had strong personal views on the matter, never did. This quality, which contributes to the readability of Motley, lessens markedly his value as a historian. Moreover, Prescott in retrospect appears to have been more shrewd in his historical characterizations than Motley, even if (or perhaps because) he was less forceful about them. This is perfectly clear, for example, in the treatment which the two gave to Philip II. Motley's Philip appears in the full horror of the black legend of the Spanish monarch, so diabolical that he loses credibility as a human being. Prescott, on the other hand, though critical, was also incisive enough to see those qualities in Philip which form the staple of modern attempts to revive his reputation, especially the qualities of diligence and devotion in his work of governing.

Just as there are those who would rank Motley above Prescott, so are there those who would accord Parkman a higher rank. And in truth, the two should not be ranked far apart. Parkman was in some senses a more economical, a more compact writer, and there is little disagreement that he was a very effective stylist. Yet there is a case for ranking Prescott higher on the grounds of his technical mastery of a complex and broader field and because he directed his interests (and subsequently the interests of American historians in general) outside of a nationally conceived frame of reference.

No judgment of Prescott could, however, be complete without taking into account the two most notable assaults on his reputation as a historian: the first by Theodore Parker, the second by the anthropological school of Lewis H. Morgan. Of these attacks, Parker's is perhaps the more telling. Parker's protests were those that have been echoed by modern critics of the romantic historians. Prescott is accused of having focused attention too narrowly on political and military history. Even in doing that, Parker argued, he did not do his work thoroughly enough. Parker found Prescott's treatment of the Spanish constitution at the time of Ferdinand and Isabella unsatisfactory. The legal complexities were not analyzed; the source of revenue not sufficiently explained. Prescott, he suggested, revealed far too little interest in social and economic data and instead cluttered his work with needless details of dress at royal pageants. Moreover, Parker waxed indignant indeed over the lack of mention of the common man; this he felt was true not only in Prescott's treatment of Spain but also in the accounts of the New World where the sufferings of the Indians were played down. Above all, he argued, Prescott's history was not philosophical; it was no better than a collection of annals and stood in the same relation to true history as a collection of memorials did to real biography. Prescott, he complained, knew nothing of philosophy and very little of political economy. The works told the facts for the facts' sake and told no more; they were hence limited, unsympathetic, uninspired.

To some of Parker's criticisms, the obvious retort is that they are absurd. This is noticeably true of Parker's allegation that Prescott was indifferent to the sufferings of the Indians. Some of the criticisms merit more attention. It is true that Prescott did ignore some of the things that Parker mentioned; Prescott was not interested, for example, in making an analysis of the effects of governmental taxation on the Spanish rural population. In ignoring these aspects, he was a child of his age.

But a more positive defense of Prescott can be offered. What Parker ignored in his criticism is that there are different sorts of history. There is narrative history and there is sociological history; both have their merits and both have their shortcomings. Prescott was a master of the first and did not indulge in the second. But to demand that he should have paid more attention to sociological factors is to demand that he should have written a totally different set of books. The historian is, after all, free to choose his subject, and Prescott's concentration on the regal history of Spain was a valid

choice and a valuable one as well. He was writing the history of a monarchy and its imperial advance, not a study of Spanish society. To the extent to which history is concerned with telling a story, it cannot escape narrative, any more than it can escape the sort of detail which Parker wanted when it is concerned with analysis of a period. Both concerns are legitimate parts of the subject, and Prescott's reputation as a historian cannot be damaged permanently by observing that he concentrated on one at the expense of the other.

The attack by the anthropologists seemed at the time to be the more serious one, but it is now almost totally discredited. In a famous essay, Morgan suggested that Prescott had grossly overestimated the degree of civilization of the Aztecs and the Incas and that he had used without proper caution suspect Spanish sources. The most recent workers in the field of pre-Columbian archaeology would disagree sharply. While they would not accept Prescott's account of the Aztec and Inca civilizations in its entirety, they would find it a more accurate view than Morgan's debunking. In fact, in respect to the very rudimentary knowledge of the subject in his own time, Prescott's account could only be called remarkable. Once again, it was the basic honesty of his research approach which made Prescott's contribution significant. Where Morgan and his followers worked from a preconceived theory back to the facts, Prescott tried to work as objectively as possible on the basis of all the information available to him. In his research, Prescott relied heavily on available Spanish sources. These were what Morgan called into question, yet later scholarship was to vindicate Prescott, for the Spanish sources are now treated with much of the respect which Prescott accorded them. One should also remember that although Prescott worked only from printed sources in dealing with archaeology and anthropology, he was thorough and critical in his research. He was able, for example, to see through the fantastic element which so fascinated his contemporaries like Lord Kingsborough in Great Britain. Attempts to link similarities in Aztec re-

ligion to tales of the lost tribes of Israel were rightly dismissed by Prescott as "moonshine."

It is most noteworthy, of course, that none of the attacks cut into Prescott's reading public. Partly for the very reasons which his antagonists criticized—because he was detached, because he did not write into his history a lesson that was not there—Prescott was from the first hailed by the public and by most of the critics. By the public he has been hailed ever since, and few have been the critics or historians who have not done the same.

To abridge Prescott into a single volume has involved the elimination of much that is worthy of inclusion. There is some evidence that Prescott conceived his works in totality as the history of the rise and decline of an empire, and although each work stands as a separate unit, I have tried to connect the passages in such a way as to illustrate the development of that theme. Fortunately, some of Prescott's best set pieces, such as his description of the Battle of Lepanto, fit well into such a scheme. I have also included some of the "obituaries" which Prescott used to summarize characters in order to illustrate his biographical approach. Unfortunately, one part which has had to be cut is his discussion of the pre-Columbian Indians. It illustrates well his historical research, but, as I have indicated, it stands as prologue to the real narrative drama in which he truly reveals his technique. For economy of space, I have omitted all of Prescott's footnotes. As he once commented, he had "suffered the scaffolding to remain after the building had been completed." In general, his notes were used to give sources verifying his text; he seldom used them (except in the cases where he analyzed other historians) to expand on it, and, for this reason, I have decided that they could in this edition be set aside. I have added a few explanatory notes of my own when I have felt them to be necessary.

Roger Howell, Jr.

BIBLIOGRAPHICAL NOTE

There are many editions of Prescott's works and a number of modern reprintings of individual titles. The best editions of his writings are:

The Works of W. H. Prescott, ed. J. F. Kirk (Philadelphia, 1874), 16 volumes

The Works of W. H. Prescott, ed. W. H. Monroe (Philadelphia, 1904), 24 volumes

C. H. Gardiner, ed., *The Literary Memoranda of William Hickling Prescott* (Norman, Okla., 1961), 2 volumes

C. H. Gardiner, ed., *The Papers of William Hickling Prescott* (Urbana, Ill., 1964)

C. L. Penney, ed., *Prescott's Unpublished Letters to Gayangos* (New York, 1927)

R. Wolcott, ed., *The Correspondence of William Hickling Prescott* (Boston, 1925)

An annotated bibliography of Prescott's published works, edited by C. H. Gardiner (Washington, 1958), provides a useful summary of the various editions. There are three notable lives of Prescott. In many ways, the most useful was that written by his friend George Ticknor (Boston, 1864), although it did not employ fully many of the materials available such as Prescott's literary memoranda. Subsequent lives were written by R. Ogden (Cambridge, Mass., 1904) and H. T. Peck (New York, 1905). The long introduction to W. Chavrat and M. Kraus, *William H. Prescott: Representative Selections* contains much information on his views and social attitudes. Some more recent studies which are of interest include: C. H. Gardiner, *Prescott and His Publishers* (Carbondale, Pa., 1959); D. Levin, *History as Romantic Art* (paperback edition, New York, 1963); S. E.

Morison, "Prescott: The American Thucydides," *Atlantic Monthly*, November, 1957; *Hispanic American Historical Review: Prescott Memorial Issue*, ed. H. F. Cline, C. H. Gardiner, C. Gibson (Durham, N. C., 1959).

DATES IN PRESCOTT'S LIFE

1796	Born in Salem, Massachusetts
1808-11	Attends Gardiner's school and reads at the Athenaeum
1811	Admitted to sophomore class at Harvard
1812	War declared between Great Britain and United States; Prescott blinded in the left eye
1816-17	Travels in England, France, Italy
1820	Editor of the *Club Room*
1824	Begins study of Spanish under inspiration of George Ticknor
1826	Resolves to write *Ferdinand and Isabella* and hires first secretary, James English
1837	Christmas: publication of *Ferdinand and Isabella*
1839	Begins correspondence with Gayangos
1843	Publication of *Conquest of Mexico*
1845	Publication of *Miscellanies*
1846	United States at war with Mexico
1847	Publication of *Conquest of Peru*
1848	Begins studies for *Philip II,* arranging to divide the field with Motley
1850	Entertained in Washington by President Taylor; spends four months in Europe (England, France, Belgium, Holland); awarded D.C.L. by Oxford University
1855	Publication of two volumes of *Philip II*
1856	Publication of continuation of Robertson's *Charles V;* health begins to decline
1858	Attack of apoplexy; publication of third volume of *Philip II*
1859	28 January: dies at Boston

Prescott:
The Conquest of Mexico and
The Conquest of Peru

PART I

History of the Reign of Ferdinand and Isabella The Catholic

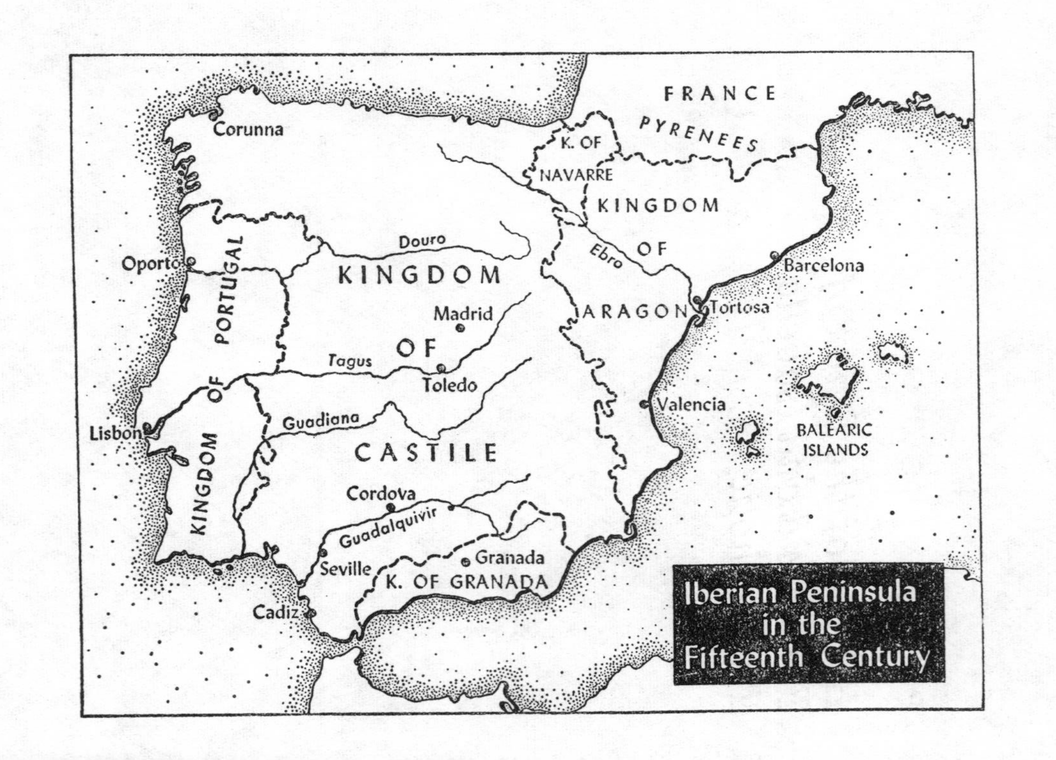
FRANCE
PYRENEES
K. OF NAVARRE
KINGDOM OF ARAGON
Ebro
Barcelona
Tortosa
Valencia
BALEARIC ISLANDS
Corunna
Oporto
KINGDOM OF PORTUGAL
Lisbon
KINGDOM OF CASTILE
Douro
Madrid
Tagus
Toledo
Guadiana
Cordova
Guadalquivir
Seville
Cadiz
Granada
K. OF GRANADA
Iberian Peninsula in the Fifteenth Century

1. *The Marriage of Ferdinand and Isabella**

[Prescott began his account of the reign of Ferdinand and Isabella with a survey of the monarchy of Castile before the fifteenth century and of the constitution of Aragon down to the middle of the century. This preliminary survey leads to the first main part of the work, a section devoted to an analysis (as Prescott put it) of "the period when the different kingdoms of Spain were first united under one monarchy and a thorough reform was introduced into their internal administration . . . the period exhibiting most fully the domestic policy of Ferdinand and Isabella." The marriage itself, which produced the union of the crowns of Castile and Aragon, took place under difficult circumstances. The princess was strongly opposed by her brother, Henry IV of Castile. Henry had been deposed in absentia *by dissident elements in the kingdom in 1465 in favor of Isabella's brother Alfonso. Within three years, Alfonso was dead. An apparent reconciliation was then reached between Isabella and Henry IV; this was embodied in the treaty of Toros de Guisando (9 September, 1468), which provided the "new and legitimate basis" referred to in the opening sentence. By the terms of the agreement, Isabella was declared the lawful successor to the crowns of Castile and Leon after Henry IV. This was done at the expense of the pretensions of Joanna, whom Henry IV always seems to have cherished as his offspring, despite imputations of illegitimacy.]*

* **From *Ferdinand and Isabella,* Part I, chap. 3.**

The new and legitimate basis on which the pretensions of Isabella to the throne now rested drew the attention of neighboring princes, who contended with each other for the honor of her hand. Among these suitors was a brother of Edward the Fourth of England, not improbably Richard, duke of Gloucester, since Clarence was then engaged in his intrigues with the earl of Warwick, which led a few months later to his marriage with the daughter of that nobleman. Had she listened to his proposals, the duke would in all likelihood have exchanged his residence in England for Castile, where his ambition, satisfied with the certain reversion of a crown, might have been spared the commission of the catalogue of crimes which blackens his memory.

Another suitor was the duke of Guienne, the unfortunate brother of Louis the Eleventh, and at that time the presumptive heir of the French monarchy. Although the ancient intimacy which subsisted between the royal families of France and Castile in some measure favored his pretensions, the disadvantages resulting from such a union were too obvious to escape attention. The two countries were too remote from each other, and their inhabitants too dissimilar in character and institutions, which had molded them into a common resem-ing as one people under a common sovereign. Should the duke of Guienne fail in the inheritance of the crown, it was argued, he would be every way an unequal match for the heiress of Castile; should he succeed to it, it might be feared that, in case of a union, the smaller kingdom would be considered only as an appendage, and sacrificed to the interests of the larger.

The person on whom Isabella turned the most favorable eye was her kinsman, Ferdinand of Aragon. The superior advantages of a connection which should be the means of uniting the people of Aragon and Castile into one nation were indeed manifest. They were the descendants of one common stock, speaking one language, and living under the influence of similar institutions, which had molded them into a common resemblance of character and manners. From their geographical position, too, they seemed destined by nature to be one nation; and while separately they were condemned to the rank of petty and subordinate states, they might hope, when consolidated into one monarchy, to rise at once to the first class of European powers. While arguments of this public nature pressed on the mind of Isabella, she was not insensible to those which most powerfully affect the female heart. Ferdinand was then in the bloom of life, and distinguished for the comeliness of his person. In the busy scenes in which he had been engaged from his boyhood, he had displayed a chivalrous valor, combined with maturity of judgment far above his years. Indeed, he was decidedly superior to his rivals in personal merit and attractions. But while private inclinations thus happily coincided with considerations of expediency for inclining her to prefer the Aragonese match, a scheme was devised in another quarter for the express purpose of defeating it.

A fraction of the royal party, with the family of Mendoza at their head, had retired in disgust with the convention of Toros de Guisando, and openly espoused the cause of the princess Joanna. They even instructed her to institute an appeal before the tribunal of the supreme pontiff, and caused a placard, exhibiting a protest against the validity of the late proceedings, to be nailed secretly in the night to the gate of Isabella's mansion. Thus were sown the seeds of new dissensions before the old were completely eradicated. With this disaffected party the marquis of Villena, who, since his reconciliation, had resumed his ancient ascendency over Henry, now associated himself. Nothing, in the opinion of this nobleman, could be more repugnant to his interests than the projected union between the houses of Castile and Aragon; to the latter of which once belonged the ample domains of his own marquisate, which he imagined would be held by a very precarious tenure should any of this family obtain a footing in Castile.

In the hope of counteracting this project, he endeavored to revive the obsolete pretensions of Alfonso, king of Portugal; and the more effectually to secure the co-operation of Henry, he connected with his scheme a proposition for marrying his daughter Joanna with the son and heir of the Portuguese monarch; and thus this unfortunate princess might be enabled to assume at once a station suitable to her birth, and at some future opportunity assert with success her claim to the Castilian crown. In furtherance of this complicated intrigue, Alfonso was invited to renew his addresses to Isabella in a more public manner than he had hitherto done; and a pompous embassy, with the archbishop of Lisbon at its head, appeared at Ocaña, where Isabella was then residing, bearing the proposals of their master. The princess returned, as before, a decided though temperate refusal. Henry, or rather the marquis of Villena, piqued at this opposition to his wishes, resolved to intimidate her into compliance, and menaced her with imprisonment in the royal fortress at Madrid. Neither her tears nor entreaties would have availed against this tyrannical proceeding; and the marquis was only deterred from putting it in execution by his fear of the inhabitants of Ocaña, who openly espoused the cause of Isabella. Indeed, the common people of Castile very generally supported her in her preference of the Aragonese match. Boys paraded the streets, bearing banners emblazoned with the arms of Aragon and singing verses prophetic of the glories of the auspicious union. They even assembled round the palace gates and insulted the ears of Henry and his minister by the repetition of satirical stanzas which contrasted Alfonso's years with the youthful graces of Ferdinand. Notwithstanding this popular expression of opinion, however, the constancy of Isabella might at length have yielded to the importunity of her persecutors had she not been encouraged by her friend the archbishop of Toledo, who had warmly entered into the interests of Aragon and who promised, should matters come to extremity, to march in person to her relief at the head of a sufficient force to insure it. (1469.)

Isabella, indignant at the oppressive treatment which she experienced from her brother, as well as at his notorious infraction of almost every article in the treaty of Toros de Guisando, felt herself released from her corresponding engagements and determined to conclude the negotiations relative to her marriage without further deference to his opinion. Before taking any decisive step, however, she was desirous of obtaining the concurrence of the leading nobles of her party. This was effected without difficulty through the intervention of the archbishop of Toledo and of Don Frederick Henriquez, admiral of Castile and the maternal grandfather of Ferdinand, a person of high consideration, both from his rank and character, and connected by blood with the principal families in the kingdom. Fortified by their approbation, Isabella dismissed the Aragonese envoy with a favorable answer to his master's suit.

Her reply was received with almost as much satisfaction by the old king of Aragon, John the Second, as by his son. This monarch, who was one of the shrewdest princes of his time, had always been deeply sensible of the importance of consolidating the scattered monarchies of Spain under one head. He had solicited the hand of Isabella for his son when she possessed only a contingent reversion of the crown. But when her succession had been settled on a more secure basis, he lost no time in effecting this favorite object of his policy. With the consent of the states, he had transferred to his son the title of King of Sicily and associated him with himself in the government at home in order to give him greater consequence in the eyes of his mistress. He then despatched a confidential agent into Castile with instructions to gain over to his interests all who exercised any influence on the mind of the princess, furnishing him for this purpose with *cartes blanches*, signed by himself and Ferdinand, which he was empowered to fill at his discretion.

Between parties thus favorably disposed there was no unnecessary delay. The marriage articles were signed, and sworn to by Ferdinand at Cervera on the 7th of January, 1469. He promised faithfully to respect the laws and usages of Castile; to fix his residence in that kingdom and not to quit it without the consent of Isabella; to alienate no property belonging to the crown; to prefer no foreigners to municipal offices and indeed to make no appointments of a civil or military nature without her consent and approbation; and to resign to her exclusively the right of nomination to ecclesiastical benefices. All ordinances of a public nature were to be subscribed equally by both. Ferdinand engaged, moreover, to prosecute the war against the Moors; to respect King Henry; to suffer every noble to remain unmolested in the possession of his dignities; and not to demand restitution of the domains formerly owned by his father in Castile. The treaty concluded with a specification of a magnificent dower to be settled on Isabella, far more ample than that usually assigned to the queens of Aragon. The circumspection of the framers of this instrument is apparent from the various provisions introduced into it solely to calm the apprehensions and to conciliate the good will of the party disaffected to the marriage; while the national partialities of the Castilians in general were gratified by the jealous restrictions imposed on Ferdinand and the relinquishment of all the essential rights of sovereignty to his consort.

While these affairs were in progress, Isabella's situation was becoming extremely critical. She had availed herself of the absence of her brother and the marquis of Villena in the south, whither they had gone for the purpose of suppressing the still lingering spark of insurrection, to transfer her residence from Ocaña to Madrigal, where, under the protection of her mother, she intended to abide the issue of the pending negotiations with Aragon. Far, however, from escaping the vigilant eye of the marquis of Villena by this movement, she laid herself more open to it. She found the bishop of Burgos, the nephew of the marquis, stationed at Madrigal, where he served as an effectual spy upon her actions. Her most confidential servants were corrupted and conveyed intelligence of her proceedings to her enemy. Alarmed at the actual progress made in the negotiations for her marriage, the marquis was now convinced that he could only hope to defeat them by resorting to the coercive system which he had before abandoned. He accordingly instructed the archbishop of Seville to march at once to Madrigal with a sufficient force to secure Isabella's person; and letters were at the same time addressed by Henry to the citizens of that place, menacing them with his resentment if they should presume to interpose in her behalf. The timid inhabitants disclosed the purport of the mandate to Isabella and besought her to provide for her own safety. This was perhaps the most critical period in her life. Betrayed by her own domestics, deserted even by those friends of her own sex who might have afforded her sympathy and counsel, but who fled affrighted from the scene of danger, and on the eve of falling into the snares of her enemies, she beheld the sudden extinction of those hopes which she had so long and so fondly cherished.

In this exigency, she contrived to convey a knowledge of her situation to Admiral Henriquez and the archbishop of Toledo. The active prelate, on receiving the summons, collected a body of horse and, reinforced by the admiral's troops, advanced with such expedition to Madrigal that he succeeded in anticipating the arrival of the enemy. Isabella received her friends with unfeigned satisfaction; and bidding adieu to her dismayed guardian, the bishop of Burgos, and his attendants, she was borne off by her little army in a sort of military triumph to the friendly city of Valladolid, where she was welcomed by the citizens with a general burst of enthusiasm.

In the meantime, Gutierre de Cardenas, one of the household of the princess, and Alonso de Palencia, the faithful chronicler of these events, were despatched into Aragon in order to quicken Ferdinand's operations during the auspicious interval afforded by the absence of Henry in Andalusia. On arriving at the frontier town of Osma, they were dismayed to find that the bishop of that place, together with the duke of Medina Celi, on whose active co-operation they had relied for the safe introduction of Ferdinand into Castile, had been gained over to the interests of the marquis of Villena. The envoys, however, adroitly concealing the real object of their mission, were permitted to pass unmolested to Saragossa, where Ferdinand was then residing. They could not have arrived at a more inopportune season. The old king of Aragon was in the very heat of the war against the insurgent Catalans, headed by the victorious John of Anjou. Although so sorely pressed, his forces were on the eve of disbanding for want of the requisite funds to maintain them. His exhausted treasury did not contain more than three hundred *enriques*.[1] In this exigency he was agitated by the most distressing doubts. As he could spare neither the funds nor the force necessary for covering his son's entrance into Castile, he must either send him unprotected into a hostile country already aware of his intended enterprise and in arms to defeat it, or abandon the long-cherished object of his policy at the moment when his plans were ripe for execution. Unable to extricate himself from this dilemma, he referred the whole matter to Ferdinand and his council.

It was at length determined that the prince should undertake the journey, accompanied by half-a-dozen attendants only, in the disguise of merchants by the direct route from Saragossa; while another party, in order to divert the attention of the Castilians, should proceed in a different direction with all the ostentation of a public embassy from the king of Aragon to Henry the Fourth. The distance was not great which Ferdinand and his suite were to travel before reaching a place of safety; but this intervening country was patrolled by squadrons of cavalry for the purpose of intercepting their progress, and the whole extent of the frontier, from Almazan to Guadalajara, was defended by a line of fortified castles in the hands of the family of Mendoza. The greatest circumspection, therefore, was necessary. The party journeyed chiefly in the night: Ferdinand assumed the disguise of a servant and, when they halted on the road, took care of the mules and served his companions at table. In this guise, with no other disaster except that of leaving at an inn the purse which contained the funds for the expedition, they arrived, late on the second night, at a little place called the

[1] A gold coin named after Henry II.

Burgo, or Borough, of Osma, which the count of Trevino, one of the partisans of Isabella, had occupied with a considerable body of men-at-arms. On knocking at the gate, cold and faint with travelling, during which the prince had allowed himself to take no repose, they were saluted by a large stone discharged by a sentinel from the battlements, which, glancing near Ferdinand's head, had well-nigh brought his romantic enterprise to a tragical conclusion; when his voice was recognized by his friends within, and the trumpets proclaiming his arrival, he was received with great joy and festivity by the count and his followers. The remainder of his journey, which he commenced before dawn, was performed under the convoy of a numerous and well-armed escort; and on the 9th of October he reached Dueñas in the kingdom of León, where the Castilian nobles and cavaliers of his party eagerly thronged to render him the homage due to his rank.

The intelligence of Ferdinand's arrival diffused universal joy in the little court of Isabella at Valladolid. Her first step was to transmit a letter to her brother Henry, in which she informed him of the presence of the prince in his dominions and of their intended marriage. She excused the course she had taken by the embarrassments in which she had been involved by the malice of her enemies. She represented the political advantages of the connection and the sanction it had received from the Castilian nobles; and she concluded with soliciting his approbation of it, giving him at the same time affectionate assurances of the most dutiful submission on the part both of Ferdinand and of herself. Arrangements were then made for an interview between the royal pair, in which some courtly parasites would fain have persuaded their mistress to require some act of homage from Ferdinand in token of the inferiority of the crown of Aragon to that of Castile: a proposition which she rejected with her usual discretion.

Agreeably to these arrangements, Ferdinand, on the evening of the 15th of October, passed privately from

Dueñas, accompanied by only four attendants, to the neighboring city of Valladolid, where he was received by the archbishop of Toledo and conducted to the apartment of his mistress. Ferdinand was at this time in the eighteenth year of his age. His complexion was fair, though somewhat bronzed by constant exposure to the sun; his eye quick and cheerful; his forehead ample, and approaching to baldness. His muscular and well-proportioned frame was invigorated by the toils of war, and by the chivalrous exercises in which he delighted. He was one of the best horsemen in his court and excelled in field-sports of every kind. His voice was somewhat sharp, but he possessed a fluent eloquence; and when he had a point to carry, his address was courteous and even insinuating. He secured his health by extreme temperance in his diet and by such habits of activity that it was said he seemed to find repose in business. Isabella was a year older than her lover. In stature she was somewhat above the middle size. Her complexion was fair; her hair of a bright chestnut color, inclining to red; and her mild blue eye beamed with intelligence and sensibility. She was exceedingly beautiful; "the handsomest lady," says one of her household, "whom I ever beheld, and the most gracious in her manners." The portrait still existing of her in the royal palace is conspicuous for an open symmetry of features, indicative of the natural serenity of temper and that beautiful harmony of intellectual and moral qualities which most distinguished her. She was dignified in her demeanor and modest even to a degree of reserve. She spoke the Castilian language with more than usual elegance, and early imbibed a relish for letters, in which she was superior to Ferdinand, whose education in this particular seems to have been neglected. It is not easy to obtain a dispassionate portrait of Isabella. The Spaniards who revert to her glorious reign are so smitten with her moral perfections that, even in depicting her personal life, they borrow somewhat of the exaggerated coloring of romance.

The interview lasted more than two hours, when

Ferdinand retired to his quarters at Dueñas as privately as he came. The preliminaries of the marriage, however, were first adjusted; but so great was the poverty of the parties that it was found necessary to borrow money to defray the expenses of the ceremony. Such were the humiliating circumstances attending the commencement of a union destined to open the way to the highest prosperity and grandeur of the Spanish monarchy!

The marriage between Ferdinand and Isabella was publicly celebrated, on the morning of the 19th of October, 1469, in the palace of John de Vivero, the temporary residence of the princess and subsequently appropriated to the chancery of Valladolid. The nuptials were solemnized in the presence of Ferdinand's grandfather, the admiral of Castile, of the archbishop of Toledo, and a multitude of persons of rank as well as of inferior condition, amounting in all to no less than two thousand. A papal bull of dispensation was produced by the archbishop, relieving the parties from the impediment incurred by their falling within the prohibited degrees of consanguinity. This spurious document was afterwards discovered to have been devised by the old king of Aragon, Ferdinand, and the archbishop, who were deterred from applying to the court of Rome by the zeal with which it openly espoused the interests of Henry, and who knew that Isabella would never consent to a union repugnant to the canons of the established church and one which involved such heavy ecclesiastical censures. A genuine bull of dispensation was obtained, some years later, from Sixtus the Fourth; but Isabella, whose honest mind abhorred everything like artifice, was filled with no little uneasiness and mortification at the discovery of the imposition. The ensuing week was consumed in the usual festivities of this joyous season, at the expiration of which the new-married pair attended publicly the celebration of mass, agreeably to the usage of the time, in the collegiate church of Santa María.

An embassy was despatched by Ferdinand and Isabella to Henry to acquaint him with their proceedings and again request his approbation of them. They repeated their assurances of loyal submission, and accompanied the message with a copious extract from such of the articles of marriage as, by their import, would be most likely to conciliate his favorable disposition. Henry coldly replied that "he must advise with his ministers."

2. *The War of Granada**

[The winning of security for Ferdinand and Isabella came as the result of war. Henry IV, who represented a serious threat to them, died in 1474, but the pretensions of Joanna remained to menace them. Her supporters turned to the elderly Alfonso V of Portugal, a spurned suitor of Isabella, offering him both Joanna's hand and the throne. The Portuguese monarch led his army into Castile to gain these prizes, but he was defeated after five years of fighting. In 1479 he retired to Portugal and Joanna withdrew to a convent. Prescott's account of these events is here omitted. His narrative is resumed with the story of the completion of the reconquest, the recapture of Moslem Spain by the Christians. The reconquest itself had begun as early as 718 at Covadonga, where a small Moslem force was defeated by the Christians in a skirmish. By the time of Ferdinand and Isabella, only the kingdom of Granada remained, the last relic of Moslem domination of Spain, and to the reduction of it

* From *Ferdinand and Isabella,* Part I, chap. 13.

their attention was turned. The first major stroke of the War of Granada was the capture of the fortress of Alhama in 1482, which Prescott treated in chapter 9. Five years later, the Christian forces were able to attack the second most important city in Granada, the port of Malaga.]

This ancient city, which, under the Spanish Arabs in the twelfth and thirteenth centuries, formed the capital of an independent principality, was second only to the metropolis itself in the kingdom of Granada. Its fruitful environs furnished abundant articles of export, while its commodious port on the Mediterranean opened a traffic with the various countries washed by that inland sea and with the remoter regions of India. Owing to these advantages, the inhabitants acquired unbounded opulence, which showed itself in the embellishments of their city, whose light forms of architecture, mingling after the Eastern fashion with odoriferous gardens and fountains of sparkling water, presented an appearance most refreshing to the senses in this sultry climate.

The city was encompassed by fortifications of great strength and in perfect repair. It was commanded by a citadel connected by a covered way with a second fortress, impregnable from its position, denominated Gebalfaro, which stood along the declivities of the bold sierra of the Axarquia,[1] whose defiles had proved so disastrous to the Christians. The city lay between two spacious suburbs, the one on the land side being also encircled by a formidable wall and the other declining towards the sea, showing an expanse of olive, orange, and pomegranate gardens, intermingled with the rich vineyards that furnished the celebrated staple for its export.

Malaga was well prepared for a siege by supplies of artillery and ammunition. Its ordinary garrison was reinforced by volunteers from the neighboring towns and by a corps of African mercenaries, Gomeres, as they were called, men of ferocious temper but of tried valor and military discipline. The command of this important

[1] A defeat of the Spaniards in 1483 by El Zagal.

post had been intrusted by El Zagal[1] to a noble Moor, named Hamet Zeli, whose renown in the present war had been established by his resolute defence of Ronda.

Ferdinand, while lying before Velez, received intelligence that many of the wealthy burghers of Malaga were inclined to capitulate at once rather than hazard the demolition of their city by an obstinate resistance. He instructed the marquis of Cadiz, therefore, to open a negotiation with Hamet Zeli, authorizing him to make the most liberal offers to the alcayde himself, as well as his garrison and the principal citizens of the place, on condition of immediate surrender. The sturdy chief, however, rejected the proposal with disdain, replying that he had been commissioned by his master to defend the place to the last extremity and that the Christian king could not offer a bribe large enough to make him betray his trust. Ferdinand, finding little prospect of operating on this Spartan temper, broke up his camp before Velez on the 7th of May and advanced with his whole army as far as Bezmillana, a place on the seaboard about two leagues distant from Malaga.

The line of march now lay through a valley commanded at the extremity nearest the city by two eminences, the one on the sea-coast, the other facing the fortress of the Gebalfaro and forming part of the wild sierra which overshadowed Malaga on the north. The enemy occupied both these important positions. A corps of Galicians was sent forward to dislodge them from the eminence towards the sea. But it failed in the assault and, notwithstanding it was led up a second time by the commander of León and the brave Garcilasso de la Vega, was again repulsed by the intrepid foe.

A similar fate attended the assault on the sierra, which was conducted by the troops of the royal household. They were driven back on the vanguard, which had halted in the valley under command of the grand master of St. James, prepared to support the attack on either side. Being reinforced, the Spaniards returned to the charge with the most determined resolution. They were

[1] King of Granada, 1485–1487.

encountered by the enemy with equal spirit. The latter, throwing away their lances, precipitated themselves on the ranks of the assailants, making use only of their daggers, grappling closely man to man, till both rolled promiscuously together down the steep sides of the ravine. No mercy was asked or shown. None thought of sparing or of spoiling, for hatred, says the chronicler, was stronger than avarice. The main body of the army, in the meanwhile, pent up in the valley, were compelled to witness the mortal conflict and listen to the exulting cries of the enemy, which, after the Moorish custom, rose high and shrill above the din of battle, without being able to advance a step in support of their companions, who were again forced to give way before their impetuous adversaries and fall back on the vanguard under the grand master of St. James. Here, however, they speedily rallied and, being reinforced, advanced to the charge a third time with such inflexible courage as bore down all opposition, and compelled the enemy, exhausted, or rather overpowered by superior numbers, to abandon his position. At the same time the rising ground on the sea-side was carried by the Spaniards under the commander of León and Garcilasso de la Vega, who, dividing their forces, charged the Moors so briskly in front and rear that they were compelled to retreat on the neighboring fortress of Gebalfaro.

As it was evening before these advantages were obtained, the army did not defile into the plains around Malaga before the following morning, when dispositions were made for its encampment. The eminence on the sierra, so bravely contested, was assigned, as the post of greatest danger, to the marquis duke of Cadiz. It was protected by strong works lined with artillery, and a corps of two thousand five hundred horse and fourteen thousand foot was placed under the immediate command of the nobleman. A line of defence was constructed along the declivity from this redoubt to the sea-shore. Similar works, consisting of a deep trench and palisades or, where the soil was too rocky to admit of them, of an embankment or mound of earth, were formed in front of the encampment, which embraced the whole circuit of the city; and the blockade was completed by a fleet of armed vessels, galleys, and caravels, which rode in the harbor under the command of the Catalan admiral, Requesens, and effectually cut off all communication by water.

The old chronicler Bernaldez warms at the aspect of the fair city of Malaga, thus encompassed by Christian legions, whose deep lines, stretching far over hill and valley, reached quite round from one arm of the sea to the other. In the midst of this brilliant encampment was seen the royal pavilion, proudly displaying the united banners of Castile and Aragon and forming so conspicuous a mark for the enemy's artillery that Ferdinand, after imminent hazard, was at length compelled to shift his quarters. The Christians were not slow in erecting counterbatteries; but the work was obliged to be carried on at night in order to screen them from the fire of the besieged.

The first operations of the Spaniards were directed against the suburb, on the land side of the city. The attack was intrusted to the count of Cifuentes, the nobleman who had been made prisoner in the affair of the Axarquia and subsequently ransomed. The Spanish ordnance was served with such effect that a practicable breach was soon made in the wall. The combatants now poured their murderous volleys on each other through the opening, and at length met on the ruins of the breach. After a desperate struggle, the Moors gave way. The Christians rushed into the inclosure, at the same time effecting a lodgment on the rampart, and although a part of it, undermined by the enemy, gave way with a terrible crash, they still kept possession of the remainder, and at length drove their antagonists, who suddenly retreated step by step, within the fortifications of the city. The lines were then drawn close around the place. Every avenue of communication was strictly guarded, and every preparation was made for reducing the town by regular blockade.

In addition to the cannon brought round by water

from Velez, the heavier lombards,[1] which from the difficulty of transportation had been left during the late siege of Antequera, were now conducted, across roads levelled for the purpose, to the camp. Supplies of marble bullets were also brought from the ancient and depopulated city of Algezira, where they had lain ever since its capture in the preceding century by Alfonso the Eleventh. The camp was filled with operatives employed in the manufacture of balls and powder, which were stored in subterranean magazines, and in the fabrication of those various kinds of battering enginery which continued in use long after the introduction of gunpowder.

During the early part of the siege, the camp experienced some temporary inconvenience from the occasional interruption of the supplies transported by water. Rumors of the appearance of the plague in some of the adjacent villages caused additional uneasiness; and deserters who passed into Malaga reported these particulars with the usual exaggeration and encouraged the besieged to persevere by the assurance that Ferdinand could not much longer keep the field and that the queen had actually written to advise his breaking up the camp. Under these circumstances, Ferdinand saw at once the importance of the queen's presence in order to dispel the delusion of the enemy and to give new heart to his soldiers. He accordingly sent a message to Cordova, where she was holding her court, requesting her appearance in the camp.

Isabella had proposed to join her husband before Velez, on receiving tidings of El Zagal's march from Granada, and had actually enforced levies of all persons capable of bearing arms, between twenty and seventy years of age, throughout Andalusia, but subsequently disbanded them on learning the discomfiture of the Moorish army. Without hesitation, she now set forward, accompanied by the cardinal of Spain and other dignitaries of the church together with the infanta Isabella and a courtly train of ladies and cavaliers in

[1] A kind of cannon.

attendance on her person. She was received at a short distance from the camp by the marquis of Cadiz and the grand master of St. James, and escorted to her quarters amidst the enthusiastic greetings of the soldiery. Hope now brightened every countenance. A grace seemed to be shed over the rugged features of war; and the young gallants thronged from all quarters to the camp, eager to win the guerdon of valor from the hands of those from whom it is most grateful to receive it.

Ferdinand, who had hitherto brought into action only the lighter pieces of ordnance, from a willingness to spare the noble edifices of the city, now pointed his heaviest guns against its walls. Before opening his fire, however, he again summoned the place, offering the usual liberal terms in case of immediate compliance and engaging otherwise "with the blessing of God, to make them all slaves"! But the heart of the alcayde was hardened like that of Pharaoh, says the Andalusian chronicler, and the people were swelled with vain hopes so that their ears were closed against the proposal; orders were even issued to punish with death any attempt at a parley. On the contrary, they made answer by a more lively cannonade than before along the whole line of ramparts and fortresses which overhung the city. Sallies were also made at almost every hour of the day and night on every assailable point of the Christian lines, so that the camp was kept in perpetual alarm. In one of the nocturnal sallies, a body of two thousand men from the castle of Gebalfaro succeeded in surprising the quarters of the marquis of Cadiz, who, with his followers, was exhausted by fatigue and watching during the two preceding nights. The Christians, bewildered with the sudden tumult which broke their slumber, were thrown into the greatest confusion; and the marquis, who rushed half armed from his tent, found no little difficulty in bringing them to order and beating off the assailants, after receiving a wound in the arm from an arrow; while he had a still narrower escape from the ball of an arquebuse that penetrated his buckler and hit him below the cuirass, but fortunately so much spent as to do him no injury.

The Moors were not unmindful of the importance of Malaga or the gallantry with which it was defended. They made several attempts to relieve it, the failure of which was owing less to the Christians than to treachery and their own miserable feuds. A body of cavalry, which El Zagal despatched from Guadix to throw succors into the beleaguered city, was encountered and cut to pieces by a superior force of the young king Abdallah, who consummated his baseness by sending an embassy to the Christian camp, charged with a present of Arabian horses sumptuously caparisoned to Ferdinand and of costly silks and Oriental perfumes to the queen; at the same time complimenting them on their successes and soliciting the continuance of their friendly dispositions towards himself. Ferdinand and Isabella requited this act of humiliation by securing to Abdallah's subjects the right of cultivating their fields in quiet and of trafficking with the Spaniards in every commodity save military stores. At this paltry price did the dastard prince consent to stay his arm at the only moment when it could be used effectually for his country.

More serious consequences were like to have resulted from an attempt made by another party of Moors from Guadix to penetrate the Christian lines. Part of them succeeded and threw themselves into the besieged city. The remainder were cut in pieces. There was one, however, who, making no show of resistance, was taken prisoner without harm to his person. Being brought before the marquis of Cadiz, he informed that nobleman that he could make some important disclosures to the sovereigns. He was accordingly conducted to the royal tent; but, as Ferdinand was taking his siesta in the sultry hour of the day, the queen, moved by divine inspiration, according to the Castilian historian, deferred the audience till her husband should awake, and commanded the prisoner to be detained in the adjoining tent. This was occupied by Dona Beatrix de Bobadilla, marchioness of Moya, Isabella's early friend, who happened to be at that time engaged in discourse with a

Portuguese nobleman, Don Alvaro, son of the duke of Braganza.

The Moor did not understand the Castilian language, and, deceived by the rich attire and courtly bearing of these personages, he mistook them for the king and queen. While in the act of refreshing himself with a glass of water, he suddenly drew a dagger from beneath the broad folds of his *albornoz,* or Moorish mantle, which he had been incautiously suffered to retain, and darting on the Portuguese prince, gave him a deep wound on the head, and then, turning like lightning on the marchioness, aimed a stroke at her, which fortunately glanced without injury, the point of the weapon being turned by the heavy embroidery of her robes. Before he could repeat his blow, the Moorish Scaevola, with a fate very different from that of his Roman prototype,[1] was pierced with a hundred wounds by the attendants, who rushed to the spot alarmed by the cries of the marchioness, and his mangled remains were soon after discharged from a catapult into the city; a foolish bravado, which the besieged requited by slaying a Galician gentleman and sending his corpse astride upon a mule through the gates of the town into the Christian camp.

This daring attempt on the lives of the king and queen spread general consternation throughout the army. Precautions were taken for the future by ordinances prohibiting the introduction of any unknown person armed, or any Moor whatever, into the royal quarters; and the bodyguard was augmented by the addition of two hundred hidalgos[2] of Castile and Aragon, who, with their retainers, were to keep constant watch over the persons of the sovereigns.

Meanwhile, the city of Malaga, whose natural population was greatly swelled by the influx of its foreign auxiliaries, began to be straitened for supplies, while its distress was aggravated by the spectacle of abundance which reigned throughout the Spanish camp. Still,

[1] The legendary Roman hero Scaevola, ca. sixth century B.C.
[2] Noblemen.

however, the people, overawed by the soldiery, did not break out into murmurs, nor did they relax in any degree the pertinacity of their resistance. Their drooping spirits were cheered by the predictions of a fanatic, who promised that they should eat the grain which they saw in the Christian camp; a prediction which came to be verified, like most others that are verified at all, in a very different sense from that intended or understood.

The incessant cannonade kept up by the besieging army, in the meantime, so far exhausted their ammunition that they were constrained to seek supplies from the most distant parts of the kingdom and from foreign countries. The arrival of two Flemish transports at this juncture from the emperor of Germany, whose interest had been roused in the crusade, afforded a seasonable reinforcement of military stores and munitions.

The obstinate defence of Malaga had given the siege such celebrity that volunteers, eager to share in it, flocked from all parts of the Peninsula to the royal standard. Among others, the duke of Medina Sidonia, who had furnished his quota of troops at the opening of the campaign, now arrived in person with a reinforcement, together with a hundred galleys freighted with supplies, and a loan of twenty thousand *doblas*[1] of gold to the sovereigns for the expenses of the war. Such was the deep interest in it excited throughout the nation, and the alacrity which every order of men exhibited in supporting its enormous burdens.

The Castilian army, swelled by these daily augmentations, varied in its amount, according to different estimates, from sixty to ninety thousand men. Throughout this immense host the most perfect discipline was maintained. Gaming was restrained by ordinances interdicting the use of dice and cards, of which the lower orders were passionately fond. Blasphemy was severely punished. Prostitutes, the common pest of a camp, were excluded; and so entire was the subordination that not a knife was drawn and scarcely a brawl occurred, says the historian, among the motley multitude. Besides the

[1] A gold coin of fluctuating value.

higher ecclesiastics who attended the court, the camp was well supplied with holy men, priests, friars, and the chaplains of the great nobility, who performed the exercises of religion in their respective quarters with all the pomp and splendor of the Roman Catholic worship, exalting the imaginations of the soldiers into the high devotional feeling which became those who were fighting the battles of the Cross.

Hitherto, Ferdinand, relying on the blockade and yielding to the queen's desire to spare the lives of her soldiers, had formed no regular plan of assault upon the town. But as the season rolled on without the least demonstration of submission on the part of the besieged, he resolved to storm the works, which, if attended by no other consequences, might at least serve to distress the enemy and hasten the hour of surrender. Large wooden towers on rollers were accordingly constructed and provided with an apparatus of drawbridges and ladders, which, when brought near to the ramparts, would open a descent into the city. Galleries were also wrought, some for the purpose of penetrating into the place and others to sap the foundations of the walls. The whole of these operations was placed under the direction of Francisco Ramirez, the celebrated engineer of Madrid.

But the Moors anticipated the completion of these formidable preparations by a brisk, well-concerted attack on all points of the Spanish lines. They countermined the assailants and, encountering them in the subterraneous passages, drove them back, and demolished the frame-work of the galleries. At the same time, a little squadron of armed vessels, which had been riding in safety under the guns of the city, pushed out and engaged the Spanish fleet. Thus the battle raged with fire and sword, above and under ground, along the ramparts, the ocean, and the land, at the same time. Even Pulgar[1] cannot withhold his tribute of admiration to this unconquerable spirit in an enemy wasted by all the ex-

[1] Hernando del Pulgar (1430?–1491), secretary and chronicler of Ferdinand and Isabella.

tremities of famine and fatigue. "Who does not marvel," he says, "at the bold heart of these infidels in battle, their prompt obedience to their chiefs, their dexterity in the wiles of war, their patience under privation, and undaunted perseverance in their purposes?"

A circumstance occurred in a sortie from the city, indicating a trait of character worth recording. A noble Moor, named Abrahen Zenete, fell in with a number of Spanish children who had wandered from their quarters. Without injuring them, he touched them gently with the handle of his lance, saying, "Get ye gone, varlets, to your mothers." On being rebuked by his comrades, who inquired why he had let them escape so easily, he replied, "Because I saw no beard upon their chins." "An example of magnanimity," says the Curate of Los Palacios, "truly wonderful in a heathen, and which might have reflected credit on a Christian hidalgo."

But no virtue or valor could avail the unfortunate Malagans against the overwhelming force of their enemies, who, driving them back from every point, compelled them, after a desperate struggle of six hours, to shelter themselves within the defences of the town. The Christians followed up their success. A mine was sprung near a tower connected by a bridge of four arches with the main works of the place. The Moors, scattered and intimidated by the explosion, retreated across the bridge; and the Spaniards, carrying the tower, whose guns completely enfiladed it, obtained possession of this important pass into the beleaguered city. For these and other signal services during the siege, Francisco Ramirez, the master of the ordnance, received the honors of knighthood from the hand of King Ferdinand.

The citizens of Málaga, dismayed at beholding the enemy established in their defences and fainting under exhaustion from a siege which had already lasted more than three months, now began to murmur at the obstinacy of the garrison and to demand a capitulation. Their magazines of grain were emptied, and for some weeks they had been compelled to devour the flesh of horses, dogs, cats, and even the boiled hides of these animals or, in default of other nutriment, vine-leaves dressed with oil, and leaves of the palm-tree, pounded fine and baked into a sort of cake. In consequence of this loathsome and unwholesome diet, diseases were engendered. Multitudes were seen dying about the streets. Many deserted to the Spanish camp, eager to barter their liberty for bread; and the city exhibited all the extremities of squalid and disgusting wretchedness, bred by pestilence and famine among an overcrowded population. The sufferings of the citizens softened the stern heart of the alcayde, Hamet Zeli, who at length yielded to their importunities and, withdrawing his forces into the Gebalfaro, consented that the Malagans should make the best terms they could with their conqueror.

A deputation of the principal inhabitants, with an eminent merchant named Ali Dordux at their head, was then despatched to the Christian quarters with the offer of the city to capitulate on the same liberal conditions which had been uniformly granted by the Spaniards. The king refused to admit the embassy into his presence and haughtily answered, through the commander of León, that "these terms had been twice offered to the people of Malaga, and rejected; that it was too late for them to stipulate conditions, and nothing now remained but to abide by those which he, as their conqueror, should vouchsafe to them."

Ferdinand's answer spread general consternation throughout Malaga. The inhabitants saw too plainly that nothing was to be hoped from an appeal to sentiments of humanity. After a tumultuous debate, the deputies were despatched a second time to the Christian camp, charged with propositions in which concession was mingled with menace. They represented that the severe response of King Ferdinand to the citizens had rendered them desperate; that they were willing to resign to him their fortifications, their city—in short, their property of every description—on his assurance of their personal security and freedom; if he refused this, they would take their Christian captives, amounting to five or six hundred, from the dungeons in which they lay and hang them like dogs over the battlements; and then, placing their old men, women, and children in the fortress, they would set fire to the town and cut a way for themselves through their enemies, or fall in the attempt. "So," they continued, "if you gain a victory, it will be such a one as shall make the name of Malaga ring throughout the world, and to ages yet unborn!" Ferdinand, unmoved by these menaces, coolly replied that he saw no occasion to change his former determination, but they might rest assured, if they harmed a single hair of a Christian, he would put every soul in the place—man, woman, and child—to the sword.

The anxious people, who thronged forth to meet the embassy on its return to the city, were overwhelmed with the deepest gloom at its ominous tidings. Their fate was now sealed. Every avenue to hope seemed closed by the stern response of the victor. Yet hope will still linger; and although there were some frantic enough to urge the execution of their desperate menaces, the greater number of the inhabitants, and among them those most considerable for wealth and influence, preferred the chance of Ferdinand's clemency to certain, irretrievable ruin.

For the last time, therefore, the deputies issued from the gates of the city, charged with an epistle to the sovereigns from their unfortunate countrymen, in which, after deprecating their anger and lamenting their own blind obstinacy, they reminded their highnesses of the liberal terms which their ancestors had granted to Cordova, Antequera, and other cities after a defence as pertinacious as their own. They expatiated on the fame which the sovereigns had established by the generous policy of their past conquests and, appealing to their magnanimity, concluded with submitting themselves, their families, and their fortunes to their disposal. Twenty of the principal citizens were then delivered up as hostages for the peaceable demeanor of the city until its occupation by the Spaniards. "Thus," says the Curate of Los Palacios, "did the Almighty harden the hearts of these heathen, like to those of the Egyptians, in order that they might receive the full wages of the manifold oppressions which they had wrought on his people, from the days of King Roderic to the present time!"

On the appointed day, the commander of León rode through the gates of Malaga at the head of his well-appointed chivalry and took possession of the *alcazaba*, or lower citadel. The troops were then posted at their respective stations along the fortifications, and the banners of Christian Spain triumphantly unfurled from the towers of the city, where the crescent had been displayed for an uninterrupted period of nearly eight centuries.

The first act was to purify the town from the numerous dead bodies and other offensive matter which had accumulated during this long siege and lay festering in the streets, poisoning the atmosphere. The principal mosque was next consecrated with due solemnity to the service of Santa María de la Encarnacion. Crosses and bells, the symbols of Christian worship, were distributed in profusion among the sacred edifices; where, says the Catholic chronicler last quoted, "the celestial music of their chimes, sounding at every hour of the day and night, caused perpetual torment to the ears of the infidel."

On the eighteenth day of August, being somewhat more than three months from the date of opening trenches, Ferdinand and Isabella made their entrance into the conquered city, attended by the court, the clergy, and the whole of their military array. The procession moved in solemn state up the principal streets, now deserted and hushed in ominous silence, to the new cathedral of St. Mary, where mass was performed; and as the glorious anthem of the *Te Deum* rose for the first time within its ancient walls, the sovereigns, together with the whole army, prostrated themselves in grateful adoration of the Lord of hosts, who had thus reinstated them in the domains of their ancestors.

The most affecting incident was afforded by the multitude of Christian captives who were rescued from the Moorish dungeons. They were brought before the sovereigns, with their limbs heavily manacled, their beards descending to their waists, and their sallow visages emaciated by captivity and famine. Every eye was suffused with tears at the spectacle. Many recognized their ancient friends, of whose fate they had long been ignorant. Some had lingered in captivity ten or fifteen years; and among them were several belonging to the best families in Spain. On entering the presence, they would have testified their gratitude by throwing themselves at the feet of the sovereigns; but the latter, raising them up and mingling their tears with those of the liberated captives, caused their fetters to be removed and, after administering to their necessities, dismissed them with liberal presents.

The fortress of Gebalfaro surrendered on the day after the occupation of Malaga by the Spaniards. The gallant Zegri chieftain, Hamet Zeli, was loaded with chains; and being asked why he had persisted so obstinately in his rebellion, boldly answered, "Because I was commissioned to defend the place to the last extremity; and if I had been properly supported, I would have died sooner than surrender now!"

The doom of the vanquished was now to be pronounced. On entering the city, orders had been issued to the Spanish soldiery prohibiting them under the severest penalties from molesting either the persons or property of the inhabitants. These latter were directed to remain in their respective mansions with a guard set over them, while the cravings of appetite were supplied by a liberal distribution of food. At length, the whole population of the city, comprehending every age and sex, was commanded to repair to the great courtyard of the *alcazaba,* which was overlooked on all sides by lofty ramparts garrisoned by the Spanish soldiery. To this place, the scene of many a Moorish triumph, where the spoil of the border foray had been often displayed, and which might still be emblazoned with the trophy of many a Christian banner, the people of Malaga now directed their steps. As the multitude swarmed through the streets, filled with boding apprehensions of their fate, they wrung their hands and, raising their eyes to heaven, uttered the most piteous lamentations. "O Malaga," they cried, "renowned and beautiful city, how are thy sons about to forsake thee! Could not thy soil, on which they first drew breath, be suffered to cover them in death? Where is now the strength of thy towers, where the beauty of thy edifices? The strength of thy walls, alas! could not avail thy children, for they had sorely displeased their Creator. What shall become of thy old men and thy matrons, or of thy young maidens delicately nurtured within thy halls, when they shall feel the iron yoke of bondage? Can thy barbarous conquerors without remorse thus tear asunder the dearest ties of life?" Such are the melancholy strains in which the Castilian chronicler has given utterance to the sorrows of the captive city.

The dreadful doom of slavery was pronounced on the assembled multitude. One-third was to be transported into Africa in exchange for an equal number of Christian captives detained there; and all who had relatives or friends in this predicament were required to furnish a specification of them. Another third was appropriated to reimburse the state for the expenses of the war. The remainder were to be distributed as presents at home and abroad. Thus, one hundred of the flower of the African warriors were sent to the pope, who incorporated them into his guard, and converted them all in the course of the year, says the Curate of Los Palacios, into very good Christians. Fifty of the most beautiful Moorish girls were presented by Isabella to the queen of Naples, thirty to the queen of Portugal, others to the ladies of her court; and the residue of both sexes were apportioned among the nobles, cavaliers, and inferior members of the army, according to their respective rank and services.

As it was apprehended that the Malagans, rendered desperate by the prospect of a hopeless, interminable captivity, might destroy or secrete their jewels, plate, and other precious effects, in which this wealthy city abounded, rather than suffer them to fall into the hands of their enemies, Ferdinand devised a politic expedient for preventing it. He proclaimed that he would receive a certain sum, if paid within nine months, as the ransom of the whole population, and that their personal effects should be admitted in part payment. This sum averaged about thirty *doblas* a head, including in the estimate all those who might die before the determination of the period assigned. The ransom thus stipulated proved more than the unhappy people could raise, either by themselves or agents employed to solicit contributions among their brethren of Granada and Africa; at the same time, it so far deluded their hopes that they gave in a full inventory of their effects to the treasury. By this shrewd device Ferdinand obtained complete possession both of the persons and property of his victims.

Malaga was computed to contain from eleven to fifteen thousand inhabitants, exclusive of several thousand foreign auxiliaries, within its gates at the time of surrender. One cannot, at this day, read the melancholy details of its story without feelings of horror and indignation. It is impossible to vindicate the dreadful sentence passed on this unfortunate people for a display of heroism which should have excited admiration in every generous bosom. It was obviously most repugnant to Isabella's natural disposition and must be admitted to leave a stain on her memory which no coloring of history can conceal. It may find some palliation, however, in the bigotry of the age, the more excusable in a woman, whom education, general example, and natural distrust of herself, accustomed to rely, in matters of conscience, on the spiritual guides whose piety and professional learning seemed to qualify them for the trust. Even in this very transaction she fell far short of the suggestions of some of her counsellors, who urged her to put every inhabitant without exception to the sword; which, they affirmed, would be a just requital of their obstinate rebellion and would prove a wholesome warning to others! We are not told who the advisers of this precious measure were; but the whole experience of this reign shows that we shall scarcely wrong the clergy much by imputing it to them. That their arguments could warp so enlightened a mind as that of Isabella from the natural principles of justice and humanity furnishes a remarkable proof of the ascendence which the priesthood usurped over the most gifted intellects, and of their gross abuse of it, before the Reformation--by breaking the seals set on the sacred volume—opened to mankind the uncorrupted channel of divine truth.

The fate of Malaga may be said to have decided that of Granada. The latter was now shut out from the most important ports along her coasts; and she was environed on every point of her territory by her warlike foe, so that she could hardly hope more from subsequent efforts, however strenuous and united, than to postpone the inevitable hour of dissolution. The cruel treatment of Malaga was the prelude to the long series of persecutions which awaited the wretched Moslems in the land of their ancestors; in that land over which the "star of Islamism," to borrow their own metaphor, had shone in full brightness for nearly eight centuries, but where it was now fast descending amid clouds and tempests to the horizon.

The first care of the sovereigns was directed towards repeopling the depopulated city with their own subjects. Houses and lands were freely granted to such as would settle there. Numerous towns and villages with a wide circuit of territory were placed under its civil jurisdiction, and it was made the head of a diocese embracing most of the recent conquests in the south and west of Granada. These inducements, combined with the natural advantages of position and climate, soon caused the tide of Christian population to flow into the deserted city; but it was very long before it again reached the degree of commercial consequence to which it had been raised by the Moors.

After these salutary arrangements, the Spanish sovereigns led back their victorious legions in triumph to Cordova; whence dispersing to their various homes, they prepared, by a winter's repose, for new campaigns and more brilliant conquests.

[*The capture of Malaga may, as Prescott indicated, have decided the fate of the major Moorish city, Granada, but the final reduction of the capital did not occur until 1492, a year as significant in the internal history of Spain as it was in the history of exploration. The war* *in Granada was now prosecuted on a more enlarged scale than it had been. The formidable Moorish leader El Zagal was defeated; the important towns of Baza and Almeria were taken; but in the winter of 1490 Granada still remained a Moorish stronghold under the leadership of King Abdallah.**]

The winter of 1490 was busily occupied with preparations for the closing campaign against Granada. Ferdinand took command of the army in the month of April, 1491, with the purpose of sitting down before the Moorish capital, not to rise until its final surrender. The troops, which mustered in the Val de Velillos, are computed by most historians at fifty thousand horse and foot, although Martyr,[1] who served as a volunteer, swells the number to eighty thousand. They were drawn from the different cities, chiefly, as usual, from Andalusia, which had been stimulated to truly gigantic efforts throughout this protracted war, and from the nobility of every quarter, many of whom, wearied out with the contest, contented themselves with sending their quotas, while many others, as the marquises of Cadiz and Villena, the counts of Tendilla, Cabra, and Ureña, and Alonso de Aguilar, appeared in person, eager, as they had borne the brunt of so many hard campaigns, to share in the closing scene of triumph.

On the 26th of the month the army encamped near the fountain of Ojos de Huescar, in the vega, about two leagues distant from Granada. Ferdinand's first movement was to detach a considerable force, under the marquis of Villena, which he subsequently supported in person with the remainder of the army, for the purpose of scouring the fruitful regions of the Alpujarras, which served as the granary of the capital. This service was performed with such unsparing rigor that no less than twenty-four towns and hamlets in the mountains were ransacked and razed to the ground. After this, Ferdinand returned loaded with spoil to his former posi-

* From *Ferdinand and Isabella*, Part I, chap. 15.

[1] Peter Martyr (1457–1526), Italian humanist and historian.

tion on the banks of the Xenil, in full view of the Moorish metropolis, which seemed to stand alone, like some sturdy oak, the last of the forest, bidding defiance to the storm which had prostrated all its brethren.

Notwithstanding the failure of all external resources, Granada was still formidable from its local position and its defences. On the east it was fenced in by a wild mountain barrier, the Sierra Nevada, whose snow-clad summits diffused a grateful coolness over the city through the sultry heats of summer. The side towards the vega, facing the Christian encampment, was encircled by walls and towers of massive strength and solidity. The population, swelled to two hundred thousand by the immigration from the surrounding country, was likely, indeed, to be a burden in a protracted siege; but among them were twenty thousand, the flower of the Moslem chivalry, who had escaped the edge of the Christian sword. In front of the city, for an extent of nearly ten leagues, lay unrolled the magnificent vega—

> *"Fresca y regalada vega,*
> *Dulce recreacion de damas*
> *Y de hombres gloria immensa"*[1]

whose prolific beauties could scarcely be exaggerated in the most florid strains of the Arabian minstrel and which still bloomed luxuriant, notwithstanding the repeated ravages of the preceding season.

The inhabitants of Granada were filled with indignation at the sight of their enemy, thus encamped under the shadow, as it were, of their battlements. They sallied forth in small bodies, or singly, challenging the Spaniards to equal encounter. Numerous were the combats which took place between the high-mettled cavaliers on both sides, who met on the level arena, as on a tilting-ground, where they might display their prowess in the presence of the assembled beauty and chivalry of their respective nations: for the Spanish camp was

[1] "Fresh and pleasant plain, sweet recreation of ladies and great glory of men."

graced, as usual, by the presence of Queen Isabella and the infantas, with the courtly train of ladies who had accompanied their royal mistress from Alcala la Real. The Spanish ballads glow with picturesque details of these knightly tourneys, forming the most attractive portion of this romantic minstrelsy, which, celebrating the prowess of Moslem as well as Christian warriors, sheds a dying glory round the last hours of Granada.

The festivity which reigned throughout the camp on the arrival of Isabella did not divert her attention from the stern business of war. She superintended the military preparations and personally inspected every part of the encampment. She appeared on the field superbly mounted and dressed in complete armor; and as she visited the different quarters and reviewed her troops, she administered words of commendation or sympathy, suited to the condition of the soldier.

On one occasion she expressed a desire to take a nearer survey of the city. For this purpose a house was selected, affording the best point of view, in the little village of Zubia, at no great distance from Granada. The king and queen stationed themselves before a window which commanded an unbroken prospect of the Alhambra and the most beautiful quarter of the town. In the meanwhile, a considerable force, under the marquis duke of Cadiz, had been ordered, for the protection of the royal persons, to take up a position between the village and the city of Granada, with strict injunctions on no account to engage the enemy, as Isabella was unwilling to stain the pleasures of the day with unnecessary effusion of blood.

The people of Granada, however, were too impatient long to endure the presence and, as they deemed it, the bravado of their enemy. They burst forth from the gates of the capital, dragging along with them several pieces of ordnance, and commenced a brisk assault on the Spanish lines. The latter sustained the shock with firmness till the marquis of Cadiz, seeing them thrown into some disorder, found it necessary to assume the offensive and, mustering his followers around him, made one of those desperate charges which had so often broken the enemy. The Moorish cavalry faltered, but might have disputed the ground had it not been for the infantry, which, composed of the rabble population of the city, was easily thrown into confusion and hurried the horse along with it. The rout now became general. The Spanish cavaliers, whose blood was up, pursued to the very gates of Granada; "and not a lance," says Bernaldez,[1] "that day, but was dyed in the blood of the infidel." Two thousand of the enemy were slain and taken in the engagement, which lasted only a short time; and the slaughter was stopped only by the escape of the fugitives within the walls of the city.

About the middle of July, an accident occurred in the camp, which was like to have been attended with fatal consequences. The queen was lodged in a superb pavilion belonging to the marquis of Cadiz and always used by him in the Moorish war. By the carelessness of one of her attendants, a lamp was placed in such a situation that during the night, perhaps owing to a gust of wind, it set fire to the drapery or loose hangings of the pavilion, which was instantly in a blaze. The flame communicated with fearful rapidity to the neighboring tents, made of light, combustible materials, and the camp was menaced with general conflagration. This occurred at the dead of night, when all but the sentinels were buried in sleep. The queen, and her children, whose apartments were near hers, were in great peril and escaped with difficulty, though fortunately without injury. The alarm soon spread. The trumpets sounded to arms, for it was supposed to be some night attack of the enemy. Ferdinand, snatching up his arms hastily, put himself at the head of his troops, but, soon ascertaining the nature of the disaster, contented himself with posting the marquis of Cadiz, with a strong body of horse, over against the city in order to repel any sally from that quarter. None, however, was attempted, and the fire was at length extinguished without personal injury, though not without loss of much valuable proper-

[1] Andres Bernaldez, Curate of Los Palacios (1488–1513), a major authority on the Moorish war.

ty in jewels, plate, brocade, and other costly decorations of the tents of the nobility.

In order to guard against a similar disaster, as well as to provide comfortable winter-quarters for the army should the siege be so long protracted as to require it, it was resolved to build a town of substantial edifices on the place of the present encampment. The plan was immediately put in execution. The work was distributed in due proportions among the troops of the several cities and of the great nobility; the soldier was on a sudden converted into an artisan, and, instead of war, the camp echoed with the sounds of peaceful labor.

In less than three months this stupendous task was accomplished. The spot so recently occupied by light, fluttering pavilions was thickly covered with solid structures of stone and mortar, comprehending, besides dwelling-houses, stables for a thousand horses. The town was thrown into a quadrangular form, traversed by two spacious avenues intersecting each other at right angles in the center, in the form of a cross, with stately portals at each of the four extremities. Inscriptions on blocks of marble in the various quarters recorded the respective shares of the several cities in the execution of the work. When it was completed, the whole army was desirous that the new city should bear the name of their illustrious queen; but Isabella modestly declined this tribute and bestowed on the place the title of Santa Fe, in token of the unshaken trust manifested by her people throughout this war in Divine Providence. With this name it still stands as it was erected in 1491, a monument of the constancy and enduring patience of the Spaniards, "the only city in Spain," in the words of a Castilian writer, "that has never been contaminated by the Moslem heresy."

The erection of Santa Fe by the Spaniards struck a greater damp into the people of Granada than the most successful military achievement could have done. They beheld the enemy setting foot on their soil with a resolution never more to resign it. They already began to suffer from the rigorous blockade, which effectually excluded supplies from their own territories, while all communication with Africa was jealously intercepted. Symptoms of insubordination had begun to show themselves among the overgrown population of the city, as it felt more and more the pressure of famine. In this crisis the unfortunate Abdallah and his principal counsellors became convinced that the place could not be maintained much longer; and at length, in the month of October, propositions were made, through the vizier Abul Cazim Abdelmalic, to open a negotiation for the surrender of the place. The affair was to be conducted with the utmost caution; since the people of Granada, notwithstanding their precarious condition and their disquietude, were buoyed up by indefinite expectations of relief from Africa or some other quarter.

The Spanish sovereigns intrusted the negotiation to their secretary, Fernando de Zafra, and to Gonsalvo de Cordova, the latter of whom was selected for this delicate business from his uncommon address and his familiarity with the Moorish habits and language. Thus the capitulation of Granada was referred to the man who acquired in her long wars the military science which enabled him, at a later period, to foil the most distinguished generals of Europe.

The conferences were conducted by night with the utmost secrecy, sometimes within the walls of Granada and at others in the little hamlet of Churriana, about a league distant from it. At length, after large discussion on both sides, the terms of capitulation were definitively settled, and ratified by the respective monarchs on the 25th of November, 1491.

The conditions were of similar though somewhat more liberal import than those granted to Baza. The inhabitants of Granada were to retain possession of their mosques, with the free exercise of their religion, with all its peculiar rites and ceremonies; they were to be judged by their own laws, under their own cadis or magistrates, subject to the general control of the Castilian governor; they were to be unmolested in their ancient usages, manners, language, and dress; to be protected in the full enjoyment of their property, with the right of disposing of it on their own account and of migrating when and where they would; and to be furnished with vessels for the conveyance of such as chose within three years to pass into Africa. No heavier taxes were to be imposed than those customarily paid to their Arabic sovereigns, and none whatever before the expiration of three years. King Abdallah was to reign over a specified territory in the Alpujarras, for which he was to do homage to the Castilian Crown. The artillery and the fortifications were to be delivered into the hands of the Christians, and the city was to be surrendered in sixty days from the date of the capitulation. Such were the principal terms of the surrender of Granada, as authenticated by the most accredited Castilian and Arabic authorities; which I have stated the more precisely, as affording the best data for estimating the extent of Spanish perfidy in later times.

The conferences could not be conducted so secretly but that some report of them got air among the populace of the city, who now regarded Abdallah with an evil eye for his connection with the Christians. When the fact of the capitulation became known, the agitation speedily mounted into an open insurrection, which menaced the safety of the city as well as of Abdallah's person. In this alarming state of things, it was thought best by that monarch's counsellors to anticipate the appointed day of surrender; and the 2nd of January, 1492, was accordingly fixed on for that purpose.

Every preparation was made by the Spaniards for performing this last act of the drama with suitable pomp and effect. The mourning which the court had put on for the death of Prince Alonso of Portugal, occasioned by a fall from his horse a few months after his marriage with the infanta Isabella, was exchanged for gay and magnificent apparel. On the morning of the 2nd, the whole Christian camp exhibited a scene of the most animating bustle. The grand cardinal Mendoza was sent forward at the head of a large detachment, comprehending his household troops and the veteran infantry grown grey in the Moorish wars, to occupy the Alhambra preparatory to the entrance of the sovereigns. Ferdinand stationed himself at some distance in the rear, near an Arabian mosque, since consecrated as the hermitage of St. Sebastian. He was surrounded by his courtiers, with their stately retinues, glittering in gorgeous panoply and proudly displaying the armorial bearings of their ancient houses. The queen halted still farther in the rear, at the village of Armilla.

As the column under the grand cardinal advanced up the Hill of Martyrs, over which a road had been constructed for the passage of the artillery, he was met by the Moorish prince Abdallah, attended by fifty cavaliers, who, descending the hill, rode up to the position occupied by Ferdinand on the banks of the Xenil. As the Moor approached the Spanish king, he would have thrown himself from his horse and saluted his hand in token of homage; but Ferdinand hastily prevented him, embracing him with every mark of sympathy and regard. Abdallah then delivered up the keys of the Alhambra to his conqueror, saying, "They are thine, O king, since Allah so decrees it: use thy success with clemency and moderation." Ferdinand would have uttered some words of consolation to the unfortunate prince, but he moved forward with a dejected air to the spot occupied by Isabella, and after similar acts of obeisance, passed on to join his family, who had preceded him with his most valuable effects on the route to the Alpujarras.

The sovereigns during this time awaited with impatience the signal of the occupation of the city by the cardinal's troops, which, winding slowly along the outer circuit of the walls, as previously arranged, in order to spare the feelings of the citizens as far as possible, entered by what is now called the gate of Los Molinos. In a short time, the large silver cross, borne by Ferdinand throughout the crusade, was seen sparkling in the sunbeams, while the standards of Castile and St. Jago waved triumphantly from the red towers of the Alhambra. At this glorious spectacle the choir of the royal chapel broke forth into the solemn anthem of the *Te Deum;* and the whole army, penetrated with deep emotion, prostrated themselves on their knees in adoration of the Lord of hosts, who had at length granted the consummation of their wishes in this last and glorious triumph of the Cross. The grandees who surrounded Ferdinand then advanced towards the queen and, kneeling down, saluted her hand in token of homage to her as sovereign of Granada. The procession took up its march towards the city, "the king and queen moving in the midst," says an historian, "emblazoned with royal magnificence; and as they were in the prime of life, and had now achieved the completion of this glorious conquest, they seemed to represent even more than their wonted majesty. Equal with each other, they were raised far above the rest of the world. They appeared, indeed, more than mortal, and as if sent by heaven for the salvation of Spain."

In the meanwhile the Moorish king, traversing the route of the Alpujarras, reached a rocky eminence which commanded a last view of Granada. He checked his horse, and, as his eye for the last time wandered over the scenes of his departed greatness, his heart swelled, and he burst into tears. "You do well," said his more masculine mother, "to weep like a woman for what you could not defend like a man!" "Alas!" exclaimed the unhappy exile, "when were woes ever equal to mine!" The scene of this event is still pointed out to the traveller by the people of the district; and the rocky height from which the Moorish chief took his sad farewell of the princely abodes of his youth is commemorated by the poetical title of *El ultimo Sospiro del Moro,* "The Last Sigh of the Moor."

The sequel of Abdallah's history is soon told. Like his uncle, El Zagal, he pined away in his barren domain of the Alpujarras, under the shadow, as it were, of his ancient palaces. In the following year he passed over to Fez with his family, having commuted his petty sovereignty for a considerable sum of money paid him by Ferdinand and Isabella, and soon after fell in battle in the service of an African prince, his kinsman. "Wretched man," exclaims a caustic chronicler of his nation, "who could lose his life in another's cause, though he did not dare to die in his own! Such," continues the Arabian, with characteristic resignation, "was the immutable decree of destiny. Blessed be Allah, who exalteth and debaseth the kings of the earth, according to his divine will, in whose fulfilment consists that eternal justice which regulates all human affairs." The portal through which King Abdallah for the last time issued from his capital was at his request walled up, that none other might again pass through it. In this condition it remains to this day, a memorial of the sad destiny of the last of the kings of Granada.

The fall of Granada excited a general sensation throughout Christendom, where it was received as counterbalancing, in a manner, the loss of Constantinople nearly half a century before. At Rome the event was commemorated by a solemn procession of the pope and cardinals to St. Peter's, where high mass was celebrated, and the public rejoicing continued for several days. The intelligence was welcomed with no less satisfaction in England, where Henry the Seventh was seated on the throne.

Thus ended the war of Granada, which is often compared by the Castilian chroniclers to that of Troy in its duration, and which certainly fully equalled the latter in variety of picturesque and romantic incidents and in circumstances of poetical interest. With the surrender of its capital terminated the Arabian empire in the Peninsula after an existence of seven hundred and forty-one years from the date of the original conquest. The consequences of this closing war were of the highest moment to Spain. The most obvious was the recovery of an extensive territory, hitherto held by a people whose difference of religion, language, and general habits made them not only incapable of assimilating with their Christian neighbors but almost their natural enemies; while their local position was a matter of just concern, as interposed between the great divisions of the Spanish monarchy and opening an obvious avenue to invasion from Africa. By the new conquest, moreover, the Spaniards gained a large extent of country, possessing the highest capacities for production in its natural fruitfulness of soil, the temperature of climate, and the state of cultivation to which it had been brought by its ancient occupants; while its shores were lined with commodious havens that afforded every facility for commerce. The scattered fragments of the ancient Visigothic empire were now again, with the exception of the little state of Navarre, combined into one great monarchy, as originally destined by nature: and Christian Spain gradually rose, by means of her new acquisitions, from a subordinate situation to the level of a first-rate European power.

The moral influence of the Moorish war, its influence on the Spanish character, was highly important. The inhabitants of the great divisions of the country, as in most countries during the feudal ages, had been brought too frequently into collision with each other to allow the existence of a pervading national feeling. This was particularly the case in Spain, where independent states insensibly grew out of the detached fragments of territory recovered at different times from the Moorish monarchy. The war of Granada subjected all the various sections of the country to one common action under the influence of common motives of the most exciting interest; while it brought them in conflict with a race the extreme repugnance of whose institutions and character to their own served greatly to nourish the nationality of sentiment. In this way the spark of patriotism was kindled throughout the whole nation, and the most distant provinces of the Peninsula were knit together by a bond of union which has remained indissoluble.

The consequences of these wars in a military aspect are also worthy of notice. Up to this period, war had been carried on by irregular levies, extremely limited in numerical amount and in period of service, under little subordination, except to their own immediate chiefs, and wholly unprovided with the apparatus required for extended operations. The Spaniards were even lower than most of the European nations in military science, as is apparent from the infinite pains of Isabella to avail herself of all foreign resources for their improvement. In the war of Granada, masses of men were brought together far greater than had hitherto been known in modern warfare. They were kept in the field not only through long campaigns but far into the winter: a thing altogether unprecedented. They were made to act in concert, and the numerous petty chiefs brought into complete subjection to one common head, whose personal character enforced the authority of station. Lastly, they were supplied with all the requisite munitions through the providence of Isabella, who introduced into the service the most skilful engineers from other countries and kept in pay bodies of mercenaries—as the Swiss, for example, reputed the best-disciplined troops of that day. In this admirable school the Spanish soldier was gradually trained to patient endurance, fortitude, and thorough subordination; and those celebrated captains were formed, with that invincible infantry, which in the beginning of the sixteenth century spread the military fame of their country over all Christendom.

But, with all our sympathy for the conquerors, it is impossible without a deep feeling of regret to contemplate the decay and final extinction of a race who had made such high advances in civilization as the Spanish Arabs; to see them driven from the stately palaces reared by their own hands, wandering as exiles over the lands which still blossomed with the fruits of their industry, and wasting away under persecution, until their very name as a nation was blotted out from the map of history. It must be admitted, however, that they had long since reached their utmost limit of advancement as a people. The light shed over their history shines from distant ages; for during the later period of their existence they appear to have reposed in a state of torpid, luxurious indulgence, which would seem to argue that, when causes of external excitement were withdrawn, the inherent vices of their social institutions had incapacitated them for the further production of excellence. In this impotent condition, it was wisely ordered that their territory should be occupied by people whose religion and more liberal form of government, however frequently misunderstood or perverted, qualified them for advancing still higher the interests of humanity.

It will not be amiss to terminate the narrative of the war of Granada with some notice of the fate of Rodrigo Ponce de León, marquis duke of Cadiz; for he may be regarded in a peculiar manner as the hero of it, having struck the first stroke by the surprise of Alhama and witnessed every campaign till the surrender of Granada. A circumstantial account of his last moments is afforded by the pen of his worthy countryman, the Andalusian Curate of Los Palacios. The gallant marquis survived the close of the war only a short time, terminating his days at his mansion in Seville on the 28th of August, 1492, by a disorder brought on by fatigue and incessant exposure. He had reached the forty-ninth year of his age and, although twice married, left no legitimate issue. In his person he was of about the middle stature, of a compact, symmetrical frame, a fair complexion, with light hair inclining to red. He was an excellent horseman and well skilled in most of the exercises of chivalry. He had the rare merit of combining sagacity with intrepidity in action. Though somewhat impatient and slow to forgive, he was frank and generous, a warm friend, and a kind master to his vassals.

He was strict in his observance of the Catholic worship, punctilious in keeping all the church festivals and in enforcing their observance throughout his domains; and in war he was a most devout champion of the Virgin. He was ambitious of acquisitions, but lavish in expenditure, especially in the embellishment and fortification of his towns and castles; spending on Alcala de Guadaira, Xerez, and Alanis the enormous sum of seventeen million *maravedis*.[1] To the ladies he was courteous, as became a true knight. At his death, the king and queen with the whole court went into mourning; "for he was a much-loved cavalier," says the Curate, "and was esteemed, like the Cid,[2] both by friend and foe; and no Moor durst abide in that quarter of the field where his banner was displayed."

His body, after lying in state for several days in his

[1] The Castilian money of account.

[2] The Cid was Ruy Diaz de Bivar (1040–1099), a Castilian hero.

palace at Seville, with his trusty sword by his side, with which he had fought all his battles, was borne in solemn procession by night through the streets of the city, which was everywhere filled with the deepest lamentation, and was finally deposited in the great chapel of the Augustine church, in the tomb of his ancestors. Ten Moorish banners, which he had taken in battle with the infidel before the war of Granada, were borne along at his funeral, "and still wave over his sepulchre," says Bernaldez, "keeping alive the memory of his exploits, as undying as his soul." The banners have long since moldered into dust; the very tomb which contained his ashes has been sacrilegiously demolished; but the fame of the hero will survive as long as anything like respect for valor, courtesy, unblemished honor, or any other attribute of chivalry shall be found in Spain.

*3. The Italian Wars**

[The conquest of the Moors and the establishment of internal order was only a part of the history of Spain during the reigns of Ferdinand and Isabella. In the second part of his work, Prescott turned to consider "the period when, the interior organization of the monarchy having been completed, the Spanish nation entered on its schemes of discovery and conquest . . . the period illustrating more particularly the foreign policy of Ferdinand and Isabella." The conquest of Granada in 1492 allowed Ferdinand to pursue a more active policy abroad than had typified the early part of the reign. This involved some major adjustments, especially in regard to France. Cas-

* From *Ferdinand and Isabella,* Part II, chap. 12.

tile had been traditionally friendly to France; Aragon had been hostile. In the period after 1492, it was the Aragonese policy that predominated. Attention was directed to two areas, the Catalan-French border and Italy; when the French king Charles VIII seized Naples in 1495, Italy became the focus of Spanish foreign policy and war with France became a necessity. During campaigns in 1495 to 1497 and 1501 to 1504, Gonzalo de Cordoba, the Great Captain, shaped the mighty Spanish army that was to be such an essential part of the Spanish preponderance of the sixteenth and seventeenth centuries. Prescott was strongly attracted to the romantic figure of Gonzalo; he wrote of him: "His characteristics were prudence, coolness, steadiness of purpose, and intimate knowledge of man; he understood above all the temper of his own countrymen; he may be said in some degree to have formed their military character." Prescott's narrative is here resumed during Gonzalo's campaign in Italy in 1503. Gonzalo had marched out of the town of Barleta and had encamped near Cerignola; the French army under the Duke of Nemours pursued him.]

The weather, although only at the latter end of April, was extremely sultry; the troops, notwithstanding Gonsalvo's orders on crossing the river Ofanto, the ancient Aufidus, had failed to supply themselves with sufficient water for the march; parched with heat and dust, they were soon distressed by excessive thirst; and as the burning rays of the noontide sun beat fiercely on their heads, many of them, especially those cased in heavy armor, sank down on the road, fainting with exhaustion and fatigue. Gonsalvo was seen in every quarter, administering to the necessities of his men and striving to reanimate their drooping spirits. At length, to relieve them, he commanded that each trooper should take one of the infantry on his crupper, setting the example himself by mounting a German ensign behind him on his own horse.

In this way the whole army arrived early in the afternoon before Cerignola, a small town on an eminence about sixteen miles from Barleta, where the nature of the ground afforded the Spanish general a favorable position for his camp. The sloping sides of the hill were covered with vineyards, and its base was protected by a ditch of considerable depth. Gonsalvo saw at once the advantages of the ground. His men were jaded by the march; but there was no time to lose, as the French, who, on his departure from Barleta, had been drawn up under the walls of Canossa, were now rapidly advancing. All hands were put in requisition, therefore, for widening the trench, in which they planted sharp-pointed stakes; while the earth which they excavated enabled them to throw up a parapet of considerable height on the side next the town. On this rampart he mounted his little train of artillery, consisting of thirteen guns, and behind it drew up his forces in order of battle.

Before these movements were completed in the Spanish camp, the bright arms and banners of the French were seen glistening in the distance amid the tall fennel and cane-brakes with which the country was thickly covered. As soon as they had come in view of the Spanish encampment, they were brought to a halt, while a council of war was called to determine the expediency of giving battle that evening. The duke of Nemours would have deferred it till the following morning, as the day was already far spent and allowed no time for reconnoitring the position of his enemy. But Ives d'Alègre, Chandieu, the commander of the Swiss, and some other officers were for immediate action, representing the importance of not balking the impatience of the soldiers, who were all hot for the assault. In the course of the debate, Alègre was so much heated as to throw out some rash taunts on the courage of the viceroy, which the latter would have avenged on the spot had not his arm been arrested by Louis d'Ars. He had the weakness, however, to suffer them to change his cooler purpose, exclaiming, "We will fight to-night, then; and perhaps those who vaunt the loudest will be found to trust more to their spurs than their swords"; a prediction bitterly justified by the event.

While this dispute was going on, Gonsalvo gained time for making the necessary disposition of his troops. In the center he placed his German auxiliaries, armed with their long pikes, and on each wing the Spanish infantry under the command of Pedro Navarro, Diego de Paredes, Pizarro, and other illustrious captains. The defence of the artillery was committed to the left wing. A considerable body of men-at-arms, including those recently equipped from the spoils of Ruvo, was drawn up within the intrenchments, in a quarter affording a convenient opening for a sally, and placed under the orders of Mendoza and Fabrizio Colonna, whose brother Prospero and Pedro de la Paz took charge of the light cavalry, which was posted without the lines to annoy the advance of the enemy and act on any point, as occasion might require. Having completed his preparations, the Spanish general coolly waited the assault of the French.

The duke of Nemours had marshalled his forces in a very different order. He distributed them into three battles or divisions, stationing his heavy horse, composing altogether, as Gonsalvo declared, "the finest body of cavalry seen for many years in Italy," under the command of Louis d'Ars, on the right. The second and center division, formed somewhat in the rear of the right, was made up of the Swiss and Gascon infantry, headed by the brave Chandieu; and his left, consisting chiefly of his light cavalry and drawn up, like the last, somewhat in the rear of the preceding, was intrusted to Alègre.

It was within half an hour of sunset when the duke of Nemours gave orders for the attack and, putting himself at the head of the gendarmerie on the right, spurred at full gallop against the Spanish left. The hostile armies were nearly equal, amounting to between six and seven thousand men each. The French were superior in the number and condition of their cavalry, rising to a third of their whole force; while Gonsalvo's strength lay chiefly in his infantry, which had acquired a lesson of tactics under him that raised it to a level with the best in Europe.

As the French advanced, the guns on the Spanish left poured a lively fire into their ranks, when, a spark accidentally communicating with the magazine of powder, the whole blew up with a tremendous explosion. The Spaniards were filled with consternation; but Gonsalvo, converting the misfortune into a lucky omen, called out, "Courage, soldiers! these are the beacon-lights of victory! We have no need of our guns at close quarters."

In the meantime, the French van under Nemours, advancing rapidly under the dark clouds of smoke which rolled heavily over the field, were unexpectedly brought up by the deep trench, of whose existence they were unapprised. Some of the horse were precipitated into it, and all received a sudden check, until Nemours, finding it impossible to force the works in this quarter, rode along their front in search of some practicable passage. In doing this, he necessarily exposed his flank to the fatal aim of the Spanish arquebusiers. A shot from one of them took effect on the unfortunate young nobleman, and he fell, mortally wounded, from his saddle.

At this juncture, the Swiss and Gascon infantry, briskly moving up to second the attack of the now disordered horse, arrived before the intrenchments. Undismayed by this formidable barrier, their commander, Chandieu, made the most desperate attempts to force a passage; but the loose earth freshly turned up afforded no hold to the feet, and his men were compelled to recoil from the dense array of German pikes which bristled over the summit of the breastwork. Chandieu, their leader, made every effort to rally and bring them back to the charge, but in the act of doing this was hit by a ball, which stretched him lifeless in the ditch; his burnished arms and the snow-white plumes above his helmet making him a conspicuous mark for the enemy.

All was now confusion. The Spanish arquebusiers, screened by their defences, poured a galling fire into the dense masses of the enemy, who were mingled together indiscriminately, horse and foot, while, the leaders being down, no one seemed capable of bringing them to order. At this critical moment, Gonsalvo, whose eagle eye took in the operations of the whole field, ordered a general charge along the line; and the Spaniards, leaping their intrenchments, descended with the fury of an avalanche on their foes, whose wavering columns, completely broken by the violence of the shock, were seized with a panic and fled, scarcely offering any resistance. Louis d'Ars, at the head of such of the men-at-arms as could follow him, went off in one direction and Ives d'Alègre, with his light cavalry, which had hardly come into action, in another; thus fully verifying the ominous prediction of his commander. The slaughter fell most heavily on the Swiss and Gascon foot, whom the cavalry under Mendoza and Pedro de la Paz rode down and cut to pieces without sparing, till the shades of evening shielded them at length from their pitiless pursuers.

Prospero Colonna pushed on to the French encampment, where he found the tables in the duke's tent spread for his evening repast, of which the Italian general and his followers did not fail to make good account—a trifling incident that well illustrates the sudden reverses of war.

The Great Captain passed the night on the field of battle, which on the following morning presented a ghastly spectacle of the dying and the dead. More than three thousand French are computed by the best accounts to have fallen. The loss of the Spaniards, covered as they were by their defences, was inconsiderable. All the enemy's artillery, consisting of thirteen pieces, his baggage, and most of his colors fell into their hands. Never was there a more complete victory, achieved too within the space of little more than an hour. The body of the unfortunate Nemours, which was recognized by one of his pages from the rings on the fingers, was found under a heap of slain, much disfigured. It appeared that he had received three several wounds, disproving, if need were, by his honorable death, the injurious taunts of Alègre. Gonsalvo was affected even to tears at beholding the mutilated remains of his young and gallant adversary, who, whatever judgment might be formed of his capacity as a leader, was allowed to have all the qualities which belong to a true knight. With him perished the last scion of the illustrious house of Armagnac. Gonsalvo ordered his remains to be conveyed to Barleta, where they were laid in the cemetery of the convent of St. Francis, with all the honors due to his high station.

The Spanish commander lost no time in following up his blow, well aware that it is quite as difficult to improve a victory as to win one. The French had rushed into battle with too much precipitation to agree on any plan of operations or any point on which to rally in case of defeat. They accordingly scattered in different directions, and Pedro de la Paz was despatched in pursuit of Louis d'Ars, who threw himself into Venosa, where he kept the enemy at bay for many months longer. Paredes kept close on the scent of Alègre, who, finding the gates shut against him wherever he passed, at length took shelter in Gaeta, on the extreme point of the Neapolitan territory. There he endeavored to rally the scattered relics of the field of Cerignola and to establish a strong position, from which the French, when strengthened by fresh supplies from home, might recommence operations for the recovery of the kingdom.

The day after the battle of Cerignola the Spaniards received tidings of another victory, scarcely less important, gained over the French in Calabria the preceding week. The army sent out under Portocarrero had reached that coast early in March; but soon after its arrival its gallant commander fell ill and died. The dying general named Don Fernando de Andrada as his successor; and this officer, combining his forces with those before in the country under Cardona and Benavides, encountered the French commander D'Aubigny in a pitched battle not far from Seminara on Friday the 21st of April. It was near the same spot on which the latter had twice beaten the Spaniards. But the star of France was on the wane; and the gallant old officer had the mortification to see his little corps of veterans completely routed after a sharp engagement of less than an hour, while he himself was retrieved with difficulty from the hands of the enemy by the valor of his Scottish guard.

The Great Captain and his army, highly elated with the news of this fortunate event, which annihilated the French power in Calabria, began their march on Naples, Fabrizio Colonna having been first detached into the Abruzzi to receive the submission of the people in that quarter. The tidings of the victory had spread far and wide; and as Gonsalvo's army advanced, they beheld the ensigns of Aragon floating from the battlements of the towns upon their route, while the inhabitants came forth to greet the conqueror, eager to testify their devotion to the Spanish cause. The army halted at Benevento; and the general sent his summons to the city of Naples, inviting it in the most courteous terms to resume its ancient allegiance to the legitimate branch of Aragon. It was hardly to be expected that the allegiance of a people who had so long seen their country set up as a mere stake for political gamesters should sit very closely upon them, or that they should care to peril their lives on the transfer of a crown which had shifted on the heads of half-a-dozen proprietors in as many successive years. With the same ductile enthusiasm, therefore, with which they had greeted the accession of Charles the Eighth and of Louis the Twelfth, they now welcomed the restoration of the ancient dynasty of Aragon; and deputies from the principal nobility and citizens waited on the Great Captain at Acerra, where they tendered him the key of the city and requested the confirmation of their rights and privileges.

Gonsalvo, having promised this in the name of his royal master, on the following morning, the 14th of May, 1503, made his entrance in great state into the capital, leaving his army without the walls. He was escorted by the military of the city under a royal canopy borne by the deputies. The streets were strewed with flowers, the edifices decorated with appropriate emblems and devices, and wreathed with banners emblazoned with the united arms of Aragon and Naples. As he passed along, the city rang with the acclamations of countless multitudes who thronged the streets; while

every window and housetop was filled with spectators, eager to behold the man who, with scarcely any other resources than those of his own genius, had so long defied, and at length completely foiled, the power of France.

On the following day a deputation of the nobility and people waited on the Great Captain at his quarters and tendered him the usual oaths of allegiance for his master, King Ferdinand, whose accession finally closed the series of revolutions which had so long agitated this unhappy country.

The city of Naples was commanded by two strong fortresses still held by the French, which, being well victualled and supplied with ammunition, showed no disposition to surrender. The Great Captain determined, therefore, to reserve a small corps for their reduction, while he sent forward the main body of his army to besiege Gaeta. But the Spanish infantry refused to march until the heavy arrears, suffered to accumulate through the negligence of the government, were discharged; and Gonsalvo, afraid of awakening the mutinous spirit which he had once found it so difficult to quell, was obliged to content himself with sending forward his cavalry and German levies, and to permit the infantry to take up its quarters in the capital under strict orders to respect the persons and property of the citizens.

He now lost no time in pressing the siege of the French fortresses, whose impregnable situation might have derided the efforts of the most formidable enemy in the ancient state of military science. But the reduction of these places was intrusted to Pedro Navarro, the celebrated engineer, whose improvements in the art of mining have gained him the popular reputation of being its inventor, and who displayed such unprecedented skill on this occasion as makes it a memorable epoch in the annals of war.

Under his directions, the small tower of St. Vincenzo having been first reduced by a furious cannonade, a mine was run under the outer defences of the great fortress called Castel Nuovo. On the 21st of May the mine was sprung, a passage was opened over the prostrate ramparts, and the assailants, rushing in with Gonsalvo and Navarro at their head before the garrison had time to secure the drawbridge, applied their ladders to the walls of the castle and succeeded in carrying the place by escalade after a desperate struggle, in which the greater part of the French were slaughtered. An immense booty was found in the castle. The Angevin party had made it a place of deposit for their most valuable effects, gold, jewels, plate, and other treasures, which, together with its well-stored magazines of grain and ammunition, became the indiscriminate spoil of the victors. As some of these, however, complained of not getting their share of the plunder, Gonsalvo, giving full scope in the exultation of the moment to military license, called out, gaily, "Make amends for it, then, by what you can find in my quarters!" The words were not uttered to deaf ears. The mob of soldiery rushed to the splendid palace of the Angevin prince of Salerno, then occupied by the Great Captain, and in a moment its sumptuous furniture, paintings, and other costly decorations, together with the contents of its generous cellar, were seized and appropriated without ceremony by the invaders, who thus indemnified themselves at their general's expense for the remissness of the government.

After some weeks of protracted operations, the remaining fortress, Castel d'Uovo, as it was called, opened its gates to Navarro; and a French fleet, coming into the harbor, had the mortification to find itself fired on from the walls of the place it was intended to relieve. Before this event, Gonsalvo, having obtained funds from Spain for paying off his men, quit the capital and directed his march on Gaeta. The important results of his victories were now fully disclosed. D'Aubigny, with the wreck of the forces escaped from Seminara, had surrendered. The two Abruzzi, the Capitanate, all the Basilicate, except Venosa, still held by Louis d'Ars, and indeed every considerable place in the kingdom had tendered its submission, with the exception of Gaeta. Summoning, therefore, to his aid Andrada, Navarro, and his other officers, the Great Captain resolved to concentrate all his strength on this point, designing to press the siege and thus exterminate at a blow the feeble remains of the French power in Italy. The enterprise was attended with more difficulty than he had anticipated.

[*Gaeta did not easily fall to Gonzalo. There, as Prescott commented, he "experienced an opposition to which, of late, he had been wholly unaccustomed." Moreover, he received intelligence that the French had crossed the Tiber and were in full march toward him. It was not until half a year later that he was able to bring his campaign to a close. Finally routing his enemies on the Garigliano River between Naples and Gaeta, he was at last able to enter the stronghold which had long eluded him. The victory brought his military career to an end; Prescott took advantage of this to add to the narrative a section explaining the military significance of the new Spanish army.**]

On the 3rd of January, 1504, Gonsalvo made his entry into Gaeta; and the thunders of his ordnance, now for the first time heard from its battlements, announced that this strong key to the dominions of Naples had passed into the hands of Aragon. After a short delay for the refreshment of his troops, he set out for the capital. But, amidst the general jubilee which greeted his return, he was seized with a fever, brought on by the incessant fatigue and high mental excitement in which he had been kept for the last four months. The attack was severe, and the event for some time doubtful. During this state of suspense the public mind was in the deepest agitation. The popular manners of Gonsalvo had won the hearts of the giddy people of Naples, who transferred their affections, indeed, as readily as their allegiances; and prayers and vows for his restoration were offered up in all the churches and monasteries of the city. His excellent constitution at length got the better of his disease. As soon as this favorable result was ascertained, the whole population, rushing to the other extreme, abandoned itself to a delirium of joy; and, when he was sufficiently recovered to give them audience, men

* From *Ferdinand and Isabella*, Part II, chap. 15.

of all ranks thronged to Castel Nuovo, to tender their congratulations and obtain a sight of the hero who now returned to their capital for the third time with the laurel of victory on his brow. Every tongue, says his enthusiastic biographer, was eloquent in his praise: some dwelling on his noble port and the beauty of his countenance; others on the elegance and amenity of his manners; and all dazzled by a spirit of munificence which would have become royalty itself.

The tide of panegyric was swelled by more than one bard who sought, though with indifferent success, to catch inspiration from so glorious a theme, trusting doubtless that his liberal hand would not stint the recompense to the precise measure of desert. Amid this general burst of adulation, the muse of Sannazaro,[1] worth all his tribe, was alone silent; for the trophies of the conqueror were raised on the ruins of that royal house under which the bard had been so long sheltered; and this silence, so rare in his tuneful brethren, must be admitted to reflect more credit on his name than the best he ever sung.

The first business of Gonsalvo was to call together the different orders of the state and receive their oaths of allegiance to King Ferdinand. He next occupied himself with the necessary arrangements for the reorganization of the government and for reforming various abuses which had crept into the administration of justice, more particularly. In these attempts to introduce order he was not a little thwarted, however, by the insubordination of his own soldiery. They loudly clamored for the discharge of the arrears, still shamefully protracted, till, their discontent swelling to open mutiny, they forcibly seized on two of the principal places in the kingdom as security for the payment. Gonsalvo chastised their insolence by disbanding several of the most refractory companies and sending them home for punishment. He endeavored to relieve them in part by raising contributions from the Neapolitans. But the soldiers took the matter into their own hands, oppressing the un-

[1] Jacopo Sannazaro, Italian Renaissance poet, author of *Arcadia*.

fortunate people on whom they were quartered in a manner which rendered their condition scarcely more tolerable than when exposed to the horrors of actual war. This was the introduction, according to Guicciardini,[1] of those systematic military exactions in time of peace which became so common afterwards in Italy, adding an inconceivable amount to the long catalogue of woes which afflicted that unhappy land.

Amidst his manifold duties, Gonsalvo did not forget the gallant officers who had borne with him the burdens of war; and he requited their services in a princely style, better suited to his feelings than his interests, as subsequently appeared. Among them were Navarro, Mendoza, Andrada, Benavides, Leyva, the Italians Alviano and the two Colonnas, most of whom lived to display the lessons of tactics which they learned under this great commander on a still wider theatre of glory in the reign of Charles the Fifth. He made them grants of cities, fortresses, and extensive lands, according to their various claims, to be held as fiefs of the Crown. All this was done with the previous sanction of his royal master, Ferdinand the Catholic. They did some violence, however, to his more economical spirit, and he was heard somewhat peevishly to exclaim, "It boots little for Gonsalvo de Cordova to have won a kingdom for me, if he lavishes it all away before it comes into my hands." It began to be perceived at court that the Great Captain was too powerful for a subject.

Meanwhile, Louis the Twelfth was filled with serious apprehensions for the fate of his possessions in the north of Italy. His former allies, the emperor Maximilian and the republic of Venice, the latter more especially, had shown many indications not merely of coldness to himself but of a secret understanding with his rival, the Spanish king. The restless pope, Julius the Second, had schemes of his own wholly independent of France. The republics of Pisa and Genoa, the latter one of her avowed dependencies, had entered into correspondence

[1] Francesco Guicciardini (1483–1540), Italian lawyer and historian.

with the Great Captain and invited him to assume their protection; while several of the disaffected party in Milan had assured him of their active support in case he would march with a sufficient force to overturn the existing government. Indeed, not only France but Europe in general expected that the Spanish commander would avail himself of the present crisis to push his victorious arms into upper Italy, revolutionize Tuscany in his way, and, wresting Milan from the French, drive them, crippled and disheartened by their late reverses, beyond the Alps.

But Gonsalvo had occupation enough on his hands in settling the disordered state of Naples. King Ferdinand, his sovereign, notwithstanding the ambition of universal conquest absurdly imputed to him by the French writers, had no design to extend his acquisitions beyond what he could permanently maintain. His treasury, never overflowing, was too deeply drained by the late heavy demands on it for him so soon to embark on another perilous enterprise, that must rouse anew the swarms of enemies who seemed willing to rest in quiet after their long and exhausting struggle; nor is there any reason to suppose he sincerely contemplated such a movement for a moment.

The apprehension of it, however, answered Ferdinand's purpose by preparing the French monarch to arrange his differences with his rival, as the latter now earnestly desired, by negotiation. Indeed, two Spanish ministers had resided during the greater part of the war at the French court, with the view of improving the first opening that should occur for accomplishing this object; and by their agency a treaty was concluded, to continue for three years, which guaranteed to Aragon the undisturbed possession of her conquests during that period. The chief articles provided for the immediate cessation of hostilities between the belligerents and the complete re-establishment of their commercial relations and intercourse, with the exception of Naples, from which the French were to be excluded. The Spanish Crown was to have full power to reduce all refractory places in that kingdom; and the contracting parties solemnly pledged themselves each to render no assistance, secretly or openly, to the enemies of the other. The treaty, which was to run from the 25th of February, 1504, was signed by the French king and the Spanish plenipotentiaries at Lyons on the 11th of that month, and ratified by Ferdinand and Isabella at the convent of Santa María de la Mejorada, the 31st of March following.

There was still a small spot in the heart of Naples, comprehending Venosa and several adjoining towns, where Louis d'Ars and his brave associates yet held out against the Spanish arms. Although cut off by the operation of this treaty from the hope of further support from home, the French knight disdained to surrender, but sallied out at the head of his little troop of gallant veterans and thus, armed at all points, says Brantôme,[1] with lance in rest, took his way through Naples and the center of Italy. He marched in battle array, levying contributions for his support on the places through which he passed. In this manner he entered France, and presented himself before the court at Blois. The king and queen, delighted with his prowess, came forward to welcome him, and made good cheer, says the old chronicler, for himself and his companions, whom they recompensed with liberal largesses, proffering at the same time any boon to the brave knight which he should demand for himself. The latter in return simply requested that his old comrade Ives d'Alègre should be recalled from exile. This trait of magnanimity, when contrasted with the general ferocity of the times, has something in it inexpressibly pleasing. It shows, like others recorded of the French gentlemen of that period, that the age of chivalry—the chivalry of romance, indeed—had not wholly passed away.

The pacification of Lyons sealed the fate of Naples and, while it terminated the wars in that kingdom, closed the military career of Gonsalvo de Cordova. It is impossible to contemplate the magnitude of the results

[1] Pierre de Bourdeilles Brantôme (1535?–1614), French historian.

achieved with such slender resources, and in the face of such overwhelming odds, without deep admiration for the genius of the man by whom they were accomplished.

His success, it is true, is imputable in part to the signal errors of his adversaries. The magnificent expedition of Charles the Eighth failed to produce any permanent impression, chiefly in consequence of the precipitation with which it had been entered into, without sufficient concert with the Italian states, who became a formidable enemy when united in his rear. He did not even avail himself of his temporary acquisition of Naples to gather support from the attachment of his new subjects. Far from incorporating with them, he was regarded as a foreigner and an enemy, and, as such, expelled by the joint action of all Italy from its bosom as soon as it had recovered sufficient strength to rally.

Louis the Twelfth profited by the errors of his predecessor. His acquisitions in the Milanese formed a basis for future operations; and by negotiation and otherwise he secured the alliance and the interests of the various Italian governments on his side. These preliminary arrangements were followed by preparations every way commensurate with his object. He failed in the first campaign, however, by intrusting the command to incompetent hands, consulting birth rather than talent or experience.

In the succeeding campaigns, his failure, though partly chargeable on himself, was less so than on circumstances beyond his control. The first of these was the long detention of the army before Rome by Cardinal D'Amboise, and its consequent exposure to the unexampled severity of the ensuing winter; a second was the fraudulent conduct of the commissaries, implying, no doubt, some degree of negligence in the person who appointed them; and lastly, the want of a suitable commander-in-chief of the army. La Tremouille being ill and D'Aubigny a prisoner in the hands of the enemy, there appeared no one among the French qualified to cope with the Spanish general. The marquis of Mantua, independently of the disadvantage of being a foreigner, was too timid in council and dilatory in conduct to be any way competent to this difficult task.

If his enemies, however, committed great errors, it is altogether owing to Gonsalvo that he was in a situation to take advantage of them. Nothing could be more unpromising than his position on first entering Calabria. Military operations had been conducted in Spain on principles totally different from those which prevailed in the rest of Europe. This was the case especially in the late Moorish wars, where the old tactics and the character of the ground brought light cavalry chiefly into use. This, indeed, constituted his principal strength at this period; for his infantry, though accustomed to irregular service, was indifferently armed and disciplined. An important revolution, however, had occurred in the other parts of Europe. The infantry had there regained the superiority which it maintained in the days of the Greeks and Romans. The experiment had been made on more than one bloody field; and it was found that the solid columns of Swiss and German pikes not only bore down all opposition in their onward march, but presented an impregnable barrier, not to be shaken by the most desperate charges of the best heavy-armed cavalry. It was against these dreaded battalions that Gonsalvo was now called to measure for the first time the bold but rudely armed and comparatively raw recruits from Galicia and Asturias.

He lost his first battle, into which, it should be remembered, he was precipitated against his will. He proceeded afterwards with the greatest caution, gradually familiarizing his men with the aspect and usages of the enemy whom they held in such awe, before bringing them again to a direct encounter. He put himself to school during this whole campaign, carefully acquainting himself with the tactics, discipline, and novel arms of his adversaries, and borrowing just so much as he could incorporate into the ancient system of the Spaniards without discarding the latter altogether. Thus, while he retained the short sword and buckler of his countrymen, he fortified his battalions with a large number of spearmen, after the German fashion. The arrangement is highly commended by the sagacious Machiavelli, who considers it as combining the advantages of both systems; since, while the long spear served all the purposes of resistance, or even of attack on level ground, the short swords and targets enabled their wearers, as already noticed, to cut in under the dense array of hostile pikes and bring the enemy to close quarters, where his formidable weapon was of no avail.

While Gonsalvo made this innovation in the arms and tactics, he paid equal attention to the formation of a suitable character in his soldiery. The circumstances in which he was placed at Barleta, and on the Garigliano, imperatively demanded this. Without food, clothes, or pay, without the chance even of retrieving his desperate condition by venturing a blow at the enemy, the Spanish soldier was required to remain passive. To do this demanded patience, abstinence, strict subordination, and a degree of resolution far higher than that required to combat obstacles, however formidable in themselves, where active exertion, which tasks the utmost energies of the soldier, renews his spirits and raises them to a contempt of danger. It was calling on him, in short, to begin with achieving that most difficult of all victories, the victory over himself.

All this the Spanish commander effected. He infused into his men a portion of his own invincible energy. He inspired a love of his person, which led them to emulate his example, and a confidence in his genius and resources, which supported them under all their privations by a firm reliance on a fortunate issue. His manners were distinguished by a graceful courtesy, less encumbered with etiquette than was usual with persons of his high rank in Castile. He knew well the proud and independent feelings of the Spanish soldier, and, far from annoying him by unnecessary restraints, showed the most liberal indulgence at all times. But his kindness was tempered with severity, which displayed itself, on such occasions as required interposition, in a manner that rarely failed to repress everything like insubordination. The reader will readily recall an example of this in the mutiny before Tarento;[1] and it was doubtless by the assertion of similar power that he was so long able to keep in check his German mercenaries, distinguished above the troops of every other nation by their habitual license and contempt of authority.

While Gonsalvo relied so freely on the hardy constitution and patient habits of the Spaniards, he trusted no less to the deficiency of these qualities in the French, who, possessing little of the artificial character formed under the stern training of later times, resembled their Gaulish ancestors in the facility with which they could be brought to rally. In this he did not miscalculate. The French infantry, drawn from the militia of the country, hastily collected and soon to be disbanded, and the independent nobility and gentry who composed the cavalry service were alike difficult to be brought within the strict curb of military rule. The severe trials which steeled the souls and gave sinewy strength to the constitutions of the Spanish soldiers impaired those of their enemies, introduced divisions into their councils, and relaxed the whole tone of discipline. Gonsalvo watched the operation of all this and, coolly awaiting the moment when his weary and disheartened adversary should be thrown off his guard, collected all his strength for a decisive blow, by which to terminate the action. Such was the history of those memorable campaigns which closed with the brilliant victories of Cerignola and the Garigliano.

In a review of his military conduct, we must not overlook his politic deportment towards the Italians, altogether the reverse of the careless and insolent bearing of the French. He availed himself liberally of their superior science, showing great deference and confiding the most important trusts to their officers. Far from the reserve usually shown to foreigners, he appeared insensible to national distinctions and ardently embraced them as companions-in-arms, embarked in a common cause with himself. In their tourney with the French before Barleta, to which the whole nation attached such

[1] A mutiny occurred in the Spanish army besieging Tarento in 1502. It was put down by Gonsalvo.

importance as a vindication of national honor, they were entirely supported by Gonsalvo, who furnished them with arms, secured a fair field of fight, and shared the triumph of the victors as that of his own countrymen—paying those delicate attentions which cost far less, indeed, but to an honorable mind are of greater value, than more substantial benefits. He conciliated the good-will of the Italian states by various important services; of the Venetians, by his gallant defence of their possessions in the Levant; of the people of Rome, by delivering them from the pirates of Ostia; while he succeeded, notwithstanding the excesses of his soldiery, in captivating the giddy Neapolitans to such a degree, by his affable manners and splendid style of life, as seemed to efface from their minds every recollection of the last and most popular of their monarchs, the unfortunate Frederick.

The distance of Gonsalvo's theatre of operations from his own country, apparently most discouraging, proved extremely favorable to his purposes. The troops, cut off from retreat by a wide sea and an impassable mountain barrier, had no alternative but to conquer or to die. Their long continuance in the field without disbanding gave them all the stern, inflexible qualities of a standing army; and as they served through so many successive campaigns under the banner of the same leader, they were drilled in a system of tactics far steadier and more uniform than could be acquired under a variety of commanders, however able. Under these circumstances, which so well fitted them for receiving impressions, the Spanish army was gradually molded into the form determined by the will of its great chief.

When we look at the amount of forces at the disposal of Gonsalvo, it appears so paltry, especially compared with the gigantic apparatus of later wars, that it may well suggest disparaging ideas of the whole contest. To judge correctly, we must direct our eyes to the result. With this insignificant force we shall then see the kingdom of Naples conquered and the best generals and armies of France annihilated; an important innovation effected in military science; the art of mining, if not invented, carried to unprecedented perfection; a thorough reform introduced in the arms and discipline of the Spanish soldier; and the organization completed of that valiant infantry which is honestly eulogized by a French writer as irresistible in attack and impossible to rout, and which carried the banners of Spain victorious for more than a century over the most distant parts of Europe.

*4. The Death of Isabella: Her Character and Person**

[By 1504, Spain had taken great forward strides. The Italian conquests had led to the acquisition of an important kingdom in the heart of Europe. Across the Atlantic, a new world was being opened to her explorers. But, as Prescott wrote, "in this noontide of her success, she was to experience a fatal shock in the loss of that illustrious personage who had so long and so gloriously presided over her destinies." On 26 November, 1504, Isabella died. She had been the essential heroine in Prescott's story, and in an extended obituary account he sought to sum up her character. The breaking of the narrative in order to insert a retrospective section on the character and life of a main figure is typical of Prescott's writing; he did the same with all his major characters. In the case of Isabella, the digression underlines the extent to which she was treated as a romantic heroine by Prescott and also points out the way she had become for him a figure representative of the whole sweep of Spanish history. Her

* From *Ferdinand and Isabella,* Part II, chap. 16.

character was further developed by contrasts. The relentlessly pursued comparison with Elizabeth of England (with whose career Prescott assumed his readers would be familiar) is given here; in chapter 24 (not printed here), Prescott contrasted her with her husband Ferdinand.]

Her person, as mentioned in the early part of the narrative, was of the middle height and well-proportioned. She had a clear, fresh complexion, with light-blue eyes and auburn hair—a style of beauty exceedingly rare in Spain. Her features were regular and universally allowed to be uncommonly handsome. The illusion which attaches to rank, more especially when united with engaging manners, might lead us to suspect some exaggeration in the encomiums so liberally lavished on her. But they would seem to be in a great measure justified by the portraits that remain of her, which combine a faultless symmetry of features with singular sweetness and intelligence of expression.

Her manners were most gracious and pleasing. They were marked by natural dignity and modest reserve, tempered by an affability which flowed from the kindliness of her disposition. She was the last person to be approached with undue familiarity; yet the respect which she imposed was mingled with the strongest feelings of devotion and love. She showed great tact in accommodating herself to the peculiar situation and character of those around her. She appeared in arms at the head of her troops and shrunk from none of the hardships of war. During the reforms introduced into the religious houses, she visited the nunneries in person, taking her needlework with her and passing the day in the society of the inmates. When travelling in Galicia, she attired herself in the costume of the country, borrowing for that purpose the jewels and other ornaments of the ladies there, and returning them with liberal additions. By this condescending and captivating deportment, as well as by her higher qualities, she gained an ascendency over her turbulent subjects which no king of Spain could ever boast.

She spoke the Castilian with much elegance and correctness. She had an easy fluency of discourse, which, though generally of a serious complexion, was occasionally seasoned with agreeable sallies, some of which have passed into proverbs. She was temperate even to abstemiousness in her diet, seldom or never tasting wine, and so frugal in her table that the daily expenses for herself and family did not exceed the moderate sum of forty ducats. She was equally simple and economical in her apparel. On all public occasions, indeed, she displayed a royal magnificence; but she had no relish for it in private, and she freely gave away her clothes and jewels as presents to her friends. Naturally of a sedate though cheerful temper, she had little taste for the frivolous amusements which make up so much of a court life; and if she encouraged the presence of minstrels and musicians in her palace, it was to wean her young nobility from the coarser and less intellectual pleasures to which they were addicted.

Among her moral qualities, the most conspicuous, perhaps, was her magnanimity. She betrayed nothing little or selfish, in thought or action. Her schemes were vast, and executed in the same noble spirit in which they were conceived. She never employed doubtful agents or sinister measures, but the most direct and open policy. She scorned to avail herself of advantages offered by the perfidy of others. Where she had once given her confidence, she gave her hearty and steady support; and she was scrupulous to redeem any pledge she had made to those who ventured in her cause, however unpopular. She sustained Ximenes[1] in all his obnoxious but salutary reforms. She seconded Columbus in the prosecution of his arduous enterprise and shielded him from the calumny of his enemies. She did the same good service to her favorite, Gonsalvo de Cordova; and the day of her death was felt, and, as it proved, truly felt, by both as the last of their good fortune. Artifice and duplicity were so abhorrent to her character, and so averse from her

[1] Francisco Jimenez de Cisneros (1436–1517), Archbishop of Toledo from 1495.

domestic policy, that when they appear in the foreign relations of Spain it is certainly not imputable to her. She was incapable of harboring any petty distrust or latent malice; and, although stern in the execution and exaction of public justice, she made the most generous allowance, and even sometimes advances, to those who had personally injured her.

But the principle which gave a peculiar coloring to every feature of Isabella's mind was piety. It shone forth from the very depths of her soul with a heavenly radiance which illuminated her whole character. Fortunately, her earliest years had been passed in the rugged school of adversity, under the eye of a mother who implanted in her serious mind such strong principles of religion as nothing in after-life had power to shake. At an early age, in the flower of youth and beauty, she was introduced to her brother's court; but its blandishments, so dazzling to a young imagination, had no power over hers; for she was surrounded by a moral atmosphere of purity,

> "Driving far off each thing of sin and guilt."[1]

Such was the decorum of her manners that, though encompassed by false friends and open enemies, not the slightest reproach was breathed on her fair name in this corrupt and calumnious court.

She gave a liberal portion of her time to private devotions, as well as to the public exercises of religion. She expended large sums in useful charities, especially in the erection of hospitals and churches, and the more doubtful endowments of monasteries. Her piety was strikingly exhibited in that unfeigned humility which, although the very essence of our faith, is so rarely found; and most rarely in those whose great powers and exalted stations seem to raise them above the level of ordinary mortals. A remarkable illustration of this is afforded in the queen's correspondence with Talavera, in which her meek and docile spirit is strikingly contrasted

[1] The quotation is from Milton.

with the Puritanical intolerance of her confessor. Yet Talavera was sincere and benevolent at heart. Unfortunately, the royal conscience was at times committed to very different keeping, and that humility which, as we have repeatedly had occasion to notice, made her defer so reverentially to her ghostly advisers led, under the fanatic Torquemada, the confessor of her early youth, to those deep blemishes on her administration, the establishment of the Inquisition and the exile of the Jews.

But though blemishes of the deepest dye on her administration, they are certainly not to be regarded as such on her moral character. It will be difficult to condemn her, indeed, without condemning the age; for these very acts are not only excused but extolled by her contemporaries as constituting her strongest claims to renown and to the gratitude of her country. They proceeded from the principle, openly avowed by the court of Rome, that zeal for the purity of the faith could atone for every crime. This immoral maxim, flowing from the head of the church, was echoed in a thousand different forms by the subordinate clergy and greedily received by a superstitious people. It was not to be expected that a solitary woman, filled with natural diffidence of her own capacity on such subjects, should array herself against those venerated counsellors whom she had been taught from her cradle to look to as the guides and guardians of her conscience.

However mischievous the operations of the Inquisition may have been in Spain, its establishment, in point of principle, was not worse than many other measures which have passed with far less censure, though in a much more advanced and civilized age. Where, indeed, during the sixteenth and the greater part of the seventeenth century was the principle of persecution abandoned by the dominant party, whether Catholic or Protestant? And where that of toleration asserted, except by the weaker? It is true, to borrow Isabella's own expression in her letter to Talavera, the prevalence of a bad custom cannot constitute its apology. But it should serve much to mitigate our condemnation of the queen that she fell into no greater error, in the imperfect light in which she lived, than was common to the greatest minds in a later and far riper period.

Isabella's actions, indeed, were habitually based on principle. Whatever errors of judgment be imputed to her, she most anxiously sought in all situations to discern and discharge her duty. Faithful in the dispensation of justice, no bribe was large enough to ward off the execution of the law. No motive, not even conjugal affection, could induce her to make an unsuitable appointment to public office. No reverence for the ministers of religion could lead her to wink at their misconduct; nor could the deference she entertained for the head of the church allow her to tolerate his encroachments on the rights of her crown. She seemed to consider herself especially bound to preserve entire the peculiar claims and privileges of Castile, atfer its union under the same sovereign with Aragon. And although, "while her own will was law," says Peter Martyr, "she governed in such a manner that it might appear the joint action of both Ferdinand and herself," yet she was careful never to surrender into his hands one of those prerogatives which belonged to her as queen-proprietor of the kingdom.

Isabella's measures were characterized by that practical good sense without which the most brilliant parts may work more to the woe than to the weal of mankind. Though engaged all her life in reforms, she had none of the failings so common in reformers. Her plans, though vast, were never visionary. The best proof of this is that she lived to see most of them realized.

She was quick to discern objects of real utility. She saw the importance of the new discovery of printing, and liberally patronized it, from the first moment it appeared. She had none of the exclusive, local prejudices too common with her countrymen. She drew talent from the most remote quarters to her dominions by munificent rewards. She imported foreign artisans for her manufactures, foreign engineers and officers for the discipline of her army, and foreign scholars to imbue her martial subjects with more cultivated tastes. She consulted the useful in all her subordinate regulations; in her sumptuary laws, for instance, directed against the fashionable extravagances of dress, and the ruinous ostentation so much affected by the Castilians in their weddings and funerals. Lastly, she showed the same perspicacity in the selection of her agents, well knowing that the best measures become bad in incompetent hands.

But although the skilful selection of her agents was an obvious cause of Isabella's success, yet another, even more important, is to be found in her own vigilance and untiring exertions. During the first busy and bustling years of her reign, these exertions were of incredible magnitude. She was almost always in the saddle, for she made all her journeys on horseback: and she travelled with a rapidity which made her always present on the spot where her presence was needed. She was never intimidated by the weather or the state of her own health; and this reckless exposure undoubtedly contributed much to impair her excellent constitution.

She was equally indefatigable in her mental application. After assiduous attention to business through the day, she was often known to sit up all night dictating despatches to her secretaries. In the midst of these overwhelming cares she found time to supply the defects of early education by learning Latin, so as to understand it without difficulty, whether written or spoken, and indeed, in the opinion of a competent judge, to attain a critical accuracy in it. As she had little turn for light amusements, she sought relief from graver cares by some useful occupation appropriate to her sex; and she left ample evidence of her skill in this way, in the rich specimens of embroidery, wrought with her own fair hands, with which she decorated the churches. She was careful to instruct her daughters in these more humble departments of domestic duty; for she thought nothing too humble to learn which was useful.

With all her high qualifications, Isabella would have been still unequal to the achievement of her grand designs, without possessing a degree of fortitude rare in either sex; not the courage which implies contempt of personal danger—though of this she had a larger share than falls to most men; nor that which supports its possessor under the extremities of bodily pain—though of this she gave ample evidence, since she endured the greatest suffering her sex is called to bear without a groan; but that moral courage which sustains the spirit in the dark hour of adversity and, gathering light from within to dispel the darkness, imparts its own cheering influence to all around. This was shown remarkably in the stormy season which ushered in her accession, as well as through the whole of the Moorish war. It was her voice that decided never to abandon Alhama. Her remonstrances compelled the king and nobles to return to the field, when they had quit it after an ineffectual campaign. As dangers and difficulties multiplied, she multiplied resources to meet them; and when her soldiers lay drooping under the evils of some protracted siege, she appeared in the midst, mounted on her war-horse, with her delicate limbs cased in knightly mail and, riding through their ranks, breathed new courage into their hearts by her own intrepid bearing. To her personal efforts, indeed, as well as counsels, the success of this glorious war may be mainly imputed; and the unsuspicious testimony of the Venetian minister, Navagiero, a few years later shows that the nation so considered it. "Queen Isabel," says he, "by her singular genius, masculine strength of mind, and other virtues most unusual in our own sex as well as hers, was not merely of great assistance in, but the chief cause of, the conquest of Granada. She was, indeed, a most rare and virtuous lady, one of whom the Spaniards talk far more than of the king, sagacious as he was and uncommon for his time."

Happily, these masculine qualities in Isabella did not extinguish the softer ones which constitute the charm of her sex. Her heart overflowed with affectionate sensibility to her family and friends. She watched over the declining days of her aged mother, and ministered to her sad infirmities with all the delicacy of filial tenderness. We have seen abundant proofs how fondly and faithfully she loved her husband to the last, though this love was not always as faithfully requited. For her children she lived more than for herself; and for them too she died, for it was their loss and their afflictions which froze the current of her blood before age had time to chill it. Her exalted state did not remove her above the sympathies of friendship. With her friends she forgot the usual distinctions of rank, sharing in their joys, visiting and consoling them in sorrow and sickness, and condescending in more than one instance to assume the office of executrix on their decease. Her heart, indeed, was filled with benevolence to all mankind. In the most fiery heat of war she was engaged in devising means for mitigating its horrors. She is said to have been the first to introduce the benevolent institution of camp hospitals; and we have seen, more than once, her lively solicitude to spare the effusion of blood even of her enemies. But it is needless to multiply examples of this beautiful but familiar trait in her character.

It is in these more amiable qualities of her sex that Isabella's superiority becomes most apparent over her illustrious namesake, Elizabeth of England, whose history presents some features parallel to her own. Both were disciplined in early life by the teachings of that stern nurse of wisdom, Adversity. Both were made to experience the deepest humiliation at the hands of their nearest relative, who should have cherished and protected them. Both succeeded in establishing themselves on the throne after the most precarious vicissitudes. Each conducted her kingdom, through a long and triumphant reign, to a height of glory which it had never before reached. Both lived to see the vanity of all earthly grandeur, and to fall the victims of an inconsolable melancholy; and both left behind an illustrious name, unrivalled in the subsequent annals of their country.

But with these few circumstances of their history the resemblance ceases. Their characters afford scarcely a point of contact. Elizabeth, inheriting a large share of the bold and bluff King Harry's temperament, was haughty, arrogant, coarse, and irascible; while with these fiercer qualities she mingled deep dissimulation and strange irresolution. Isabella, on the other hand, tempered the dignity of royal station with the most bland and courteous manners. Once resolved, she was constant in her purposes, and her conduct in public and private life was characterized by candor and integrity. Both may be said to have shown that magnanimity which is implied by the accomplishment of great objects in the face of great obstacles. But Elizabeth was desperately selfish; she was incapable of forgiving, not merely a real injury, but the slightest affront to her vanity; and she was merciless in exacting retribution. Isabella, on the other hand, lived only for others, was ready at all times to sacrifice self to considerations of public duty, and, far from personal resentments, showed the greatest condescension and kindness to those who had most sensibly injured her; while her benevolent heart sought every means to mitigate the authorized severities of the law, even towards the guilty.

Both possessed rare fortitude. Isabella, indeed, was placed in situations which demanded more frequent and higher displays of it than her rival; but no one will doubt a full measure of this quality in the daughter of Henry the Eighth. Elizabeth was better educated, and every way more highly accomplished, than Isabella. But the latter knew enough to maintain her station with dignity; and she encouraged learning by a munificent patronage. The masculine powers and passions of Elizabeth seemed to divorce her in a great measure from the peculiar attributes of her sex, at least from those which constitute its peculiar charm; for she had abundance of its foibles: a coquetry and love of admiration which age could not chill; a levity, most careless, if not criminal; and a fondness for dress and tawdry magnificence of ornament, which was ridiculous, or disgusting, according to the different periods of life in which it was indulged. Isabella, on the other hand, distinguished through life for decorum of manners and purity beyond the breath of calumny, was content with the legitimate affection which she could inspire within the range of her domestic circle. Far from a frivolous affectation of ornament or dress, she was most simple in her own attire and seemed to set no value on her jewels but as they could serve the necessities of the state; when they could be no longer useful in this way, she gave them away, as we have seen, to her friends.

Both were uncommonly sagacious in the selection of their ministers; though Elizabeth was drawn into some errors in this particular by her levity, as was Isabella by religious feeling. It was this, combined with her excessive humility, which led to the only grave errors in the administration of the latter. Her rival fell into no such errors; and she was a stranger to the amiable qualities which led to them. Her conduct was certainly not controlled by religious principle; and though the bulwark of the Protestant faith, it might be difficult to say whether she were at heart most a Protestant or a Catholic. She viewed religion in its connection with the state—in other words, with herself; and she took measures for enforcing conformity to her own views, not a whit less despotic, and scarcely less sanguinary, than those countenanced for conscience's sake by her more bigoted rival.

This feature of bigotry, which has thrown a shade over Isabella's otherwise beautiful character, might lead to a disparagement of her intellectual power compared with that of the English queen. To estimate this aright, we must contemplate the results of their respective reigns. Elizabeth found all the materials of prosperity at hand, and availed herself of them most ably to build up a solid fabric of national grandeur. Isabella created these materials. She saw the faculties of her people locked up in a death-like lethargy, and she breathed into them the breath of life for those great and heroic enterprises which terminated in such glorious consequences to the monarchy. It is when viewed from the depressed position of her early days that the achievements of her reign seem scarcely less than miraculous. The masculine genius of the English queen stands out relieved beyond its natural dimensions by its separation from the softer qualities of her sex; while her rival's, like some vast but symmetrical edifice, loses in appearance somewhat of its actual grandeur from the perfect harmony of its proportions.

The circumstances of their deaths, which were somewhat similar, displayed the great dissimilarity of their characters. Both pined amidst their royal state, a prey to incurable despondency, rather than any marked bodily distemper. In Elizabeth it sprung from wounded vanity, a sullen conviction that she had outlived the admiration on which she had so long fed—and even the solace of friendship and the attachment of her subjects. Nor did she seek consolation where alone it was to be found, in that sad hour. Isabella, on the other hand, sank under a too-acute sensibility to the sufferings of others. But, amidst the gloom which gathered around her, she looked with the eye of faith to the brighter prospects which unfolded of the future; and when she resigned her last breath, it was amidst the tears and universal lamentations of her people.

It is in this undying, unabated attachment of the nation, indeed, that we see the most unequivocal testimony to the virtues of Isabella. In the downward progress of things in Spain, some of the most ill-advised measures of her administration have found favor and been perpetuated, while the more salutary have been forgotten. This may lead to a misconception of her real merits. In order to estimate these, we must listen to the voice of her contemporaries, the eyewitnesses of the condition in which she found the state, and in which she left it. We shall then see but one judgment formed of her, whether by foreigners or natives. The French and Italian writers equally join in celebrating the triumphant glories of her reign, and her magnanimity, wisdom, and purity of character. Her own subjects extol her as "the most brilliant exemplar of every virtue," and mourn over the day of her death as "the last of the prosperity and happiness of their country"; while those who had nearer access to her person are unbounded in their admiration of those amiable qualities whose full power is revealed only in the unrestrained intimacies of domestic life. The judgment of posterity has ratified the sentence of her own age. The most enlightened Spaniards of the present day, by no means insensible to the errors of her government, but more capable of appreciating its merits than those of a less instructed age, bear honorable testimony to her deserts; and, while they pass over the bloated magnificence of succeeding monarchs, who arrest the popular eye, dwell with enthusiasm on Isabella's character, as the most truly great in their line of princes.

5. *The Administration of Ferdinand and Isabella: A Review**

[With the death of Isabella, Prescott's narrative loses some of its interest. In the course of working on the last portion of the book, he wrote to Bancroft: "I have little more to do than bury and write the epitaphs of the Great Captain, Ximenes, and Ferdinand. Columbus and Isabella are already sent to their account. So my present occupation seems to be that of a sexton, and I begin to weary of it." Nonetheless, Prescott ended the book on a brilliant note by reviewing the reign and assessing its place in Spanish history. The last portion of this review is printed here. It is of particular interest because of Prescott's comments on national character. The good seeds cast in the reign of Ferdinand and Isabella yielded good fruit in the following reigns, but in the long run, Prescott argued, the ancient liberties of the country were undermined and the "foul mist" of the Inquisition cast its blight on the country. The real glory of Spain, he felt, was reflected under the Catholic kings, rather than in the so-called "Golden Age" of their successors.]

* From *Ferdinand and Isabella,* Part II, chap. 26.

The petty states, which had before swarmed over the Peninsula, neutralizing each other's operations and preventing any effective movement abroad, were now amalgamated into one whole. Sectional jealousies and antipathies, indeed, were too sturdily rooted to be wholly extinguished; but they gradually subsided under the influence of a common government and community of interests. A more enlarged sentiment was infused into the people, who, in their foreign relations, at least, assumed the attitude of one great nation. The names of Castilian and Aragonese were merged in the comprehensive one of Spaniard; and Spain, with an empire which stretched over three-quarters of the globe and which almost realized the proud boast that the sun never set within her borders, now rose, not to the first class only, but to the first place, in the scale of European powers.

The extraordinary circumstances of the country tended naturally to nourish the lofty, romantic qualities and the somewhat exaggerated tone of sentiment which always pervaded the national character. The age of chivalry had not faded away in Spain, as in most other lands. It was fostered, in time of peace, by the tourneys, jousts, and other warlike pageants which graced the court of Isabella. It gleamed out, as we have seen, in the Italian campaigns under Gonsalvo de Cordova, and shone forth in all its splendors in the war of Granada. "This was a right gentle war," says Navagiero,[1] in a passage too pertinent to be omitted, "in which, as firearms were comparatively little used, each knight had the opportunity of showing his personal prowess; and rare was it that a day passed without some feat of arms and valorous exploit. The nobility and chivalry of the land all thronged there to gather renown. Queen Isabel, who attended with her whole court, breathed courage into every heart. There was scarce a cavalier who was not enamored of some one or other of her ladies, the witness of his passion by his valiant deeds. What knight so weapons or some token of her favor, admonished him

[1] Andreas Navagiero (1483–1529), Venetian historian.

to bear himself like a true knight, and show the strength of his passion by his valiant deeds. "What knight so craven, then," exclaims the chivalrous Venetian, "that he would not have been more than a match for the stoutest adversary; or who would not sooner have lost his life a thousand times than return dishonored to the lady of his love? In truth," he concludes, "this conquest may be said to have been achieved by love, rather than by arms."

The Spaniard was a knight-errant, in its literal sense, roving over seas on which no bark had ever ventured, among islands and continents where no civilized man had ever trodden and which fancy peopled with all the marvels and drear enchantments of romance—courting danger in every form, combating everywhere, and everywhere victorious. The very odds presented by the defenceless natives among whom he was cast, "a thousand of whom," to quote the words of Columbus, "were not equal to three Spaniards," was in itself typical of his profession; and the brilliant destinies to which the meanest adventurer was often called, now carving out with his good sword some "El Dorado" more splendid than fancy had dreamed of, and now overturning some old barbaric dynasty, were full as extraordinary as the wildest chimeras which Ariosto ever sang or Cervantes satirized.[1]

His countrymen who remained at home, feeding greedily on the reports of his adventures, lived almost equally in an atmosphere of romance. A spirit of chivalrous enthusiasm penetrated the very depths of the nation, swelling the humblest individual with lofty aspirations and a proud consciousness of the dignity of his nature. "The princely disposition of the Spaniards," says a foreigner of the time, "delighteth me much, as well as the gentle nurture and noble conversation, not merely of those of high degree, but of the citizen, peasant, and common laborer." What wonder that such sentiments should be found incompatible with sober, methodical

[1] Ludovico Ariosto (1474–1523), Italian poet, author of *Orlando Furioso;* Miguel de Cervantes (1547–1616), Spanish writer, author of *Don Quixote.*

habits of business, or that the nation indulging them should be seduced from the humble paths of domestic industry to a brilliant and bolder career of adventure? Such consequences became too apparent in the following reign.

In noticing the circumstances that conspired to form the national character, it would be unpardonable to omit the establishment of the Inquisition, which contributed so largely to counterbalance the benefits resulting from Isabella's government; an institution which has done more than any other to stay the proud march of human reason; which, by imposing uniformity of creed, has proved the fruitful parent of hypocrisy and superstition; which has soured the sweet charities of human life and, settling like a foul mist on the goodly promise of the land, closed up the fair buds of science and civilization ere they were fully opened. Alas! that such a blight should have fallen on so gallant and generous a people! That it should have been brought on it, too, by one of such unblemished patriotism and purity of motive as Isabella! How must her virtuous spirit, if it be permitted the departed good to look down on the scene of their earthly labors, mourn over the misery and moral degradation entailed on her country by this one act! So true is it that the measures of this great queen have had a permanent influence, whether for good or for evil, on the destinies of her country.

The immediate injury inflicted on the nation by the spirit of bigotry in the reign of Ferdinand and Isabella, although greatly exaggerated, was doubtless serious enough. Under the otherwise beneficent operation of their government, however, the healthful and expansive energies of the state were sufficient to heal up these and deeper wounds, and still carry it onward in the career of prosperity. With this impulse, indeed, the nation continued to advance higher and higher, in spite of the system of almost unmingled evil pursued in the following reigns. The glories of this later period, of the age of Charles the Fifth, as it is called, must find their true source in the measures of his illustrious predecessors. It was in their court that Boscan, Garcilasso, Mendoza, and the other master-spirits were trained, who molded Castilian literature into the new and more classical forms of later times. It was under Gonsalvo de Cordova that Leyva, Pescara, and those great captains with their invincible legions were formed, who enabled Charles the Fifth to dictate laws to Europe for half a century. And it was Columbus who not only led the way but animated the Spanish navigator with the spirit of discovery. Scarcely was Ferdinand's reign brought to a close before Magellan completed (1520) what that monarch had projected, the circumnavigation of the southern continent; the victorious banners of Cortes had already (1518) penetrated into the golden realms of Montezuma; and Pizarro, a very few years later (1524), following up the lead of Balboa, embarked on the enterprise which ended in the downfall of the splendid dynasty of the Incas.

Thus it is that the seed sown under a good system continues to yield fruit under a bad one. The season of the most brilliant results, however, is not always that of the greatest national prosperity. The splendors of foreign conquest in the boasted reign of Charles the Fifth were dearly purchased by the decline of industry at home and the loss of liberty. The patriot will see little to cheer him in this "golden age" of the national history, whose outward show of glory will seem to his penetrating eye only the hectic brilliancy of decay. He will turn to an earlier period, when the nation, emerging from the sloth and license of a barbarous age, seemed to renew its ancient energies and to prepare like a giant to run its course; and glancing over the long interval since elapsed, during the first half of which the nation wasted itself on schemes of mad ambition, and in the latter has sunk into a state of paralytic torpor, he will fix his eye on the reign of Ferdinand and Isabella as the most glorious epoch in the annals of his country.

PART II

The Conquest of Mexico

*1. The Discovery of Mexico: Cortes Destroys His Ships**

[*After he had completed his work on Ferdinand and Isabella, Prescott turned to a consideration of Spain's activities in the New World. He wrote to Irving: "Soon after I had despatched their Catholic Highnesses, Ferdinand and Isabella, I found the want of my old companions in the long hours of an idle man's life, and, as I looked round for something else, the History of Cortes and Pizarro struck me as the best subject." The book begins with a lengthy survey of Aztec civilization (see the Introduction for comments on its accuracy); this has been omitted here although Prescott always felt that the preliminary scene-painting was an important part of his histories. The narrative part of the history is concerned with the varying fortunes of the band of Spaniards under Cortes, the small army of conquerors who were to overthrow the Aztec empire. The Spaniards had investigated the coast of Yucatan as early as 1517. The lure of gold led Velasquez, the governor of Cuba, to send out further expeditions, and the commander of the third expedition was Hernando Cortes,* alcalde *of the city of Santiago, an adventurer who had come to the New World in 1504 in search of fortune. Cortes bypassed the authority of Velasquez and set himself directly under the king so that, for much of his campaign, he had, in effect, an enemy behind him in Velasquez as well as the Indians before him. In 1519 he sailed to Mexico. Initial*

* **From *The Conquest of Mexico*, Book II, chap. 8.**

resistance by the Indians at Tabasco was strong, but the small Spanish force was able to establish a foothold on the mainland. Problems remained; not the least of these was the interplay between the ambiguous relation of Cortes to Velasquez and the desire of some men in the expedition to return home. These troubles came to a head in a conspiracy led by a priest, Juan Diaz, to seize a ship and return to Cuba. The plot was revealed and a number of men condemned. Prescott's narrative is taken up at this point.]

The arrangements being now finally settled at the Villa Rica, Cortes sent forward Alvarado[1] with a large part of the army to Cempoalla, where he soon after joined them with the remainder. The late affair of the conspiracy seems to have made a deep impression on his mind. It showed him that there were timid spirits in the camp on whom he could not rely and who, he feared, might spread the seeds of disaffection among their companions. Even the more resolute, on any occasion of disgust or disappointment hereafter, might falter in purpose and, getting possession of the vessels, abandon the enterprise. This was already too vast, and the odds were too formidable, to authorize expectation of success with diminution of numbers. Experience showed that this was always to be apprehended while means of escape were at hand. The best chance for success was to cut off these means. He came to the daring resolution to destroy the fleet without the knowledge of his army.

When arrived at Cempoalla, he communicated his design to a few of his devoted adherents, who entered warmly into his views. Through them he readily persuaded the pilots, by means of those golden arguments which weigh more than any other with ordinary minds, to make such a report of the condition of the fleet as suited his purpose. The ships, they said, were grievously

[1] Pedro de Alvarado, one of the captains of Cortes, later governor of Guatemala.

racked by the heavy gales they had encountered, and, what was worse, the worms had eaten into their sides and bottoms until most of them were not sea-worthy, and some, indeed, could scarcely now be kept afloat.

Cortes received the communication with surprise; "for he could well dissemble," observes Las Casas,[1] with his usual friendly comment, "when it suited his interests." "If it be so," he exclaimed, "we must make the best of it! Heaven's will be done!" He then ordered five of the worst-conditioned to be dismantled, their cordage, sails, iron, and whatever was movable, to be brought on shore, and the ships to be sunk. A survey was made of the others, and, on a similar report, four more were condemned in the same manner. Only one small vessel remained!

When the intelligence reached the troops in Cempoalla, it caused the deepest consternation. They saw themselves cut off by a single blow from friends, family, country! The stoutest hearts quailed before the prospect of being thus abandoned on a hostile shore, a handful of men arrayed against a formidable empire. When the news arrived of the destruction of the five vessels first condemned, they had acquiesced in it as a necessary measure, knowing the mischievous activity of the insects in these tropical seas. But when this was followed by the loss of the remaining four, suspicions of the truth flashed on their minds. They felt they were betrayed. Murmurs, at first deep, swelled louder and louder, menacing open mutiny. "Their general," they said, "had led them like cattle to be butchered in the shambles!" The affair wore a most alarming aspect. In no situation was Cortes ever exposed to greater danger from his soldiers.

His presence of mind did not desert him at this crisis. He called his men together and, employing the tones of persuasion rather than authority, assured them that a survey of the ships showed they were not fit for service. If he had ordered them to be destroyed, they should con-

[1] Bartolomé de las Casas (1474–1566), a Dominican who is noted for his efforts to secure fair treatment of the Indians in the New World.

sider, also, that his was the greatest sacrifice, for they were his property—all, indeed, he possessed in the world. The troops, on the other hand, would derive one great advantage from it, by the addition of a hundred able-bodied recruits, before required to man the vessels. But even if the fleet had been saved, it could have been of little service in their present expedition, since they would not need it if they succeeded, while they would be too far in the interior to profit by it if they failed. He besought them to turn their thoughts in another direction. To be thus calculating chances and means of escape was unworthy of brave souls. They had set their hands to work; to look back, as they advanced, would be their ruin. They had only to resume their former confidence in themselves and their general, and success was certain. "As for me," he concluded, "I have chosen my part. I will remain here, while there is one to bear me company. If there be any so craven, as to shrink from sharing the dangers of our glorious enterprise, let them go home, in God's name. There is still one vessel left. Let them take that and return to Cuba. They can tell there how they deserted their commander and their comrades, and patiently wait till we return loaded with the spoils of the Aztecs."

The politic orator had touched the right chord in the bosoms of the soldiers. As he spoke, their resentment gradually died away. The faded visions of future riches and glory, rekindled by his eloquence, again floated before their imaginations. The first shock over, they felt ashamed of their temporary distrust. The enthusiasm for their leader revived, for they felt that under his banner only they could hope for victory; and, as he concluded, they testified the revulsion of their feelings by making the air ring with their shouts, "To Mexico! to Mexico!"

The destruction of his fleet by Cortes is, perhaps, the most remarkable passage in the life of this remarkable man. History, indeed, affords examples of a similar expedient in emergencies somewhat similar; but none where the chances of success were so precarious, and defeat would be so disastrous. Had he failed, it might well seem an act of madness. Yet it was the fruit of deliberate calculation. He had set fortune, fame, life itself, all upon the cast, and must abide the issue. There was no alternative in his mind but to succeed or perish. The measure he adopted greatly increased the chance of success. But to carry it into execution, in the face of an incensed and desperate soldiery, was an act of resolution that has few parallels in history.

2. The Entrance to Cholula and the Massacre*

[In mid-August, 1519, the small Spanish force set out on the march toward Tenochtitlan, the Aztec capital; they numbered about fifteen horse and 400 infantry, accompanied by some Indian porters and a few native nobles with their retainers. A brief campaign was fought against the Indian state of Tlaxcala; the successful conclusion of this brought the Tlaxcalans into Cortes' camp as allies. As the Spaniards pushed on, consternation grew in the Aztec capital. Cortes and his band seemed to be the fulfillment of ancient prophecies about the return of a conquering ruler from the East to reclaim his kingdom. Moreover, the threat posed by the Spaniards was even greater after they had gained the Tlaxcalans to their side, for the latter were ancient and traditional foes of the Aztec rulers of Tenochtitlan. After three weeks in Tlaxcala, Cortes resumed his march toward Mexico, accompanied by a host of Tlaxcalan soldiers. The first major city which they encountered was Cholula, an ally of the Aztecs; their reception was initially friendly.]

*** From *The Conquest of Mexico*, Book III, chaps. 6-7.**

On the following morning he made his entrance at the head of his army into Cholula, attended by no other Indians than those from Cempoalla, and a handful of Tlascalans to take charge of the baggage. His allies, at parting, gave him many cautions respecting the people he was to visit, who, while they affected to despise them as a nation of traders, employed the dangerous arms of perfidy and cunning. As the troops drew near the city, the road was lined with swarms of people of both sexes and every age—old men tottering with infirmity, women with children in their arms—all eager to catch a glimpse of the strangers, whose persons, weapons, and horses were objects of intense curiosity to eyes which had not hitherto ever encountered them in battle. The Spaniards, in turn, were filled with admiration at the aspect of the Cholulans, much superior in dress and general appearance to the nations they had hitherto seen. They were particularly struck with the costume of the higher classes, who wore fine embroidered mantles, resembling the graceful *albornoz,* or Moorish cloak, in their texture and fashion. They showed the same delicate taste for flowers as the other tribes of the plateau, decorating their persons with them and tossing garlands and bunches among the soldiers. An immense number of priests mingled with the crowd, swinging their aromatic censers, while music from various kinds of instruments gave a lively welcome to the visitors and made the whole scene one of gay, bewildering enchantment. If it did not have the air of a triumphal procession so much as at Tlascala, where the melody of instruments was drowned by the shouts of the multitude, it gave a quiet assurance of hospitality and friendly feeling not less grateful.

The Spaniards were also struck with the cleanliness of the city, the width and great regularity of the streets, which seemed to have been laid out on a settled plan, with the solidity of the houses, and the number and size of the pyramidal temples. In the court of one of these, and its surrounding buildings, they were quartered.

They were soon visited by the principal lords of the place, who seemed solicitous to provide them with accommodations. Their table was plentifully supplied, and, in short, they experienced such attentions as were calculated to dissipate their suspicions, and made them impute those of their Tlascalan friends to prejudice and old national hostility.

In a few days the scene changed. Messengers arrived from Montezuma, who, after a short and unpleasant intimation to Cortes that his approach occasioned much disquietude to their master, conferred separately with the Mexican ambassadors still in the Castilian camp and then departed, taking one of the latter along with them. From this time, the deportment of their Cholulan hosts underwent a visible alteration. They did not visit the quarters as before and, when invited to do so, excused themselves on pretence of illness. The supply of provisions was stinted, on the ground that they were short of maize. These symptoms of alienation, independently of temporary embarrassment, caused serious alarm in the breast of Cortes for the future. His apprehensions were not allayed by the reports of the Cempoallans, who told him that in wandering round the city they had seen several streets barricaded, the *azoteas*, or flat roofs of the houses, loaded with huge stones and other missiles, as if preparatory to an assault, and in some places they had found holes covered over with branches, and upright stakes planted within, as if to embarrass the movements of the cavalry. Some Tlascalans coming in, also, from their camp informed the general that a great sacrifice, mostly of children, had been offered up in a distant quarter of the town to propitiate the favor of the gods, apparently for some intended enterprise. They added that they had seen numbers of the citizens leaving the city with their women and children, as if to remove them to a place of safety. These tidings confirmed the worst suspicions of Cortes, who had no doubt that some hostile scheme was in agitation. If he had felt any, a discovery by Marina,[1] the good angel of the expedition, would have turned these doubts into certainty.

The amiable manners of the Indian girl had won her

[1] An Indian girl given to Cortes as a slave in Tabasco on his first arrival in Yucatan. She became an interpreter for him and bore him a son.

the regard of the wife of one of the caciques, who repeatedly urged Marina to visit her house, darkly intimating that in this way she would escape the fate that awaited the Spaniards. The interpreter, seeing the importance of obtaining further intelligence at once, pretended to be pleased with the proposal and affected, at the same time, great discontent with the white men, by whom she was detained in captivity. Thus throwing the credulous Cholulan off her guard, Marina gradually insinuated herself into her confidence so far as to draw from her a full account of the conspiracy.

It originated, she said, with the Aztec emperor, who had sent rich bribes to the great caciques, and to her husband among others, to secure them in his views. The Spaniards were to be assaulted as they marched out of the capital, when entangled in its streets, in which numerous impediments had been placed to throw the cavalry into disorder. A force of twenty thousand Mexicans was already quartered at no great distance from the city, to support the Cholulans in the assault. It was confidently expected that the Spaniards, thus embarrassed in their movements, would fall an easy prey to the superior strength of their enemy. A sufficient number of prisoners was to be reserved to grace the sacrifices of Cholula; the rest were to be led in fetters to the capital of Montezuma.

While this conversation was going on, Marina occupied herself with putting up such articles of value and wearing apparel as she proposed to take with her in the evening, when she could escape unnoticed from the Spanish quarters to the house of her Cholulan friend, who assisted her in the operation. Leaving her visitor thus employed, Marina found an opportunity to steal away for a few moments and, going to the general's apartment, disclosed to him her discoveries. He immediately caused the cacique's wife to be seized, and on examination she fully confirmed the statement of his Indian mistress.

The intelligence thus gathered by Cortes filled him with the deepest alarm. He was fairly taken in the snare. To fight or to fly seemed equally difficult. He was in a city of enemies, where every house might be converted into a fortress, and where such embarrassments were thrown in the way as might render the maneuvers of his artillery and horse nearly impracticable. In addition to the wily Cholulans, he must cope, under all these disadvantages, with the redoubtable warriors of Mexico. He was like a traveller who has lost his way in the darkness among precipices, where any step may dash him to pieces and where to retreat or to advance is equally perilous.

He was desirous to obtain still further confirmation and particulars of the conspiracy. He accordingly induced two of the priests in the neighborhood, one of them a person of much influence in the place, to visit his quarters. By courteous treatment and liberal largesses of the rich presents he had received from Montezuma—thus turning his own gifts against the giver—he drew from them a full confirmation of the previous report. The emperor had been in a state of pitiable vacillation since the arrival of the Spaniards. His first orders to the Cholulans were to receive the strangers kindly. He had recently consulted his oracles anew and obtained for answer that Cholula would be the grave of his enemies; for the gods would be sure to support him in avenging the sacrilege offered to the Holy City. So confident were the Aztecs of success that numerous manacles, or poles with thongs which served as such, were already in the place to secure the prisoners.

Cortes, now feeling himself fully possessed of the facts, dismissed the priests with injunctions of secrecy, scarcely necessary. He told them it was his purpose to leave the city on the following morning and requested that they would induce some of the principal caciques to grant him an interview in his quarters. He then summoned a council of his officers, though, as it seems, already determined as to the course he was to take.

The members of the council were differently affected by the startling intelligence according to their different characters. The more timid, disheartened by the prospect of obstacles which seemed to multiply as they drew nearer the Mexican capital, were for retracing their steps and seeking shelter in the friendly city of Tlascala. Others, more persevering but prudent, were for taking the more northerly route originally recommended by their allies. The greater part supported the general, who was ever of opinion that they had no alternative but to advance. Retreat would be ruin. Halfway measures were scarcely better and would infer a timidity which must discredit them with both friend and foe. Their true policy was to rely on themselves—to strike such a blow as should intimidate their enemies and show them that the Spaniards were as incapable of being circumvented by artifice as of being crushed by weight of numbers and courage in the open field.

When the caciques, persuaded by the priests, appeared before Cortes, he contented himself with gently rebuking their want of hospitality and assured them the Spaniards would be no longer a burden to their city, as he proposed to leave it early on the following morning. He requested, moreover, that they would furnish a reinforcement of two thousand men to transport his artillery and baggage. The chiefs, after some consultation, acquiesced in a demand which might in some measure favor their own designs.

On their departure, the general summoned the Aztec ambassadors before him. He briefly acquainted them with his detection of the treacherous plot to destroy his army, the contrivance of which, he said, was imputed to their master, Montezuma. It grieved him much, he added, to find the emperor implicated in so nefarious a scheme and that the Spaniards must now march as enemies against the prince whom they had hoped to visit as a friend.

The ambassadors, with earnest protestations, asserted their entire ignorance of the conspiracy and their belief that Montezuma was equally innocent of a crime which they charged wholly on the Cholulans. It was clearly the policy of Cortes to keep on good terms with the Indian monarch, to profit as long as possible by his good offices and to avail himself of his fancied security—such feelings of security as the general could inspire him with—to cover his own future operations. He affected to give credit, therefore, to the assertion of the envoys and declared his unwillingness to believe that a monarch who had rendered the Spaniards so many friendly offices would now consummate the whole by a deed of such unparalleled baseness. The discovery of their twofold duplicity, he added, sharpened his resentment against the Cholulans, on whom he would take such vengeance as should amply requite the injuries done both to Montezuma and the Spaniards. He then dismissed the ambassadors, taking care, notwithstanding this show of confidence, to place a strong guard over them to prevent communication with the citizens.

That night was one of deep anxiety to the army. The ground they stood on seemed loosening beneath their feet, and any movement might be the one marked for their destruction. Their vigilant general took all possible precautions for their safety, increasing the number of the sentinels and posting his guns in such a manner as to protect the approaches to the camp. His eyes, it may well be believed, did not close during the night. Indeed every Spaniard lay down in his arms, and every horse stood saddled and bridled, ready for instant service. But no assault was meditated by the Indians, and the stillness of the hour was undisturbed except by the occasional sounds heard in a populous city, even when buried in slumber, and by the hoarse cries of the priests from the turrets of the *teocallis*,[1] proclaiming through their trumpets the watches of the night.

With the first streak of morning light, Cortes was seen on horseback, directing the movements of his little band. The strength of his forces he drew up in the great square or court, surrounded partly by buildings, as before noticed, and in part by a high wall. There were three gates of entrance, at each of which he placed a strong guard. The rest of his troops, with his great guns, he posted without the enclosure in such a manner as to command the avenues and secure those within from interruption in their bloody work. Orders

[1] Temples.

had been sent the night before to the Tlascalan chiefs to hold themselves ready, at a concerted signal, to march into the city and join the Spaniards.

The arrangements were hardly completed before the Cholulan caciques appeared, leading a body of levies, *tamanes,* even more numerous than had been demanded. They were marched at once into the square commanded, as we have seen, by the Spanish infantry, which was drawn up under the walls. Cortes then took some of the caciques aside. With a stern air, he bluntly charged them with the conspiracy, showing that he was well acquainted with all the particulars. He had visited their city, he said, at the invitation of their emperor; had come as a friend; had respected the inhabitants and their property; and, to avoid all cause of umbrage, had left a great part of his forces without the walls. They had received him with a show of kindness and hospitality, and, reposing on this, he had been decoyed into the snare and found this kindness only a mask to cover the blackest perfidy.

The Cholulans were thunderstruck at the accusation. An undefined awe crept over them as they gazed on the mysterious strangers and felt themselves in the presence of beings who seemed to have the power of reading the thoughts scarcely formed in their bosoms. There was no use in prevarication or denial before such judges. They confessed the whole and endeavored to excuse themselves by throwing the blame on Montezuma. Cortes, assuming an air of higher indignation at this, assured them that the pretence should not serve, since, even if well founded, it would be no justification; and he would now make such an example of them for their treachery that the report of it should ring throughout the wide borders of Anahuac![1]

The fatal signal, the discharge of an arquebuse, was then given. In an instant every musket and crossbow was levelled at the unfortunate Cholulans in the court-

[1] *Anahuac* means "near the water." It was first applied to the country around the lakes in the Valley of Mexico and later extended to the more remote regions incorporated within the Aztec confederacy.

yard, and a frightful volley poured into them as they stood crowded together like a herd of deer in the center. They were taken by surprise, for they had not heard the preceding dialogue with the chiefs. They made scarcely any resistance to the Spaniards, who followed up the discharge of their pieces by rushing on them with their swords; and, as the half-naked bodies of the natives afforded no protection, they hewed them down with as much ease as the reaper mows down the ripe corn in harvest time. Some endeavored to scale the walls, but only afforded a surer mark to the arquebusiers and archers. Others threw themselves into the gateways, but were received on the long pikes of the soldiers who guarded them. Some few had better luck in hiding themselves under the heaps of slain with which the ground was soon loaded.

While this work of death was going on, the countrymen of the slaughtered Indians, drawn together by the noise of the massacre, had commenced a furious assault on the Spaniards from without. But Cortes had placed his battery of heavy guns in a position that commanded the avenues, and swept off the files of the assailants as they rushed on. In the intervals between the discharges, which, in the imperfect state of the science in that day, were much longer than in ours, he forced back the press by charging with the horse into the midst. The steeds, the guns, the weapons of the Spaniards were all new to the Cholulans. Notwithstanding the novelty of the terrific spectacle, the flash of fire-arms mingling with the deafening roar of the artillery as its thunders reverberated among the buildings, the despairing Indians pushed on to take the places of their fallen comrades.

While this fierce struggle was going forward, the Tlascalans, hearing the concerted signal, had advanced with quick pace into the city. They had bound, by order of Cortes, wreaths of sedge round their heads that they might the more surely be distinguished from the Cholulans. Coming up in the very heat of the engagement, they fell on the defenceless rear of the townsmen, who, trampled down under the heels of the Castilian cavalry on one side and galled by their vindictive enemies on the other, could no longer maintain their ground. They gave way, some taking refuge in the nearest buildings, which, being partly of wood, were speedily set on fire. Others fled to the temples. One strong party, with a number of priests at its head, got possession of the great *teocalli*. There was a vulgar tradition, already alluded to, that, on removal of part of the walls, the god would send forth an inundation to overwhelm his enemies. The superstitious Cholulans with great difficulty succeeded in wrenching away some of the stones in the walls of the edifice. But dust, not water, followed. Their false gods deserted them in the hour of need. In despair they flung themselves into the wooden turrets that crowned the temple, and poured down stones, javelins, and burning arrows on the Spaniards as they climbed the great staircase, which, by a flight of one hundred and twenty steps, scaled the face of the pyramid. But the fiery shower fell harmless on the steel bonnets of the Christians, while they availed themselves of the burning shafts to set fire to the wooden citadel, which was speedily wrapt in flames. Still the garrison held out, and though quarter, it is said, was offered, only one Cholulan availed himself of it. The rest threw themselves headlong from the parapet or perished miserably in the flames.

All was now confusion and uproar in the fair city which had so lately reposed in security and peace. The groans of the dying, the frantic supplications of the vanquished for mercy were mingled with the loud battle-cries of the Spaniards as they rode down their enemy, and with the shrill whistle of the Tlascalans, who gave full scope to the long-cherished rancor of ancient rivalry. The tumult was still further swelled by the incessant rattle of musketry and the crash of falling timbers, which sent up a volume of flame that outshone the ruddy light of morning, making altogether a hideous confusion of sights and sounds that converted the Holy City into a pandemonium. As resistance slackened, the victors broke into the houses and sacred places, plundering them of whatever valuables they contained, plate, jewels, which were found in some quantity, wearing-apparel and provisions, the two last coveted even more than the former by the simple Tlascalans, thus facilitating a division of the spoil, much to the satisfaction of their Christian confederates. Amidst this universal license, it is worthy of remark, the commands of Cortes were so far respected that no violence was offered to women or children, though these, as well as numbers of the men, were made prisoners, to be swept into slavery by the Tlascalans. These scenes of violence had lasted some hours, when Cortes, moved by the entreaties of some Cholulan chiefs who had been reserved from the massacre, backed by the prayers of the Mexican envoys, consented, out of regard, as he said, to the latter, the representatives of Montezuma, to call off the soldiers and put a stop, as well as he could, to further outrage. Two of the caciques were also permitted to go to their countrymen with assurances of pardon and protection to all who would return to their obedience.

These measures had their effect. By the joint efforts of Cortes and the caciques, the tumult was with much difficulty appeased. The assailants, Spaniards and Indians, gathered under their respective banners, and the Cholulans, relying on the assurance of their chiefs, gradually returned to their homes.

The first act of Cortes was to prevail on the Tlascalan chiefs to liberate their captives. Such was their deference to the Spanish commander that they acquiesced, though not without murmurs, contenting themselves, as they best could, with the rich spoil rifled from the Cholulans, consisting of various luxuries long since unknown in Tlascala. His next care was to cleanse the city from its loathsome impurities, particularly from the dead bodies which lay festering in heaps in the streets and great square. The general, in his letter to Charles the Fifth, admits three thousand slain; most accounts say six, and some swell the amount yet higher. As the eldest and principal cacique was among the number, Cortes assisted the Cholulans in installing a successor in his place. By these pacific measures, confidence was gradually restored. The people in the environs, reassured, flocked into the capital to supply the place of the diminished population. The markets were again opened, and the usual avocations of an orderly, industrious community were resumed. Still, the long piles of black and smoldering ruins proclaimed the hurricane which had so lately swept over the city, and the walls surrounding the scene of slaughter in the great square, which were standing more than fifty years after the event, told the sad tale of the Massacre of Cholula.

This passage in their history is one of those that have left a dark stain on the memory of the Conquerors. Nor can we contemplate at this day, without a shudder, the condition of this fair and flourishing capital thus invaded in its privacy and delivered over to the excesses of a rude and ruthless soldiery. But, to judge the action fairly, we must transport ourselves to the age when it happened. The difficulty that meets us in the outset is to find a justification of the right of conquest at all. But it should be remembered that religious infidelity, at this period, and till much later, was regarded—no matter whether founded on ignorance or education, whether hereditary or acquired, heretical or pagan—as a sin to be punished with fire and fagot in this world and eternal suffering in the next. This doctrine, monstrous as it is, was the creed of the Romish, in other words, of the Christian Church—the basis of the Inquisition and of those other species of religious persecutions which have stained the annals, at some time or other, of nearly every nation in Christendom. Under this code, the territory of the heathen, wherever found, was regarded as a sort of religious waif, which, in default of a legal proprietor, was claimed and taken possession of by the Holy See, and as such was freely given away by the head of the church to any temporal potentate whom he pleased that would assume the burden of conquest. Thus, Alexander the Sixth generously granted a large portion of the Western Hemisphere to the Spaniards, and of the Eastern to the Portuguese. These lofty pretensions of the successors of the humble fisherman of Galilee, far from being nominal, were acknowledged and appealed to as conclusive in controversies between nations.

With the right of conquest thus conferred, came also the obligation, on which it may be said to have been founded, to retrieve the nations sitting in darkness from eternal perdition. This obligation was acknowledged by the best and the bravest, the gownsman in his closet, the missionary, and the warrior in the crusade. However much it may have been debased by temporal motives and mixed up with worldly considerations of ambition and avarice, it was still active in the mind of the Christian conqueror. We have seen how far paramount it was to every calculation of personal interest in the breast of Cortes. The concession of the pope then, founded on and enforcing the imperative duty of conversion, was the assumed basis—and, in the apprehension of that age, a sound one—of the right of conquest.

The right could not, indeed, be construed to authorize any unnecessary act of violence to the natives. The present expedition, up to the period of its history at which we are now arrived, had probably been stained with fewer of such acts than almost any similar enterprise of the Spanish discoverers in the New World. Throughout the campaign, Cortes had prohibited all wanton injuries to the natives in person or property and had punished the perpetrators of them with exemplary severity. He had been faithful to his friends and, with perhaps a single exception, not unmerciful to his foes. Whether from policy or principle, it should be recorded to his credit; though, like every sagacious mind, he may have felt that principle and policy go together.

He had entered Cholula as a friend, at the invitation of the Indian emperor, who had a real, if not avowed, control over the state. He had been received as a friend, with every demonstration of good will; when, without any offence of his own or his followers, he found they were to be the victims of an insidious plot, that they were standing on a mine which might be sprung at any moment and bury them all in its ruins. His safety, as he truly considered, left no alternative but to anticipate the blow of his enemies. Yet who can doubt that the punishment thus inflicted was excessive, that the same end might have been attained by directing the blow against the guilty chiefs, instead of letting it fall on the ignorant rabble, who but obeyed the commands of their masters? But when was it ever seen that fear, armed with power, was scrupulous in the exercise of it, or that the passions of a fierce soldiery, inflamed by conscious injuries, could be regulated in the moment of explosion?

We shall, perhaps, pronounce more impartially on the conduct of the Conquerors if we compare it with that of our own contemporaries under somewhat similar circumstances. The atrocities of Cholula were not so bad as those inflicted on the descendants of these very Spaniards, in the late war of the Peninsula, by the most polished nations of our time; by the British at Badajoz, for example—at Taragona, and a hundred other places, by the French.[1] The wanton butchery, the ruin of property, and, above all, those outrages worse than death, from which the female part of the population were protected at Cholula, show a catalogue of enormities quite as black as those imputed to the Spaniards and without the same apology for resentment—with no apology indeed, but that afforded by a brave and patriotic resistance. The consideration of these events, which, from their familiarity, make little impression on our senses, should render us more lenient in our judgments of the past, showing, as they do, that man in a state of excitement, savage or civilized, is much the same in every age. It may teach us—it is one of the best lessons of history—that, since such are the inevitable evils of war, even among the most polished people, those who hold the destinies of nations in their hands, whether rulers or legislators, should submit to every sacrifice, save that of honor, before authorizing an appeal to arms. The extreme solicitude to avoid these calamities, by the aid of peaceful congresses and impartial mediation, is, on the whole, the strongest evidence, stronger than that afforded by the progress of science and art, of our boasted advance in civilization.

[1] Prescott refers here to the war of the British against the French in Portugal and Spain, 1808–1814.

It is far from my intention to vindicate the cruel deeds of the old Conquerors. Let them lie heavy on their heads. They were an iron race, who perilled life and fortune in the cause; and, as they made little account of danger and suffering for themselves, they had little sympathy to spare for their unfortunate enemies. But, to judge them fairly, we must not do it by the lights of our own age. We must carry ourselves back to theirs and take the point of view afforded by the civilization of their time. Thus only can we arrive at impartial criticism in reviewing the generations that are past. We must extend to them the same justice which we shall have occasion to ask from posterity, when, by the light of a higher civilization, it surveys the dark or doubtful passages in our own history, which hardly arrest the eye of the contemporary.

But whatever be thought of this transaction in a moral view, as a stroke of policy it was unquestionable. The nations of Anahuac had beheld, with admiration mingled with awe, the little band of Christian warriors steadily advancing along the plateau in face of every obstacle, overturning army after army with as much ease, apparently, as the good ship throws off the angry billows from her bows; or rather like the lava, which, rolling from their own volcanoes, holds on its course unchecked by obstacles, rock, tree, or building, bearing them along or crushing and consuming them in its fiery path. The prowess of the Spaniards—"the white gods," as they were often called—made them to be thought invincible. But it was not till their arrival at Cholula that the natives learned how terrible was their vengeance; and they trembled!

None trembled more than the Aztec emperor on his throne among the mountains. He read in these events the dark characters traced by the finger of Destiny. He felt his empire melting away like a morning mist. He might well feel so. Some of the most important cities in the neighborhood of Cholula, intimidated by the fate of that capital, now sent their envoys to the Castilian camp, tendering their allegiance and propitiating the favor of the strangers by rich presents of gold and slaves. Montezuma, alarmed at these signs of defection, took counsel again of his impotent deities; but, although the altars smoked with fresh hecatombs of human victims, he obtained no cheering response. He determined, therefore, to send another embassy to the Spaniards, disavowing any participation in the conspiracy of Cholula. . . .

*3. The March to Mexico and the Entrance into Tenochtitlan**

[*Following the forcible reduction of Cholula, Cortes and his men, their force now swelled by 4,000 Indian allies, continued over the mountains toward Mexico. They were encouraged by the frequent complaints which they heard concerning the harshness of Aztec rule. The Indian emperor, Montezuma, cast into a state of depression by his faith in the ancient prophecies, allowed them to continue their march. The passage through the mountains was far from easy; harassed by icy winds and other natural hazards, Cortes and his army pushed on.*]

The troops, refreshed by a night's rest, succeeded, early on the following day, in gaining the crest of the sierra of Ahualco, which stretches like a curtain between the two great mountains on the north and south. Their progress was now comparatively easy, and they marched forward with a buoyant step, as they felt they were treading the soil of Montezuma.

They had not advanced far, when, turning an angle of the sierra, they suddenly came on a view which more than compensated the toils of the preceding day. It was

* From *The Conquest of Mexico*, Book III, chaps. 8–9.

that of the Valley of Mexico, or Tenochtitlan, as more commonly called by the natives; which, with its picturesque assemblage of water, woodland, and cultivated plains, its shining cities and shadowy hills, was spread out like some gay and gorgeous panorama before them. In the highly rarefied atmosphere of these upper regions, even remote objects have a brilliancy of coloring and a distinctness of outline which seem to annihilate distance. Stretching far away at their feet were seen noble forests of oak, sycamore, and cedar, and beyond, yellow fields of maize and the towering maguey, intermingled with orchards and blooming gardens; for flowers, in such demand for their religious festivals, were even more abundant in this populous valley than in other parts of Anahuac. In the center of the great basin were beheld the lakes, occupying then a much larger portion of its surface than at present; their borders thickly studded with towns and hamlets, and, in the midst—like some Indian empress with her coronal of pearls—the fair city of Mexico, with her white towers and pyramidal temples, reposing, as it were, on the bosom of the waters, the far-famed "Venice of the Aztecs." High over all rose the royal hill of Chapoltepec, the residence of the Mexican monarchs, crowned with the same grove of gigantic cypresses which at this day fling their broad shadows over the land. In the distance beyond the blue waters of the lake, and nearly screened by intervening foliage, was seen a shining speck, the rival capital of Tezcuco, and, still further on, the dark belt of porphyry, girding the Valley around, like a rich setting which Nature had devised for the fairest of her jewels.

Such was the beautiful vision which broke on the eyes of the Conquerors. And even now, when so sad a change has come over the scene; when the stately forests have been laid low, and the soil, unsheltered from the fierce radiance of a tropical sun, is in many places abandoned to sterility; when the waters have retired, leaving a broad and ghastly margin white with the incrustation of salts, while the cities and hamlets on their borders have moldered into ruins—even now that deso-

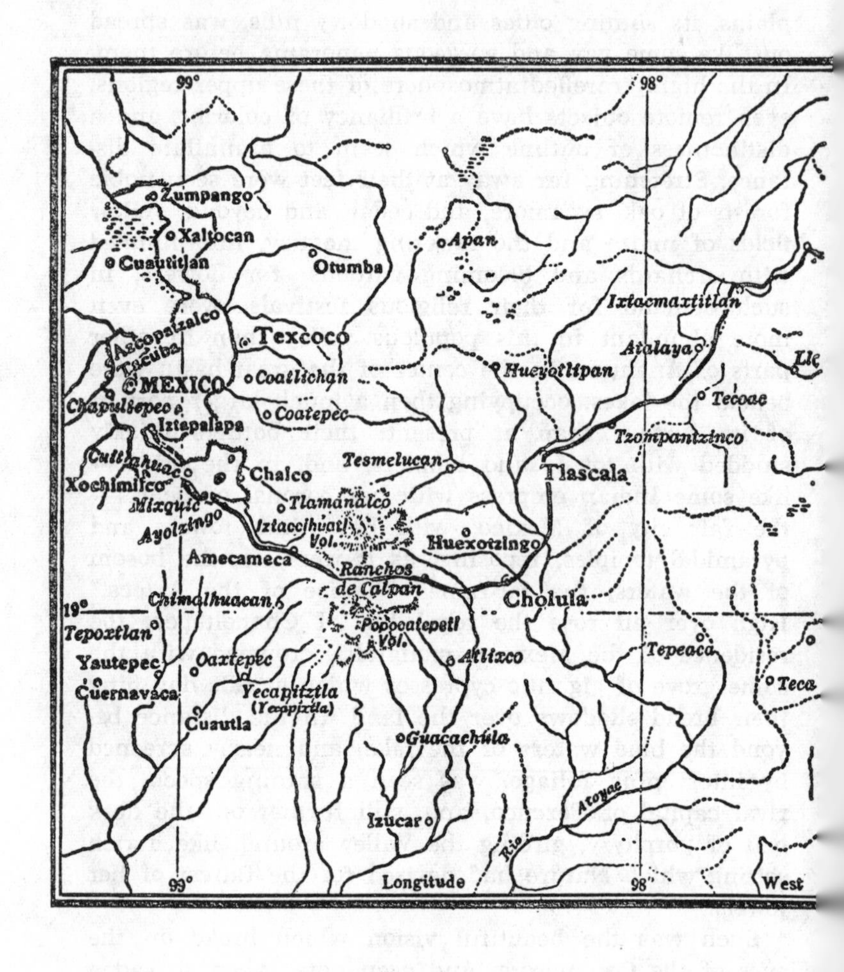
99°
98°
Zumpango
Xaltocan
Cuautitlan
Otumba
Apan
Ixtacmaxtitlan
Azcopotzalco
Tacuba
Texcoco
Atalaya
MEXICO
Coatlichan
Hueyotlipan
Chapultepec
Iztapalapa
Coatepec
Tecoac
Tzompantzinco
Cultlahuac
Tesmelucan
Tlascala
Xochimilco
Chalco
Mixquic
Tlamanalco
Ayolzingo
Iztaccihuatl
Vol.
Huexotzingo
Amecameca
Ranchos
de Calpan
Chimalhuacan
Cholula
19°
Tepoxtlan
Popocatepetl
Vol.
Tepeaca
Yautepec
Oaxtepec
Atlixco
Cuernavaca
Yecapitztla
(Yecapixtla)
Teca
Cuautla
Guacachula
Atoyac
Izucar
Rio
99°
Longitude
98°
West

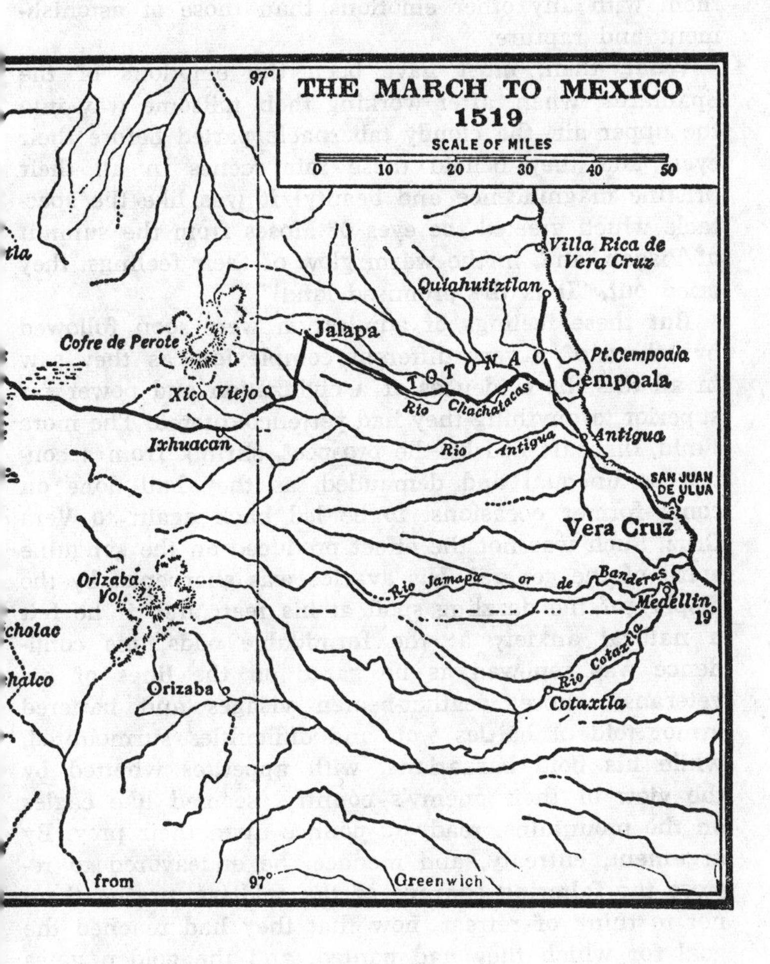
THE MARCH TO MEXICO
1519
SCALE OF MILES
0 10 20 30 40 50
97°
Villa Rica de
Vera Cruz
Quiahuitztlan
Jalapa
Cofre de Perote
TOTONAC
Pt.Cempoala
Cempoala
Xico Viejo
Rio Chachatacas
Ixhuacan
Rio Antigua
Antigua
SAN JUAN
DE ULUA
Vera Cruz
Orizaba
Vol.
Rio Jamapa or de Banderas
Medellin
19°
Orizaba
Rio Cotaxtla
Cotaxtla
from
97°
Greenwich

lation broods over the landscape, so indestructible are the lines of beauty which Nature has traced on its features that no traveller, however cold, can gaze on them with any other emotions than those of astonishment and rapture.

What, then, must have been the emotions of the Spaniards, when, after working their toilsome way into the upper air, the cloudy tabernacle parted before their eyes, and they beheld these fair scenes in all their pristine magnificence and beauty! It was like the spectacle which greeted the eyes of Moses from the summit of Pisgah, and, in the warm glow of their feelings, they cried out, "It is the promised land!"

But these feelings of admiration were soon followed by others of a very different complexion, as they saw in all this the evidences of a civilization and power far superior to anything they had yet encountered. The more timid, disheartened by the prospect, shrunk from a contest so unequal and demanded, as they had done on some former occasions, to be led back again to Vera Cruz. Such was not the effect produced on the sanguine spirit of the general. His avarice was sharpened by the display of the dazzling spoil at his feet; and, if he felt a natural anxiety at the formidable odds, his confidence was renewed as he gazed on the lines of his veterans, whose weather-beaten visages and battered armor told of battles won and difficulties surmounted, while his bold barbarians, with appetites whetted by the view of their enemy's country, seemed like eagles on the mountains, ready to pounce upon their prey. By argument, entreaty, and menace, he endeavored to restore the faltering courage of the soldiers, urging them not to think of retreat, now that they had reached the goal for which they had panted, and the golden gates were opened to receive them. In these efforts he was well seconded by the brave cavaliers, who held honor as dear to them as fortune; until the dullest spirits caught somewhat of the enthusiasm of their leaders, and the general had the satisfaction to see his hesitating columns, with their usual buoyant step, once more on their march down the slopes of the sierra.

With every step of their progress, the woods became thinner; patches of cultivated land more frequent; and hamlets were seen in the green and sheltered nooks, the inhabitants of which, coming out to meet them, gave the troops a kind reception. Everywhere they heard complaints of Montezuma, especially of the unfeeling manner in which he carried off their young men to recruit his armies, and their maidens for his harem. These symptoms of discontent were noticed with satisfaction by Cortes, who saw that Montezuma's "mountain throne," as it was called, was indeed seated on a volcano, with the elements of combustion so active within that it seemed as if any hour might witness an explosion. He encouraged the disaffected natives to rely on his protection, as he had come to redress their wrongs. He took advantage, moreover, of their favorable dispositions to scatter among them such gleams of spiritual light as time and the preaching of Father Olmedo could afford.

He advanced by easy stages, somewhat retarded by the crowd of curious inhabitants gathered on the highways to see the strangers and halting at every spot of interest or importance. On the road he was met by another embassy from the capital. It consisted of several Aztec lords, freighted, as usual, with a rich largess of gold and robes of delicate furs and feathers. The message of the emperor was couched in the same deprecatory terms as before. He even condescended to bribe the return of the Spaniards by promising, in that event, four loads of gold to the general and one to each of the captains, with a yearly tribute to their sovereign. So effectually had the lofty and naturally courageous spirit of the barbarian monarch been subdued by the influence of superstition!

But the man whom the hostile array of armies could not daunt was not to be turned from his purpose by a woman's prayers. He received the embassy with his usual courtesy, declaring, as before, that he could not answer to his own sovereign, if he were now to return without visiting the emperor in his capital. It would be much easier to arrange matters by a personal interview than by distant negotiations. The Spaniards came in the spirit of peace. Montezuma would so find it; but, should their presence prove burdensome to him, it would be easy for them to relieve him of it.

The Aztec monarch, meanwhile, was a prey to the most dismal apprehensions. It was intended that the embassy above noticed should reach the Spaniards before they crossed the mountains. When he learned that this was accomplished and that the dread strangers were on their march across the Valley, the very threshold of his capital, the last spark of hope died away in his bosom. Like one who suddenly finds himself on the brink of some dark and yawning gulf, he was too much bewildered to be able to rally his thoughts or even to comprehend his situation. He was the victim of an absolute destiny, against which no foresight or precautions could have availed. It was as if the strange beings who had thus invaded his shores had dropped from some distant planet, so different were they from all he had ever seen, in appearance and manners; so superior —though a mere handful in numbers—to the banded nations of Anahuac in strength and science and all the fearful accompaniments of war! They were now in the Valley. The huge mountain-screen which nature had so kindly drawn around it for its defence, had been overleaped. The golden visions of security and repose, in which he had so long indulged, the lordly sway descended from his ancestors, his broad imperial domain were all to pass away. It seemed like some terrible dream—from which he was now, alas! to awake to a still more terrible reality.

In a paroxysm of despair he shut himself up in his palace, refused food, and sought relief in prayer and in sacrifice. But the oracles were dumb. He then adopted the more sensible expedient of calling a council of his principal and oldest nobles. Here was the same division of opinion which had before prevailed. Cacama, the young king of Tezcuco, his nephew, counselled him to receive the Spaniards courteously, as ambassadors, so styled by themselves, of a foreign prince. Cuitlahua, Montezuma's more warlike brother, urged him to muster his forces on the instant and drive back the invaders from his capital, or die in its defence. But the monarch found it difficult to rally his spirits for this final struggle. With downcast eye and dejected mien he exclaimed, "Of what avail is resistance when the gods have declared themselves against us! Yet I mourn most for the old and infirm, the women and children, too feeble to fight or to fly. For myself and the brave men around me, we must bare our breasts to the storm, and meet it as we may!" Such are the sorrowful and sympathetic tones in which the Aztec emperor is said to have uttered the bitterness of his grief. He would have acted a more glorious part had he put his capital in a posture of defence and prepared, like the last of the Palaeologi,[1] to bury himself under its ruins.

He straightway prepared to send a last embassy to the Spaniards, with his nephew, the lord of Tezcuco, at its head, to welcome them to Mexico.

The Christian army, meanwhile, had advanced as far as Amaquemecan, a well-built town of several thousand inhabitants. They were kindly received by the cacique, lodged in large, commodious stone buildings, and at their departure presented, among other things, with gold to the amount of three thousand *castellanos*.[2] Having halted there a couple of days, they descended among flourishing plantations of maize and of maguey, the latter of which might be called the Aztec vineyards, towards the lake of Chalco. Their first resting-place was Ajotzinco, a town of considerable size, with a great part of it then standing on piles in the water. It was the first specimen which the Spaniards had seen of this maritime architecture. The canals, which intersected the city instead of streets, presented an animated scene, from the number of barks which glided up and down, freighted with provisions and other articles for the inhabitants. The Spaniards were particularly struck with the style and commodious structure of the houses, built chiefly of stone, and with the general aspect of wealth and even elegance which prevailed there.

[1] Constantine XI, the last Byzantine emperor, who died in 1453 when the Turks captured Constantinople.

[2] An old Spanish coin.

Though received with the greatest show of hospitality, Cortes found some occasion for distrust in the eagerness manifested by the people to see and approach the Spaniards. Not content with gazing at them in the roads, some even made their way stealthily into their quarters, and fifteen or twenty unhappy Indians were shot down by the sentinels as spies. Yet there appears, as well as we can judge at this distance of time, to have been no real ground for such suspicion. The undisguised jealousy of the court and the cautions he had received from his allies, while they very properly put the general on his guard, seem to have given an unnatural acuteness, at least in the present instance, to his perceptions of danger.

Early on the following morning, as the army was preparing to leave the place, a courier came, requesting the general to postpone his departure till after the arrival of the king of Tezcuco, who was advancing to meet him. It was not long before he appeared, borne in a palanquin, or litter, richly decorated with plates of gold and precious stones, having pillars curiously wrought, supporting a canopy of green plumes, a favorite color with the Aztec princes. He was accompanied by a numerous suite of nobles and inferior attendants. As he came into the presence of Cortes, the lord of Tezcuco descended from his palanquin, and the obsequious officers swept the ground before him as he advanced. He appeared to be a young man of about twenty-five years of age, with a comely presence, erect and stately in his deportment. He made the Mexican salutation usually addressed to persons of high rank, touching the earth with his right hand and raising it to his head. Cortes embraced him as he rose, when the young prince informed him that he came as the representative of Montezuma to bid the Spaniards welcome to his capital. He then presented the general with three pearls of uncommon size and lustre. Cortes, in return, threw over Cacama's neck a chain of cut glass, which, where glass was as rare as diamonds, might be admitted to have a value as real as the latter. After this interchange of courtesies and the most friendly and respectful assurances on the part of Cortes, the Indian prince withdrew, leaving the Spaniards strongly impressed with the superiority of his state and bearing over anything they had hitherto seen in the country.

Resuming its march, the army kept along the southern borders of the lake of Chalco, overshadowed at that time by noble woods and by orchards glowing with autumnal fruits, of unknown names, but rich and tempting hues. More frequently it passed through cultivated fields waving with the yellow harvest and irrigated by canals introduced from the neighboring lake; the whole showing a careful and economical husbandry, essential to the maintenance of a crowded population.

Leaving the mainland, the Spaniards came on the great dike or causeway, which stretches some four or five miles in length and divides Lake Chalco from Xochicalco on the west. It was a lance in breadth in the narrowest part and in some places wide enough for eight horsemen to ride abreast. It was a solid structure of stone and lime, running directly through the lake, and struck the Spaniards as one of the most remarkable works which they had seen in the country.

As they passed along, they beheld the gay spectacle of multitudes of Indians darting up and down in their light pirogues,[1] eager to catch a glimpse of the strangers or bearing the products of the country to the neighboring cities. They were amazed also by the sight of the *chinampas,* or floating gardens—those wandering islands of verdure, to which we shall have occasion to return hereafter—teeming with flowers and vegetables and moving like rafts over the waters. All round the margin, and occasionally far in the lake, they beheld little towns and villages, which, half concealed by the foliage and gathered in white clusters round the shore, looked in the distance like companies of wild swans riding quietly on the waves. A scene so new and wonderful filled their rude hearts with amazement. It seemed like enchantment; and they could find nothing to compare it with but the magical pictures in the *Amadis de*

[1] A kind of boat, generally small and propelled by paddles.

Gaula. Few pictures, indeed, in that or any other legend of chivalry could surpass the realities of their own experience. The life of the adventurer in the New World was romance put into action. What wonder, then, if the Spaniard of that day, feeding his imagination with dreams of enchantment at home and with its realities abroad, should have displayed a Quixotic enthusiasm—a romantic exaltation of character not to be comprehended by the colder spirits of other lands!

Midway across the lake the army halted at the town of Cuitlahuac, a place of moderate size but distinguished by the beauty of the buildings—the most beautiful, according to Cortes, that he had yet seen in the country. After taking some refreshment at this place, they continued their march along the dike. Though broader in this northern section, the troops found themselves much embarrassed by the throng of Indians, who, not content with gazing on them from the boats, climbed up the causeway and lined the sides of the roads. The general, afraid that his ranks might be disordered and that too great familiarity might diminish a salutary awe in the natives, was obliged to resort not merely to command but menace to clear a passage. He now found, as he advanced, a considerable change in the feelings shown towards the government. He heard only of the pomp and magnificence, nothing of the oppressions of Montezuma. Contrary to the usual fact, it seemed that the respect for the court was greatest in its immediate neighborhood.

From the causeway, the army descended on that narrow point of land which divides the waters of the Chalco from the Tezcucan lake, but which in those days was overflowed for many a mile now laid bare. Traversing this peninsula, they entered the royal residence of Iztapalapan, a place containing twelve or fifteen thousand houses, according to Cortes. It was governed by Cuitlahua, the emperor's brother, who, to do greater honor to the general, had invited the lords of some neighboring cities, of the royal house of Mexico, like himself, to be present at the interview. This was conducted with much ceremony, and, after the usual presents of gold and delicate stuffs, a collation was served to the Spaniards in one of the great halls of the palace. The excellence of the architecture here, also, excited the admiration of the general, who did not hesitate in the glow of his enthusiasm to pronounce some of the buildings equal to the best in Spain. They were of stone, and the spacious apartments had roofs of odorous cedar-wood, while the walls were tapestried with fine cottons stained with brilliant colors.

But the pride of Iztapalapan, on which its lord had freely lavished his care and his revenues, was its celebrated gardens. They covered an immense tract of land, were laid out in regular squares, and the paths intersecting them were bordered with trellises, supporting creepers and aromatic shrubs that loaded the air with their perfumes. The gardens were stocked with fruit-trees, imported from distant places, and with the gaudy family of flowers which belong to the Mexican flora, scientifically arranged, and growing luxuriant in the equable temperature of the table-land. The natural dryness of the atmosphere was counteracted by means of aqueducts and canals that carried water into all parts of the grounds.

In one quarter was an aviary, filled with numerous kinds of birds, remarkable in this region both for brilliancy of plumage and of song. The gardens were intersected by a canal communicating with the lake of Tezcuco and of sufficient size for barges to enter from the latter. But the most elaborate piece of work was a huge reservoir of stone, filled to a considerable height with water well supplied with different sorts of fish. This basin was sixteen hundred paces in circumference and was surrounded by a walk, made also of stone, wide enough for four persons to go abreast. The sides were curiously sculptured, and a flight of steps led to the water below, which fed the aqueducts above noticed or, collected into fountains, diffused a perpetual moisture.

Such are the accounts transmitted of these celebrated gardens, at a period when similar horticultural establishments were unknown in Europe; and we might well doubt their existence in this semi-civilized land were it not a matter of such notoriety at the time and so explicitly attested by the invaders. But a generation had scarcely passed after the Conquest before a sad change came over these scenes so beautiful. The town itself was deserted, and the shore of the lake was strewed with the wreck of buildings which once were its ornament and its glory. The gardens shared the fate of the city. The retreating waters withdrew the means of nourishment, converting the flourishing plains into a foul and unsightly morass, the haunt of loathsome reptiles; and the water-fowl built her nest in what had once been the palaces of princes!

In the city of Iztapalapan, Cortes took up his quarters for the night. We may imagine what a crowd of ideas must have pressed on the mind of the Conqueror as, surrounded by these evidences of civilization, he prepared, with his handful of followers, to enter the capital of a monarch, who, as he had abundant reason to know, regarded him with distrust and aversion. This capital was now but a few miles distant, distinctly visible from Iztapalapan. And as its long lines of glittering edifices, struck by the rays of the evening sun, trembled on the dark blue waters of the lake, it looked like a thing of fairy creation, rather than the work of mortal hands. Into this city of enchantment Cortes prepared to make his entry on the following morning.

With the first faint streak of dawn, the Spanish general was up, mustering his followers. They gathered, with beating hearts, under their respective banners as the trumpet sent forth its spirit-stirring sounds across water and woodland, till they died away in distant echoes among the mountains. The sacred flames on the altars of numberless *teocallis*, dimly seen through the grey mists of morning, indicated the site of the capital, till temple, tower, and palace were fully revealed in the glorious illumination which the sun, as he rose above the eastern barrier, poured over the beautiful valley. It was the 8th of November, 1519; a conspicuous day in history, as that on which the Europeans first set foot in the capital of the Western World.

Cortes with his little body of horse formed a sort of

advanced guard to the army. Then came the Spanish infantry, who in a summer's campaign had acquired the discipline and the weather-beaten aspect of veterans. The baggage occupied the center; and the rear was closed by the dark files of Tlascalan warriors. The whole number must have fallen short of seven thousand, of which less than four hundred were Spaniards.

For a short distance, the army kept along the narrow tongue of land that divides the Tezcucan from the Chalcan waters, when it entered on the great dike which, with the exception of an angle near the commencement, stretches in a perfectly straight line across the salt floods of Tezcuco to the gates of the capital. It was the same causeway, or rather the basis of that which still forms the great southern avenue of Mexico. The Spaniards had occasion more than ever to admire the mechanical science of the Aztecs, in the geometrical precision with which the work was executed as well as the solidity of its construction. It was composed of huge stones well laid in cement and wide enough, throughout its whole extent, for ten horsemen to ride abreast.

They saw, as they passed along, several large towns, resting on piles and reaching far into the water—a kind of architecture which found great favor with the Aztecs, being in imitation of that of their metropolis. The busy population obtained a good subsistence from the manufacture of salt, which they extracted from waters of the great lake. The duties on the traffic in this article were a considerable source of revenue to the crown.

Everywhere the Conquerors beheld the evidence of a crowded and thriving population, exceeding all they had yet seen. The temples and principal buildings of the cities were covered with a hard white stucco, which glistened like enamel in the level beams of the morning. The margin of the great basin was more thickly gemmed than that of Chalco with towns and hamlets. The water was darkened by swarms of canoes filled with Indians, who clambered up the sides of the causeway and gazed with curious astonishment on the strangers. And here, also, they beheld those fairy islands of flowers, overshadowed occasionally by trees of considerable size, rising and falling with the gentle undulation of the billows. At the distance of half a league from the capital, they encountered a solid work, or curtain of stone, which traversed the dike. It was twelve feet high, was strengthened by towers at the extremities, and in the center was a battlemented gateway, which opened a passage to the troops. It was called the Fort of Xoloc, and became memorable in after times as the position occupied by Cortes in the famous siege of Mexico.

Here they were met by several hundred Aztec chiefs, who came out to announce the approach of Montezuma and to welcome the Spaniards to his capital. They were dressed in the fanciful gala costume of the country, with the *maxtlatl,* or cotton sash, around their loins and a broad mantle of the same material, or of the brilliant feather-embroidery, flowing gracefully down their shoulders. On their necks and arms they displayed collars and bracelets of turquoise mosaic, with which delicate plumage was curiously mingled, while their ears, under-lips, and occasionally their noses were garnished with pendants formed of precious stones, or crescents of fine gold. As each cacique made the usual formal salutation of the country separately to the general, the tedious ceremony delayed the march more than an hour. After this, the army experienced no further interruption till it reached a bridge near the gates of the city. It was built of wood, since replaced by one of stone, and was thrown across an opening of the dike, which furnished an outlet to the waters when agitated by the winds or swollen by a sudden influx in the rainy season. It was a drawbridge; and the Spaniards, as they crossed it, felt how truly they were committing themselves to the mercy of Montezuma, who, by thus cutting off their communications with the country, might hold them prisoners in his capital.

In the midst of these unpleasant reflections, they beheld the glittering retinue of the emperor emerging from the great street which led then, as it still does, through the heart of the city. Amidst a crowd of Indian nobles, preceded by three officers of state bearing golden wands, they saw the royal palanquin blazing with burnished gold. It was borne on the shoulders of nobles, and over it a canopy of gaudy feather-work, powdered with jewels and fringed with silver, was supported by four attendants of the same rank. They were bare-footed and walked with a slow, measured pace and with eyes bent on the ground. When the train had come within a convenient distance, it halted, and Montezuma, descending from his litter, came forward leaning on the arms of the lords of Tezcuco and Iztapalapan, his nephew and brother, both of whom, as we have seen, had already been made known to the Spaniards. As the monarch advanced under the canopy, the obsequious attendants strewed the ground with cotton tapestry, that his imperial feet might not be contaminated by the rude soil. His subjects of high and low degree, who lined the sides of the causeway, bent forward with their eyes fastened on the ground as he passed, and some of the humbler class prostrated themselves before him. Such was the homage paid to the Indian despot, showing that the slavish forms of Oriental adulation were to be found among the rude inhabitants of the Western World.

Montezuma wore the girdle and ample square cloak, *tilmatli,* of his nation. It was made of the finest cotton, with the embroidered ends gathered in a knot round his neck. His feet were defended by sandals having soles of gold, and the leathern thongs which bound them to his ankles were embossed with the same metal. Both the cloak and sandals were sprinkled with pearls and precious stones, among which the emerald and the *chalchivitl*—a green stone of higher estimation than any other among the Aztecs—were conspicuous. On his head he wore no other ornament than a *panache* of plumes of the royal green, which floated down his back, the badge of military, rather than of regal, rank.

He was at this time about forty years of age. His person was tall and thin, but not ill made. His hair, which was black and straight, was not very long; to wear it short was considered unbecoming persons of rank. His beard was thin; his complexion somewhat paler than is often found in his dusky, or rather copper-colored, race. His features, though serious in their expression, did not wear the look of melancholy, indeed, of dejection, which characterizes his portrait and which may well have settled on them at a later period. He moved with dignity, and his whole demeanor, tempered by an expression of benignity not to have been anticipated from the reports circulated of his character, was worthy of a great prince. Such is the portrait left to us of the celebrated Indian emperor in this his first interview with the white men.

The army halted as he drew near. Cortes, dismounting, threw his reins to a page and, supported by a few of the principal cavaliers, advanced to meet him. The interview must have been one of uncommon interest to both. In Montezuma, Cortes beheld the lord of the broad realms he had traversed, whose magnificence and power had been the burden of every tongue. In the Spaniard, on the other hand, the Aztec prince saw the strange being whose history seemed to be so mysteriously connected with his own—the predicted one of his oracles, whose achievements proclaimed him something more than human. But, whatever may have been the monarch's feelings, he so far suppressed them as to receive his guest with princely courtesy and to express his satisfaction at personally seeing him in his capital. Cortes responded by the most profound expressions of respect, while he made ample acknowledgments for the substantial proofs which the emperor had given the Spaniards of his munificence. He then hung round Montezuma's neck a sparkling chain of colored crystal, accompanying this with a movement as if to embrace him, when he was restrained by the two Aztec lords, shocked at the menaced profanation of the sacred person of their master. After the interchange of these civilities, Montezuma appointed his brother to conduct the Spaniards to their residence in the capital and, again entering his litter, was borne off amidst prostrate crowds in the same state in which he had come. The Spaniards quickly followed and, with colors flying and music playing, soon made their entrance into the southern quarter of Tenochtitlan.

Here, again, they found fresh cause for admiration

in the grandeur of the city and the superior style of its architecture. The dwellings of the poorer class were, indeed, chiefly of reeds and mud. But the great avenue through which they were now marching was lined with the houses of the nobles, who were encouraged by the emperor to make the capital their residence. They were built of a red porous stone drawn from quarries in the neighborhood and, though they rarely rose to a second story, often covered a large space of ground. The flat roofs, *azoteas*, were protected by stone parapets, so that every house was a fortress. Sometimes these roofs resembled parterres of flowers, so thickly were they covered with them, but more frequently these were cultivated in broad terraced gardens, laid out between the edifices. Occasionally a great square or market-place intervened, surrounded by its porticoes of stone and stucco; or a pyramidal temple reared its colossal bulk, crowned with its tapering sanctuaries and altars blazing with inextinguishable fires. The great street facing the southern causeway, unlike most others in the place, was wide and extended some miles in nearly a straight line, as before noticed, through the center of the city. A spectator standing at one end of it, as his eyes ranged along the deep vista of temples, terraces, and gardens, might clearly discern the other, with the blue mountains in the distance, which, in the transparent atmosphere of the table-land, seemed almost in contact with the buildings.

But what most impressed the Spaniards was the throngs of people who swarmed through the streets and on the canals, filling every doorway and window and clustering on the roofs of the buildings. "I well remember the spectacle," exclaims Bernal Diaz;[1] "it seems now, after so many years, as present to my mind as if it were but yesterday." But what must have been the sensations of the Aztecs themselves, as they looked on the portentous pageant! as they heard, now for the first time, the well-cemented pavement ring under the iron tramp of the horses—the strange animals which fear had clothed in such supernatural terrors; as they

[1] Bernal Diaz del Castillo, *conquistador* and author of *The Discovery and Conquest of Mexico*, a major source on the subject.

gazed on the children of the East, revealing their celestial origin in their fair complexions; saw the bright falchions and bonnets of steel, a metal to them unknown, glancing like meteors in the sun, while sounds of unearthly music—at least, such as their rude instruments had never wakened—floated in the air! But every other emotion was lost in that of deadly hatred, when they beheld their detested enemy, the Tlascalan, stalking in defiance, as it were, through their streets and staring around with looks of ferocity and wonder, like some wild animal of the forest who had strayed by chance from his native fastnesses into the haunts of civilization.

As they passed down the spacious street, the troops repeatedly traversed bridges suspended above canals, along which they saw the Indian barks gliding swiftly with their little cargoes of fruits and vegetables for the markets of Tenochtitlan. At length, they halted before a broad area near the center of the city, where rose the huge pyramidal pile dedicated to the patron war-god of the Aztecs, second only in size, as well as sanctity, to the temple of Cholula, and covering the same ground now in part occupied by the great cathedral of Mexico.

Facing the western gate of the inclosure of the temple stood a low range of stone buildings, spreading over a wide extent of ground, the palace of Axayacatl, Montezuma's father, built by that monarch about fifty years before. It was appropriated as the barracks of the Spaniards. The emperor himself was in the court-yard, waiting to receive them. Approaching Cortes, he took from a vase of flowers, borne by one of his slaves, a massy collar, in which the shell of a species of craw-fish, much prized by the Indians, was set in gold and connected by heavy links of the same metal. From this chain depended eight ornaments, also of gold, made in resemblance of the same shell-fish, a span in length each and of delicate workmanship; for the Aztec goldsmiths were confessed to have shown skill in their craft not inferior to their brethren of Europe. Montezuma, as he hung the gorgeous collar round the general's neck, said,

"This palace belongs to you, Malinche"[1] (the epithet by which he always addressed him), "and your brethren. Rest after your fatigues, for you have much need to do so, and in a little while I will visit you again." So saying, he withdrew with his attendants, evincing, in this act, a delicate consideration not to have been expected in a barbarian.

Cortes' first care was to inspect his new quarters. The building, though spacious, was low, consisting of one floor, except, indeed, in the center, where it rose to an additional story. The apartments were of great size and afforded accommodations, according to the testimony of the Conquerors themselves, for the whole army! The hardy mountaineers of Tlascala were, probably, not very fastidious and might easily find a shelter in the out-buildings or under temporary awnings in the ample court-yards. The best apartments were hung with gay cotton draperies, the floors covered with mats or rushes. There were, also, low stools made of single pieces of wood elaborately carved, and in most of the apartments beds made of the palm-leaf, woven into a thick mat, with coverlets, and sometimes canopies of cotton. These mats were the only beds used by the natives, whether of high or low degree.

After a rapid survey of this gigantic pile, the general assigned to his troops their respective quarters and took as vigilant precautions for security as if he had anticipated a siege instead of a friendly entertainment. The place was encompassed by a stone wall of considerable thickness, with towers or heavy buttresses at intervals, affording a good means of defence. He planted his cannon so as to command the approaches, stationed his sentinels along the works, and, in short, enforced in every respect as strict military discipline as had been observed in any part of the march. He well knew the importance to his little band, at least for the present, of conciliating the good will of the citizens; and, to avoid all possibility of collision, he prohibited any sol-

[1] A corruption of Marina's Indian name, Malinal. Cortes was frequently referred to as Captain Malinche or as Malintzin (also derived from Malinal with *tzin*, or lord, added on).

dier from leaving his quarters without orders, under pain of death. Having taken these precautions, he allowed his men to partake of the bountiful collation which had been prepared for them.

They had been long enough in the country to become reconciled to, if not to relish, the peculiar cooking of the Aztecs. The appetite of the soldier is not often dainty, and on the present occasion it cannot be doubted that the Spaniards did full justice to the savory productions of the royal kitchen. During the meal they were served by numerous Mexican slaves, who were, indeed, distributed through the palace, anxious to do the bidding of the strangers. After the repast was concluded, and they had taken their *siesta,* not less important to a Spaniard than food itself, the presence of the emperor was again announced.

Montezuma was attended by a few of his principal nobles. He was received with much deference by Cortes; and, after the parties had taken their seats, a conversation commenced between them through the aid of Doña Marina, while the cavaliers and Aztec chieftains stood around in respectful silence.

Montezuma made many inquiries concerning the country of the Spaniards, their sovereign, the nature of his government, and especially their own motives in visiting Anahuac. Cortes explained these motives by the desire to see so distinguished a monarch and to declare to him the true Faith professed by the Christians. With rare discretion, he contented himself with dropping this hint, for the present, allowing it to ripen in the mind of the emperor till a future conference. The latter asked whether those white men who in the preceding year had landed on the eastern shores of his empire were their countrymen. He showed himself well-informed of the proceedings of the Spaniards from their arrival in Tabasco to the present time, information of which had been regularly transmitted in the hieroglyphical paintings. He was curious, also, in regard to the rank of his visitors in their own country, inquiring if they were the kinsmen of the sovereign. Cortes replied, they were kinsmen of one another and subjects of their great monarch, who held them all in peculiar estimation. Before his departure, Montezuma made himself acquainted with the names of the principal cavaliers and the position they occupied in the army.

At the conclusion of the interview, the Aztec prince commanded his attendants to bring forward the presents prepared for his guests. They consisted of cotton dresses, enough to supply every man, it is said, including the allies, with a suit! And he did not fail to add the usual accompaniment of gold chains and other ornaments, which he distributed in profusion among the Spaniards. He then withdrew with the same ceremony with which he had entered, leaving every one deeply impressed with his munificence and his affability, so unlike what they had been taught to expect by what they now considered an invention of the enemy.

That evening, the Spaniards celebrated their arrival in the Mexican capital by a general discharge of artillery. The thunders of the ordnance, reverberating among the buildings and shaking them to their foundations, the stench of the sulphurous vapor that rolled in volumes above the walls of the encampment, reminding the inhabitants of the explosions of the great *volcan*, filled the hearts of the superstitious Aztecs with dismay. It proclaimed to them that their city held in its bosom those dread beings whose path had been marked with desolation and who could call down the thunderbolts to consume their enemies! It was doubtless the policy of Cortes to strengthen this superstitious feeling as far as possible and to impress the natives, at the outset, with a salutary awe of the supernatural powers of the Spaniards.

On the following morning, the general requested permission to return the emperor's visit by waiting on him in his palace. This was readily granted, and Montezuma sent his officers to conduct the Spaniards to his presence. Cortes dressed himself in his richest habit and left the quarters attended by Alvarado, Sandoval, Velasquez, and Ordaz, together with five or six of the common file.

The royal habitation was at no great distance. It

stood on the ground, to the south-west of the cathedral, since covered in part by the *Casa del Estado*, the palace of the dukes of Monteleone, the descendants of Cortes. It was a vast, irregular pile of low stone buildings, like that garrisoned by the Spaniards. So spacious was it, indeed, that, as one of the Conquerors assures us, although he had visited it more than once, for the express purpose, he had been too much fatigued each time by wandering through the apartments ever to see the whole of it. It was built of the red porous stone of the country, *tetzontli*, was ornamented with marble, and on the façade over the principal entrance were sculptured the arms or device of Montezuma, an eagle bearing an ocelot in his talons.

In the courts through which the Spaniards passed, fountains of crystal water were playing, fed from the copious reservoir on the distant hill of Chapoltepec and supplying in their turn more than a hundred baths in the interior of the palace. Crowds of Aztec nobles were sauntering up and down in these squares and in the outer halls, loitering away their hours in attendance on the court. The apartments were of immense size, though not lofty. The ceilings were of various sorts of odoriferous wood ingeniously carved; the floors covered with mats of the palm-leaf. The walls were hung with cotton richly stained, with the skins of wild animals, or gorgeous draperies of feather-work wrought in imitation of birds, insects, and flowers, with the nice art and glowing radiance of colors that might compare with the tapestries of Flanders. Clouds of incense rolled up from censers and diffused intoxicating odors through the apartments. The Spaniards might well have fancied themselves in the voluptuous precincts of an Eastern harem, instead of treading the halls of a wild barbaric chief in the Western World.

On reaching the hall of audience, the Mexican officers took off their sandals, and covered their gay attire with a mantle of *nequen*, a coarse stuff made of the fibres of the maguey, worn only by the poorest classes. This act of humiliation was imposed on all, except the members of his own family, who approached the sovereign. Thus bare-footed, with downcast eyes and formal obeisance, they ushered the Spaniards into the royal presence.

They found Montezuma seated at the further end of a spacious saloon and surrounded by a few of his favorite chiefs. He received them kindly, and very soon Cortes, without much ceremony, entered on the subject which was uppermost in his thoughts. He was fully aware of the importance of gaining the royal convert, whose example would have such an influence on the conversion of his people. The general, therefore, prepared to display the whole store of his theological science with the most winning arts of rhetoric he could command, while the interpretation was conveyed through the silver tones of Marina, as inseparable from him, on these occasions, as his shadow.

He set forth, as clearly as he could, the ideas entertained by the Church in regard to the holy mysteries of the Trinity, the Incarnation, and the Atonement. From this he ascended to the origin of things, the creation of the world, the first pair, paradise, and the fall of man. He assured Montezuma that the idols he worshipped were Satan under different forms. A sufficient proof of it was the bloody sacrifices they imposed, which he contrasted with the pure and simple rite of the mass. Their worship would sink him in perdition. It was to snatch his soul, and the souls of his people, from the flames of eternal fire by opening to them a purer faith that the Christians had come to his land. And he earnestly besought him not to neglect the occasion but to secure his salvation by embracing the Cross, the great sign of human redemption.

The eloquence of the preacher was wasted on the insensible heart of his royal auditor. It doubtless lost somewhat of its efficacy, strained through the imperfect interpretation of so recent a neophyte as the Indian damsel. But the doctrines were too abstruse in themselves to be comprehended at a glance by the rude intellect of a barbarian. And Montezuma may have, perhaps, thought it was not more monstrous to feed on the flesh of a fellow-creature than on that of the Creator himself.

He was, besides, steeped in the superstitions of his country from his cradle. He had been educated in the straitest sect of her religion, had been himself a priest before his election to the throne, and was now the head both of the religion and the state. Little probability was there that such a man would be open to argument or persuasion, even from the lips of a more practised polemic than the Spanish commander. How could he abjure the faith that was intertwined with the dearest affections of his heart and the very elements of his being? How could he be false to the gods who had raised him to such prosperity and honors, and whose shrines were intrusted to his especial keeping?

He listened, however, with silent attention, until the general had concluded his homily. He then replied that he knew the Spaniards had held this discourse wherever they had been. He doubted not their God was, as they said, a good being. His gods, also, were good to him. Yet what his visitor said of the creation of the world was like what he had been taught to believe. It was not worth while to discourse further of the matter. His ancestors, he said, were not the original proprietors of the land. They had occupied it but a few ages and had been led there by a great Being, who, after giving them laws and ruling over the nation for a time, had withdrawn to the regions where the sun rises. He had declared, on his departure, that he or his descendants would again visit them and resume his empire. The wonderful deeds of the Spaniards, their fair complexions, and the quarter whence they came all showed they were his descendants. If Montezuma had resisted their visit to his capital, it was because he had heard such accounts of their cruelties—that they sent the lightning to consume his people or crushed them to pieces under the hard feet of the ferocious animals on which they rode. He was now convinced that these were idle tales, that the Spaniards were kind and generous in their natures; they were mortals, of a different race, indeed, from the Aztecs, wiser and more valiant—and for this he honored them.

"You, too," he added, with a smile, "have been told,

perhaps, that I am a god, and dwell in palaces of gold and silver. But you see it is false. My houses, though large, are of stone and wood like those of others; and as to my body," he said, baring his tawny arm, "you see it is flesh and bone like yours. It is true, I have a great empire, inherited from my ancestors; lands, and gold, and silver. But your sovereign beyond the waters is, I know, the rightful lord of all. I rule in his name. You, Malinche, are his ambassador; you and your brethren shall share these things with me. Rest now from your labors. You are here in your own dwellings, and everything shall be provided for your subsistence. I will see that your wishes shall be obeyed in the same way as my own." As the monarch concluded these words, a few natural tears suffused his eyes, while the image of ancient independence, perhaps, flitted across his mind.

Cortes, while he encouraged the idea that his own sovereign was the great Being indicated by Montezuma, endeavored to comfort the monarch by the assurance that his master had no desire to interfere with his authority otherwise than, out of pure concern for his welfare, to effect his conversion and that of his people to Christianity. Before the emperor dismissed his visitors he consulted his munificent spirit, as usual, by distributing rich stuffs and trinkets of gold among them, so that the poorest soldier, says Bernal Diaz, one of the party, received at least two heavy collars of the precious metal for his share. The iron hearts of the Spaniards were touched with the emotion displayed by Montezuma, as well as by his princely spirit of liberality. As they passed him, the cavaliers, with bonnet in hand, made him the most profound obeisance, and, "on the way home," continues the same chronicler, "we could discourse of nothing but the gentle breeding and courtesy of the Indian monarch, and of the respect we entertained for him."

Speculations of a graver complexion must have pressed on the mind of the general as he saw around him the evidences of a civilization, and consequently power, for which even the exaggerated reports of the natives—discredited from their apparent exaggeration—had not prepared him. In the pomp and burdensome ceremonial of the court, he saw that nice system of subordination and profound reverence for the monarch which characterize the semi-civilized empires of Asia. In the appearance of the capital, its massy yet elegant architecture, its luxurious social accommodations, its activity in trade, he recognized the proofs of the intellectual progress, mechanical skill, and enlarged resources of an old and opulent community; while the swarms in the streets attested the existence of a population capable of turning these resources to the best account.

In the Aztec he beheld a being unlike either the rude republican Tlascalan or the effeminate Cholulan, but combining the courage of the one with the cultivation of the other. He was in the heart of a great capital, which seemed like an extensive fortification, with its dikes and its drawbridges, where every house might be easily converted into a castle. Its insular position removed it from the continent, from which, at the mere nod of the sovereign, all communication might be cut off, and the whole warlike population be at once precipitated on him and his handful of followers. What could superior science avail against such odds?

As to the subversion of Montezuma's empire, now that he had seen him in his capital, it must have seemed a more doubtful enterprise than ever. The recognition which the Aztec prince had made of the feudal supremacy, if I may so say, of the Spanish sovereign was not to be taken too literally. Whatever show of deference he might be disposed to pay the latter under the influence of his present—perhaps temporary—delusion, it was not to be supposed that he would so easily relinquish his actual power and possessions or that his people would consent to it. Indeed, his sensitive apprehensions in regard to this very subject, on the coming of the Spaniards, were sufficient proof of the tenacity with which he clung to his authority. It is true that Cortes had a strong lever for future operations in the superstitious reverence felt for himself both by prince and people. It was undoubtedly his policy to maintain this sentiment unimpaired in both, as far as possible. But, before settling any plan of operations, it was necessary to make himself personally acquainted with the topography and local advantages of the capital, the character of its population, and the real nature and amount of its resources. With this view, he asked the emperor's permission to visit the principal public edifices.

*4. The Seizure of Montezuma**

[*Cortes had been welcomed into Tenochtitlan, but, as he well knew, his position was somewhat precarious. After a week in which the issues were debated, Cortes decided to seize Montezuma and compel him to move to the Spanish quarters. A pretext for this audacious action was found in the murder of some Spaniards near Vera Cruz by an officer of the Aztec ruler named Quauhpopoca; the blame for the deed was cast on the emperor. After a night of prayer, Cortes, with two interpreters and six armed companions, entered Montezuma's palace.*]

The little party were graciously received by the emperor, who soon, with the aid of the interpreters, became interested in a sportive conversation with the Spaniards, while he indulged his natural munificence by giving them presents of gold and jewels. He paid the Spanish general the particular compliment of offering him one of his daughters as his wife, an honor which the latter respectfully declined, on the ground that he was already accommodated with one in Cuba and that his religion forbade a plurality.

When Cortes perceived that a sufficient number of his

* From *The Conquest of Mexico,* Book IV, chap. 3.

soldiers were assembled, he changed his playful manner and with a serious tone briefly acquainted Montezuma with the treacherous proceedings in the *tierra caliente* and the accusation of him as their author. The emperor listened to the charge with surprise and disavowed the act, which he said could only have been imputed to him by his enemies. Cortes expressed his belief in his declaration, but added that, to prove it true, it would be necessary to send for Quauhpopoca and his accomplices that they might be examined and dealt with according to their deserts. To this Montezuma made no objection. Taking from his wrist, to which it was attached, a precious stone, the royal signet, on which was cut the figure of the war-god, he gave it to one of his nobles with orders to show it to the Aztec governor and require his instant presence in the capital, together with all those who had been accessory to the murder of the Spaniards. If he resisted, the officer was empowered to call in the aid of the neighboring towns to enforce the mandate.

When the messenger had gone, Cortes assured the monarch that this prompt compliance with his request convinced him of his innocence. But it was important that his own sovereign should be equally convinced of it. Nothing would promote this so much as for Montezuma to transfer his residence to the palace occupied by the Spaniards, till on the arrival of Quauhpopoca the affair could be fully investigated. Such an act of condescension would, of itself, show a personal regard for the Spaniards, incompatible with the base conduct alleged against him, and would fully absolve him from all suspicion!

Montezuma listened to this proposal, and the flimsy reasoning with which it was covered, with looks of profound amazement. He became pale as death; but in a moment his face flushed with resentment as with the pride of offended dignity he exclaimed, "When was it ever heard that a great prince, like myself, voluntarily left his own palace to become a prisoner in the hands of strangers!"

Cortes assured him he would not go as a prisoner.

He would experience nothing but respectful treatment from the Spaniards, would be surrounded by his own household, and hold intercourse with his people as usual. In short, it would be but a change of residence, from one of his palaces to another, a circumstance of frequent occurrence with him.—It was in vain. "If I should consent to such a degradation," he answered, "my subjects never would!" When further pressed, he offered to give up one of his sons and one of his daughters to remain as hostages with the Spaniards, so that he might be spared this disgrace.

Two hours passed in this fruitless discussion, till a high-mettled cavalier, Velasquez de León, impatient of the long delay and seeing that the attempt, if not the deed, must ruin them, cried out, "Why do we waste words on this barbarian? We have gone too far to recede now. Let us seize him and, if he resists, plunge our swords into his body!" The fierce tone and menacing gestures with which this was uttered alarmed the monarch, who inquired of Marina what the angry Spaniard said. The interpreter explained it in as gentle a manner as she could, beseeching him "to accompany the white men to their quarters, where he would be treated with all respect and kindness, while to refuse them would but expose himself to violence, perhaps to death." Marina, doubtless, spoke to her sovereign as she thought, and no one had better opportunity of knowing the truth than herself.

This last appeal shook the resolution of Montezuma. It was in vain that the unhappy prince looked around for sympathy or support. As his eyes wandered over the stern visages and iron forms of the Spaniards, he felt that his hour was indeed come; and, with a voice scarcely audible from emotion, he consented to accompany the strangers—to quit the palace, whither he was never more to return. Had he possessed the spirit of the first Montezuma, he would have called his guards around him and left his life-blood on the threshold, sooner than have been dragged a dishonored captive across it. But his courage sank under the circumstances. He felt he was the instrument of an irresistible Fate!

No sooner had the Spaniards got his consent than orders were given for the royal litter. The nobles, who bore and attended it, could scarcely believe their senses when they learned their master's purpose. But pride now came to Montezuma's aid, and, since he must go, he preferred that it should appear to be with his own free-will. As the royal retinue, escorted by the Spaniards, marched through the street with downcast eyes and dejected mien, the people assembled in crowds, and a rumor ran among them that the emperor was carried off by force to the quarters of the white men. A tumult would have soon arisen but for the intervention of Montezuma himself, who called out to the people to disperse, as he was visiting his friends of his own accord; thus sealing his ignominy by a declaration which deprived his subjects of the only excuse for resistance. On reaching the quarters, he sent out his nobles with similar assurances to the mob and renewed orders to return to their homes.

He was received with ostentatious respect by the Spaniards and selected the suite of apartments which best pleased him. They were soon furnished with fine cotton tapestries, feather-work, and all the elegances of Indian upholstery. He was attended by such of his household as he chose, his wives and his pages, and was served with his usual pomp and luxury at his meals. He gave audience, as in his own palace, to his subjects, who were admitted to his presence, few, indeed, at a time, under the pretext of greater order and decorum. From the Spaniards themselves he met with a formal deference. No one, not even the general himself, approached him without doffing his casque and rendering the obeisance due to his rank. Nor did they ever sit in his presence without being invited by him to do so.

With all this studied ceremony and show of homage, there was one circumstance which too clearly proclaimed to his people that their sovereign was a prisoner. In the front of the palace a patrol of sixty men was established, and the same number in the rear. Twenty of each corps mounted guard at once, maintaining a careful watch day and night. Another body, under command of Velasquez de León, was stationed in the royal antechamber. Cortes punished any departure from duty or relaxation of vigilance in these sentinels with the utmost severity. He felt, as, indeed, every Spaniard must have felt, that the escape of the emperor now would be their ruin. Yet the task of this unintermitting watch sorely added to their fatigues. "Better this dog of a king should die," cried a soldier one day, "than that we should wear out our lives in this manner." The words were uttered in the hearing of Montezuma, who gathered something of their import, and the offender was severely chastised by order of the general. Such instances of disrespect, however, were very rare. Indeed, the amiable deportment of the monarch, who seemed to take pleasure in the society of his jailers and who never allowed a favor or attention from the meanest soldier to go unrequited, inspired the Spaniards with as much attachment as they were capable of feeling—for a barbarian.

Things were in this posture, when the arrival of Quauhpopoca from the coast was announced. He was accompanied by his son and fifteen Aztec chiefs. He had travelled all the way borne, as became his high rank, in a litter. On entering Montezuma's presence, he threw over his dress the coarse robe of *nequen* and made the usual humiliating acts of obeisance. The poor parade of courtly ceremony was the more striking when placed in contrast with the actual condition of the parties.

The Aztec governor was coldly received by his master, who referred the affair (had he the power to do otherwise?) to the examination of Cortes. It was, doubtless, conducted in a sufficiently summary manner. To the general's query whether the cacique was the subject of Montezuma, he replied, "And what other sovereign could I serve?" implying that his sway was universal. He did not deny his share in the transaction, nor did he seek to shelter himself under the royal authority till sentence of death was passed on him and his followers, when they all laid the blame of their proceedings on Montezuma. They were condemned to be burnt alive in the area before the palace. The funeral piles were made of heaps of arrows, javelins, and other weapons, drawn by the emperor's permission from the arsenals round the great *teocalli,* where they had been stored to supply means of defense in times of civic tumult or insurrection. By this politic precaution Cortes proposed to remove a ready means of annoyance in case of hostilities with the citizens.

To crown the whole of these extraordinary proceedings, Cortes, while preparations for the execution were going on, entered the emperor's apartment attended by a soldier bearing fetters in his hands. With a severe aspect, he charged the monarch with being the original contriver of the violence offered to the Spaniards, as was now proved by the declaration of his own instruments. Such a crime, which merited death in a subject, could not be atoned for, even by a sovereign, without some punishment. So saying, he ordered the soldier to fasten the fetters on Montezuma's ankles. He coolly waited till it was done, then, turning his back on the monarch, quitted the room.

Montezuma was speechless under the infliction of this last insult. He was like one struck down by a heavy blow, that deprives him of all his faculties. He offered no resistance. But, though he spoke not a word, low, ill-suppressed moans, from time to time, intimated the anguish of his spirit. His attendants, bathed in tears, offered him their consolations. They tenderly held his feet in their arms and endeavored, by inserting their shawls and mantles, to relieve them from the pressure of the iron. But they could not reach the iron which had penetrated into his soul. He felt that he was no more a king.

Meanwhile, the execution of the dreadful doom was going forward in the court-yard. The whole Spanish force was under arms, to check any interruption that might be offered by the Mexicans. But none was attempted. The populace gazed in silent wonder, regarding it as the sentence of the emperor. The manner of the execution, too, excited less surprise, from their familiarity with similar spectacles, aggravated, indeed, by additional horrors in their own diabolical sacrifices. The Aztec lord and his companions, bound hand and foot to the blazing piles, submitted without a cry or a complaint to their terrible fate. Passive fortitude is the virtue of the Indian warrior; and it was the glory of the Aztec, as of the other races on the North American continent, to show how the spirit of the brave man may triumph over torture and the agonies of death.

When the dismal tragedy was ended, Cortes re-entered Montezuma's apartment. Kneeling down, he unclasped his shackles with his own hand, expressing at the same time his regret that so disagreeable a duty as that of subjecting him to such a punishment had been imposed on him. This last indignity had entirely crushed the spirit of Montezuma; and the monarch, whose frown, but a week since, would have made the nations of Anahuac tremble to their remotest borders, was now craven enough to thank his deliverer for his freedom, as for a great and unmerited boon!

Not long after, the Spanish general, conceiving that his royal captive was sufficiently humbled, expressed his willingness that he should return, if he inclined, to his own palace. Montezuma declined it; alleging, it is said, that his nobles had more than once importuned him to resent his injuries by taking arms against the Spaniards and that, were he in the midst of them, it would be difficult to avoid it or to save his capital from bloodshed and anarchy. The reason did honor to his heart, if it was the one which influenced him. It is probable that he did not care to trust his safety to those haughty and ferocious chieftains who had witnessed the degradation of their master and must despise his pusillanimity as a thing unprecedented in an Aztec monarch. It is also said that, when Marina conveyed to him the permission of Cortes, the other interpreter, Aguilar, gave him to understand the Spanish officers never would consent that he should avail himself of it.

Whatever were his reasons, it is certain that he declined the offer; and the general, in a well-feigned or real ecstasy, embraced him, declaring, "that he loved him as a brother, and that every Spaniard would be zealously devoted to his interests, since he had shown himself so mindful of theirs!" Honeyed words, "which," says the shrewd old chronicler who was present, "Montezuma was wise enough to know the worth of."

The events recorded in this chapter are certainly some of the most extraordinary on the page of history. That a small body of men, like the Spaniards, should have entered the palace of a mighty prince, have seized his person in the midst of his vassals, have borne him off a captive to their quarters; that they should have put to an ignominious death before his face his high officers, for executing probably his own commands, and have crowned the whole by putting the monarch in irons like a common malefactor; that this should have been done, not to a drivelling dotard in the decay of his fortunes, but to a proud monarch in the plenitude of his power, in the very heart of his capital, surrounded by thousands and tens of thousands who trembled at his nod and would have poured out their blood like water in his defence; that all this should have been done by a mere handful of adventurers—is a thing too extravagant, altogether too improbable, for the pages of romance! It is, nevertheless, literally true. Yet we shall not be prepared to acquiesce in the judgments of contemporaries, who regarded these acts with admiration. We may well distrust any grounds on which it is attempted to justify the kidnapping of a friendly sovereign—by those very persons, too, who were reaping the full benefit of his favors.

To view the matter differently, we must take the position of the Conquerors and assume with them the original right of conquest. Regarded from this point of view, many difficulties vanish. If conquest were a duty, whatever was necessary to effect it was right also. Right and expedient become convertible terms. And it can hardly be denied that the capture of the monarch was expedient if the Spaniards would maintain their hold on the empire.

The execution of the Aztec governor suggests other considerations. If he were really guilty of the perfidious act imputed to him by Cortes, and if Montezuma disavowed it, the governor deserved death, and the general was justified by the law of nations in inflicting it. It is by no means so clear, however, why he should have involved so many in this sentence, most, perhaps all, of whom must have acted under his authority. The cruel manner of the death will less startle those who are familiar with the established penal codes in most civilized nations in the sixteenth century.

But, if the governor deserved death, what pretence was there for the outrage on the person of Montezuma? If the former was guilty, the latter surely was not. But, if the cacique only acted in obedience to orders, the responsibility was transferred to the sovereign who gave the orders. They could not both stand in the same category.

It is vain, however, to reason on the matter on any abstract principles of right and wrong or to suppose that the Conquerors troubled themselves with the refinements of casuistry. Their standard of right and wrong, in reference to the natives, was a very simple one. Despising them as an outlawed race without God in the world, they, in common with their age, held it to be their "mission" (to borrow the cant phrase of our own day) to conquer and to convert. The measures they adopted certainly facilitated the first great work of conquest. By the execution of the caciques, they struck terror not only into the capital but throughout the country. It proclaimed that not a hair of a Spaniard was to be touched with impunity! By rendering Montezuma contemptible in his own eyes and those of his subjects, Cortes deprived him of the support of his people and forced him to lean on the arm of the stranger. It was a politic proceeding—to which few men could have been equal who had a touch of humanity in their natures.

A good criterion of the moral sense of the actors in these events is afforded by the reflections of Bernal Diaz, made some fifty years, it will be remembered, after the events themselves, when the fire of youth had become extinct, and the eye, glancing back through the vista of half a century, might be supposed to be unclouded by the passions and prejudices which throw their mist over the present. "Now that I am an old man," says the veteran, "I often entertain myself with calling to mind the heroical deeds of early days, till they are as fresh as the events of yesterday. I think of the seizure of the Indian monarch, his confinement in irons, and the execution of his officers, till all these things seem actually passing before me. And, as I ponder on our exploits, I feel that it was not of ourselves that we performed them, but that it was the providence of God which guided us. Much food is there here for meditation!" There is so, indeed, and for a meditation not unpleasing, as we reflect on the advance, in speculative morality, at least, which the nineteenth century has made over the sixteenth. But should not the consciousness of this teach us charity? Should it not make us the more distrustful of applying the standard of the present to measure the actions of the past?

*5. The Destruction of the Great Temple**

[From the time of his seizure, Montezuma resigned himself to his fate. Cortes' position was soon compromised, however, from a different direction. Five months after his arrival in the capital, he found himself threatened in the rear by the arrival of Panfilo Narvaez, a lieutenant of Velasquez, who occupied the land to the south in the name of the governor of Cuba. Leaving Pedro de Alvarado to control Tenochtitlan, Cortes marched off to the south with a portion of his men to combat this new threat. While he was successfully accomplishing this (and, in the process, increasing the size of his army fourfold), re-

* From *The Conquest of Mexico,* Book V, chap. 2.

volt broke out in Tenochtitlan, stirred up by a slaughter of Aztec nobles during a religious celebration. Cortes rushed back to the sullen and hostile capital. He attempted to appease the people by presenting Montezuma to them. This met with no success; Montezuma was felled by a stone thrown by his own people and died three days later. In desperation, the surrounded Spaniards decided to storm the great teocalli *or temple overlooking their quarters.*]

Opposite to the Spanish quarters, at only a few rods' distance, stood the great *teocalli* of Huitzilopochtli.[1] This pyramidal mound, with the sanctuaries that crowned it, rising altogether to the height of near a hundred and fifty feet, afforded an elevated position that completely commanded the palace of Axayacatl, occupied by the Christians. A body of five or six hundred Mexicans, many of them nobles and warriors of the highest rank, had got possession of the *teocalli*, whence they discharged such a tempest of arrows on the garrison that no one could leave his defences for a moment without imminent danger; while the Mexicans, under shelter of the sanctuaries, were entirely covered from the fire of the besieged. It was obviously necessary to dislodge the enemy, if the Spaniards would remain longer in their quarters.

Cortes assigned this service to his chamberlain, Escobar, giving him a hundred men for the purpose, with orders to storm the *teocalli* and set fire to the sanctuaries. But that officer was thrice repulsed in the attempt and, after the most desperate efforts, was obliged to return with considerable loss and without accomplishing his object.

Cortes, who saw the immediate necessity of carrying the place, determined to lead the storming party himself. He was then suffering much from the wound in his left hand, which had disabled it for the present. He made the arm serviceable, however, by fastening his buckler

[1] The war god and principal deity of the Aztecs.

to it and, thus crippled, sallied out at the head of three hundred chosen cavaliers and several thousand of his auxiliaries.

In the court-yard of the temple he found a numerous body of Indians prepared to dispute his passage. He briskly charged them, but the flat, smooth stones of the pavement were so slippery that the horses lost their footing and many of them fell. Hastily dismounting, they sent back the animals to their quarters, and, renewing the assault, the Spaniards succeeded without much difficulty in dispersing the Indian warriors and opening a free passage for themselves to the *teocalli.* This building, as the reader may remember, was a large pyramidal structure, about three hundred feet square at the base. A flight of stone steps on the outside, at one of the angles of the mound, led to a platform, or terraced walk, which passed round the building until it reached a similar flight of stairs directly over the preceding, that conducted to another landing as before. As there were five bodies or divisions of the *teocalli,* it became necessary to pass round its whole extent four times, or nearly a mile, in order to reach the summit, which, it may be recollected, was an open area, crowned only by the two sanctuaries dedicated to the Aztec deities.

Cortes, having cleared a way for the assault, sprang up the lower stairway, followed by Alvarado, Sandoval, Ordaz, and the other gallant cavaliers of his little band, leaving a file of arquebusiers and a strong corps of Indian allies to hold the enemy in check at the foot of the monument. On the first landing, as well as on the several galleries above, and on the summit, the Aztec warriors were drawn up to dispute his passage. From their elevated position they showered down volleys of lighter missiles, together with heavy stones, beams, and burning rafters, which, thundering along the stairway, overturned the ascending Spaniards and carried desolation through their ranks. The more fortunate, eluding or springing over these obstacles, succeeded in gaining the first terrace, where, throwing themselves on their enemies, they compelled them, after a short resistance, to fall back. The assailants pressed on, effectually supported by a brisk fire of the musketeers from below, which so much galled the Mexicans in their exposed situation that they were glad to take shelter on the broad summit of the *teocalli.*

Cortes and his comrades were close upon their rear, and the two parties soon found themselves face to face on this aerial battle-field, engaged in mortal combat in presence of the whole city, as well as of the troops in the court-yard, who paused, as if by mutual consent, from their own hostilities, gazing in silent expectation on the issue of those above. The area, though somewhat smaller than the base of the *teocalli,* was large enough to afford a fair field of fight for a thousand combatants. It was paved with broad, flat stones. No impediment occurred over its surface, except the huge sacrificial block and the temples of stone which rose to the height of forty feet at the further extremity of the arena. One of these had been consecrated to the Cross; the other was still occupied by the Mexican war-god. The Christian and the Aztec contended for their religions under the very shadow of their respective shrines; while the Indian priests, running to and fro, with their hair wildly streaming over their sable mantles, seemed hovering in mid-air, like so many demons of darkness urging on the work of slaughter!

The parties closed with the desperate fury of men who had no hope but in victory. Quarter was neither asked nor given; and to fly was impossible. The edge of the area was unprotected by parapet or battlement. The least slip would be fatal; and the combatants, as they struggled in mortal agony, were sometimes seen to roll over the sheer sides of the precipice together. Cortes himself is said to have had a narrow escape from this dreadful fate. Two warriors, of strong, muscular frames, seized on him and were dragging him violently towards the brink of the pyramid. Aware of their intention, he struggled with all his force and, before they could accomplish their purpose, succeeded in tearing himself from their grasp and hurling one of them over the walls with his own arm! The story is not improbable in itself, for Cortes was a man of uncommon agility and strength. It has been often repeated, but not by contemporary history.

The battle lasted with unintermitting fury for thre hours. The number of the enemy was double that of th Christians; and it seemed as if it were a contest whic must be determined by numbers and brute force, rathe than by superior science. But it was not so. The invulnerable armor of the Spaniard, his sword of matchless temper, and his skill in the use of it gave him advantages which far outweighed the odds of physica strength and numbers. After doing all that the courag of despair could enable men to do, resistance grew fainter and fainter on the side of the Aztecs. One afte another they had fallen. Two or three priests only survived to be led away in triumph by the victors. Ever other combatant was stretched a corpse on the blood arena or had been hurled from the giddy heights. Ye the loss of the Spaniards was not inconsiderable. I amounted to forty-five of their best men, and nearly al the remainder were more or less injured in the desperat conflict.

The victorious cavaliers now rushed towards the sanctuaries. The lower story was of stone; the two upper wer of wood. Penetrating into their recesses, they had th mortification to find the image of the Virgin and th Cross removed. But in the other edifice they still behel the grim figure of Huitzilopotchli, with his censer o smoking hearts, and the walls of his oratory reeking wit gore—not improbably of their own countrymen! Wit shouts of triumph the Christians tore the uncouth monster from his niche and tumbled him, in the presenc of the horror-struck Aztecs, down the steps of the *teocalli.* They then set fire to the accursed building. Th flame speedily ran up the slender towers, sending fort an ominous light over city, lake, and valley, to the remotest hut among the mountains. It was the funera pyre of paganism and proclaimed the fall of that sanguinary religion which had so long hung like a dar cloud over the fair regions of Anahuac!

Having accomplished this good work, the Spaniard descended the winding slopes of the *teocalli* with mor free and buoyant step, as if conscious that the blessing of Heaven now rested on their arms. They passed through the dusky files of Indian .warriors in the court-yard, too much dismayed by the appalling scenes they had witnessed to offer resistance, and reached their own quarters in safety. That very night they followed up the blow by a sortie on the sleeping town and burned three hundred houses, the horrors of conflagration being made still more impressive by occurring at the hour when the Aztecs, from their own system of warfare, were least prepared for them.

Hoping to find the temper of the natives somewhat subdued by these reverses, Cortes now determined, with his usual policy, to make them a vantage-ground for proposing terms of accommodation. He accordingly invited the enemy to a parley, and, as the principal chiefs, attended by their followers, assembled in the great square, he mounted the turret before occupied by Montezuma and made signs that he would address them. Marina, as usual, took her place by his side as his interpreter. The multitude gazed with earnest curiosity on the Indian girl, whose influence with the Spaniards was well known and whose connection with the general, in particular, had led the Aztecs to designate him by her Mexican name of Malinche. Cortes, speaking through the soft, musical tones of his mistress, told his audience they must now be convinced that they had nothing further to hope from opposition to the Spaniards. They had seen their gods trampled in the dust, their altars broken, their dwellings burned, their warriors falling on all sides. "All this," continued he, "you have brought on yourselves by your rebellion. Yet for the affection the sovereign whom you have so unworthily treated still bears you, I would willingly stay my hand, if you will lay down your arms, and return once more to your obedience. But, if you do not," he concluded, "I will make your city a heap of ruins, and leave not a soul alive to mourn over it!"

But the Spanish commander did not yet comprehend the character of the Aztecs, if he thought to intimidate them by menaces. Calm in their exterior and slow to move, they were the more difficult to pacify when roused; and now that they had been stirred to their inmost depths, it was no human voice that could still the tempest. It may be, however, that Cortes did not so much misconceive the character of the people. He may have felt that an authoritative tone was the only one he could assume with any chance of effect in his present position, in which milder and more conciliatory language would, by intimating a consciousness of inferiority, have too certainly defeated its own object.

It was true, they answered, he had destroyed their temples, broken in pieces their gods, massacred their countrymen. Many more, doubtless, were yet to fall under their terrible swords. But they were content so long as for every thousand Mexicans they could shed the blood of a single white man! "Look out," they continued, "on our terraces and streets, see them still thronged with warriors as far as your eyes can reach. Our numbers are scarcely diminished by our losses. Yours, on the contrary, are lessening every hour. You are perishing from hunger and sickness. Your provisions and water are failing. You must soon fall into our hands. The bridges are broken down, and you cannot escape! There will be too few of you left to glut the vengeance of our gods!" As they concluded, they sent a volley of arrows over the battlements, which compelled the Spaniards to descend and take refuge in their defences.

The fierce and indomitable spirit of the Aztecs filled the besieged with dismay. All, then, that they had done and suffered, their battles by day, their vigils by night, the perils they had braved, even the victories they had won, were of no avail. It was too evident that they had no longer the spring of ancient superstition to work upon in the breasts of the natives, who, like some wild beast that has burst the bonds of his keeper, seemed now to swell and exult in the full consciousness of their strength. The annunciation respecting the bridges fell like a knell on the ears of the Christians. All that they had heard was too true—and they gazed on one another with looks of anxiety and dismay.

*6. The Noche Triste**

[It was now apparent that the Spaniards could not win the city. To remain meant certain death by one means or another, and, consequently, the decision was reached to abandon Tenochtitlan. The costly and painful retreat of the beleaguered conquerors forms one of the saddest pages in the history of the conquest. To Prescott, as to the Spaniards, the retreat was "this terrible passage of the causeway; more disastrous than those occasioned by any other reverse which has stained the Spanish arms in the New World; and which has branded the night on which it happened, in the national annals, with the name of the noche triste, *the sad or melancholy night."]*

There was no longer any question as to the expediency of evacuating the capital. The only doubt was as to the time of doing so and the route. The Spanish commander called a council of officers to deliberate on these matters. It was his purpose to retreat on Tlascala and in that capital to decide, according to circumstances, on his future operations. After some discussion, they agreed on the causeway of Tlacopan as the avenue by which to leave the city. It would, indeed, take them back by a circuitous route, considerably longer than either of those by which they had approached the capital. But, for that reason, it would be less likely to be guarded, as least suspected; and the causeway itself being shorter than either of the other entrances, would sooner place the army in comparative security on the mainland.

*** From *The Conquest of Mexico*, Book V, chap. 3.**

There was some difference of opinion in respect to the hour of departure. The day-time, it was argued by some, would be preferable, since it would enable them to see the nature and extent of their danger and to provide against it. Darkness would be much more likely to embarrass their own movements than those of the enemy, who were familiar with the ground. A thousand impediments would occur in the night, which might prevent their acting in concert, or obeying, or even ascertaining, the orders of the commander. But on the other hand it was urged that the night presented many obvious advantages in dealing with a foe who rarely carried his hostilities beyond the day. The late active operations of the Spaniards had thrown the Mexicans off their guard, and it was improbable they would anticipate so speedy a departure of their enemies. With celerity and caution they might succeed, therefore, in making their escape from the town, possibly over the causeway, before their retreat should be discovered; and, could they once get beyond that pass of peril, they felt little apprehension for the rest.

These views were fortified, it is said, by the counsels of a soldier named Botello, who professed the mysterious science of judicial astrology. He had gained credit with the army by some predictions which had been verified by the events; those lucky hits which make chance pass for calculation with the credulous multitude. This man recommended to his countrymen by all means to evacuate the place in the night, as the hour most propitious to them, although he should perish in it. The event proved the astrologer better acquainted with his own horoscope than with that of others.

It is possible Botello's predictions had some weight in determining the opinion of Cortes. Superstition was the feature of the age, and the Spanish general, as we have seen, had a full measure of its bigotry. Seasons of gloom, moreover, dispose the mind to a ready acquiescence in the marvellous. It is, however, quite as probable that he made use of the astrologer's opinion, finding it coincided with his own, to influence that of his men and inspire them with higher confidence. At all events, it was decided to abandon the city that very night.

The general's first care was to provide for the safe transportation of the treasure. Many of the common soldiers had converted their share of the prize, as we have seen, into gold chains, collars, or other ornaments, which they easily carried about their persons. But the royal fifth, together with that of Cortes himself, and much of the rich booty of the principal cavaliers had been converted into bars and wedges of solid gold and deposited in one of the strong apartments of the palace. Cortes delivered the share belonging to the crown to the royal officers, assigning them one of the strongest horses and a guard of Castilian soldiers to transport it. Still, much of the treasure belonging both to the crown and to individuals was necessarily abandoned, from the want of adequate means of conveyance. The metal lay scattered in shining heaps along the floor, exciting the cupidity of the soldiers. "Take what you will of it," said Cortes to his men. "Better you should have it than these Mexican hounds. But be careful not to overload yourselves. He travels safest in the dark who travels lightest." His own more wary followers took heed to his counsel, helping themselves to a few articles of least bulk, though, it might be, of greatest value. But the troops of Narvaez, pining for riches, of which they had heard so much and hitherto seen so little, showed no such discretion. To them it seemed as if the very mines of Mexico were turned up before them, and, rushing on the treacherous spoil, they greedily loaded themselves with as much of it, not merely as they could accommodate about their persons, but as they could stow away in wallets, boxes, or any other mode of conveyance at their disposal.

Cortes next arranged the order of march. The van, composed of two hundred Spanish foot, he placed under the command of the valiant Gonzalo de Sandoval, supported by Diego de Ordaz, Francisco de Lujo, and about twenty other cavaliers. The rearguard, constituting the strength of the infantry, was intrusted to Pedro de Alvarado and Velasquez de Leon. The general himself took charge of the "battle," or center, in which went the baggage, some of the heavy guns, most of which, however, remained in the rear, the treasure, and the prisoners. These consisted of a son and two daughters of Montezuma, Cacama, the deposed lord of Tezcuco, and several other nobles, whom Cortes retained as important pledges in his future negotiations with the enemy. The Tlascalans were distributed pretty equally among the three divisions; and Cortes had under his immediate command a hundred picked soldiers, his own veterans most attached to his service, who, with Christoval de Olid, Francisco de Morla, Alonso de Avila, and two or three other cavaliers, formed a select corps, to act wherever occasion might require.

The general had already superintended the construction of a portable bridge to be laid over the open canals in the causeway. This was given in charge to an officer named Magarino, with forty soldiers under his orders, all pledged to defend the passage to the last extremity. The bridge was to be taken up when the entire army had crossed one of the breaches and transported to the next. There were three of these openings in the causeway, and most fortunate would it have been for the expedition if the foresight of the commander had provided the same number of bridges. But the labor would have been great, and time was short.

At midnight the troops were under arms, in readiness for the march. Mass was performed by Father Olmedo, who invoked the protection of the Almighty through the awful perils of the night. The gates were thrown open, and, on the first of July, 1520, the Spaniards for the last time sallied forth from the walls of the ancient fortress, the scene of so much suffering and such indomitable courage.

The night was cloudy, and a drizzling rain, which fell without intermission, added to the obscurity. The great square before the palace was deserted, as, indeed, it had been since the fall of Montezuma. Steadily, and as noiselessly as possible, the Spaniards held their way along the great street of Tlacopan, which so lately had resounded to the tumult of battle. All was now hushed in silence; and they were all reminded of the past by the occasional presence of some solitary corpse or a dark heap of the slain, which too plainly told where the strife had been hottest. As they passed along the lanes and alleys which opened into the great street, or looked down the canals, whose polished surface gleamed with a sort of ebon lustre through the obscurity of night, they easily fancied that they discerned the shadowy forms of their foe lurking in ambush and ready to spring on them. But it was only fancy; and the city slept undisturbed even by the prolonged echoes of the tramp of the horses and the hoarse rumbling of the artillery and baggage-trains. At length a lighter space beyond the dusky line of buildings showed the van of the army that it was emerging on the open causeway. They might well have congratulated themselves on having thus escaped the dangers of an assault in the city itself, and that a brief time would place them in comparative safety on the opposite shore. But the Mexicans were not all asleep.

As the Spaniards drew near the spot where the street opened on the causeway, and were preparing to lay the portable bridge across the uncovered breach which now met their eyes, several Indian sentinels, who had been stationed at this, as at the other approaches to the city, took the alarm and fled, rousing their countrymen by their cries. The priests, keeping their night watch on the summit of the *teocallis,* instantly caught the tidings and sounded their shells, while the huge drum in the desolate temple of the war-god sent forth those solemn tones, which, heard only in seasons of calamity, vibrated through every corner of the capital. The Spaniards saw that no time was to be lost. The bridge was brought forward and fitted with all possible expedition. Sandoval was the first to try its strength and, riding across, was followed by his little body of chivalry, his infantry, and Tlascalan allies, who formed the first division of the army. Then came Cortes and his squadrons, with the baggage, ammunition wagons, and a part of the artillery. But before they had time to defile across the narrow passage, a gathering sound was heard, like that of a mighty forest agitated by the winds. It grew louder and louder, while on the dark waters of the lake was heard a splashing noise, as of many oars. Then came a few stones and arrows striking at random among the hurrying troops. They fell every moment faster and more furious, till they thickened into a terrible tempest, while the very heavens were rent with the yells and war-cries of myriads of combatants, who seemed all at once to be swarming over land and lake!

The Spaniards pushed steadily on through this arrowy sleet, though the barbarians, dashing their canoes against the sides of the causeway, clambered up and broke in upon their ranks. But the Christians, anxious only to make their escape, declined all combat except for self-preservation. The cavaliers, spurring forward their steeds, shook off their assailants and rode over their prostrate bodies, while the men on foot with their good swords or the butts of their pieces drove them headlong again down the sides of the dike.

But the advance of several thousand men, marching, probably, on a front of not more than fifteen or twenty abreast, necessarily required much time, and the leading files had already reached the second breach in the causeway before those in the rear had entirely traversed the first. Here they halted, as they had no means of effecting a passage, smarting all the while under unintermitting volleys from the enemy, who were clustered thick on the waters around this second opening. Sorely distressed, the vanguard sent repeated messages to the rear to demand the portable bridge. At length the last of the army had crossed, and Magarino and his sturdy followers endeavored to raise the ponderous framework. But it stuck fast in the sides of the dike. In vain they strained every nerve. The weight of so many men and horses, and above all of the heavy artillery, had wedged the timbers so firmly in the stones and earth that it was beyond their power to dislodge them. Still they labored amidst a torrent of missiles, until, many of them slain and all wounded, they were obliged to abandon the attempt.

The tidings soon spread from man to man, and no sooner was their dreadful import comprehended than a cry of despair arose, which for a moment drowned all the noise of conflict. All means of retreat were cut off. Scarcely hope was left. The only hope was in such desperate exertions as each could make for himself. Order and subordination were at an end. Intense danger produced intense selfishness. Each thought only of his own life. Pressing forward, he trampled down the weak and the wounded, heedless whether it were friend or foe. The leading files, urged on by the rear, were crowded on the brink of the gulf. Sandoval, Ordaz, and the other cavaliers dashed into the water. Some succeeded in swimming their horses across; others failed, and some, who reached the opposite bank, being overturned in the ascent, rolled headlong with their steeds into the lake. The infantry followed pell-mell, heaped promiscuously on one another, frequently pierced by the shafts or struck down by the war-clubs of the Aztecs; while many an unfortunate victim was dragged half-stunned on board their canoes, to be reserved for a protracted but more dreadful death.

The carnage raged fearfully along the length of the causeway. Its shadowy bulk presented a mark of sufficient distinctness for the enemy's missiles, which often prostrated their own countrymen in the blind fury of the tempest. Those nearest the dike, running their canoes alongside with a force that shattered them to pieces, leaped on the land and grappled with the Christians, until both came rolling down the side of the causeway together. But the Aztec fell among his friends, while his antagonist was borne away in triumph to the sacrifice. The struggle was long and deadly. The Mexicans were recognized by their white cotton tunics, which showed faint through the darkness. Above the combatants rose a wild and discordant clamor, in which horrid shouts of vengeance were mingled with groans of agony, with invocations of the saints and the blessed Virgin, and with the screams of women; for there were several women, both native and Spaniards, who had accompanied the Christian camp. Among these, one named Maria de Estrada is particularly noticed for the courage she displayed, battling with broadsword and target like the staunchest of the warriors.

The opening in the causeway, meanwhile, was filled up with the wreck of matter which had been forced into it, ammunition wagons, heavy guns, bales of rich stuffs scattered over the waters, chests of solid ingots, and bodies of men and horses, till over this dismal ruin a passage was gradually formed, by which those in the rear were enabled to clamber to the other side. Cortes, it is said, found a place that was fordable, where, halting with the water up to his saddle-girths, he endeavored to check the confusion and lead his followers by a safer path to the opposite bank. But his voice was lost in the wild uproar, and finally, hurrying on with the tide, he pressed forwards with a few trusty cavaliers, who remained near his person, to the van; but not before he had seen his favorite page, Juan de Salazar, struck down, a corpse, by his side. Here he found Sandoval and his companions, halting before the third and last breach, endeavoring to cheer on their followers to surmount it. But their resolution faltered. It was wide and deep; though the passage was not so closely beset by the enemy as the preceding ones. The cavaliers again set the example by plunging into the water. Horse and foot followed as they could, some swimming, others with dying grasp clinging to the manes and tails of the struggling animals. Those fared best, as the general had predicted, who travelled lightest; and many were the unfortunate wretches, who, weighed down by the fatal gold which they loved so well, were buried with it in the salt floods of the lake. Cortes, with his gallant comrades Olid, Morla, Sandoval, and some few others, still kept in the advance, leading his broken remnant off the fatal causeway. The din of battle lessened in the distance, when the rumor reached them that the rearguard would be wholly overwhelmed without speedy relief. It seemed almost an act of desperation; but the generous hearts of the Spanish cavaliers did not stop to calculate danger when the cry for succor reached them. Turning their horses' bridles, they galloped back to the theatre of action, worked their way through the press, swam the canal, and placed themselves in the thick of the *mêlée* on the opposite bank.

The first grey of the morning was now coming over the waters. It showed the hideous confusion of the scene which had been shrouded in the obscurity of night. The dark masses of combatants, stretching along the dike, were seen struggling for mastery, until the very causeway on which they stood appeared to tremble and reel to and fro, as if shaken by an earthquake; while the bosom of the lake, as far as the eye could reach, was darkened by canoes crowded with warriors, whose spears and bludgeons, armed with blades of "volcanic glass," gleamed in the morning light.

The cavaliers found Alvarado unhorsed and defending himself with a poor handful of followers against an overwhelming tide of the enemy. His good steed, which had borne him through many a hard fight, had fallen under him. He was himself wounded in several places and was striving in vain to rally his scattered column, which was driven to the verge of the canal by the fury of the enemy, then in possession of the whole rear of the causeway, where they were reinforced every hour by fresh combatants from the city. The artillery in the earlier part of the engagement had not been idle, and its iron shower, sweeping along the dike, had mowed down the assailants by hundreds. But nothing could resist their impetuosity. The front ranks, pushed on by those behind, were at length forced up to the pieces and, pouring over them like a torrent, overthrew men and guns in one general ruin. The resolute charge of the Spanish cavaliers, who had now arrived, created a temporary check and gave time for their countrymen to make a feeble rally. But they were speedily borne down by the returning flood. Cortes and his companions were compelled to plunge again into the lake—though all did not escape. Alvarado stood on the brink for a moment, hesitating what to do. Unhorsed as he was, to throw himself into the water in the face of the hostile canoes that now swarmed around the opening afforded but a desperate chance of safety. He had but a second for thought. He was a man of powerful frame, and despair gave him unnatural energy. Setting his long lance firmly on the wreck which strewed the bottom of the lake, he sprung forward with all his might and cleared the wide gap at a leap! Aztecs and Tlascalans gazed in stupid amazement, exclaiming, as they beheld the incredible feat, "This is truly the *Tonatiuh*—the child of the Sun!" The breadth of the opening is not given. But it was so great that the valorous Captain Diaz, who well remembered the place, says the leap was impossible to any man. Other contemporaries, however, do not discredit the story. It was, beyond doubt, a matter of popular belief at the time; it is to this day familiarly known to every inhabitant of the capital; and the name of the *Salto de Alvarado*, "Alvarado's leap," given to the spot, still commemorates an exploit which rivalled those of the demigods of Grecian fable.

Cortes and his companions now rode forward to the front, where the troops in a loose, disorderly manner were marching off the fatal causeway. A few only of the enemy hung on their rear or annoyed them by occasional flights of arrows from the lake. The attention of the Aztecs was diverted by the rich spoil that strewed the battle-ground; fortunately for the Spaniards, who, had their enemy pursued with the same ferocity with which he had fought, would, in their crippled condition, have been cut off, probably to a man. But little molested, therefore, they were allowed to defile through the adjacent village, or suburbs, it might be called, of Popotla.

The Spanish commander there dismounted from his jaded steed and, sitting down on the steps of an Indian temple, gazed mournfully on the broken files as they passed before him. What a spectacle did they present! The cavalry, most of them dismounted, were mingled with the infantry, who dragged their feeble limbs along with difficulty; their shattered mail and tattered garments dripping with the salt ooze, showing through their rents many a bruise and ghastly wound; their bright arms soiled, their proud crests and banners gone, the baggage, artillery—all, in short, that constitutes the pride and panoply of glorious war, forever lost. Cortes, as he looked wistfully on their thinned and disordered ranks, sought in vain for many a familiar face and missed more than one dear companion who had stood side by side with him through all the perils of the Conquest. Though accustomed to control his emotions or, at least, to conceal them, the sight was too much for him. He covered his face with his hands, and the tears which trickled down revealed too plainly the anguish of his soul.

*7. The Siege and Surrender of Tenochtitlan**

[The fortunes of the Spaniards were at a low ebb. Gradually, however, the power of the army was recouped, and once again the force was supplied with an ample provision of men, horses, and artillery. To cope with reducing Tenochtitlan, surrounded as it was with water, Cortes developed a bold new plan of building a fleet of thirteen ships to be transported across the mountains in sections. On 26 December, 1520, a half a year after the flight from Tenochtitlan, Cortes set out once again from Tlaxcala, to which he had retreated. The Aztecs were now under a new and more effective leader, Guatemozin (or Guatemoc). Montezuma's immediate successor had died from the plague after a reign of only eighty days. The new ruler, Guatemozin, became for Prescott a symbol of the noble, war-like, and less civilized Indian; his leadership, in any case, was clearly more decisive than that of the vacillating Montezuma. The Aztecs put up a spirited defense, but they were unable to prevent their capital from

* From *The Conquest of Mexico,* Book VI, chaps. 6–8.

being surrounded. For several months, the Spaniards maintained the blockade, gradually starving the city—an Old World type of war, complete with supporting naval power, brought into play to conquer the New. The following account of the final victory of the Spanish over their Aztec enemies, comprising three chapters of Prescott's narrative, is printed completely, with the exception of one small deletion.]

Famine was now gradually working its way into the heart of the beleaguered city. It seemed certain that, with this strict blockade, the crowded population must in the end be driven to capitulate, though no arm should be raised against them. But it required time; and the Spaniards, though constant and enduring by nature, began to be impatient of hardships scarcely inferior to those experienced by the besieged. In some respects their condition was even worse, exposed, as they were, to the cold, drenching rains, which fell with little intermission, rendering their situation dreary and disastrous in the extreme.

In this state of things there were many who would willingly have shortened their sufferings and taken the chance of carrying the place by a *coup de main*. Others thought it would be best to get possession of the great market of Tlatelolco, which, from its situation in the north-western part of the city, might afford the means of communication with the camps of both Alvarado and Sandoval. This place, encompassed by spacious porticoes, would furnish accommodations for a numerous host; and, once established in the capital, the Spaniards would be in a position to follow up the blow with far more effect than at a distance.

These arguments were pressed by several of the officers, particularly by Alderete, the royal treasurer, a person of much consideration, not only from his rank but from the capacity and zeal he had shown in the service. In deference to their wishes, Cortes summoned a council of war and laid the matter before it. The treasurer's views were espoused by most of the high-mettled cavaliers, who looked with eagerness to any change of their present forlorn and wearisome life; and Cortes, thinking it probably more prudent to adopt the less expedient course than to enforce a cold and reluctant obedience to his own opinion, suffered himself to be overruled.

A day was fixed for the assault, which was to be made simultaneously by the two divisions under Alvarado and the commander-in-chief. Sandoval was instructed to draw off the greater part of his forces from the northern causeway and to unite himself with Alvarado, while seventy picked soldiers were to be detached to the support of Cortes.

On the appointed morning, the two armies, after the usual celebration of mass, advanced along their respective causeways against the city. They were supported, in addition to the brigantines, by a numerous fleet of Indian boats, which were to force a passage up the canals, and by a countless multitude of allies, whose very numbers served in the end to embarrass their operations. After clearing the suburbs, three avenues presented themselves, which all terminated in the square of Tlatelolco. The principal one, being of much greater width than the other two, might rather be called a causeway than a street, since it was flanked by deep canals on either side. Cortes divided his force into three bodies. One of them he placed under Alderete, with orders to occupy the principal street. A second he gave in charge to Andres de Tapia and Jorge de Alvarado, the former a cavalier of courage and capacity, the latter a younger brother of Don Pedro and possessed of the intrepid spirit which belonged to that chivalrous family. These were to penetrate by one of the parallel streets, while the general himself, at the head of the third division, was to occupy the other. A small body of cavalry, with two or three field-pieces, was stationed as a reserve in front of the great street of Tacuba, which was designated as the rallying point for the different divisions.

Cortes gave the most positive instructions to his captains not to advance a step without securing the means of retreat, by carefully filling up the ditches and the openings in the causeway. The neglect of this precaution by Alvarado, in an assault which he had made on the city but a few days before, had been attended with such serious consequences to his army that Cortes rode over, himself, to his officer's quarters for the purpose of publicly reprimanding him for his disobedience of orders. On his arrival at the camp, however, he found that his offending captain had conducted the affair with so much gallantry that the intended reprimand—though well deserved—subsided into a mild rebuke.

The arrangements being completed, the three divisions marched at once up the several streets. Cortes, dismounting, took the van of his own squadron, at the head of his infantry. The Mexicans fell back as he advanced, making less resistance than usual. The Spaniards pushed on, carrying one barricade after another and carefully filling up the gaps with rubbish so as to secure themselves a footing. The canoes supported the attack by moving along the canals and grappling with those of the enemy; while numbers of the nimble-footed Tlascalans, scaling the terraces, passed on from one house to another, where they were connected, hurling the defenders into the streets below. The enemy, taken apparently by surprise, seemed incapable of withstanding for a moment the fury of the assault; and the victorious Christians, cheered on by the shouts of triumph which arose from their companions in the adjoining streets, were only the more eager to be first at the destined goal.

Indeed, the facility of his success led the general to suspect that he might be advancing too fast, that it might be a device of the enemy to draw them into the heart of the city and then surround or attack them in the rear. He had some misgivings, moreover, lest his too ardent officers, in the heat of the chase, should, notwithstanding his commands, have overlooked the necessary precaution of filling up the breaches. He accordingly brought his squadron to a halt, prepared to baffle any insidious movement of his adversary. Meanwhile he received more than one message from Alderete, informing him that he had nearly gained the market. This only increased the general's apprehension that, in the rapidity of his advance, he might have neglected to secure the ground. He determined to trust no eyes but his own and, taking a small body of troops, proceeded at once to reconnoitre the route followed by the treasurer.

He had not proceeded far along the great street, or causeway, when his progress was arrested by an opening ten or twelve paces wide and filled with water at least two fathoms deep, by which a communication was formed between the canals on the opposite sides. A feeble attempt had been made to stop the gap with the rubbish of the causeway, but in too careless a manner to be of the least service; and a few straggling stones and pieces of timber only showed that the work had been abandoned almost as soon as begun. To add to his consternation, the general observed that the sides of the causeway in this neighborhood had been pared off—and, as was evident, very recently. He saw in all this the artifice of the cunning enemy and had little doubt that his hot-headed officer had rushed into a snare deliberately laid for him. Deeply alarmed, he set about repairing the mischief as fast as possible by ordering his men to fill up the yawning chasm.

But they had scarcely begun their labors when the hoarse echoes of conflict in the distance were succeeded by a hideous sound of mingled yells and war-whoops that seemed to rend the very heavens. This was followed by a rushing noise, as of the tread of thronging multitudes, showing that the tide of battle was turned back from its former course and was rolling on towards the spot where Cortes and his little band of cavaliers were planted.

His conjecture proved too true. Alderete had followed the retreating Aztecs with an eagerness which increased with every step of his advance. He had carried the barricades, which had defended the breach, without much difficulty and, as he swept on, gave orders that the opening should be stopped. But the blood of the high-spirited cavaliers was warmed by the chase, and no one cared to be detained by the ignoble occupation of filling up the ditches, while he could gather laurels so easily in the fight; and they all pressed on, exhorting and cheering one another with the assurance of being the first to reach the square of Tlatelolco. In this way they suffered themselves to be decoyed into the heart of the city; when suddenly the horn of Guatemozin—the sacred symbol, heard only in seasons of extraordinary peril—sent forth a long and piercing note from the summit of a neighboring *teocalli.* In an instant, the flying Aztecs, as if maddened by the blast, wheeled about and turned on their pursuers. At the same time, countless swarms of warriors from the adjoining streets and lanes poured in upon the flanks of the assailants, filling the air with the fierce, unearthly cries which had reached the ears of Cortes and drowning, for a moment, the wild dissonance which reigned in the other quarters of the capital.

The army, taken by surprise and shaken by the fury of the assault, were thrown into the utmost disorder. Friends and foes, white men and Indians, were mingled together in one promiscuous mass; spears, swords, and war-clubs were brandished together in the air. Blows fell at random. In their eagerness to escape, they trod down one another. Blinded by the missiles which now rained on them from the *azoteas,* they staggered on, scarcely knowing in what direction, or fell, struck down by hands which they could not see. On they came like a rushing torrent sweeping along some steep declivity, and rolling in one confused tide towards the open breach, on the further side of which stood Cortes and his companions, horror-struck at the sight of the approaching ruin. The foremost files soon plunged into the gulf, treading one another under the flood, some striving ineffectually to swim, others, with more success, to clamber over the heaps of their suffocated comrades. Many, as they attempted to scale the opposite sides of the slippery dike, fell into the water, or were hurried off by the warriors in the canoes, who added to the horrors of the rout by the fresh storm of darts and javelins which they poured on the fugitives.

Cortes, meanwhile, with his brave followers, kept his station undaunted on the other side of the breach. "I had made up my mind," he says, "to die rather than desert my poor followers in their extremity!" With outstretched hands he endeavored to rescue as many as he could from the watery grave and from the more appalling fate of captivity. He as vainly tried to restore something like presence of mind and order among the distracted fugitives. His person was too well known to the Aztecs, and his position now made him a conspicuous mark for their weapons. Darts, stones, and arrows fell around him as thick as hail, but glanced harmless from his steel helmet and armor of proof. At length a cry of "Malinche, Malinche!" arose among the enemy; and six of their number, strong and athletic warriors, rushing on him at once, made a violent effort to drag him on board their boat. In the struggle he received a severe wound in the leg, which, for the time, disabled it. There seemed to be no hope for him; when a faithful follower, Christoval de Olea, perceiving his general's extremity, threw himself on the Aztecs and with a blow cut off the arm of one savage and then plunged his sword in the body of another. He was quickly supported by a comrade named Lerma and by a Tlascalan chief, who, fighting over the prostrate body of Cortes, despatched three more of the assailants, though the heroic Olea paid dearly for his self-devotion, as he fell mortally wounded by the side of his general.

The report soon spread among the soldiers that their commander was taken; and Quiñones, the captain of his guard, with several others pouring in to the rescue, succeeded in disentangling Cortes from the grasp of his enemies who were struggling with him in the water, and raising him in their arms, placed him again on the causeway. One of his pages, meanwhile, had advanced some way through the press, leading a horse for his master to mount. But the youth received a wound in the throat from a javelin, which prevented him from effecting his object. Another of his attendants was more successful. It was Guzman, his chamberlain; but, as he held the bridle, while Cortes was assisted into the saddle, he was snatched away by the Aztecs and, with the swiftness of thought, hurried off by their canoes. The general still lingered, unwilling to leave the spot whilst his presence could be of the least service. But the faithful Quiñones, taking his horse by the bridle, turned his head from the breach, exclaiming at the same time that "his master's life was too important to the army to be thrown away there."

Yet it was no easy matter to force a passage through the press. The surface of the causeway, cut up by the feet of men and horses, was knee-deep in mud and in some parts was so much broken that the water from the canals flowed over it. The crowded mass, in their efforts to extricate themselves from their perilous position, staggered to and fro like a drunken man. Those on the flanks were often forced by the lateral pressure of their comrades down the slippery sides of the dike, where they were picked up by the canoes of the enemy, whose shouts of triumph proclaimed the savage joy with which they gathered in every new victim for the sacrifice. Two cavaliers, riding by the general's side, lost their footing and rolled down the declivity into the water. One was taken and his horse killed. The other was happy enough to escape. The valiant ensign, Corral, had a similar piece of good fortune. He slipped into the canal, and the enemy felt sure of their prize, when he again succeeded in recovering the causeway with the tattered banner of Castile still flying above his head. The barbarians set up a cry of disappointed rage, as they lost possession of a trophy, to which the people of Anahuac attached, as we have seen, the highest importance, hardly inferior in their eyes to the capture of the commander-in-chief himself.

Cortes at length succeeded in regaining the firm ground and reaching the open place before the great street of Tacuba. Here, under a sharp fire of the artillery, he rallied his broken squadrons, and charging at the head of the little body of horse, which, not having been brought into action, were still fresh, he beat off the enemy. He then commanded the retreat of the two other divisions. The scattered forces again united; and the general, sending forward his Indian confederates, took the rear with a chosen body of cavalry to cover the retreat of the army, which was effected with but little additional loss.

Andres de Tapia was despatched to the western causeway to acquaint Alvarado and Sandoval with the failure of the enterprise. Meanwhile the two captains had penetrated far into the city. Cheered by the triumphant shouts of their countrymen in the adjacent streets, they had pushed on with extraordinary vigor that they might not be outstripped in the race of glory. They had almost reached the market-place, which lay nearer to their quarters than to the general's, when they heard the blast from the dread horn of Guatemozin, followed by the overpowering yell of the barbarians, which had so startled the ears of Cortes; till at length the sounds of the receding conflict died away in the distance. The two captains now understood that the day must have gone hard with their countrymen. They soon had further proof of it, when the victorious Aztecs, returning from the pursuit of Cortes, joined their forces to those engaged with Sandoval and Alvarado and fell on them with redoubled fury. At the same time they rolled on the ground two or three of the bloody heads of the Spaniards, shouting the name of "Malinche." The captains, struck with horror at the spectacle—though they gave little credit to the words of the enemy—instantly ordered a retreat. Indeed, it was not in their power to maintain their ground against the furious assaults of the besieged, who poured on them swarm after swarm with a desperation of which, says one who was there, "although it seems as if it were now present to my eyes, I can give but a faint idea to the reader. God alone could have brought us off safe from the perils of that day." The fierce barbarians followed up the Spaniards to their very intrenchments. But here they were met, first by the cross-fire of the brigantines, which, dashing through the palisades planted to obstruct their movements, completely enfiladed the causeway, and next by that of the small battery erected in front of the camp, which, under the management of a skillful engineer named Medrano, swept the whole length of the defile. Thus galled in front and on flank, the shattered columns of the Aztecs were compelled to give way and take shelter under the defences of the city.

The greatest anxiety now prevailed in the camp regarding the fate of Cortes; for Tapia had been detained on the road by scattered parties of the enemy, whom Guatemozin had stationed there to interrupt the communications between the camps. He arrived, at length, however, though bleeding from several wounds. His intelligence, while it reassured the Spaniards as to the general's personal safety, was not calculated to allay their uneasiness in other respects.

Sandoval, in particular, was desirous to acquaint himself with the actual state of things and the further intentions of Cortes. Suffering as he was from three wounds, which he had received in that day's fight, he resolved to visit in person the quarters of the commander-in-chief. It was mid-day—for the busy scenes of the morning had occupied but a few hours—when Sandoval remounted the good steed, on whose strength and speed he knew he could rely. It was a noble animal, well known throughout the army and worthy of its gallant rider, whom it had carried safe through all the long marches and bloody battles of the Conquest. On the way he fell in with Guatemozin's scouts, who gave him chase and showered around him volleys of missiles, which fortunately found no vulnerable point in his own harness or that of his well-barbed charger.

On arriving at the camp, he found the troops there much worn and dispirited by the disaster of the morning. They had good reason to be so. Besides the killed and a long file of wounded, sixty-two Spaniards, with a multitude of allies, had fallen alive into the hands of the enemy—an enemy who was never known to spare a captive. The loss of two field-pieces and seven horses crowned their own disgrace and the triumphs of the Aztecs. This loss, so insignificant in European warfare, was a great one here, where both horses and artillery, the most powerful arms of war against the barbarians, were not to be procured without the greatest cost and difficulty.

Cortes, it was observed, had borne himself throughout

this trying day with his usual intrepidity and coolness. The only time he was seen to falter was when the Mexicans threw down before him the heads of several Spaniards, shouting at the same time, "Sandoval," "Tonatiuh," the well-known epithet of Alvarado. At the sight of the gory trophies he grew deadly pale; but, in a moment recovering his usual confidence, he endeavored to cheer up the drooping spirits of his followers. It was with a cheerful countenance that he now received his lieutenant; but a shade of sadness was visible through this outward composure, showing how the catastrophe of the *puente cuidada*, "the sorrowful bridge," as he mournfully called it, lay heavy at his heart.

To the cavalier's anxious inquiries as to the cause of the disaster, he replied: "It is for my sins that it has befallen me, son Sandoval"; for such was the affectionate epithet with which Cortes often addressed his best-beloved and trusty officer. He then explained to him the immediate cause, in the negligence of the treasurer. Further conversation followed, in which the general declared his purpose to forego active hostilities for a few days. "You must take my place," he continued, "for I am too much crippled at present to discharge my duties. You must watch over the safety of the camps. Give especial heed to Alvarado's. He is a gallant soldier, I know it well; but I doubt the Mexican hounds may, some hour, take him at disadvantage." These few words showed the general's own estimate of his two lieutenants, both equally brave and chivalrous, but the one uniting with these qualities the circumspection so essential to success in perilous enterprises, in which the other was signally deficient. The future conqueror of Guatemala had to gather wisdom, as usual, from the bitter fruits of his own errors. It was under the training of Cortes that he learned to be a soldier. The general, having concluded his instructions, affectionately embraced his lieutenant and dismissed him to his quarters.

It was late in the afternoon when he reached them; but the sun was still lingering above the western hills and poured his beams wide over the Valley, lighting up the old towers and temples of Tenochtitlan with a mellow radiance that little harmonized with the dark scenes of strife in which the city had so lately been involved. The tranquillity of the hour, however, was on a sudden broken by the strange sounds of the great drum in the temple of the war-god—sounds which recalled the *noche triste,* with all its terrible images, to the minds of the Spaniards, for that was the only occasion on which they had ever heard them. They intimated some solemn act of religion within the unhallowed precincts of the *teocalli;* and the soldiers, startled by the mournful vibrations, which might be heard for leagues across the Valley, turned their eyes to the quarter whence they proceeded. They there beheld a long procession winding up the huge sides of the pyramid; for the camp of Alvarado was pitched scarcely a mile from the city, and objects are distinctly visible, at a great distance, in the transparent atmosphere of the table-land.

As the long file of priests and warriors reached the flat summit of the *teocalli,* the Spaniards saw the figures of several men stripped to their waists, some of whom, by the whiteness of their skins, they recognized as their own countrymen. They were the victims for sacrifice. Their heads were gaudily decorated with coronals of plumes, and they carried fans in their hands. They were urged along by blows and compelled to take part in the dances in honor of the Aztec war-god. The unfortunate captives, then stripped of their sad finery, were stretched, one after another, on the great stone of sacrifice. On its convex surface, their breasts were heaved up conveniently for the diabolical purpose of the priestly executioner, who cut asunder the ribs by a strong blow with his sharp razor of *itztli* and, thrusting his hand into the wound, tore away the heart, which, hot and reeking, was deposited on the golden censer before the idol. The body of the slaughtered victim was then hurled down the steep stairs of the pyramid, which, it may be remembered, were placed at the same angle of the pile, one flight below another; and the mutilated remains were gathered up by the savages beneath, who soon prepared with them the cannibal repast which completed the work of abomination!

We may imagine with what sensations the stupefied Spaniards must have gazed on this horrid spectacle, so near that they could almost recognize the persons of their unfortunate friends, see the struggles and writhing of their bodies, hear—or fancy that they heard—their screams of agony! yet so far removed that they could render them no assistance. Their limbs trembled beneath them as they thought what might one day be their own fate; and the bravest among them, who had hitherto gone to battle as careless and light-hearted as to the banquet or the ball-room, were unable, from this time forward, to encounter their ferocious enemy without a sickening feeling, much akin to fear, coming over them.

Such was not the effect produced by this spectacle on the Mexican forces, gathered at the end of the causeway. Like vultures maddened by the smell of distant carrion, they set up a piercing cry and, as they shouted that "such should be the fate of all their enemies," swept along in one fierce torrent over the dike. But the Spaniards were not to be taken by surprise; and, before the barbarian horde had come within their lines, they opened such a deadly fire from their battery of heavy guns, supported by the musketry and crossbows, that the assailants were compelled to fall back slowly, but fearfully mangled, to their former position.

The five following days passed away in a state of inaction, except, indeed, so far as was necessary to repel the sorties made from time to time by the militia of the capital. The Mexicans, elated with their success, meanwhile, abandoned themselves to jubilee; singing, dancing, and feasting on the mangled relics of their wretched victims. Guatemozin sent several heads of the Spaniards, as well as of the horses, round the country, calling on his old vassals to forsake the banners of the white men, unless they would share the doom of the enemies of Mexico. The priests now cheered the young monarch and the people with the declaration that the dread Huitzilopochtli, their offended deity, appeased by the sacrifices offered up on his altars, would again take the Aztecs under his protection and deliver their enemies, before the expiration of eight days, into their hands.

This comfortable prediction, confidently believed by the Mexicans, was thundered in the ears of the besieging army in tones of exultation and defiance. However it may have been contemned by the Spaniards, it had a very different effect on their allies. The latter had begun to be disgusted with a service so full of peril and suffering and already protracted far beyond the usual term of Indian hostilities. They had less confidence than before in the Spaniards. Experience had shown that they were neither invincible nor immortal, and their recent reverses made them even distrust the ability of the Christians to reduce the Aztec metropolis. They recalled to mind the ominous words of Xicotencatl,[1] that "so sacrilegious a war could come to no good for the people of Anahuac." They felt that their arm was raised against the gods of their country. The prediction of the oracle fell heavy on their hearts. They had little doubt of its fulfilment and were only eager to turn away the bolt from their own heads by a timely secession from the cause.

They took advantage, therefore, of the friendly cover of night to steal away from their quarters. Company after company deserted in this manner, taking the direction of their respective homes. Those belonging to the great towns of the valley, whose allegiance was the most recent, were the first to cast it off. Their example was followed by the older confederates, the militia of Cholula, Tepeaca, Tezcuco, and even the faithful Tlascala. There were, it is true, some exceptions to these, and among them, Ixtilxochitl, the young lord of Tezcuco, and Chichemecatl, the valiant Tlascalan chieftain, who, with a few of their immediate followers, still remained true to the banner under which they had enlisted. But their number was insignificant. The Spaniards beheld with dismay the mighty array, on which they relied for support, thus silently melting away be-

[1] Xicotencatl, leader of the armies of Tlascala.

fore the breath of superstition. Cortes alone maintained a cheerful countenance. He treated the prediction with contempt, as an invention of the priests, and sent his messengers after the retreating squadrons, beseeching them to postpone their departure or at least to halt on the road, till the time, which would soon elapse, should show the falsehood of the prophecy.

The affairs of the Spaniards at this crisis must be confessed to have worn a gloomy aspect. Deserted by their allies, with their ammunition nearly exhausted, cut off from the customary supplies from the neighborhood, harassed by unintermitting vigils and fatigues, smarting under wounds, of which every man in the army had his share, with an unfriendly country in their rear, and a mortal foe in front, they might well be excused for faltering in their enterprise. They found abundant occupation by day in foraging the country, and in maintaining their position on the causeways against the enemy, now made doubly daring by success and by the promises of their priests; while at night their slumbers were disturbed by the beat of the melancholy drum, the sounds of which, booming far over the waters, tolled the knell of their murdered comrades. Night after night fresh victims were led up to the great altar of sacrifice; and while the city blazed with the illuminations of a thousand bonfires on the terraced roofs of the dwellings and in the areas of the temples, the dismal pageant, showing through the fiery glare like the work of the ministers of hell, was distinctly visible from the camp below. One of the last of the sufferers was Guzman, the unfortunate chamberlain of Cortes, who lingered in captivity eighteen days before he met his doom.

Yet in this hour of trial the Spaniards did not falter. Had they faltered, they might have learned a lesson of fortitude from some of their own wives, who continued with them in the camp and who displayed a heroism, on this occasion, of which history has preserved several examples. One of these, protected by her husband's armor, would frequently mount guard in his place when he was wearied. Another, hastily putting on a soldier's *escaupil*[1] and seizing a sword and lance, was seen, on one occasion, to rally her retreating countrymen and lead them back against the enemy. Cortes would have persuaded these Amazonian dames to remain at Tlascala; but they proudly replied, "It was the duty of Castilian wives not to abandon their husbands in danger, but to share it with them—and die with them, if necessary." And well did they do their duty.

Amidst all the distresses and multiplied embarrassments of their situation, the Spaniards still remained true to their purpose. They relaxed in no degree the severity of the blockade. Their camps still occupied the only avenues to the city; and their batteries, sweeping the long defiles at every fresh assault of the Aztecs, mowed down hundreds of the assailants. Their brigantines still rode on the waters, cutting off the communication with the shore. It is true, indeed, the loss of the auxiliary canoes left a passage open for the occasional introduction of supplies to the capital. But the whole amount of these supplies was small; and its crowded population, while exulting in their temporary advantage and the delusive assurances of their priests, were beginning to sink under the withering grasp of an enemy within, more terrible than the one which lay before their gates.

Thus passed away the eight days prescribed by the oracle; and the sun, which rose upon the ninth, beheld the fair city still beset on every side by the inexorable foe. It was a great mistake of the Aztec priests—one not uncommon with false prophets, anxious to produce a startling impression on their followers—to assign so short a term for the fulfilment of their prediction.

The Tezcucan and Tlascalan chiefs now sent to acquaint their troops with the failure of the prophecy and to recall them to the Christian camp. The Tlascalans, who had halted on the way, returned, ashamed of their credulity, and with ancient feelings of animosity, heightened by the artifice of which they had

[1] The *ichcahuipilli,* or tunic stuffed with cotton, used by the Indians as armor.

been the dupes. Their example was followed by many of the other confederates, with the levity natural to a people whose convictions are the result, not of reason but of superstition. In a short time the Spanish general found himself at the head of an auxiliary force, which, if not so numerous as before, was more than adequate to all his purposes. He received them with politic benignity; and, while he reminded them that they had been guilty of a great crime in thus abandoning their commander, he was willing to overlook it in consideration of their past services. They must be aware that these services were not necessary to the Spaniards, who had carried on the siege with the same vigor during their absence as when they were present. But he was unwilling that those who had shared the dangers of the war with him should not also partake of its triumphs and be present at the fall of their enemy, which he promised, with a confidence better founded than that of the priests in their prediction, should not be long delayed.

Yet the menaces and machinations of Guatemozin were still not without effect in the distant provinces. Before the full return of the confederates, Cortes received an embassy from Cuernavaca, ten or twelve leagues distant, and another from some friendly towns of the Otomies, still farther off, imploring his protection against their formidable neighbors, who menaced them with hostilities as allies of the Spaniards. As the latter were then situated, they were in a condition to receive succor much more than to give it. Most of the officers were accordingly opposed to granting a request compliance with which must still further impair their diminished strength. But Cortes knew the importance, above all, of not betraying his own inability to grant it. "The greater our weakness," he said, "the greater need have we to cover it under a show of strength."

He immediately detached Tapia with a body of about a hundred men in one direction and Sandoval with a somewhat larger force in the other, with orders that their absence should not in any event be prolonged beyond ten days. The two captains executed their commission promptly and effectually. They each met and defeated his adversary in a pitched battle, laid waste the hostile territories, and returned within the time prescribed. They were soon followed by ambassadors from the conquered places, soliciting the alliance of the Spaniards; and the affair terminated by an accession of new confederates, and, what was more important, a conviction in the old that the Spaniards were both willing and competent to protect them.

Fortune, who seldom dispenses her frowns or her favors single-handed, further showed her good-will to the Spaniards at this time by sending a vessel into Vera Cruz laden with ammunition and military stores. It was part of the fleet destined for the Florida coast by the romantic old knight, Ponce de León. The cargo was immediately taken by the authorities of the port and forwarded, without delay, to the camp, where it arrived most seasonably, as the want of powder, in particular, had begun to be seriously felt. With strength thus renovated, Cortes determined to resume active operations, but on a plan widely differing from that pursued before.

In the former deliberations on the subject, two courses, as we have seen, presented themselves to the general. One was to intrench himself in the heart of the capital, and from this point carry on hostilities; the other was the mode of proceeding hitherto followed. Both were open to serious objections, which he hoped would be obviated by the one now adopted. This was to advance no step without securing the entire safety of the army, not only on its immediate retreat but in its future inroads. Every breach in the causeway, every canal in the streets was to be filled up in so solid a manner that the work should not be again disturbed. The materials for this were to be furnished by the buildings, every one of which, as the army advanced, whether public or private, hut, temple, or palace, was to be demolished! Not a building in their path was to be spared. They were all indiscriminately to be levelled until, in the Conqueror's own language, "the water should be converted into dry land," and a smooth and open ground be afforded for the maneuvers of the cavalry and artillery.

Cortes came to this terrible determination with great difficulty. He sincerely desired to spare the city, "the most beautiful thing in the world," as he enthusiastically styled it, and which would have formed the most glorious trophy of his conquest. But, in a place where every house was a fortress and every street was cut up by canals so embarrassing to his movements, experience proved it was vain to think of doing so and becoming master of it. There was as little hope of a peaceful accommodation with the Aztecs, who, so far from being broken by all they had hitherto endured and the long perspective of future woes, showed a spirit as haughty and implacable as ever.

The general's intentions were learned by the Indian allies with unbounded satisfaction; and they answered his call for aid by thousands of pioneers, armed with their *coas*, or hoes of the country, all testifying the greatest alacrity in helping on the work of destruction. In a short time the breaches in the great causeways were filled up so effectually that they were never again molested. Cortes himself set the example by carrying stones and timber with his own hands. The buildings in the suburbs were then thoroughly levelled, the canals were filled up with the rubbish, and a wide space around the city was thrown open to the maneuvers of the cavalry, who swept over it free and unresisted. The Mexicans did not look with indifference on these preparations to lay waste their town and leave them bare and unprotected against the enemy. They made incessant efforts to impede the labors of the besiegers, but the latter, under cover of their guns, which kept up an unintermitting fire, still advanced in the work of desolation.

The gleam of fortune, which had so lately broken out on the Mexicans, again disappeared; and the dark mist, after having been raised for a moment, settled on the doomed capital more heavily than before. Famine, with all her hideous train of woes, was making rapid strides among its accumulated population. The stores provided for the siege were exhausted. The casual supply of human victims, or that obtained by some straggling pirogue from the neighboring shores, was too inconsiderable to be widely felt. Some forced a scanty sustenance from a mucilaginous substance, gathered in small quantities on the surface of the lake and canals. Others appeased the cravings of appetite by devouring rats, lizards, and the like loathsome reptiles, which had not yet deserted the starving city. Its days seemed to be already numbered. But the page of history has many an example to show that there are no limits to the endurance of which humanity is capable when animated by hatred and despair.

With the sword thus suspended over it, the Spanish commander, desirous to make one more effort to save the capital, persuaded three Aztec nobles, taken in one of the late actions, to bear a message from him to Guatemozin; though they undertook it with reluctance, for fear of the consequences to themselves. Cortes told the emperor that all had now been done that brave men could do in defence of their country. There remained no hope, no chance of escape for the Mexicans. Their provisions were exhausted; their communications were cut off; their vassals had deserted them; even their gods had betrayed them. They stood alone, with the nations of Anahuac banded against them. There was no hope but in immediate surrender. He besought the young monarch to take compassion on his brave subjects, who were daily perishing before his eyes; and on the fair city, whose stately buildings were fast crumbling into ruins. "Return to the allegiance," he concludes, "which you once proffered to the sovereign of Castile. The past shall be forgotten. The persons and property, in short, all the rights of the Aztecs shall be respected. You shall be confirmed in your authority, and Spain will once more take your city under her protection."

The eye of the young monarch kindled, and his dark cheek flushed with sudden anger, as he listened to proposals so humiliating. But, though his bosom glowed with the fiery temper of the Indian, he had the qualities of a "gentle cavalier," says one of his enemies, who knew him well. He did no harm to the envoys; but, after the heat of the moment had passed off, he gave the matter a calm consideration and called a council of his wise men and warriors to deliberate upon it. Some were for accepting the proposals, as offering the only chance of preservation. But the priests took a different view of the matter. They knew that the ruin of their own order must follow the triumph of Christianity. "Peace was good," they said, "but not with the white men." They reminded Guatemozin of the fate of his uncle Montezuma, and the requital he had met with for all his hospitality: of the seizure and imprisonment of Cacama, the cacique of Tezcuco; of the massacre of the nobles by Alvarado; of the insatiable avarice of the invaders, which had stripped the country of its treasures; of their profanation of the temples; of the injuries and insults which had stripped the country of its treasures; of their and their religion. "Better," they said, "to trust in the promises of their own gods, who had so long watched over the nation. Better, if need be, give up our lives at once for our country than drag them out in slavery and suffering among the false strangers."

The eloquence of the priests, artfully touching the various wrongs of his people, roused the hot blood of Guatemozin. "Since it is so," he abruptly exclaimed, "let us think only of supplying the wants of the people. Let no man, henceforth, who values his life talk of surrender. We can at least die like warriors."

The Spaniards waited two days for the answer to their embassy. At length, it came in a general sortie of the Mexicans, who, pouring through every gate of the capital, like a river that has burst its banks, swept on, wave upon wave, to the very intrenchments of the besiegers, threatening to overwhelm them by their numbers. Fortunately, the position of the latter on the dikes secured their flanks, and the narrowness of the defile gave their small battery of guns all the advantages of a larger one. The fire of artillery and musketry blazed without intermission along the several causeways, belching forth volumes of sulphurous smoke that, rolling heavily over the waters, settled dark around the Indian city and hid it from the surrounding country. The brigantines thundered, at the same time, on the flanks of the columns, which, after some ineffectual efforts to maintain themselves, rolled back in wild confusion, till their impotent fury died away in sullen murmurs within the capital.

Cortes now steadily pursued the plan he had laid down for the devastation of the city. Day after day the several armies entered by their respective quarters, Sandoval probably directing his operations against the north-eastern district. The buildings made of the porous *tetzontli,* though generally low, were so massy and extensive, and the canals were so numerous, that their progress was necessarily slow. They, however, gathered fresh accessions of strength every day from the numbers who flocked to the camp from the surrounding country and who joined in the work of destruction with a hearty good will, which showed their eagerness to break the detested yoke of the Aztecs. The latter raged with impotent anger as they beheld their lordly edifices, their temples, all they had been accustomed to venerate thus ruthlessly swept away; their canals, constructed with so much labor, and what to them seemed science, filled up with rubbish; their flourishing city, in short, turned into a desert, over which the insulting foe now rode triumphant. They heaped many a taunt on the Indian allies. "Go on," they said bitterly, "the more you destroy, the more you will have to build up again hereafter. If we conquer, you shall build for us; and if your white friends conquer, they will make you do as much for them." The event justified the prediction.

In their rage they rushed blindly on the corps which covered the Indian pioneers. But they were as often driven back by the impetuous charge of the cavalry or received on the long pikes of Chinantla, which did good service to the besiegers in their operations. At the close of day, however, when the Spaniards drew off their forces, taking care to send the multitudinous host of confederates first from the ground, the Mexicans usually rallied for a more formidable attack. Then they poured out from every lane and by-way, like so many mountain streams, sweeping over the broad level cleared by the enemy and falling impetuously on their flanks and rear. At such times they inflicted considerable loss in their turn, till an ambush, which Cortes laid for them among the buildings adjoining the great temple, did them so much mischief that they were compelled to act with more reserve.

At times the war displayed something of a chivalrous character, in the personal rencontres of the combatants. Challenges passed between them, and especially between the native warriors. These combats were usually conducted on the *azoteas,* whose broad and level surface afforded a good field of fight. On one occasion, a Mexican of powerful frame, brandishing a sword and buckler which he had won from the Christians, defied his enemies to meet him in single fight. A young page of Cortes, named Nuñez, obtained his master's permission to accept the vaunting challenge of the Aztec and, springing on the *azotea,* succeeded after a hard struggle in discomfiting his antagonist, who fought at a disadvantage with weapons in which he was unpractised, and, running him through the body, brought off his spoils in triumph and laid them at the general's feet.

The division of Cortes had now worked its way as far north as the great street of Tacuba, which opened a communication with Alvarado's camp and near which stood the palace of Guatemozin. It was a spacious stone pile that might well be called a fortress. Though deserted by its royal master, it was held by a strong body of Aztecs, who made a temporary defence, but of little avail against the battering enginery of the besiegers. It was soon set on fire, and its crumbling walls were levelled in the dust, like those other stately edifices of the capital, the boast and admiration of the Aztecs and some of the fairest fruits of their civilization. "It was a sad thing to witness their destruction," exclaims Cortes, "but it was part of our plan of operations, and we had no alternative."

These operations had consumed several weeks, so that it was now drawing towards the latter part of July. During this time, the blockade had been maintained with the utmost rigor, and the wretched inhabitants were suffering all the extremities of famine. Some few stragglers were taken, from time to time, in the neighborhood of the Christian camp, whither they had wandered in search of food. They were kindly treated, by command of Cortes, who was in hopes to induce others to follow their example and thus to afford a means of conciliating the inhabitants, which might open the way to their submission. But few were found willing to leave the shelter of the capital, and they preferred to take their chance with their suffering countrymen rather than trust themselves to the mercies of the besiegers.

From these few stragglers, however, the Spaniards heard a dismal tale of woe respecting the crowded population in the interior of the city. All the ordinary means of sustenance had long since failed, and they now supported life as they could, by means of such roots as they could dig from the earth, by gnawing the bark of trees, by feeding on the grass—on anything, in short, however loathsome, that could allay the craving of appetite. Their only drink was the brackish water of the soil saturated with the salt lake. Under this unwholesome diet, and the diseases engendered by it, the population was gradually wasting away. Men sickened and died every day, in all the excruciating torments produced by hunger, and the wan and emaciated survivors seemed only to be waiting for their time.

The Spaniards had visible confirmation of all this, as they penetrated deeper into the city and approached the district of Tlatelolco, now occupied by the besieged. They found the ground turned up in quest of roots and weeds, the trees stripped of their green stems, their foliage, and their bark. Troops of famished Indians flitted in the distance, gliding like ghosts among the scenes of their former residence. Dead bodies lay unburied in the streets and court-yards, or filled up the canals. It was a sure sign of the extremity of the Aztecs; for they held the burial of the dead as a solemn and imperative duty. In the early part of the siege, they had religiously attended to it. In its later stages, they were still careful to withdraw the dead from the public eye, by bringing their remains within the houses. But the number of these, and their own sufferings, had now so fearfully increased that they had grown indifferent to this, and they suffered their friends and their kinsmen to lie and molder on the spot where they drew their last breath!

As the invaders entered the dwellings, a more appalling spectacle presented itself; the floors covered with the prostrate forms of the miserable inmates, some in the agonies of death, others festering in their corruption; men, women, and children, inhaling the poisonous atmosphere and mingled promiscuously together; mothers with their infants in their arms perishing of hunger before their eyes, while they were unable to afford them the nourishment of nature; men crippled by their wounds, with their bodies frightfully mangled, vainly attempting to crawl away, as the enemy entered. Yet even in this state they scorned to ask for mercy and glared on the invaders with the sullen ferocity of the wounded tiger that the huntsmen have tracked to his forest cave. The Spanish commander issued strict orders that mercy should be shown to these poor and disabled victims. But the Indian allies made no distinction. An Aztec, under whatever circumstances, was an enemy; and, with hideous shouts of triumph, they pulled down the burning buildings on their heads, consuming the living and the dead in one common funeral pile!

Yet the sufferings of the Aztecs, terrible as they were, did not incline them to submission. There were many, indeed, who, from greater strength of constitution, or from the more favorable circumstances in which they were placed, still showed all their wonted energy of body and mind, and maintained the same undaunted and resolute demeanor as before. They fiercely rejected all the overtures of Cortes, declaring they would rather die than surrender, and adding, with a bitter tone of exultation, that the invaders would be at least disappointed in their expectations of treasure, for it was buried where they could never find it!

The women, it is said, shared in this desperate—it should rather be called heroic—spirit. They were indefatigable in nursing the sick and dressing their wounds; they aided the warriors in battle by supplying them with the Indian ammunition of stones and arrows, prepared their slings, strung their bows, and displayed, in short, all the constancy and courage shown by the noble maidens of Saragossa in our day and by those of Carthage in the days of antiquity.

Cortes had now entered one of the great avenues leading to the market-place of Tlatelolco, the quarter towards which the movements of Alvarado were also directed. A single canal only lay in his way; but this was of great width and stoutly defended by the Mexican archery. At this crisis, the army one evening, while in their intrenchments on the causeway, were surprised by an uncommon light that arose from the huge *teocalli* in that part of the city which, being at the north, was the most distant from their own position. This temple, dedicated to the dread war-god, was inferior only to the pyramid in the great square; and on it the Spaniards had more than once seen their unhappy countrymen led to slaughter. They now supposed that the enemy were employed in some of their diabolical ceremonies, when the flame, mounting higher and higher, showed that the sanctuaries themselves were on fire. A shout of exultation at the sight broke forth from the assembled soldiers, as they assured one another that their countrymen under Alvarado had got possession of the building.

It was indeed true. That gallant officer, whose position on the western causeway placed him near the district of Tlatelolco, had obeyed his commander's instructions to the letter, razing every building to the ground in his progress and filling up the ditches with their ruins. He, at length, found himself before the great *teocalli* in the neighborhood of the market. He ordered a company, under a cavalier named Gutierre de Badajoz, to storm the place, which was defended by a body of warriors, mingled with priests, still more wild and ferocious than the soldiery. The garrison, rushing down the winding terraces, fell on the assailants with such fury as compelled them to retreat in confusion, and with some loss. Alvarado ordered another detachment to their support. This last was engaged, at the moment, with a body of Aztecs, who hung on its rear as it wound up the galleries of the *teocalli.* Thus hemmed in between two enemies, above and below, the position of the Spaniards was critical. With sword and buckler, they plunged desperately on the ascending Mexicans and drove them into the court-yard below, where Alvarado plied them with such lively volleys of musketry as soon threw them into disorder and compelled them to abandon the ground. Being thus rid of annoyance in the rear, the Spaniards returned to the charge. They drove the enemy up the heights of the pyramid, and, reaching the broad summit, a fierce encounter followed in mid-air—such an encounter as takes place where death is the certain consequence of defeat. It ended, as usual, in the discomfiture of the Aztecs, who were either slaughtered on the spot still wet with the blood of their own victims or pitched headlong down the sides of the pyramid.

The area was covered with the various symbols of the barbarous worship of the country and with two lofty sanctuaries, before whose grinning idols were displayed the heads of several Christian captives, who had been immolated on their altars. Although overgrown by their long, matted hair and bushy beards, the Spaniards could recognize, in the livid countenances, their comrades who had fallen into the hands of the enemy. Tears fell from their eyes as they gazed on the melancholy spectacle and thought of the hideous death which their countrymen had suffered. They removed the sad relics with decent care, and after the Conquest deposited them in consecrated ground, on a spot since covered by the Church of the Martyrs.

They completed their work by firing the sanctuaries that the place might be no more polluted by these abominable rites. The flame crept slowly up the lofty pinnacles, in which stone was mingled with wood, till, at length, bursting into one bright blaze, it shot up its spiral volume to such a height that it was seen from the most distant quarters of the Valley. It was this which had been hailed by the soldiery of Cortes, and it served as the beacon-light to both friend and foe, intimating the progress of the Christian arms.

The commander-in-chief and his division, animated by the spectacle, made, in their entrance on the following day, more determined efforts to place themselves alongside of their companions under Alvarado. The broad canal, above noticed as the only impediment now lying in his way, was to be traversed; and on the further side, the emaciated figures of the Aztec warriors were gathered in numbers to dispute the passage, like the gloomy shades that wander—as ancient poets tell us—on the banks of the infernal river. They poured down, however, a storm of missiles, which were no shades, on the heads of the Indian laborers while occupied with filling up the wide gap with the ruins of the surrounding buildings. Still they toiled on in defiance of the arrowy shower, fresh numbers taking the place of those who fell. And when at length the work was completed, the cavalry rode over the rough plain at full charge against the enemy, followed by the deep array of spearmen, who bore down all opposition with their invincible phalanx.

The Spaniards now found themselves on the same ground with Alvarado's division. Soon afterwards that chief, attended by several of his staff, rode into their lines and cordially embraced his countrymen and companions in arms for the first time since the beginning of the siege. They were now in the neighborhood of the market. Cortes, taking with him a few of his cavaliers, galloped into it. It was a vast enclosure, as the reader has already seen, covering many an acre. Its dimensions were suited to the immense multitudes who gathered there from all parts of the Valley in the flourishing days of the Aztec monarchy. It was surrounded by porticoes and pavilions for the accommodation of the artisans and traders, who there displayed their various fabrics and articles of merchandise. The flat roofs of the piazzas were now covered with crowds of men and women, who gazed in silent dismay on the steel-clad horsemen that profaned these precincts with their presence for the first time since their expulsion from the capital. The multitude, composed for the most part, probably, of unarmed citizens, seemed taken by surprise; at least, they made no show of resistance; and the general, after leisurely viewing the ground, was permitted to ride back unmolested to the army.

On arriving there, he ascended the *teocalli*, from which the standard of Castile, supplanting the memorials of Aztec superstition, was now triumphantly floating. The Conqueror, as he strode among the smoking embers on the summit, calmly surveyed the scene of desolation below. The palaces, the temples, the busy marts of industry and trade, the glittering canals, covered with their rich freights from the surrounding country, the royal pomp of groves and gardens, all the splendors of the imperial city, the capital of the Western World, forever gone—and in their place a barren wilderness! How different the spectacle which the year before had met his eye, as it wandered over the scenes from the heights of the neighboring *teocalli*, with Montezuma at his side! Seven-eighths of the city were laid in ruins, with the occasional exception, perhaps, of some colossal temple that it would have required too much time to demolish. The remaining eighth, comprehending the district of Tlatelolco, was all that now remained to the Aztecs, whose population—still large after all its losses—was crowded into a compass that would hardly have afforded accommodations for a third of their number. . . .

[*Cortes followed the suggestion of a veteran of the Italian Wars and constructed a sort of catapult to aid in destroying the buildings. The machine was a total failure, the stone it launched falling back on the catapult and destroying it, much to the joy of the Aztecs and the discomfiture of Cortes.*]

There was no occasion to resort to artificial means to precipitate the ruin of the Aztecs. It was accelerated every hour by causes more potent than those arising from mere human agency. There they were, pent up in their close and suffocating quarters, nobles, commoners, and slaves, men, women, and children, some in houses, more frequently in hovels—for this part of the city was not the best—others in the open air in canoes or in the streets, shivering in the cold rains of night and scorched by the burning heat of day. An old chronicler mentions the fact of two women of rank remaining three days and nights up to their necks in the water among the reeds, with only a handful of maize for their support. The ordinary means of sustaining life were long since gone. They wandered about in search of anything, however unwholesome or revolting, that might mitigate the fierce gnawings of hunger. Some hunted for insects and worms on the borders of the lake, or gathered the salt weeds and moss from its bottom, while at times they might be seen casting a wistful look at the green hills beyond, which many of them had left to share the fate of their brethren in the capital.

To their credit, it is said by the Spanish writers that they were not driven in their extremity to violate the laws of nature by feeding on one another. But, unhappily, this is contradicted by the Indian authorities, who state that many a mother, in her agony, devoured the offspring which she had no longer the means of supporting. This is recorded of more than one siege in history; and it is the more probable here, where the sensibilities must have been blunted by familiarity with the brutal practices of the national superstition.

But all was not sufficient, and hundreds of famished wretches died every day from extremity of suffering. Some dragged themselves into the houses and drew their last breath alone and in silence. Others sank down in the public streets. Wherever they died, there they were left. There was no one to bury or to remove them. Familiarity with the spectacle made men indifferent to it. They looked on in dumb despair, waiting for their own turn. There was no complaint, no lamentation, but deep, unutterable woe.

If in other quarters of the town the corpses might be seen scattered over the streets, here they were gathered in heaps. "They lay so thick," says Bernal Diaz, "that one could not tread except among the bodies." "A man could not set his foot down," says Cortes, yet more strongly, "unless on the corpse of an Indian!" They were piled one upon another, the living mingled with the dead. They stretched themselves on the bodies of their friends and lay down to sleep there. Death was everywhere. The city was a vast charnel-house, in which all was hastening to decay and decomposition. A poisonous steam arose from the mass of putrefaction under the action of alternate rain and heat, which so tainted the whole atmosphere that the Spaniards, including the general himself, in their brief visits to the quarter, were made ill by it, and it bred a pestilence that swept off even greater numbers than the famine.

Men's minds were unsettled by these strange and accumulated horrors. They resorted to all the superstitious rites prescribed by their religion, to stay the pestilence. They called on their priests to invoke the gods in their behalf. But the oracles were dumb, or gave only gloomy responses. Their deities had deserted them, and in their place they saw signs of celestial wrath, telling of still greater woes in reserve. Many, after the siege, declared that, among other prodigies, they beheld a stream of light, of a blood-red color, coming from the north in the direction of Tepejacac, with a rushing noise, like that of a whirlwind, which swept round the district of Tlatelolco, darting out sparkles and flakes of fire, till it shot far into the center of the lake! In the disordered state of their nerves, a mysterious fear took possession of their senses. Prodigies were of familiar occurrence, and the most familiar phenomena of nature were converted into prodigies. Stunned by their calamities, reason was bewildered, and they became the sport of the wildest and most superstitious fancies.

In the midst of these awful scenes, the young emperor of the Aztecs remained, according to all accounts, calm and courageous. With his fair capital laid in ruins before his eyes, his nobles and faithful subjects dying around him, his territory rent away, foot by foot, till scarce enough remained for him to stand on, he rejected every invitation to capitulate and showed the same indomitable spirit as at the commencement of the siege. When Cortes, in the hope that the extremities of the besieged would incline them to listen to an accommodation, persuaded a noble prisoner to bear to Guatemozin his proposals to that effect, the fierce young monarch, according to the general, ordered him at once to be sacrificed. It is a Spaniard, we must remember, who tells the story.

Cortes, who had suspended hostilities for several days, in the vain hope that the distresses of the Mexicans would bend them to submission, now determined to drive them to it by a general assault. Cooped up as they were within a narrow quarter of the city, their position favored such an attempt. He commanded Alvarado to hold himself in readiness and directed Sandoval—who, besides the causeway, had charge of the fleet, which lay off the Tlatelolcan district—to support the attack by a cannonade on the houses near the water. He then led his forces into the city, or rather across the horrid waste that now encircled it.

On entering the Indian precincts, he was met by several of the chiefs, who, stretching forth their emaciated arms, exclaimed, "You are the children of the Sun. But the Sun is swift in his course. Why are you, then, so tardy? Why do you delay so long to put an end to our miseries? Rather kill us at once, that we may go to our god Huitzilopochtli, who waits for us in heaven to give us rest from our sufferings!"

Cortes was moved by their piteous appeal, and answered that he desired not their death but their submission. "Why does your master refuse to treat with me," he said, "when a single hour will suffice for me to crush him and all his people?" He then urged them to request Guatemozin to confer with him, with the assurance that he might do it in safety, as his person should not be molested.

The nobles, after some persuasion, undertook the mission; and it was received by the young monarch in a manner which showed—if the anecdote before related of him be true—that misfortune had, at length, asserted some power over his haughty spirit. He consented to the interview, though not to have it take place on that day but the following, in the great square of Tlatelolco. Cortes, well satisfied, immediately withdrew from the city and resumed his position on the causeway.

The next morning he presented himself at the place

appointed, having previously stationed Alvarado there with a strong corps of infantry to guard against treachery. The stone platform in the center of the square was covered with mats and carpets, and a banquet was prepared to refresh the famished monarch and his nobles. Having made these arrangements, he awaited the hour of the interview.

But Guatemozin, instead of appearing himself, sent his nobles, the same who had brought to him the general's invitation and who now excused their master's absence on the plea of illness. Cortes, though disappointed, gave a courteous reception to the envoys, considering that it might still afford the means of opening a communication with the emperor. He persuaded them without much entreaty to partake of the good cheer spread before them, which they did with a voracity that told how severe had been their abstinence. He then dismissed them with a seasonable supply of provisions for their master, pressing him to consent to an interview, without which it was impossible their differences could be adjusted.

The Indian envoys returned in a short time, bearing with them a present of fine cotton fabrics, of no great value, from Guatemozin, who still declined to meet the Spanish general. Cortes, though deeply chagrined, was unwilling to give up the point. "He will surely come," he said to the envoys, "when he sees that I suffer you to go and come unharmed, you who have been my steady enemies, no less than himself, throughout the war. He has nothing to fear from me." He again parted with them, promising to receive their answer the following day.

On the next morning, the Aztec chiefs, entering the Christian quarters, announced to Cortes that Guatemozin would confer with him at noon in the market-place. The general was punctual at the hour; but without success. Neither monarch nor ministers appeared there. It was plain that the Indian prince did not care to trust the promises of his enemy. A thought of Montezuma may have passed across his mind. After he had waited three hours, the general's patience was exhausted, and, as he learned that the Mexicans were busy in preparations for defense, he made immediate dispositions for the assault.

The confederates had been left without the walls; for he did not care to bring them in sight of the quarry before he was ready to slip the leash. He now ordered them to join him, and, supported by Alvarado's division, marched at once into the enemy's quarters. He found them prepared to receive him. Their most able-bodied warriors were thrown into the van, covering their feeble and crippled comrades. Women were seen occasionally mingling in the ranks and, as well as children, thronged the *azoteas*, where, with famine-stricken visages and haggard eyes, they scowled defiance and hatred on their invaders.

As the Spaniards advanced, the Mexicans set up a fierce war-cry and sent off clouds of arrows with their accustomed spirit, while the women and boys rained down darts and stones from their elevated position on the terraces. But the missiles were sent by hands too feeble to do much damage; and, when the squadrons closed, the loss of strength became still more sensible in the Aztecs. Their blows fell feebly and with doubtful aim; though some, it is true, of stronger constitution, or gathering strength from despair, maintained to the last a desperate fight.

The arquebusiers now poured in a deadly fire. The brigantines replied by successive volleys in the opposite quarter. The besieged, hemmed in, like deer surrounded by the huntsmen, were brought down on every side. The carnage was horrible. The ground was heaped up with slain, until the maddened combatants were obliged to climb over the human mounds to get at one another. The miry soil was saturated with blood, which ran off like water and dyed the canals themselves with crimson. All was uproar and terrible confusion. The hideous yells of the barbarians, the oaths and execrations of the Spaniards, the cries of the wounded, the shrieks of women and children, the heavy blows of the Conquerors, the death-struggle of their victims, the rapid, reverberating echoes of musketry, the hissing of innumerable missiles, the crash and crackling of blazing buildings, crushing hundreds in their ruins, the blinding volumes of dust and sulphurous smoke shrouding all in their gloomy canopy made a scene appalling even to the soldiers of Cortes, steeled as they were by many a rough passage of war and by long familiarity with blood and violence. "The piteous cries of the women and children, in particular," says the general, "were enough to break one's heart." He commanded that they should be spared and that all who asked it should receive quarter. He particularly urged this on the confederates and placed men among them to restrain their violence. But he had set an engine in motion too terrible to be controlled. It were as easy to curb the hurricane in its fury as the passions of an infuriated horde of savages. "Never did I see so pitiless a race," he exclaims, "or any thing wearing the form of man so destitute of humanity." They made no distinction of sex or age, and in this hour of vengeance seemed to be requiting the hoarded wrongs of a century. At length, sated with slaughter, the Spanish commander sounded a retreat. It was full time, if, according to his own statement—we may hope it is an exaggeration—forty thousand souls had perished! Yet their fate was to be envied, in comparison with that of those who survived.

Through the long night which followed, no movement was perceptible in the Aztec quarter. No light was seen there, no sound was heard, save the low moaning of some wounded or dying wretch, writhing in his agony. All was dark and silent—the darkness of the grave. The last blow seemed to have completely stunned them. They had parted with hope and sat in sullen despair, like men waiting in silence the stroke of the executioner. Yet, for all this, they showed no disposition to submit. Every new injury had sunk deeper into their souls and filled them with a deeper hatred of their enemy. Fortune, friends, kindred, home—all were gone. They were content to throw away life itself, now that they had nothing more to live for.

Far different was the scene in the Christian camp, where, elated with their recent successes, all was alive with bustle and preparation for the morrow. Bonfires were seen blazing along the causeways, lights gleamed from tents and barracks, and the sounds of music and merriment, borne over the waters, proclaimed the joy of the soldiers at the prospect of so soon terminating their wearisome campaign.

On the following morning the Spanish commander again mustered his forces, having decided to follow up the blow of the preceding day before the enemy should have time to rally, and at once to put an end to the war. He had arranged with Alvarado, on the evening previous, to occupy the market-place of Tlatelolco; and the discharge of an arquebuse was to be the signal for a simultaneous assault. Sandoval was to hold the northern causeway and, with the fleet, to watch the movements of the Indian emperor and to intercept the flight to the mainland, which Cortes knew he meditated. To allow him to effect this would be to leave a formidable enemy in his own neighborhood, who might at any time kindle the flame of insurrection throughout the country. He ordered Sandoval, however, to do no harm to the royal person and not to fire on the enemy at all, except in self-defense.

It was on the memorable 13th of August, 1521, the day of St. Hippolytus—from this circumstance selected as the patron saint of modern Mexico—that Cortes led his warlike array for the last time across the black and blasted environs which lay around the Indian capital. On entering the Aztec precincts, he paused, willing to afford its wretched inmates one more chance of escape, before striking the fatal blow. He obtained an interview with some of the principal chiefs and expostulated with them on the conduct of their prince. "He surely will not," said the general, "see you all perish, when he can so easily save you." He then urged them to prevail on Guatemozin to hold a conference with him, repeating the assurances of his personal safety.

The messengers went on their mission and soon returned with the *cihuacoatl* at their head, a magistrate of high authority among the Mexicans. He said, with a melancholy air, in which his own disappointment was visible, that "Guatemozin was ready to die where he was, but would hold no interview with the Spanish commander"; adding in a tone of resignation, "It is for you to work your pleasure." "Go, then," replied the stern Conqueror, "and prepare your countrymen for death. Their hour is come."

He still postponed the assault for several hours. But the impatience of his troops at this delay was heightened by the rumor that Guatemozin and his nobles were preparing to escape with their effects in the *piraguas* and canoes which were moored on the margin of the lake. Convinced of the fruitlessness and impolicy of further procrastination, Cortes made his final dispositions for the attack and took his own station on an *azotea,* which commanded the theatre of operations.

When the assailants came into presence of the enemy, they found them huddled together in the utmost confusion, all ages and sexes, in masses so dense that they nearly forced one another over the brink of the causeways into the water below. Some had climbed on the terraces, others feebly supported themselves against the walls of the buildings. Their squalid and tattered garments gave a wildness to their appearance, which still further heightened the ferocity of their expression, as they glared on their enemy with eyes in which hate was mingled with despair. When the Spaniards had approached within bowshot, the Aztecs let off a flight of impotent missiles, showing to the last the resolute spirit, though they had lost the strength, of their better days. The fatal signal was then given by the discharge of an arquebuse—speedily followed by peals of heavy ordnance, the rattle of fire-arms, and hellish shouts of the confederates as they sprang upon their victims. It is unnecessary to stain the page with a repetition of the horrors of the preceding day. Some of the wretched Aztecs threw themselves into the water and were picked up by the canoes. Others sunk and were suffocated in the canals. The number of these became so great that a bridge was made of their dead bodies, over which the assailants could climb to the opposite banks. Others again, especially the women, begged for mercy, which, as the chroniclers assure us, was everywhere granted by the Spaniards and, contrary to the instructions and entreaties of Cortes, everywhere refused by the confederates.

While this work of butchery was going on, numbers were observed pushing off in the barks that lined the shore and making the best of their way across the lake. They were constantly intercepted by the brigantines, which broke through the flimsy array of boats, sending off their volleys to the right and left as the crews of the latter hotly assailed them. The battle raged as fiercely on the lake as on the land. Many of the Indian vessels were shattered and overturned. Some few, however, under cover of the smoke, which rolled darkly over the waters, succeeded in clearing themselves of the turmoil and were fast nearing the opposite shore.

Sandoval had particularly charged his captains to keep an eye on the movements of any vessel in which it was at all probable that Guatemozin might be concealed. At this crisis, three or four of the largest *piraguas* were seen skimming over the water and making their way rapidly across the lake. A captain named Garci Holguin, who had command of one of the best sailers in the fleet, instantly gave them chase. The wind was favorable, and every moment he gained on the fugitives, who pulled their oars with a vigor that despair alone could have given. But it was in vain; and, after a short race, Holguin, coming alongside of one of the *piraguas*, which, whether from its appearance or from information he had received, he conjectured might bear the Indian emperor, ordered his men to level their crossbows at the boat. But, before they could discharge them, a cry arose from those in it that their lord was on board. At the same moment, a young warrior, armed with buckler and *maquahuitl*,[1] rose up, as if to beat off the assailants. But, as the Spanish captain ordered his men not to shoot, he dropped his weapons and exclaimed, "I am Guatemozin; lead me to Malinche, I am his prisoner; but let no harm come to my wife and my followers."

[1] A wooden sword with cutting edges of obsidian.

Holguin assured him that his wishes should be respected and assisted him to get on board the brigantine, followed by his wife and attendants. These were twenty in number, consisting of Coanoca, the deposed lord of Tezcuco, the lord of Tlacopan, and several other caciques and dignitaries, whose rank, probably, had secured them some exemption from the general calamities of the siege. When the captives were seated on the deck of his vessel, Holguin requested the Aztec prince to put an end to the combat by commanding his people in the other canoes to surrender. But, with a dejected air, he replied, "It is not necessary. They will fight no longer, when they see that their prince is taken." He spoke truth. The news of Guatemozin's capture spread rapidly through the fleet and on shore, where the Mexicans were still engaged in conflict with their enemies. It ceased, however, at once. They made no further resistance; and those on the water quickly followed the brigantines, which conveyed their captive monarch to land. It seemed as if the fight had been maintained thus long the better to divert the enemy's attention and cover their master's retreat.

Meanwhile Sandoval, on receiving tidings of the capture, brought his own brigantine alongside of Holguin's and demanded the royal prisoner to be surrendered to him. But his captain claimed him as his prize. A dispute arose between the parties, each anxious to have the glory of the deed and perhaps the privilege of commemorating it on his escutcheon. The controversy continued so long that it reached the ears of Cortes, who, in his station on the *azotea,* had learned with no little satisfaction the capture of his enemy. He instantly sent orders to his wrangling officers to bring Guatemozin before him that he might adjust the difference between them. He charged them, at the same time, to treat their prisoner with respect. He then made preparations for the interview, caused the terrace to be carpeted with crimson cloth and matting, and a table to be spread with provisions, of which the unhappy Aztecs stood so much in need. His lovely Indian mistress, Doña Marina, was present to act as interpreter. She had stood by his side through all the troubled scenes of the Conquest, and she was there now to witness its triumphant termination.

Guatemozin, on landing, was escorted by a company of infantry to the presence of the Spanish commander. He mounted the *azotea* with a calm and steady step and was easily to be distinguished from his attendant nobles, though his full, dark eye was no longer lighted up with its accustomed fire, and his features wore an expression of passive resignation that told little of the fierce and fiery spirit that burned within. His head was large, his limbs well proportioned, his complexion fairer than those of his bronze-colored nation, and his whole deportment singularly mild and engaging.

Cortes came forward with a dignified and studied courtesy to receive him. The Aztec monarch probably knew the person of his conqueror, for he first broke silence by saying: "I have done all that I could to defend myself and my people. I am now reduced to this state. You will deal with me, Malinche, as you list." Then, laying his hand on the hilt of a poniard stuck in the general's belt, he added, with vehemence, "Better despatch me with this, and rid me of life at once." Cortes was filled with admiration at the proud bearing of the young barbarian, showing in his reverses a spirit worthy of an ancient Roman. "Fear not," he replied, "you shall be treated with all honor. You have defended your capital like a brave warrior. A Spaniard knows how to respect valor even in an enemy." He then inquired of him where he had left the princess, his wife; and, being informed that she still remained under protection of a Spanish guard on board the brigantine, the general sent to have her escorted to his presence.

She was the youngest daughter of Montezuma and was hardly on the verge of womanhood. On the accession of her cousin, Guatemozin, to the throne, she had been wedded to him as his lawful wife. She is celebrated by her contemporaries for her personal charms; and the beautiful princess, Tecuichpo, is still commemorated by the Spaniards, since from her by a subsequent marriage are descended some of the illustrious families of their own nation. She was kindly received by Cortes, who showed her the respectful attentions suited to her rank. Her birth, no doubt, gave her an additional interest in his eyes, and he may have felt some touch of compunction as he gazed on the daughter of the unfortunate Montezuma. He invited his royal captives to partake of the refreshments which their exhausted condition rendered so necessary. Meanwhile the Spanish commander made his dispositions for the night, ordering Sandoval to escort the prisoners to Cojohuacan, whither he proposed himself immediately to follow. The other captains, Olid and Alvarado, were to draw off their forces to their respective quarters. It was impossible for them to continue in the capital, where the poisonous effluvia from the unburied carcasses loaded the air with infection. A small guard only was stationed to keep order in the wasted suburbs. It was the hour of vespers when Guatemozin surrendered, and the siege might be considered as then concluded. The evening set in dark, and the rain began to fall, before the several parties had evacuated the city.

During the night, a tremendous tempest, such as the Spaniards had rarely witnessed, and such as is known only within the tropics, burst over the Mexican Valley. The thunder, reverberating from the rocky amphitheatre of hills, bellowed over the waste of waters and shook the *teocallis* and crazy tenements of Tenochtitlan—the few that yet survived—to their foundations. The lightning seemed to cleave asunder the vault of heaven, as its vivid flashes wrapped the whole scene in a ghastly glare, for a moment, to be again swallowed up in darkness. The war of elements was in unison with the fortunes of the ruined city. It seemed as if the deities of Anahuac, scared from their ancient abodes, were borne along shrieking and howling in the blast, as they abandoned the fallen capital to its fate!

On the day following the surrender, Guatemozin requested the Spanish commander to allow the Mexicans to leave the city and to pass unmolested into the open country. To this Cortes readily assented, as, indeed, without it, he could take no steps for purifying the capital.

He gave his orders, accordingly, for the evacuation of the place, commanding that no one, Spaniard or confederate, should offer violence to the Aztecs or in any way obstruct their departure. The whole number of these is variously estimated at from thirty to seventy thousand, besides women and children, who had survived the sword, pestilence, and famine. It is certain they were three days in defiling along the several causeways—a mournful train: husbands and wives, parents and children, the sick and the wounded, leaning on one another for support as they feebly tottered along, squalid and but half covered with rags that disclosed at every step hideous gashes, some recently received, others festering from long neglect and carrying with them an atmosphere of contagion. Their wasted forms and famine-stricken faces told the whole history of the siege; and as the straggling files gained the opposite shore, they were observed to pause from time to time, as if to take one more look at the spot so lately crowned by the imperial city, once their pleasant home and endeared to them by many a glorious recollection.

On the departure of the inhabitants, measures were immediately taken to purify the place by means of numerous fires kept burning day and night, especially in the infected quarter of Tlatelolco, and by collecting the heaps of dead, which lay moldering in the streets, and consigning them to the earth. Of the whole number who perished in the course of the siege, it is impossible to form any probable computation. The accounts range widely from one hundred and twenty thousand, the lowest estimate, to two hundred and forty thousand. The number of the Spaniards who fell was comparatively small, but that of the allies must have been large, if the historian of Tezcuco is correct in asserting that thirty thousand perished of his own countrymen alone. That the number of those destroyed within the city was immense cannot be doubted, when we consider that, besides its own redundant population, it was thronged with that of the neighboring towns, who, distrusting their strength to resist the enemy, sought protection within its walls.

The booty found there—that is, the treasures of gold and jewels, the only booty of much value in the eyes of the Spaniards—fell far below their expectations. It did not exceed, according to the general's statement, a hundred and thirty thousand *castellanos* of gold, including the sovereign's share, which, indeed, taking into account many articles of curious and costly workmanship, voluntarily relinquished by the army, greatly exceeded his legitimate fifth. Yet the Aztecs must have been in possession of a much larger treasure, if it were only the wreck of that recovered from the Spaniards on the night of the memorable flight from Mexico. Some of the spoil may have been sent away from the capital, some spent in preparations for defense, and more of it buried in the earth or sunk in the water of the lake. Their menaces were not without a meaning. They had, at least, the satisfaction of disappointing the avarice of their enemies.

Cortes had no further occasion for the presence of his Indian allies. He assembled the chiefs of the different squadrons, thanked them for their services, noticed their valor in flattering terms, and, after distributing presents among them with the assurance that his master, the Emperor, would recompense their fidelity yet more largely, dismissed them to their own homes. They carried off a liberal share of the spoils, of which they had plundered the dwellings—not of a kind to excite the cupidity of the Spaniards—and returned in triumph, short-sighted triumph! at the success of their expedition and the downfall of the Aztec dynasty.

Great, also, was the satisfaction of the Spaniards at this brilliant termination of their long and laborious campaign. They were, indeed, disappointed at the small amount of treasure found in the conquered city. But the soldier is usually too much absorbed in the present to give much heed to the future; and, though their discontent showed itself afterwards in a more clamorous form, they now thought only of their triumph and abandoned themselves to jubilee. Cortes celebrated the event by a banquet, as sumptuous as circumstances would permit, to which all the cavaliers and officers were invited.

Loud and long was their revelry, which was carried to such an excess as provoked the animadversion of Father Olmedo, who intimated that this was not the fitting way to testify their sense of the favors shown them by the Almighty. Cortes admitted the justice of the rebuke but craved some indulgence for a soldier's license in the hour of victory. The following day was appointed for the commemoration of their successes in a more suitable manner.

A procession of the whole army was then formed, with Father Olmedo at its head. The soiled and tattered banners of Castile, which had waved over many a field of battle, now threw their shadows on the peaceful array of the soldiery as they slowly moved along, rehearsing the litany and displaying the image of the Virgin and the blessed symbol of man's redemption. The reverend father pronounced a discourse, in which he briefly reminded the troops of their great cause for thankfulness to Providence for conducting them safe through their long and perilous pilgrimage; and, dwelling on the responsibility incurred by their present position, he besought them not to abuse the rights of conquest but to treat the unfortunate Indians with humanity. The sacrament was then administered to the commander-in-chief and the principal cavaliers, and the services concluded with a solemn thanksgiving to the God of battles, who had enabled them to carry the banner of the Cross triumphant over this barbaric empire.

Thus, after a siege of nearly three months' duration, unmatched in history for the constancy and courage of the besieged, seldom surpassed for the severity of its sufferings, fell the renowned capital of the Aztecs. Unmatched, it may be truly said, for constancy and courage, when we recollect that the door of capitulation on the most honorable terms was left open to them throughout the whole blockade and that, sternly rejecting every proposal of their enemy, they, to a man, preferred to die rather than surrender. More than three centuries had elapsed since the Aztecs, a poor and wandering tribe from the far Northwest, had come on the plateau. There they built their miserable collection of huts on the spot

—as tradition tells us—prescribed by the oracle. Their conquests, at first confined to their immediate neighborhood, gradually covered the Valley, then, crossing the mountains, swept over the broad extent of the table-land, descended its precipitous sides, and rolled onwards to the Mexican Gulf and the distant confines of Central America. Their wretched capital, meanwhile, keeping pace with the enlargement of territory, had grown into a flourishing city, filled with buildings, monuments of art, and a numerous population, that give it the first rank among the capitals of the Western World. At this crisis, came over another race from the remote East, strangers like themselves, whose coming had also been predicted by the oracle, and, appearing on the plateau, assailed them in the very zenith of their prosperity and blotted them out from the map of nations forever! The whole story has the air of fable rather than of history: a legend of romance, a tale of the genii!

Yet we cannot regret the fall of an empire which did so little to promote the happiness of its subjects or the real interests of humanity. Notwithstanding the lustre thrown over its latter days by the glorious defence of its capital, by the mild munificence of Montezuma, by the dauntless heroism of Guatemozin, the Aztecs were emphatically a fierce and brutal race, little calculated, in their best aspects, to excite our sympathy and regard. Their civilization, such as it was, was not their own, but reflected, perhaps imperfectly, from a race whom they had succeeded in the land. It was, in respect to the Aztecs, a generous graft on a vicious stock and could have brought no fruit to perfection. They ruled over their wide domains with a sword, instead of a sceptre. They did nothing to ameliorate the condition or in any way promote the progress of the vassals. Their vassals were serfs, used only to minister to their pleasure, held in awe by armed garrisons, ground to the dust by imposts in peace, by military conscriptions in war. They did not, like the Romans, whom they resembled in the nature of their conquests, extend the rights of citizenship to the conquered. They did not amalgamate them into one great nation, with common rights and interests. They held them as aliens—even those who in the Valley were gathered round the very walls of the capital. The Aztec metropolis, the heart of the monarchy, had not a sympathy, not a pulsation, in common with the rest of the body politic. It was a stranger in its own land.

The Aztecs not only did not advance the condition of their vassals, but, morally speaking, they did much to degrade it. How can a nation where human sacrifices prevail, and especially when combined with cannibalism, further the march of civilization? How can the interests of humanity be consulted where man is levelled to the rank of the brutes that perish? The influence of the Aztecs introduced their gloomy superstition into lands before unacquainted with it, or where, at least, it was not established in any great strength. The example of the capital was contagious. As the latter increased in opulence, the religious celebrations were conducted with still more terrible magnificence, in the same manner as the gladiatorial shows of the Romans increased in pomp with the increasing splendor of the capital. Men became familiar with scenes of horror and the most loathsome abominations. Women and children—the whole nation became familiar with and assisted at them. The heart was hardened, the manners were made ferocious, the feeble light of civilization, transmitted from a milder race, was growing fainter and fainter, as thousands and thousands of miserable victims throughout the empire were yearly fattened in its cages, sacrificed on its altars, dressed and served at its banquets! The whole land was converted into a vast human shambles! The empire of the Aztecs did not fall before its time.

Whether these unparalleled outrages furnish a sufficient plea to the Spaniards for their invasion; whether, with the Protestant, we are content to find a warrant for it in the natural rights and demands of civilization, or, with the Roman Catholic, in the good pleasure of the Pope—on the one or other of which grounds, the conquests by most Christian nations in the East and the West have been defended—it is unnecessary to discuss. It is more material to inquire whether, assuming the right, the conquest of Mexico was conducted with a proper regard to the claims of humanity. And here we must admit that, with all allowance for the ferocity of the age and the laxity of its principles, there are passages which every Spaniard who cherishes the fame of his countrymen would be glad to see expunged from their history; passages not to be vindicated on the score of self-defence or of necessity of any kind, and which must for ever leave a dark spot on the annals of the Conquest. And yet, taken as a whole, the invasion, up to the capture of the capital, was conducted on principles less revolting to humanity than most, perhaps than any, of the other conquests of the Castilian crown in the New World.

It may seem slight praise to say that the followers of Cortes used no blood-hounds to hunt down their wretched victims, as in some other parts of the Continent, nor exterminated a peaceful and submissive population in mere wantonness of cruelty, as in the Islands. Yet it is something that they were not so far infected by the spirit of the age and that their swords were rarely stained with blood unless it was indispensable to the success of their enterprise. Even in the last siege of the capital, the sufferings of the Aztecs, terrible as they were, do not imply any unusual cruelty in the victors; they were not greater than those inflicted on their own countrymen at home, in many a memorable instance, by the most polished nations, not merely of ancient times but of our own. They were the inevitable consequences which follow from war, when, instead of being confined to its legitimate field, it is brought home to the hearthstone, to the peaceful community of the city—its burghers untrained to arms, its women and children yet more defenceless. In the present instance, indeed, the sufferings of the besieged were in a great degree to be charged on themselves—on their patriotic but desperate self-devotion. It was not the desire, as certainly it was not the interest, of the Spaniards to destroy the capital or its inhabitants. When any of these fell into their hands, they were kindly entertained, their wants supplied, and every means taken to infuse into them a spirit of conciliation; and this, too, it should be remembered, in despite of the dreadful doom to which they consigned their Christian captives. The gates of a fair capitulation were kept open, though unavailingly, to the last hour.

The right of conquest necessarily implies that of using whatever force may be necessary for overcoming resistance to the assertion of that right. For the Spaniards to have done otherwise than they did would have been to abandon the siege and, with it, the conquest of the country. To have suffered the inhabitants, with their high-spirited monarch, to escape would but have prolonged the miseries of war by transferring it to another and more inaccessible quarter. They literally, so far as the success of the expedition was concerned, had no choice. If our imagination is struck with the amount of suffering in this and in similar scenes of the Conquest, it should be borne in mind that it was a natural result of the great masses of men engaged in the conflict. The amount of suffering does not of itself show the amount of cruelty which caused it; and it is but justice to the Conquerors of Mexico to say that the very brilliancy and importance of their exploits have given a melancholy celebrity to their misdeeds and thrown them into somewhat bolder relief than strictly belongs to them. It is proper that thus much should be stated, not to excuse their excesses but that we may be enabled to make a more impartial estimate of their conduct as compared with that of other nations under similar circumstances, and that we may not visit them with peculiar obloquy for evils which necessarily flow from the condition of war. I have not drawn a veil over these evils; for the historian should not shrink from depicting in their true colors the atrocities of a condition over which success is apt to throw a false halo of glory, but which, bursting asunder the strong bonds of human fellowship, purchases its triumphs by arming the hand of man against his brother, makes a savage of the civilized, and kindles the fires of hell in the bosom of the savage.

Whatever may be thought of the Conquest in a moral view, regarded as a military achievement, it must fill us with astonishment. That a handful of adventurers, indifferently armed and equipped, should have landed on the shores of a powerful empire, inhabited by a fierce and warlike race, and, in defiance of the reiterated prohibitions of its sovereign, have forced their way into the interior; that they should have done this without knowledge of the language or of the land, without chart or compass to guide them, without any idea of the difficulties they were to encounter, totally uncertain whether the next step might bring them on a hostile nation or on a desert, feeling their way along in the dark, as it were; that though nearly overwhelmed by their first encounter with the inhabitants, they should have still pressed on to the capital of the empire and, having reached it, thrown themselves unhesitatingly into the midst of their enemies; that, so far from being daunted by the extraordinary spectacle there exhibited of power and civilization, they should have been but the more confirmed in their original design; that they should have seized the monarch, have executed his ministers before the eyes of his subjects, and, when driven forth with ruin from the gates, have gathered their scattered wreck together, and, after a system of operations pursued with consummate policy and daring, have succeeded in overturning the capital and establishing their sway over the country; that all this should have been so effected by a mere handful of indigent adventurers—is a fact a little short of the miraculous, too startling for the probabilities demanded by fiction, and without a parallel in the pages of history.

Yet this must not be understood too literally; for it would be unjust to the Aztecs themselves, at least to their military prowess, to regard the Conquest as directly achieved by the Spaniards alone. This would indeed be to arm the latter with the charmed shield of Ruggiero and the magic lance of Astolfo, overturning its hundreds at a touch.[1] The Indian empire was in a manner conquered by Indians. The first terrible encounter of the Spaniards with the Tlascalans, which had nearly proved

[1] Ruggiero and Astolfo, characters in Ariosto's poem, *Orlando Furioso.*

their ruin, did in fact insure their success. It secured to them a strong native support on which to retreat in the hour of trouble, and round which they could rally the kindred races of the land for one great and overwhelming assault. The Aztec monarchy fell by the hands of its own subjects, under the direction of European sagacity and science. Had it been united, it might have bidden defiance to the invaders. As it was, the capital was dissevered from the rest of the country; and the bolt, which might have passed off comparatively harmless had the empire been cemented by a common principle of loyalty and patriotism, now found its way into every crack and crevice of the ill-compacted fabric and buried it in its own ruins. Its fate may serve as a striking proof that a government which does not rest on the sympathies of its subjects cannot long abide; that human institutions, when not connected with human prosperity and progress, must fall—if not before the increasing light of civilization, by the hand of violence; by violence from within, if not from without. And who shall lament their fall?

PART III

The Conquest of Peru

1. *Francisco Pizarro: His Early History and First Expedition**

[The Conquest of Peru *was a natural sequel to Prescott's account of Cortes. In plan, the two works were similar.* The Conquest of Peru, *like the corresponding volumes on Mexico, had an introductory section on the civilization of the Indians (here omitted). The real sweep of the history was, however, the story of the conquest itself. Prescott found the history of Peru less attractive than that of Mexico; Pizarro lacked the stature of Cortes, and the framework of the narrative lacked the dramatic unity of the account of the fall of Tenochtitlan. Prescott complained of this in his journals, but it did not prevent him from weaving the history together in nearly as skillful a fashion as he had displayed in his earlier works. The South Sea had been discovered by the explorer Balboa in 1513, and, almost at once, there had grown up tales of rich lands to the south. In 1522, Pascual de Andagoya sailed south from Panama to seek these, but, after an accident, he cut his voyage short and returned home, having barely escaped the limits of the Isthmus. The captain appointed by the governor of Panama Pedrarias to succeed Andagoya died, and at this point Pizarro was to join with two others to continue the voyages of exploration. Prescott begins with a brief account of Pizarro's life up till 1522.*]

Francisco Pizarro was born in Truxillo, a city of Estremadura, in Spain. The period of his birth is uncertain;

* From *The Conquest of Peru*, Book II, chap. 2.

but probably it was not far from 1471. He was an illegitimate child, and that his parents should not have taken pains to perpetuate the date of his birth is not surprising. Few care to make a particular record of their transgressions. His father, Gonzalo Pizarro, was a colonel of infantry and served with some distinction in the Italian campaigns under the Great Captain, and afterwards in the wars of Navarre. His mother, named Francisca Gonzales, was a person of humble condition in the town of Truxillo.

But little is told of Francisco's early years, and that little not always deserving of credit. According to some, he was deserted by both parents and left as a foundling at the door of one of the principal churches of the city. It is even said that he would have perished had he not been nursed by a sow. This is a more discreditable fountain of supply than that assigned to the infant Romulus. The early history of men who have made their names famous by deeds in after-life, like the early history of nations, affords a fruitful field for invention.

It seems certain that the young Pizarro received little care from either of his parents and was suffered to grow up as nature dictated. He was neither taught to read nor write, and his principal occupation was that of a swineherd. But this torpid way of life did not suit the stirring spirit of Pizarro as he grew older and listened to the tales, widely circulated and so captivating to a youthful fancy, of the New World. He shared in the popular enthusiasm and availed himself of a favorable moment to abandon his ignoble charge and escape to Seville, the port where the Spanish adventurers embarked to seek their fortunes in the West. Few of them could have turned their backs on their native land with less cause for regret than Pizarro.

In what year this important change in his destiny took place we are not informed. The first we hear of him in the New World is at the island of Hispaniola, in 1510, where he took part in the expedition to Uraba in Tierra Firme under Alonzo de Ojeda, a cavalier whose character and achievements find no parallel but in the pages of Cervantes. Hernando Cortes, whose mother was a Pizarro and related, it is said, to the father of Francis, was then in St. Domingo and prepared to accompany Ojeda's expedition, but was prevented by a temporary lameness. Had he gone, the fall of the Aztec empire might have been postponed for some time longer, and the sceptre of Montezuma have descended in peace to his posterity. Pizarro shared in the disastrous fortunes of Ojeda's colony and by his discretion obtained so far the confidence of his commander as to be left in charge of the settlement when the latter returned for supplies to the islands. The lieutenant continued at his perilous post for nearly two months, waiting deliberately until death should have thinned off the colony sufficiently to allow the miserable remnant to be embarked in the single small vessel that remained to it.

After this, we find him associated with Balboa, the discoverer of the Pacific, and co-operating with him in establishing the settlement at Darien. He had the glory of accompanying this gallant cavalier in his terrible march across the mountains and of being among the first Europeans, therefore, whose eyes were greeted with the long-promised vision of the Southern Ocean.

After the untimely death of his commander, Pizarro attached himself to the fortunes of Pedrarias and was employed by that governor in several military expeditions, which, if they afforded nothing else, gave him the requisite training for the perils and privations that lay in the path of the future Conqueror of Peru.

In 1515 he was selected, with another cavalier named Morales, to cross the Isthmus and traffic with the natives on the shores of the Pacific. And there, while engaged in collecting his booty of gold and pearls from the neighboring islands, as his eye ranged along the shadowy line of coast till it faded in the distance, his imagination may have been first fired with the idea of, one day, attempting the conquest of the mysterious regions beyond the mountains. On the removal of the seat of government across the Isthmus to Panama, Pizarro accompanied Pedrarias, and his name became conspicuous among the cavaliers who extended the line of conquest to the north over the martial tribes of Veragua.

But all these expeditions, whatever glory they may have brought him, were productive of very little gold, and, at the age of fifty, the captain Pizarro found himself in possession only of a tract of unhealthy land in the neighborhood of the capital and of such *repartimientos*[1] of the natives as were deemed suited to his military services. The New World was a lottery, where the great prizes were so few that the odds were much against the player; yet in the game he was content to stake health, fortune, and, too often, his fair fame.

Such was Pizarro's situation when, in 1522, Andagoya returned from his unfinished enterprise to the south of Panama, bringing back with him more copious accounts than any hitherto received of the opulence and grandeur of the countries that lay beyond. It was at this time, too, that the splendid achievements of Cortes made their impression on the public mind and gave a new impulse to the spirit of adventure. The southern expeditions became a common topic of speculation among the colonists of Panama. But the region of gold, as it lay behind the mighty curtain of the Cordilleras, was still veiled in obscurity. No idea could be formed of its actual distance; and the hardships and difficulties encountered by the few navigators who had sailed in that direction gave a gloomy character to the undertaking, which had hitherto deterred the most daring from embarking in it. There is no evidence that Pizarro showed any particular alacrity in the cause. Nor were his own funds such as to warrant any expectation of success without great assistance from others. He found this in two individuals of the colony, who took too important a part in the subsequent transactions not to be particularly noticed.

One of them, Diego de Almagro, was a soldier of fortune, somewhat older, it seems probable, than Pizarro; though little is known of his birth, and even the place of it is disputed. It is supposed to have been the town of Almagro in New Castile, whence his own name, for

[1] A distribution of Indians who were expected to perform labor services.

want of a better source, was derived; for, like Pizarro, he was a foundling. Few particulars are known of him till the present period of our history; for he was one of those whom the working of turbulent times first throws upon the surface—less fortunate, perhaps, than if left in their original obscurity. In his military career, Almagro had earned the reputation of a gallant soldier. He was frank and liberal in his disposition, somewhat hasty and ungovernable in his passions, but, like men of a sanguine temperament, after the first sallies had passed away, not difficult to be appeased. He had, in short, the good qualities and the defects incident to an honest nature not improved by the discipline of early education or self-control.

The other member of the confederacy was Fernando de Luque, a Spanish ecclesiastic, who exercised the functions of vicar at Panama and had formerly filled the office of schoolmaster in the Cathedral of Darien. He seems to have been a man of singular prudence and knowledge of the world, and by his respectable qualities had acquired considerable influence in the little community to which he belonged, as well as the control of funds, which made his co-operation essential to the success of the present enterprise.

It was arranged among the three associates that the two cavaliers should contribute their little stock towards defraying the expenses of the armament, but by far the greater part of the funds was to be furnished by Luque. Pizarro was to take command of the expedition, and the business of victualling and equipping the vessels was assigned to Almagro. The associates found no difficulty in obtaining the consent of the governor to their undertaking. After the return of Andagoya, he had projected another expedition, but the officer to whom it was to be intrusted died. Why he did not prosecute his original purpose and commit the affair to an experienced captain like Pizarro does not appear. He was probably not displeased that the burden of the enterprise should be borne by others, so long as a good share of the profit went into his own coffers. This he did not overlook in his stipulations.

Thus fortified with the funds of Luque and the consent of the governor, Almagro was not slow to make preparations for the voyage. Two small vessels were purchased, the larger of which had been originally built by Balboa for himself, with a view to this same expedition. Since his death, it had lain dismantled in the harbor of Panama. It was now refitted as well as circumstances would permit, and put in order for sea, while the stores and provisions were got on board with an alacrity which did more credit, as the event proved, to Almagro's zeal than to his forecast.

There was more difficulty in obtaining the necessary complement of hands; for a general feeling of distrust had gathered round expeditions in this direction, which could not readily be overcome. But there were many idle hangers-on in the colony, who had come out to mend their fortunes and were willing to take their chance of doing so, however desperate. From such materials as these, Almagro assembled a body of somewhat more than a hundred men; and, every thing being ready, Pizarro assumed the command and, weighing anchor, took his departure from the little port of Panama, about the middle of November, 1524. Almagro was to follow in a second vessel of inferior size, as soon as it could be fitted out. . . .

[*The time of the year was extremely unsuitable for the voyage. Not only was it the rainy season, but it was also a period of contrary winds. In Prescott's words, the hardships suffered in this first trip were an "ominous commencement." Pizarro pushed on despite the difficulty, despatching a vessel back for supplies. A fearful six weeks was spent at a spot called by the Spaniards Puerto de la Hambre, the port of famine, until the relieving vessel returned. Revived by the arrival of provisions, the expedition once more pushed on.*]*

Had he struck boldly out into the deep, instead of hugging the inhospitable shore, where he had hitherto found so little to recompense him, he might have spared

* From *The Conquest of Peru,* Book II, chap. 2.

himself the repetition of wearisome and unprofitable adventures and reached by a shorter route the point of his destination. But the Spanish mariner groped his way along these unknown coasts, landing at every convenient headland, as if fearful lest some fruitful region or precious mine might be overlooked should a single break occur in the line of survey. Yet it should be remembered that, though the true point of Pizarro's destination is obvious to us, familiar with the topography of these countries, he was wandering in the dark, feeling his way along inch by inch, as it were, without chart to guide him, without knowledge of the seas or of the bearings of the coast, and even with no better defined idea of the object at which he aimed than that of a land teeming with gold, that lay somewhere at the south! It was a hunt after an *El Dorado*, on information scarcely more circumstantial or authentic than that which furnished the basis of so many chimerical enterprises in this land of wonders. Success only, the best argument with the multitude, redeemed the expeditions of Pizarro from a similar imputation of extravagance.

Holding on his southerly course under the lee of the shore, Pizarro, after a short run, found himself abreast of an open reach of country, or at least one less encumbered with wood, which rose by a gradual swell as it receded from the coast. He landed with a small body of men and, advancing a short distance into the interior, fell in with an Indian hamlet. It was abandoned by the inhabitants, who, on the approach of the invaders, had betaken themselves to the mountains; and the Spaniards, entering their deserted dwellings, found there a good store of maize and other articles of food, and rude ornaments of gold of considerable value. Food was not more necessary for their bodies than was the sight of gold, from time to time, to stimulate their appetite for adventure. One spectacle, however, chilled their blood with horror. This was the sight of human flesh, which they found roasting before the fire, as the barbarians had left it, preparatory to their obscene repast. The Spaniards, conceiving that they had fallen in with a tribe of Caribs, the only race in that part of the New

World known to be cannibals, retreated precipitately to their vessel. They were not steeled by sad familiarity with the spectacle, like the Conquerors of Mexico.

The weather, which had been favorable, now set in tempestuous, with the heavy squalls, accompanied by incessant thunder and lightning, and the rain, as usual in these tropical tempests, descended not so much in drops as in unbroken sheets of water. The Spaniards, however, preferred to take their chance on the raging elements rather than remain in the scene of such brutal abominations. But the fury of the storm gradually subsided, and the little vessel held on her way along the coast, till, coming abreast of a bold point of land named by Pizarro Punta Quemada, he gave orders to anchor. The margin of the shore was fringed with a deep belt of mangrove trees, the long roots of which, interlacing one another, formed a kind of submarine latticework that made the place difficult of approach. Several avenues, opening through this tangled thicket, led Pizarro to conclude that the country must be inhabited, and he disembarked, with the greater part of his force, to explore the interior.

He had not penetrated more than a league, when he found his conjecture verified by the sight of an Indian town of larger size than those he had hitherto seen, occupying the brow of an eminence and well defended by palisades. The inhabitants, as usual, had fled, but left in their dwellings a good supply of provisions and some gold trinkets, which the Spaniards made no difficulty of appropriating to themselves. Pizarro's flimsy bark had been strained by the heavy gales it had of late encountered, so that it was unsafe to prosecute the voyage further without more thorough repairs than could be given to her on this desolate coast. He accordingly determined to send her back with a few hands to be careened at Panama and meanwhile to establish his quarters in his present position, which was so favorable for defence. But first he despatched a small party under Montenegro to reconnoitre the country and, if possible, to open a communication with the natives.

The latter were a warlike race. They had left their

habitations in order to place their wives and children in safety. But they had kept an eye on the movements of the invaders, and when they saw their forces divided they resolved to fall upon each body singly before it could communicate with the other. So soon, therefore, as Montenegro had penetrated through the defiles of the lofty hills, which shoot out like spurs of the Cordilleras along this part of the coast, the Indian warriors, springing from their ambush, sent off a cloud of arrows and other missiles that darkened the air, while they made the forest ring with their shrill war-whoop. The Spaniards, astonished at the appearance of the savages, with their naked bodies gaudily painted, and brandishing their weapons as they glanced among the trees and straggling underbrush that choked up the defile, were taken by surprise and thrown for a moment into disarray. Three of their number were killed and several wounded. Yet, speedily rallying, they returned the discharge of the assailants with their crossbows—for Pizarro's troops do not seem to have been provided with muskets on this expedition—and then, gallantly charging the enemy, sword in hand, succeeded in driving them back into the fastnesses of the mountains. But it only led them to shift their operations to another quarter and make an assault on Pizarro before he could be relieved by his lieutenant.

Availing themselves of their superior knowledge of the passes, they reached that commander's quarters long before Montenegro, who had commenced a countermarch in the same direction; and issuing from the woods, the bold savages saluted the Spanish garrison with a tempest of darts and arrows, some of which found their way through the joints of the harness and the quilted mail of the cavaliers. But Pizarro was too well practised a soldier to be off his guard. Calling his men about him, he resolved not to abide the assault tamely in the works, but to sally out and meet the enemy on their own ground. The barbarians, who had advanced near the defences, fell back as the Spanish burst forth with their valiant leader at their head. But, soon returning with admirable ferocity to the charge, they singled out Pizarro, whom by his bold bearing and air of authority they easily recognized as the chief, and hurling at him a storm of missiles, wounded him, in spite of his armor, in no less than seven places.

Driven back by the fury of the assault directed against his own person, the Spanish commander retreated down the slope of the hill, still defending himself as he could with sword and buckler, when his foot slipped, and he fell. The enemy set up a fierce yell of triumph, and some of the boldest sprang forward to despatch him. But Pizarro was on his feet in an instant and, striking down two of the foremost with his strong arm, held the rest at bay till his soldiers could come to the rescue. The barbarians, struck with admiration at his valor, began to falter, when Montenegro, luckily coming on the ground at the moment and falling on their rear, completed their confusion; and, abandoning the field, they made the best of their way into the recesses of the mountains. The ground was covered with their slain; but the victory was dearly purchased by the death of two more Spaniards and a long list of wounded.

A council of war was then called. The position had lost its charm in the eyes of the Spaniards, who had met here with the first resistance they had yet experienced on their expedition. It was necessary to place the wounded in some secure spot, where their injuries could be attended to. Yet it was not safe to proceed farther, in the crippled state of their vessel. On the whole, it was decided to return and report their proceedings to the governor; and, though the magnificent hopes of the adventures had not been realized, Pizarro trusted that enough had been done to vindicate the importance of the enterprise and to secure the countenance of Pedrarias for the further prosecution of it.

Yet Pizarro could not make up his mind to present himself, in the present state of the undertaking, before the governor. He determined, therefore, to be set on shore with the principal part of his company at Chicama, a place on the mainland, at a short distance west of Panama. From this place, which he reached without any further accident, he despatched the vessel and in it his treasurer, Nicolas de Ribera, with the gold he had collected and with instructions to lay before the governor a full account of his discoveries and the result of the expedition.

While these events were passing, Pizarro's associate, Almagro, had been busily employed in fitting out another vessel for the expedition at the port of Panama. It was not till long after his friend's departure that he was prepared to follow him. With the assistance of Luque, he at length succeeded in equipping a small caravel and embarking a body of between sixty and seventy adventurers, mostly of the lowest order of the colonists. He steered in the track of his comrade with the intention of overtaking him as soon as possible. By a signal previously concerted of notching the trees, he was able to identify the spots visited by Pizarro—Puerto de Piñas, Puerto de la Hambre, Pueblo Quemado—touching successively at every point of the coast explored by his countrymen, though in a much shorter time. At the last-mentioned place he was received by the fierce natives with the same hostile demonstrations as Pizarro, though in the present encounter the Indians did not venture beyond their defences. But the hot blood of Almagro was so exasperated by this check that he assaulted the place and carried it sword in hand, setting fire to the outworks and dwellings and driving the wretched inhabitants into the forests.

His victory cost him dear. A wound from a javelin on the head caused an inflammation in one of his eyes, which, after great anguish, ended in the loss of it. Yet the intrepid adventurer did not hesitate to pursue his voyage, and, after touching at several places on the coast, some of which rewarded him with a considerable booty in gold, he reached the mouth of the Rio de San Juan, about the fourth degree of north latitude. He was struck with the beauty of the stream and with the cultivation on its borders, which were sprinkled with Indian cottages showing some skill in their construction and altogether intimating a higher civilization than anything he had yet seen.

Still his mind was filled with anxiety for the fate of Pizarro and his followers. No trace of them had been found on the coast for a long time, and it was evident they must have foundered at sea, or made their way back to Panama. This last he deemed most probable, as the vessel might have passed him unnoticed under the cover or the night or of the dense fogs that sometimes hang over the coast.

Impressed with this belief, he felt no heart to continue his voyage of discovery, for which, indeed, his single bark, with its small complement of men, was altogether inadequate. He proposed, therefore, to return without delay. On his way, he touched at the Isle of Pearls, and there learned the result of his friend's expedition and the place of his present residence. He directed his course at once to Chicama, where the two cavaliers soon had the satisfaction of embracing each other and recounting their several exploits and escapes. Almagro returned even better freighted with gold than his confederate, and at every step of his progress he had collected fresh confirmation of the existence of some great and opulent empire in the South. The confidence of the two friends was much strengthened by their discoveries; and they unhesitatingly pledged themselves to one another to die rather than abandon the enterprise.

The best means of obtaining the levies requisite for so formidable an undertaking—more formidable, as it now appeared to them, than before—were made the subject of long and serious discussion. It was at length decided that Pizarro should remain in his present quarters, inconvenient and even unwholesome as they were rendered by the humidity of the climate and the pestilent swarms of insects that filled the atmosphere. Almagro would pass over to Panama, lay the case before the governor, and secure, if possible, his good will towards the prosecution of the enterprise. If no obstacle were thrown in their way from this quarter, they might hope, with the assistance of Luque, to raise the necessary supplies;

while the results of the recent expedition were sufficiently encouraging to draw adventurers to their standard in a community which had a craving for excitement that gave even danger a charm and which held life cheap in comparison with gold.

*2. The Contract and the Second Expedition**

[The first expedition had hardly been a success. The adventurers had exhausted their limited financial resources, but nonetheless they did not despair, even though the situation in Panama was not conducive to their plans. Prescott here describes how they borrowed money, bought out the governor, and early in 1526 launched a second small expedition down the coast.]

On his arrival at Panama, Almagro found that events had taken a turn less favorable to his views than he had anticipated. Pedrarias, the governor, was preparing to lead an expedition in person against a rebellious officer in Nicaragua; and his temper, naturally not the most amiable, was still further soured by this defection of his lieutenant and the necessity it imposed on him of a long and perilous march. When, therefore, Almagro appeared before him with the request that he might be permitted to raise further levies to prosecute his enterprise, the governor received him with obvious dissatisfaction, listened coldly to the narrative of his losses, turned an incredulous ear to his magnificent promises for the future, and bluntly demanded an account of the lives which had been sacrificed by Pizarro's obstinacy, but which, had they been spared, might have stood him in

* From *The Conquest of Peru,* Book II, chap. 3.

good stead in his present expedition to Nicaragua. He positively declined to countenance the rash schemes of the two adventurers any longer, and the conquest of Peru would have been crushed in the bud but for the efficient interposition of the remaining associate, Fernando de Luque.

This sagacious ecclesiastic had received a very different impression from Almagro's narrative from that which had been made on the mind of the irritable governor. The actual results of the enterprise in gold and silver thus far, indeed, had been small—forming a mortifying contrast to the magnitude of their expectations. But, in another point of view, they were of the last importance, since the intelligence which the adventurers had gained in every successive stage of their progress, confirmed, in the strongest manner, the previous accounts, received from Andagoya and others, of a rich Indian empire at the south, which might repay the trouble of conquering it as well as Mexico had repaid the enterprise of Cortes. Fully entering, therefore, into the feelings of his military associates, he used all his influence with the governor to incline him to a more favorable view of Almagro's petition: and no one in the little community of Panama exercised greater influence over the councils of the executive than Father Luque, for which he was indebted no less to his discretion and acknowledged sagacity than to his professional station.

But while Pedrarias, overcome by the arguments or importunity of the churchman, yielded a reluctant assent to the application, he took care to testify his displeasure with Pizarro, on whom he particularly charged the loss of his followers, by naming Almagro as his equal in command in the proposed expedition. This mortification sunk deep into Pizarro's mind. He suspected his comrade, with what reason does not appear, of soliciting this boon from the governor. A temporary coldness arose between them, which subsided, in outward show at least, on Pizarro's reflecting that it was better to have this authority conferred on a friend than on a stranger, perhaps an enemy. But the seeds of permanent distrust were left in his bosom and lay waiting for the due season to ripen into a fruitful harvest of discord.

Pedrarias had been originally interested in the enterprise, at least so far as to stipulate for a share of the gains, though he had not contributed, as it appears, a single ducat towards the expenses. He was at length, however, induced to relinquish all right to a share of the contingent profits. But in his manner of doing so, he showed a mercenary spirit, better becoming a petty trader than a high officer of the Crown. He stipulated that the associates should secure to him the sum of one thousand *pesos de oro* in requital of his good will, and they eagerly closed with his proposal rather than be encumbered with his pretensions. For so paltry a consideration did he resign his portion of the rich spoil of the Incas! But the governor was not gifted with the eye of a prophet. His avarice was of that short-sighted kind which defeats itself. He had sacrificed the chivalrous Balboa just as that officer was opening to him the conquest of Peru, and he would now have quenched the spirit of enterprise, that was taking the same direction, in Pizarro and his associates.

Not long after this, in the following year, he was succeeded in his government by Don Pedro de los Rios, a cavalier of Cordova. It was the policy of the Castilian Crown to allow no one of the great colonial officers to occupy the same station so long as to render himself formidable by his authority. It had, moreover, many particular causes of disgust with Pedrarias. The functionary they sent out to succeed him was fortified with ample instructions for the good of the colony, and especially of the natives, whose religious conversion was urged as a capital object and whose personal freedom was unequivocally asserted, as loyal vassals of the Crown. It is but justice to the Spanish government to admit that its provisions were generally guided by a humane and considerate policy, which was as regularly frustrated by the cupidity of the colonist and the capricious cruelty of the conqueror. The few remaining years of Pedrarias were spent in petty squabbles, both of a personal and official nature; for he was still continued in office, though in one of less consideration than that which he had hitherto filled. He survived but a few years, leaving behind him a reputation not to be envied, of one who united a pusillanimous spirit with uncontrollable passion, but who displayed, notwithstanding, a certain energy of character or, to speak more correctly, an impetuosity of purpose, which might have led to good results had it taken a right direction. Unfortunately, his lack of discretion was such that the direction he took was rarely of service to his country or to himself.

Having settled their difficulties with the governor and obtained his sanction to their enterprise, the confederates lost no time in making the requisite preparations for it. Their first step was to execute the memorable contract which served as the basis of their future arrangements; and, as Pizarro's name appears in this, it seems probable that that chief had crossed over to Panama so soon as the favorable disposition of Pedrarias had been secured. The instrument, after invoking in the most solemn manner the names of the Holy Trinity and Our Lady the Blessed Virgin, sets forth that whereas the parties have full authority to discover and subdue the countries and provinces lying south of the Gulf, belonging to the empire of Peru, and as Fernando de Luque had advanced the funds for the enterprise in bars of gold of the value of twenty thousand *pesos*, they mutually bind themselves to divide equally among them the whole of the conquered territory. This stipulation is reiterated over and over again, particularly with reference to Luque, who, it is declared, is to be entitled to one-third of all lands, *repartimientos*, treasures of every kind, gold, silver, and precious stones—to one-third even of all vassals, rents, and emoluments arising from such grants as may be conferred by the Crown on either of his military associates, to be held for his own use or for that of his heirs, assigns, or legal representative.

The two captains solemnly engaged to devote themselves exclusively to the present undertaking until it is accomplished; and in case of failure in their part of the convenant they pledge themselves to reimburse Luque for his advances, for which all the property they possess shall be held responsible, and this declaration is to be a sufficient warrant for the execution of judgment against them, in the same manner as if it had proceeded from the decree of a court of justice.

The commanders, Pizarro and Almagro, made oath, in the name of God and the Holy Evangelists, sacredly to keep this convenant, swearing it on the missal, on which they traced with their own hands the sacred emblem of the cross. To give still greater efficacy to the compact, Father Luque administered the sacrament to the parties, dividing the consecrated wafer into three portions, of which each one of them partook; while the bystanders, says an historian, were affected to tears by this spectacle of the solemn ceremonial with which these men voluntarily devoted themselves to a sacrifice that seemed little short of insanity.

The instrument, which was dated March 10, 1526, was subscribed by Luque and attested by three respectable citizens of Panama, one of whom signed on behalf of Pizarro and the other for Almagro; since neither of these parties, according to the avowal of the instrument, was able to subscribe his own name.

Such was the singular compact by which three obscure individuals coolly carved out and partitioned among themselves an empire, of whose extent, power, and resources, of whose situation, of whose existence even, they had no sure or precise knowledge. The positive and unhesitating manner in which they speak of the grandeur of this empire, of its stores of wealth, so conformable to the event, but of which they could have really known so little, forms a striking contrast with the general skepticism and indifference manifested by nearly every other person, high and low, in the community of Panama.

The religious tone of the instrument is not the least remarkable feature in it, especially when we contrast this with the relentless policy pursued by the very men who were parties to it, in their conquest of the country. "In the name of the Prince of Peace," says the illustrious historian of America,[1] "they ratified a contract of which plunder and bloodshed were the objects." The reflection seems reasonable. Yet, in criticizing what is done, as well as what is written, we must take into account the spirit of the times. The invocation of Heaven was natural, where the object of the undertaking was in part a religious one. Religion entered, more or less, into the theory, at least, of the Spanish conquests in the New World. That motives of a baser sort mingled largely with these higher ones, and in different proportions according to the character of the individual, no one will deny. And few are they that have proposed to themselves a long career of action without the intermixture of some vulgar personal motive—fame, honors, or emolument. Yet that religion furnishes a key to the American crusades, however rudely they may have been conducted, is evident from the history of their origin; from the sanction openly given to them by the Head of the Church; from the throng of self-devoted missionaries who followed in the track of the conquerors to garner up the rich harvest of souls; from the reiterated instructions of the Crown, the great object of which was the conversion of the natives; from those superstitious acts of the iron-hearted soldiery themselves, which, however they may be set down to fanaticism, were clearly too much in earnest to leave any ground for the charge of hypocrisy. It was indeed a fiery cross that was borne over the devoted land, scathing and consuming it in its terrible progress; but it was still the cross, the sign of man's salvation, the only sign by which generations and generations yet unborn were to be rescued from eternal perdition.

It is a remarkable fact, which has hitherto escaped the notice of the historian, that Luque was not the real party to this contract. He represented another, who placed in his hands the funds required for the undertaking. This appears from an instrument signed by Luque himself and certified before the same notary that prepared the original contract. The instrument declares

[1] William Robertson (see Introduction).

that the sum of twenty thousand *pesos* advanced for the expedition was furnished by the Licentiate Gaspar de Espinosa, then at Panama; that the vicar acted only as his agent and by his authority; and that, in consequence, the said Espinosa and no other was entitled to a third of all the profits and acquisitions resulting from the conquest of Peru. This instrument, attested by three persons, one of them the same who had witnessed the original contract, was dated on the 6th of August, 1531. The Licentiate Espinosa was a respectable functionary, who had filled the office of principal alcalde[1] in Darien and since taken a conspicuous part in the conquest and settlement of Tierra Firme. He enjoyed much consideration for his personal character and station; and it is remarkable that so little should be known of the manner in which the convenant so solemnly made was executed in reference to him. As in the case of Columbus, it is probable that the unexpected magnitude of the results was such as to prevent a faithful adherence to the original stipulation; and yet, from the same consideration, one can hardly doubt that the twenty thousand *pesos* of the bold speculator must have brought him a magnificent return. Nor did the worthy vicar of Panama, as the history will show hereafter, go without his reward.

[*Early in the voyage, Pizarro conquered an Indian coastal town. Here he remained for a while, sending one ship under Bartolomé Ruiz to the south to explore. In his exploration, Ruiz discovered increasing signs of civilization the further to the south he went. Pizarro's men, reinforced by Almagro and others from Panama, sailed south themselves to follow up these discoveries. When they met stiff resistance at a town near the equator, they drew back, and Almagro proposed a return to Panama for supplies and to recruit volunteers. A quarrel broke out between Pizarro and Almagro, Pizarro alleging that he had to endure the suffering while Almagro had ease. Finally, Pizarro agreed to remain with part*

[1] A judge, frequently also acting as a sort of mayor.

*of the expedition on the island of Gallo, out of reach of the native attacks. It was to prove a poor resting place with little food and much rain and sickness.**]

Not long after Almagro's departure, Pizarro sent off the remaining vessel, under the pretext of its being put in repair at Panama. It probably relieved him of a part of his followers, whose mutinous spirit made them an obstacle rather than a help in his forlorn condition and with whom he was the more willing to part because of the difficulty in finding subsistence on the barren spot which he now occupied.

Great was the dismay occasioned by the return of Almagro and his followers in the little community of Panama; for the letter[1] surreptitiously conveyed in the ball of cotton fell into the hands for which it was intended, and the contents soon got abroad with the usual quantity of exaggeration. The haggard and dejected mien of the adventurers of itself told a tale sufficiently disheartening, and it was soon generally believed that the few ill-fated survivors of the expedition were detained against their will by Pizarro, to end their days with their disappointed leader on his desolate island.

Pedro de los Rios, the governor, was so much incensed at the result of the expedition and the waste of life it had occasioned to the colony that he turned a deaf ear to all the applications of Luque and Almagro for further countenance in the affair; he derided their sanguine anticipations of the future and finally resolved to send an officer to the isle of Gallo with orders to bring back every Spaniard whom he should find still living in that dreary abode. Two vessels were immediately despatched for the purpose and placed under charge of a cavalier named Tafur, a native of Cordova.

Meanwhile Pizarro and his followers were experiencing all the miseries which might have been expected from the character of the barren spot on which they were imprisoned. They were, indeed, relieved from all

* From *The Conquest of Peru*, Book II, chap. 4.

[1] A letter from several of the disaffected soldiers complaining of their condition and the cupidity of their leaders had been secreted in a ball of cotton.

apprehensions of the natives, since these had quit the island on its occupation by the white men; but they had to endure the pains of hunger even in a greater degree than they had formerly experienced in the wild woods of the neighboring continent. Their principal food was crabs and such shell-fish as they could scantily pick up along the shores. Incessant storms of thunder and lightning, for it was the rainy season, swept over the desolate island and drenched them with a perpetual flood. Thus, half-naked and pining with famine, there were few in that little company who did not feel the spirit of enterprise quenched within them, or who looked for any happier termination of their difficulties than that afforded by a return to Panama. The appearance of Tafur, therefore, with his two vessels well stored with provisions, was greeted with all the rapture that the crew of a sinking wreck might feel on the arrival of some unexpected succor; and the only thought, after satisfying the immediate cravings of hunger, was to embark and leave the detested isle for ever.

But by the same vessel letters came to Pizarro from his two confederates, Luque and Almagro, beseeching him not to despair in his present extremity, but to hold fast to his original purpose. To return under the present circumstances would be to seal the fate of the expedition; and they solemnly engaged, if he would remain firm at his post, to furnish him in a short time with the necessary means for going forward.

A ray of hope was enough for the courageous spirit of Pizarro. It does not appear that he himself had entertained, at any time, thoughts of returning. If he had, these words of encouragement entirely banished them from his bosom, and he prepared to stand the fortune of the cast on which he had so desperately ventured. He knew, however, that solicitations or remonstrances would avail little with the companions of his enterprise; and he probably did not care to win over the more timid spirits, who, by perpetually looking back, would only be a clog in his future movements. He announced his own purpose, however, in a laconic but decided manner, characteristic of a man more accustomed to act than to talk, and well calculated to make an impression on his rough followers.

Drawing his sword, he traced a line with it on the sand from east to west. Then, turning towards the south, "Friends and comrades!" he said, "on that side are toil, hunger, nakedness, the drenching storm, desertion, and death; on this side, ease and pleasure. There lies Peru with its riches; here, Panama and its poverty. Choose, each man, what best becomes a brave Castilian. For my part, I go to the south." So saying, he stepped across the line. He was followed by the brave pilot Ruiz; next by Pedro de Candia, a cavalier born, as his name imports, in one of the isles of Greece. Eleven others successively crossed the line, thus intimating their willingness to abide the fortunes of their leader, for good or for evil. Fame, to quote the enthusiastic language of an ancient chronicler, has commemorated the names of this little band, "who thus, in the face of difficulties unexampled in history, with death rather than riches for their reward, preferred it all to abandoning their honor, and stood firm by their leader as an example of loyalty to future ages."

But the act excited no such admiration in the mind of Tafur, who looked on it as one of gross disobedience to the commands of the governor and as little better than madness, involving the certain destruction of the parties engaged in it. He refused to give any sanction to it himself by leaving one of his vessels with the adventurers to prosecute their voyage, and it was with great difficulty that he could be persuaded even to allow them a part of the stores which he had brought for their support. This had no influence on their determination, and the little party, bidding adieu to their returning comrades, remained unshaken in their purpose of abiding the fortunes of their commander.

There is something striking to the imagination in the spectacle of these few brave spirits thus consecrating themselves to a daring enterprise, which seemed as far above their strength as any recorded in the fabulous annals of knight-errantry. A handful of men, without food, without clothing, almost without arms, without knowledge of the land to which they were bound, without vessel to transport them, were here left on a lonely rock in the ocean with the avowed purpose of carrying on a crusade against a powerful empire staking their lives on its success. What is there in the legends of chivalry that surpasses it? This was the crisis of Pizarro's fate. There are moments in the lives of men, which, as they are seized or neglected, decide their future destiny. Had Pizarro faltered from his strong purpose, and yielded to the occasion, now so temptingly presented, for extricating himself and his broken band from their desperate position, his name would have been buried with his fortunes, and the conquest of Peru would have been left for other and more successful adventurers. But his constancy was equal to the occasion, and his conduct here proved him competent to the perilous post he had assumed, and inspired others with a confidence in him which was the best assurance of success.

In the vessel that bore back Tafur and those who seceded from the expedition the pilot Ruiz was also permitted to return, in order to co-operate with Luque and Almagro in their application for further succor.

Not long after the departure of the ships, it was decided by Pizarro to abandon his present quarters, which had little to recommend them and which, he reflected, might now be exposed to annoyance from the original inhabitants should they take courage and return, on learning the diminished number of the white men. The Spaniards, therefore, by his orders, constructed a rude boat or raft, on which they succeeded in transporting themselves to the little island of Gorgona, twenty-five leagues to the north of their present residence. It lay about five leagues from the continent, and was uninhabited. It had some advantages over the isle of Gallo; for it stood higher above the sea and was partially covered with wood, which afforded shelter to a species of pheasant and the hare or rabbit of the country, so that the Spaniards, with their crossbows, were enabled to procure a tolerable supply of game. Cool streams that issued from the living rock furnished abundance of water, though the drenching rains that fell without intermission left them in no danger of perishing by thirst. From this annoyance they found protection in the rude huts which they constructed; though here, as in their former residence, they suffered from the no less intolerable annoyance of venomous insects, which multiplied and swarmed in the exhalations of the rank and stimulated soil. In this dreary abode Pizarro omitted no means by which to sustain the drooping spirits of his men. Morning prayers were duly said, and the evening hymn to the Virgin was regularly chanted; the festivals of the church were carefully commemorated, and every means taken by their commander to give a kind of religious character to his enterprise and to inspire his rough followers with a confidence in the protection of Heaven that might support them in their perilous circumstances.

In these uncomfortable quarters, their chief employment was to keep watch on the melancholy ocean that they might hail the first signal of the anticipated succor. But many a tedious month passed away, and no sign of it appeared. All around was the same wide waste of waters, except to the eastward, where the frozen crest of the Andes, touched with the ardent sun of the equator, glowed like a ridge of fire along the whole extent of the great continent. Every speck in the distant horizon was carefully noticed, and the drifting timber or masses of sea-weed, heaving to and fro on the bosom of the waters, was converted by their imagination into the promised vessel; till, sinking under successive disappointments, hope gradually gave way to doubt, and doubt settled into despair.

Meanwhile the vessel of Tafur had reached the port of Panama. The tidings which she brought of the inflexible obstinacy of Pizarro and his followers filled the governor with indignation. He could look on it in no other light than as an act of suicide and steadily refused to send further assistance to men who were obstinately bent on their own destruction. Yet Luque and Almagro were true to their engagements. They represented to the governor that, if the conduct of their comrade was rash, it was at least in the service of the Crown, and in prosecuting the great work of discovery, Rios had been instructed, on his taking the government, to aid Pizarro in the enterprise; and to desert him now would be to throw away the remaining chance of success and to incur the responsibility of his death and that of the brave men who adhered to him. These remonstrances, at length, so far operated on the mind of that functionary that he reluctantly consented that a vessel should be sent to the island of Gorgona, but with no more hands than were necessary to work her, and with positive instructions to Pizarro to return in six months and report himself at Panama, whatever might be the future results of his expedition.

Having thus secured the sanction of the executive, the two associates lost no time in fitting out a small vessel with stores and a supply of arms and ammunition, and despatched it to the island. The unfortunate tenants of this little wilderness, who had now occupied it for seven months, hardly dared to trust their senses when they descried the white sails of the friendly bark coming over the waters. And although, when the vessel anchored off the shore, Pizarro was disappointed to find that it brought no additional recruits for the enterprise, yet he greeted it with joy, as affording the means of solving the great problem of the existence of the rich southern empire, and of thus opening the way for its future conquest. Two of his men were so ill that it was determined to leave them in the care of some of the friendly Indians who had continued with him through the whole of his sojourn, and to call for them on his return. Taking with him the rest of his hardy followers and the natives of Tumbez, he embarked and, speedily weighing anchor, bade adieu to the "Hell," as it was called by the Spaniards, which had been the scene of so much suffering and such undaunted resolution.

Every heart was now elated with hope, as they found themselves once more on the waters, under the guidance of the good pilot, Ruiz, who, obeying the directions of the Indians, proposed to steer for the land of Tumbez, which would bring them at once into the golden empire of the Incas—the El Dorado of which they had been so long in pursuit. Passing by the dreary isle of Gallo, which they had such good cause to remember, they stood farther out to sea until they made Point Tacumez, near which they had landed on their previous voyage. They did not touch at any part of the coast, but steadily held on their way, though considerably impeded by the currents, as well as by the wind, which blew with little variation from the south. Fortunately, the wind was light, and, as the weather was favorable, their voyage, though slow, was not uncomfortable. In a few days, they came in sight of Point Pasado, the limit of the pilot's former navigation; and, crossing the line, the little bark entered upon those unknown seas which had never been ploughed by European keel before. The coast, they observed, gradually declined from its former bold and rugged character, gently sloping towards the shore and spreading out into sandy plains, relieved here and there by patches of uncommon richness and beauty; while the white cottages of the natives glistening along the margin of the sea and the smoke that rose among the distant hills intimated the increasing population of the country.

At length, after the lapse of twenty days from their departure from the island, the adventurous vessel rounded the point of St. Helena and glided smoothly into the waters of the beautiful gulf of Guayaquil. The country was here studded along the shore with towns and villages, though the mighty chain of the Cordilleras, sweeping up abruptly from the coast, left but a narrow strip of emerald verdure, through which numerous rivulets, spreading fertility around them, wound their way into the sea.

The voyagers were now abreast of some of the most stupendous heights of this magnificent range: Chimborazo, with its broad round summit, towering like the dome of the Andes, and Cotopaxi, with its dazzling cone of silvery white, that knows no change except from the action of its own volcanic fires; for this mountain is the most terrible of the American volcanoes and was in formidable activity at no great distance from the period of our narrative. Well pleased with the signs of civilization that opened on them at every league of their progress, the Spaniards at length came to anchor off the island of Santa Clara, lying at the entrance of the Bay of Tumbez.

The place was uninhabited but was recognized by the Indians on board as occasionally resorted to by the warlike people of the neighboring isle of Puna for purpose of sacrifice and worship. The Spaniards found on the spot a few bits of gold rudely wrought into various shapes and probably designed as offerings to the Indian deity. Their hearts were cheered, as the natives assured them they would see great abundance of the same precious metal in their own city of Tumbez.

The following morning they stood across the bay for this place. As they drew near, they beheld a town of considerable size, with many of the buildings apparently of stone and plaster, situated in the bosom of a fruitful meadow, which seemed to have been redeemed from the sterility of the surrounding country by careful and minute irrigation. When at some distance from shore, Pizarro saw standing towards him several large balsas, which were found to be filled with warriors going on an expedition against the island of Puna. Running alongside of the Indian flotilla, he invited some of the chiefs to come on board of his vessel. The Peruvians gazed with wonder on every object which met their eyes, and especially on their own countrymen, whom they had little expected to meet there. The latter informed them in what manner they had fallen into the hands of the strangers, whom they described as a wonderful race of beings that had come thither for no harm, but solely to be made acquainted with the country and its inhabitants. This account was confirmed by the Spanish commander, who persuaded the Indians to return in their balsas and report what they had learned to their townsmen, requesting them at the same time to provide his vessel with refreshments, as it was his desire to enter into friendly intercourse with the natives.

The people of Tumbez were gathered along the shore and were gazing with unutterable amazement on the floating castle, which, now having dropped anchor, rode lazily at its moorings in their bay. They eagerly listened to the accounts of their countrymen and instantly reported the affair to the *curaca* or ruler of the district, who, conceiving that the strangers must be beings of a superior order, prepared at once to comply with their request. It was not long before several balsas were seen steering for the vessel laden with bananas, plantains, yuca, Indian corn, sweet potatoes, pine-apples, cocoanuts, and other rich products of the bountiful vale of Tumbez. Game and fish, also, were added, with a number of llamas, of which Pizarro had seen the rude drawings belonging to Balboa, but of which till now he had met with no living specimen. He examined this curious animal, the Peruvian sheep—or, as the Spaniards called it, the "little camel" of the Indians—with much interest, greatly admiring the mixture of wool and hair which supplied the natives with the materials for their fabrics.

At that time there happened to be at Tumbez an Inca noble, or *orejon*—for so men of his rank were called by the Spaniards, from the huge ornaments of gold attached to their ears. He expressed great curiosity to see the wonderful strangers and had, accordingly, come out with the balsas for the purpose. It was easy to perceive from the superior quality of his dress, as well as from the deference paid to him by the others, that he was a person of consideration; and Pizarro received him with marked distinction. He showed him the different parts of the ship, explaining to him the uses of whatever engaged his attention and answering his numerous queries as well as he could, by means of the Indian interpreters. The Peruvian chief was especially desirous of knowing whence and why Pizarro and his followers had come to these shores. The Spanish captain replied that he was the vassal of a great prince, the greatest and most powerful in the world, and that he had come to this country to assert his master's lawful supremacy over it. He had further come to rescue the inhabitants from the darkness of unbelief in which they were now wandering. They worshipped an evil spirit, who would sink their souls into everlasting perdition; and he would give them the knowledge of the true and only God, Jesus Christ, since to believe in him was eternal salvation.

The Indian prince listened with deep attention and apparent wonder; but answered nothing. It may be that neither he nor his interpreters had any very distinct ideas of the doctrines thus abruptly revealed to them. It may be that he did not believe there was any other potentate on earth greater than the Inca; none, at least, who had a better right to rule over his dominions. And it is very possible he was not disposed to admit that the great luminary whom he worshipped was inferior to the God of the Spaniards. But whatever may have passed in the untutored mind of the barbarian, he did not give vent to it, but maintained a discreet silence, without any attempt to controvert or to convince his Christian antagonist.

He remained on board of the vessel till the hour of dinner, of which he partook with the Spaniards, expressing his satisfaction at the strange dishes, and especially pleased with the wine, which he pronounced far superior to the fermented liquors of his own country. On taking leave, he courteously pressed the Spaniards to visit Tumbez, and Pizarro dismissed him with the present, among other things, of an iron hatchet, which had greatly excited his admiration; for the use of iron was as little known to the Peruvians as to the Mexicans.

On the day following, the Spanish captain sent one of his own men, named Alonso de Molina, on shore, accompanied by a Negro who had come in the vessel from Panama, together with a present for the *curaca* of some swine and poultry, neither of which were indigenous to the New World. Towards evening his emissary returned with a fresh supply of fruits and vegetables that the friendly people sent to the vessel. Molina had a wondrous tale to tell. On landing, he was surrounded by the natives, who expressed the greatest astonishment at his dress, his fair complexion, and his long beard. The women, especially, manifested great curiosity in respect to him, and Molina seemed to be entirely won by their charms and captivating manners. He probably intimated his satisfaction by his demeanor, since they urged him to stay among them, promising in that case to provide him with a beautiful wife.

Their surprise was equally great at the complexion of his sable companion. They could not believe it was natural and tried to rub off the imaginary dye with their hands. As the African bore all this with characteristic good humor, displaying at the same time his rows of ivory teeth, they were prodigiously delighted. The animals were no less above their comprehension; and, when the cock crew, the simple people clapped their hands and inquired what he was saying. Their intellects were so bewildered by sights so novel that they seemed incapable of distinguishing between man and brute.

Molina was then escorted to the residence of the *curaca*, whom he found living in much state, with porters stationed at his doors and with a quantity of gold and silver vessels, from which he was served. He was then taken to different parts of the Indian city and saw a fortress built of rough stone and, though low, spreading over a large extent of ground. Near this was a temple; and the Spaniard's description of its decorations, blazing with gold and silver, seemed so extravagant that Pizarro, distrusting his whole account, resolved to send a more discreet and trustworthy emissary on the following day.

The person selected was Pedro de Candia, the Greek cavalier mentioned as one of the first who intimated his intention to share the fortunes of his commander. He was sent on shore dressed in complete mail as became a good knight, with his sword by his side and his arquebuse on his shoulder. The Indians were even more dazzled by his appearance than by Molina's, as the sun fell brightly on his polished armor and glanced from his military weapons. They had heard much of the formidable arquebuse from their townsmen who had come in the vessel, and they besought Candia "to let it speak to them." He accordingly set up a wooden board as a target and, taking deliberate aim, fired off the musket. The flash of the powder and the startling report of the piece as the board, struck by the ball, was shivered into splinters, filled the natives with dismay. Some fell on the ground covering their faces with their hands, and others approached the cavalier with feelings of awe, which were gradually dispelled by the assurance they received from the smiling expression of his countenance.

They then showed him the same hospitable attentions which they had paid to Molina; and his description of the marvels of the place, on his return, fell nothing short of his predecessor's. The fortress, which was surrounded by a triple row of wall, was strongly garrisoned. The temple he described as literally tapestried with plates of gold and silver. Adjoining this structure was a sort of convent appropriated to the Inca's destined brides, who manifested great curiosity to see him. Whether this was gratified is not clear; but Candia described the gardens of the convent, which he entered, as glowing with imitations of fruits and vegetables all in pure gold and silver! He had seen a number of artisans at work, whose sole business seemed to be to furnish these gorgeous decorations for the religious houses.

The reports of the cavalier may have been somewhat overcolored. It was natural that men coming from the dreary wilderness in which they had been buried the last six months should have been vividly impressed by the tokens of civilization which met them on the Peruvian coast. But Tumbez was a favorite city of the Peruvian princes. It was the most important place on the northern borders of the empire, contiguous to the recent acquisition of Quito. The great Tupac Yupanqui had established a strong fortress there and peopled it with a colony of *mitimaes*.[1] The temple, and the house occupied by the Virgins of the Sun, had been erected by Huayna Capac and were liberally endowed by that Inca, after the sumptuous fashion of the religious establishments of Peru. The town was well supplied with water by numerous aqueducts; and the fruitful valley in which it was embosomed and the ocean which bathed

[1] A *mitima* was a system used by the Incas to forestall rebellion. The inhabitants of a conquered region were moved elsewhere and their place taken by safer peasants long used to Inca domination. Tupac Yupanqui (1471–1493) was the tenth Inca; he was succeeded by Huayna Capac (1493–1525).

its shores supplied ample means of subsistence to a considerable population. But the cupidity of the Spaniards, after the Conquest, was not slow in despoiling the place of its glories; and the site of its proud towers and temples, in less than half a century after that fatal period, was to be traced only by the huge mass of ruins that encumbered the ground.

The Spaniards were nearly mad with joy, says an old writer, at receiving these brilliant tidings of the Peruvian city. All their fond dreams were now to be realized, and they had at length reached the realm which had so long flitted in visionary splender before them. Pizarro expressed his gratitude to Heaven for having crowned his labors with so glorious a result; but he bitterly lamented the hard fate which, by depriving him of his followers, denied him, at such a moment, the means of availing himself of his success. Yet he had no cause for lamentation; and the devout Catholic saw in this very circumstance a providential interposition which prevented the attempt at conquest, while such attempts would have been premature. Peru was not yet torn asunder by the dissensions of rival candidates for the throne; and, united and strong under the sceptre of a warlike monarch, she might well have bid defiance to all the forces that Pizarro could muster. "It was manifestly the work of Heaven," exclaims a devout son of the Church, "that the natives of the country should have received him in so kind and loving a spirit, as best fitted to facilitate the conquest; for it was the Lord's hand which led him and his followers to this remote region for the extension of the holy faith, and for the salvation of souls."

Having now collected all the information essential to his object, Pizarro, after taking leave of the natives of Tumbez and promising a speedy return, weighed anchor and again turned his prow towards the south. Still keeping as near as possible to the coast, that no place of importance might escape his observation, he passed Cape Blanco and, after sailing about a degree and a half, made the port of Payta. The inhabitants, who had notice of his approach, came out in their balsas to get sight of the wonderful strangers, bringing with them stores of fruits, fish, and vegetables, with the same hospitable spirit shown by their countrymen at Tumbez.

After staying here a short time and interchanging presents of trifling value with the natives, Pizarro continued his cruise; and, sailing by the sandy plains of Sechura for an extent of near a hundred miles, he doubled the Punta de Aguja and swept down the coast as it fell off towards the east, still carried forward by light and somewhat variable breezes. The weather now became unfavorable, and the voyagers encountered a succession of heavy gales, which drove them some distance out to sea and tossed them about for many days. But they did not lose sight of the mighty ranges of the Andes, which, as they proceeded towards the south, were still seen, at nearly the same distance from the shore, rolling onwards, peak after peak, with their stupendous surges of ice, like some vast ocean that had been suddenly arrested and frozen up in the midst of its wild and tumultuous career. With this landmark always in view, the navigator had little need of star or compass to guide his bark on her course.

As soon as the tempest had subsided, Pizarro stood in again for the continent, touching at the principal points as he coasted along. Everywhere he was received with the same spirit of generous hospitality, the natives coming out on their balsas to welcome him, laden with their little cargoes of fruits and vegetables, of all the luscious varieties that grow in the *tierra caliente.* All were eager to have a glimpse of the strangers, the "Children of the Sun," as the Spaniards began already to be called from their fair complexions, brilliant armor, and the thunderbolts which they bore in their hands. The most favorable reports, too, had preceded them, of the urbanity and gentleness of their manners, thus unlocking the hearts of the simple natives and disposing them to confidence and kindness. The iron-hearted soldier had not yet disclosed the darker side of his character. He was too weak to do so. The hour of conquest had not yet come.

In every place Pizarro received the same accounts of a powerful monarch who ruled over the land and held his court on the mountain plains of the interior, where his capital was depicted as blazing with gold and silver and displaying all the profusion of an Oriental satrap. The Spaniards, except at Tumbez, seem to have met with little of the precious metals among the natives on the coast. More than one writer asserts that they did not covet them or, at least, by Pizarro's orders, affected not to do so. He would not have them betray their appetite for gold, and actually refused gifts when they were proffered! It is more probable that they saw little display of wealth, except in the embellishments of the temples and other sacred buildings, which they did not dare to violate. The precious metals, reserved for the uses of religion and for persons of high degree, were not likely to abound in the remote towns and hamlets on the coast.

Yet the Spaniards met with sufficient evidence of general civilization and power to convince them that there was much foundation for the reports of the natives. Repeatedly they saw structures of stone and plaster, occasionally showing architectural skill in the execution, if not elegance of design. Wherever they cast anchor, they beheld green patches of cultivated country redeemed from the sterility of nature and blooming with the variegated vegetation of the tropics; while a refined system of irrigation, by means of aqueducts and canals, seemed to be spread like a network over the surface of the country, making even the desert to blossom as the rose. At many places where they landed they saw the great road of the Incas which traversed the sea-coast, often, indeed, lost in the volatile sands where no road could be maintained, but rising into a broad and substantial causeway, as it emerged on a firmer soil. Such a provision for internal communication was in itself no slight monument of power and civilization. . . .

*3. The Third Expedition**

[On his previous voyage, Pizarro had reached a point nine degrees south of the equator. After a trip of eighteen months, he returned to Panama, but his grand reports won no public support, and, with money gone, the adventurers, prompted by Luque, decided to appeal to the Emperor himself. In the summer of 1528 Pizarro crossed the ocean and appeared at the court of Spain, bringing with him some tangible proofs of the civilization he had found. The time was fortunate for his appeal, Cortes having also arrived recently at the court with the news of his conquests in Mexico. In 1529 a capitulation was signed by the Queen Regent on behalf of the Emperor appointing Pizarro Governor and Captain General of Peru for life. Before leaving Spain to return to the New World, Pizarro recruited his four brothers (or half-brothers) and a cousin and then left once again for Panama. Almagro was not happy with the arrangement made in the capitulation, since he had hoped for a share of the command. Once more disagreement threatened the adventurers; once more, the argument was patched up with difficulty. At the end of 1530, preparations were underway in Panama for the new voyage.]

No time was now lost in preparing for the voyage. It found little encouragement, however, among the colonists of Panama, who were too familiar with the sufferings on the former expeditions to care to undertake an-

* From *The Conquest of Peru*, Book III, chap. 1.

other, even with the rich bribe that was held out to allure them. A few of the old company were content to follow out the adventure to its close; and some additional stragglers were collected from the province of Nicaragua—a shoot, it may be remarked, from the Colony of Panama. But Pizarro made slender additions to the force brought over with him from Spain, though this body was in better condition and, in respect to arms, ammunition, and equipment generally, was on a much better footing than his former levies. The whole number did not exceed one hundred and eighty men, with twenty-seven horses for the cavalry. He had provided himself with three vessels, two of them of a good size, to take the place of those which he had been compelled to leave on the opposite side of the Isthmus at Nombre de Dios—an armament small for the conquest of an empire and far short of that prescribed by the capitulation with the Crown. With this the intrepid chief proposed to commence operations, trusting to his own successes and the exertions of Almagro, who was to remain behind for the present to muster reinforcements.

On St. John the Evangelist's day, the banners of the company and the royal standard were consecrated in the cathedral church of Panama; a sermon was preached before the little army by Fray Juan de Vargas, one of the Dominicans selected by the government for the Peruvian mission; and mass was performed, and the sacrament administered to every soldier previous to his engaging in the crusade against the infidel. Having thus solemnly invoked the blessing of Heaven on the enterprise, Pizarro and his followers went on board their vessels, which rode at anchor in the Bay of Panama, and early in January, 1531, sallied forth on his third and last expedition for the conquest of Peru.

It was his intention to steer direct for Tumbez, which held out so magnificent a show of treasure on his former voyage. But head-winds and currents, as usual, baffled his purpose, and after a run of thirteen days, much shorter than the period formerly required for the same distance, his little squadron came to anchor in the Bay of St. Matthew, about one degree north; and Pizarro, after consulting with his officers, resolved to disembark his forces and advance along the coast, while the vessels held their course at a convenient distance from the shore.

The march of the troops was severe and painful in the extreme; for the road was constantly intersected by streams, which, swollen by the winter rains, widened at their mouths into spacious estuaries. Pizarro, who had some previous knowledge of the country, acted as guide as well as commander of the expedition. He was ever ready to give aid where it was needed, encouraging his followers to ford or swim the torrents as they best could, and cheering the desponding by his own buoyant and courageous spirit.

At length they reached a thick-settled hamlet, or rather town, in the province of Coaque. The Spaniards rushed on the place, and the inhabitants, without offering resistance, fled in terror to the neighboring forests, leaving their effects—of much greater value than had been anticipated—in the hands of the invaders. "We fell on them, sword in hand," says one of the Conquerors, with some naïveté; "for, if we had advised the Indians of our approach we should never have found there such a store of gold and precious stones." The natives, however, according to another authority, stayed voluntarily; "for, as they had done no harm to the white men, they flattered themselves that there would be only an interchange of good offices with the strangers"—an expectation founded, it may be, on the good character which the Spaniards had established for themselves on their preceding visit, but in which the simple people now found themselves most unpleasantly deceived.

Rushing into the deserted dwellings, the invaders found there, besides stuffs of various kinds and food most welcome in their famished condition, a large quantity of gold and silver wrought into clumsy ornaments, together with many precious stones; for this was the region of the *esmeraldas,* or emeralds, where that valuable gem was most abundant. One of these jewels, that fell into the hands of Pizarro in this neighborhood, was as large as a pigeon's egg. Unluckily, his rude followers did not know the value of their prize; and they broke many of them in pieces by pounding them with hammers. They were led to this extraordinary proceeding, it is said, by one of the Dominican missionaries, Fray Reginaldo de Pedraza, who assured them that this was the way to prove the true emerald, which could not be broken. It was observed that the good father did not subject his own jewels to this wise experiment; but, as the stones, in consequence of it, fell in value, being regarded merely as colored glass, he carried back a considerable store of them to Panama.

The gold and silver ornaments rifled from the dwellings were brought together and deposited in a common heap; when a fifth was deducted for the Crown, and Pizarro distributed the remainder in the due proportions among the officers and privates of his company. This was the usage invariably observed on the like occasions throughout the Conquest. The invaders had embarked in a common adventure. Their interest was common, and to have allowed every one to plunder on his own account would only have led to insubordination and perpetual broils. All were required, therefore, on pain of death, to contribute whatever they obtained, whether by bargain or by rapine, to the general stock; and all were too much interested in the execution of the penalty to allow the unhappy culprit who violated the law any chance of escape.

Pizarro, with his usual policy, sent back to Panama a large quantity of the gold, no less than twenty thousand *castellanos* in value, in the belief that the sight of so much treasure, thus speedily acquired, would settle the doubt of the wavering and decide them on joining his banner. He judged right. As one of the Conquerors piously expresses it, "It pleased the Lord that we should fall in with the town of Coaque, that the riches of the land might find credit with the people and that they should flock to it."

Pizarro, having refreshed his men, continued his march along the coast, but no longer accompanied by the vessels, which had returned for recruits to Panama. The road, as he advanced, was checkered with strips of sandy waste, which, drifted about by the winds, blinded the soldiers and afforded only treacherous footing for man and beast. The glare was intense; and the rays of a vertical sun beat fiercely on the iron mail and the thick quilted doublets of cotton, till the fainting troops were almost suffocated with the heat. To add to their distresses, a strange epidemic broke out in the little army. It took the form of ulcers, or rather hideous warts of great size, which covered the body and when lanced, as was the case with some, discharged such a quantity of blood as proved fatal to the sufferer. Several died of this frightful disorder, which was so sudden in its attack, and attended with such prostration of strength, that those who lay down well at night were unable to lift their hands to their heads in the morning. The epidemic, which made its first appearance during this invasion and which did not long survive it, spread over the country, sparing neither native nor white man. It was one of those plagues from the vial of wrath, which the destroying angel, who follows in the path of the conqueror, pours out on the devoted nations.

The Spaniards rarely experienced on their march either resistance or annoyance from the inhabitants, who, instructed by the example of Coaque, fled with their effects into the woods and neighboring mountains. No one came out to welcome the strangers and offer the rites of hospitality, as on their last visit to the land. For the white men were no longer regarded as good beings that had come from heaven, but as ruthless destroyers, who, invulnerable to the assaults of the Indians, were borne along on the back of fierce animals, swifter than the wind, with weapons in their hands, that scattered fire and desolation as they went. Such were the stories now circulated of the invaders, which, preceding them everywhere on their march, closed the hearts, if not the doors, of the natives against them. Exhausted by the fatigue of travel and by disease, and grievously disappointed at the poverty of the land, which now offered no compensation for their toils, the soldiers of Pizarro cursed the hour in which they had enlisted under his standard, and the men of Nicaragua in particular, says the old chronicler, calling to mind their pleasant quarters in their luxurious land, sighed only to return to their Mahometan paradise.

At this juncture the army was gladdened by the sight of a vessel from Panama, which brought some supplies, together with the royal treasurer, the *veedor*, or inspector, the comptroller, and other high officers appointed by the Crown to attend the expedition. They had been left in Spain by Pizarro, in consequence of his abrupt departure from the country; and the Council of the Indies, on learning the circumstance, had sent instructions to Panama to prevent the sailing of his squadron from that port. But the Spanish government, with more wisdom, countermanded the order, only requiring the functionaries to quicken their own departure and take their place without loss of time in the expedition.

The Spaniards in their march along the coast had now advanced as far as Puerto Viejo. Here they were soon after joined by another small reinforcement of about thirty men, under an officer named Benalcazar, who subsequently rose to high distinction in this service. Many of the followers of Pizarro would now have halted at this spot and established a colony there. But that chief thought more of conquering than of colonizing, at least for the present; and he proposed, as his first step, to get possession of Tumbez, which he regarded as the gate of the Peruvian empire. Continuing his march, therefore, to the shores of what is now called the Gulf of Guayaquil, he arrived off the little island of Puna, lying at no great distance from the Bay of Tumbez. This island, he thought, would afford him a convenient place to encamp until he was prepared to make his descent on the Indian city.

The dispositions of the islanders seemed to favor his purpose. He had not been long in their neighborhood before a deputation of the natives, with their cacique at their head, crossed over in their balsas to the mainland to welcome the Spaniards to their residence. But the Indian interpreters of Tumbez, who had returned with Pizarro from Spain and continued with the camp, put their master on his guard against the meditated treachery of the islanders, whom they accused of designing to destroy the Spaniards by cutting the ropes that held together the floats and leaving those upon them to perish in the waters. Yet the cacique, when charged by Pizarro with this perfidious scheme, denied it with such an air of conscious innocence, that the Spanish commander trusted himself and his followers, without further hesitation, to his conveyance and was transported in safety to the shores of Puna.

Here he was received in a hospitable manner, and his troops were provided with comfortable quarters. Well satisfied with his present position, Pizarro resolved to occupy it until the violence of the rainy season was passed, when the arrival of the reinforcements he expected would put him in better condition for marching into the country of the Inca.

The island, which lies in the mouth of the river of Guayaquil and is about eight leagues in length by four in breadth at the widest part, was at that time partially covered with a noble growth of timber. But a large portion of it was subjected to cultivation and bloomed with plantations of cacao, of the sweet potato, and the different products of a tropical clime, evincing agricultural knowledge as well as industry in the population. They were a warlike race, but had received from their Peruvian foes the appellation of "perfidious." It was the brand fastened by the Roman historians on their Carthaginian enemies—with perhaps no better reason. The bold and independent islanders opposed a stubborn resistance to the arms of the Incas; and, though they had finally yielded, they had been ever since at feud, and often in deadly hostility, with their neighbors of Tumbez.

The latter no sooner heard of Pizarro's arrival on the island than, trusting probably to their former friendly relations with him, they came over in some number to the Spanish quarters. The presence of their detested rivals was by no means grateful to the jealous inhabitants of Puna, and the prolonged residence of the white men on their island could not be otherwise than burdensome. In their outward demeanor they still maintained the same show of amity; but Pizarro's interpreters again put him on his guard against the proverbial perfidy of their hosts. With his suspicions thus roused, the Spanish commander was informed that a number of the chiefs had met together to deliberate on a plan of insurrection. Not caring to wait for the springing of the mine, he surrounded the place of meeting with his soldiers and made prisoners of the suspected chieftains. According to one authority, they confessed their guilt. This is by no means certain. Nor is it certain that they meditated an insurrection. Yet the fact is not improbable in itself; though it derives little additional probability from the assertion of the hostile interpreters. It is certain, however, that Pizarro was satisfied of the existence of a conspiracy; and, without further hesitation, he abandoned his wretched prisoners, ten or twelve in number, to the tender mercies of their rivals of Tumbez, who instantly massacred them before his eyes.

Maddened by this outrage, the people of Puna sprang to arms and threw themselves at once, with fearful yells and the wildest menaces of despair, on the Spanish camp. The odds of numbers were greatly in their favor, for they mustered several thousand warriors. But the more decisive odds of arms and discipline were on the side of their antagonists; and, as the Indians rushed forward in a confused mass to the assault, the Castilians coolly received them on their long pikes or swept them down by the volleys of their musketry. Their ill-protected bodies were easily cut to pieces by the sharp sword of the Spaniard; and Hernando Pizarro, putting himself at the head of the cavalry, charged boldly into the midst and scattered them far and wide over the field, until, panic-struck by the terrible array of steel-clad horsemen and the stunning reports and the flash of fire-arms, the fugitives sought shelter in the depths of their forests. Yet the victory was owing, in degree, at least—if we may credit the Conquerors—to the interposition of Heaven; for St. Michael and his legions were seen high in the air above the combatants, contending with the arch-enemy of man, cheering on the Christians by their example!

Not more than three or four Spaniards fell in the fight; but many were wounded, and among them Hernando Pizarro, who received a severe injury in the leg from a javelin. Nor did the war end here; for the implacable islanders, taking advantage of the cover of night, or of any remissness on the part of the invaders, were ever ready to steal out of their fastnesses and spring on their enemy's camp, while, by cutting off his straggling parties and destroying his provisions, they kept him in perpetual alarm.

In this uncomfortable situation, the Spanish commander was gladdened by the appearance of two vessels off the island. They brought a reinforcement consisting of a hundred volunteers, besides horses for the cavalry. It was commanded by Hernando de Soto, a captain afterwards famous as the discoverer of the Mississippi, which still rolls its majestic current over the place of his burial—a fitting monument for his remains, as it is of his renown.

The reinforcement was most welcome to Pizarro, who had been long discontented with his position on an island, where he found nothing to compensate the life of unintermitting hostility which he was compelled to lead. With these recruits he felt himself in sufficient strength to cross over to the continent and resume military operations in the proper theatre for discovery and conquest. From the Indians of Tumbez he learned that the country had been for some time distracted by a civil war between two sons of the late monarch, competitors for the throne. This intelligence he regarded as of the utmost importance, for he remembered the use which Cortes had made of similar dissensions among the tribes of Anahuac. Indeed, Pizarro seems to have had the example of his great predecessor before his eyes on more occasions than this. But he fell far short of his model; for, notwithstanding the restraint he sometimes put upon himself, his coarser nature and more ferocious temper often betrayed him into acts more repugnant to sound policy, which would never have been countenanced by the Conqueror of Mexico.

*4. The March to the Andes**

[Attempts were made to persuade Tumbez to capitulate peacefully; eventually force had to be used. Following the reduction of Tumbez, Pizarro moved further south and established the city of San Miguel at the mouth of the Chira River to serve as his base camp. In the meantime, the powerful Inca empire, which was the object of the conqueror's expedition, had declined into a civil war. About seven years before Pizarro came to San Miguel, the Inca Huayna Capac had died. At his death he had divided the empire between the rightful heir, Huascar, and his favorite son, Atahuallpa. Just at the time when Pizarro was preparing his third expedition, war broke out between these two rivals. In the struggle the more ruthless Atahuallpa proved successful, and, establishing himself by force as the supreme ruler in the Inca empire, he set up residence at Caxamalca in northern Peru. Hearing of the civil war and its outcome, Pizarro determined to leave San Miguel and to seek out the new Inca at Caxamalca.]

On the 24th of September, 1532, five months after landing at Tumbez, Pizarro marched out at the head of his little body of adventurers from the gates of San Miguel, having enjoined it on the colonists to treat their Indian vassals with humanity and to conduct themselves in such a manner as would secure the good-will of the surrounding tribes. Their own existence, and with it the

* From *The Conquest of Peru*, Book III, chap. 3.

safety of the army and the success of the undertaking, depended on this course. In the place were to remain the royal treasurer, the *veedor*, or inspector of metals, and other officers of the crown; and the command of the garrison was intrusted to the *contador*,[1] Antonio Navarro. Then putting himself at the head of his troops, the chief struck boldly into the heart of the country in the direction where, as he was informed, lay the camp of the Inca. It was a daring enterprise, thus to venture with a handful of followers into the heart of a powerful empire, to present himself, face to face, before the Indian monarch in his own camp, encompassed by the flower of his victorious army! Pizarro had already experienced more than once the difficulty of maintaining his ground against the rude tribes of the north, so much inferior in strength and numbers to the warlike legions of Peru. But the hazard of the game, as I have already more than once had occasion to remark, constituted its great charm with the Spaniard. The brilliant achievements of his countrymen, on the like occasions, with means so inadequate, inspired him with confidence in his own good star; and this confidence was one source of his success. Had he faltered for a moment, had he stopped to calculate his chances, he must inevitably have failed; for the odds were too great to be combated by sober reason. They were only to be met triumphantly by the spirit of the knight-errant.

After crossing the smooth waters of the Piura, the little army continued to advance over a level district intersected by streams that descended from the neighboring Cordilleras. The face of the country was shagged over with forests of gigantic growth, and occasionally traversed by ridges of barren land, that seemed like shoots of the adjacent Andes, breaking up the surface of the region into little sequestered valleys of singular loveliness. The soil, though rarely watered by the rains of heaven, was naturally rich, and wherever it was refreshed with moisture, as on the margins of the streams, it was enamelled with the brightest verdure. The indus-

[1] Auditor.

try of the inhabitants, moreover, had turned these streams to the best account, and canals and aqueducts were seen crossing the low lands in all directions and spreading over the country, like a vast network, diffusing fertility and beauty around them. The air was scented with the sweet odors of flowers, and everywhere the eye was refreshed by the sight of orchards laden with unknown fruits and of fields waving with yellow grain and rich in luscious vegetables of every description that teem in the sunny clime of the equator. The Spaniards were among a people who had carried the refinements of husbandry to a greater extent than any yet found on the American continent; and, as they journeyed through this paradise of plenty, their condition formed a pleasant contrast to what they had before endured in the dreary wilderness of the mangroves.

Everywhere, too, they were received with confiding hospitality by the simple people; for which they were no doubt indebted, in a great measure, to their own inoffensive deportment. Every Spaniard seemed to be aware that his only chance of success lay in conciliating the good opinion of the inhabitants among whom he had so recklessly cast his fortunes. In most of the hamlets, and in every place of considerable size, some fortress was to be found, or royal caravansary, destined for the Inca on his progresses, the ample halls of which furnished abundant accommodations for the Spaniards, who were thus provided with quarters along their route at the charge of the very government which they were preparing to overturn.

On the fifth day after leaving San Miguel, Pizarro halted in one of these delicious valleys, to give his troops repose and to make a more complete inspection of them. Their number amounted in all to one hundred and seventy-seven, of which sixty-seven were cavalry. He mustered only three arquebusiers in his whole company, and a few crossbow-men, altogether not exceeding twenty. The troops were tolerably well equipped and in good condition. But the watchful eye of their commander noticed with uneasiness that, notwithstanding the general heartiness in the cause manifested by his followers, there were some among them whose countenances lowered with discontent and who, although they did not give vent to it in open murmurs, were far from moving with their wonted alacrity. He was aware that, if this spirit became contagious, it would be the ruin of the enterprise; and he thought it best to exterminate the gangrene at once, and at whatever cost, than to wait until it had infected the whole system. He came to an extraordinary resolution.

Calling his men together, he told them that "a crisis had now arrived in their affairs, which it demanded all their courage to meet. No man should think of going forward in the expedition who could not do so with his whole heart or who had the least misgiving as to its success. If any repented of his share in it, it was not too late to turn back. San Miguel was but poorly garrisoned, and he should be glad to see it in greater strength. Those who chose might return to this place, and they should be entitled to the same proportion of lands and Indian vassals as the present residents. With the rest, were they few or many, who chose to take their chance with him, he should pursue the adventure to the end."

It was certainly a remarkable proposal for a commander who was ignorant of the amount of disaffection in his ranks and who could not safely spare a single man from his force, already far too feeble for the undertaking. Yet, by insisting on the wants of the little colony of San Miguel, he afforded a decent pretext for the secession of the malcontents and swept away the barrier of shame which might have still held them in the camp. Notwithstanding the fair opening thus afforded, there were but few, nine in all, who availed themselves of the general's permission. Four of these belonged to the infantry, and five to the horse. The rest loudly declared their resolve to go forward with their brave leader; and, if there were some whose voices were faint amidst the general acclamation, they at least relinquished the right of complaining hereafter, since they had voluntarily rejected the permission to return. This stroke of policy in their sagacious captain was attended with the best effects. He had winnowed out the few grains of discontent which, if left to themselves, might have fermented in secret till the whole mass had swelled into mutiny. Cortes had compelled his men to go forward heartily in his enterprise by burning their vessels and thus cutting off the only means of retreat. Pizarro, on the other hand, threw open the gate to the disaffected and facilitated their departure. Both judged right, under their peculiar circumstances, and both were perfectly successful.

Feeling himself strengthened, instead of weakened, by his loss, Pizarro now resumed his march and on the second day arrived before a place called Zaran, situated in a fruitful valley among the mountains. Some of the inhabitants had been drawn off to swell the levies of Atahuallpa. The Spaniards had repeated experience on their march of the oppressive exactions of the Inca, who had almost depopulated some of the valleys to obtain reinforcements for his army. The *curaca* of the Indian town where Pizarro now arrived received him with kindness and hospitality, and the troops were quartered as usual in one of the royal *tambos,* or caravansaries, which were found in all the principal places.

Yet the Spaniards saw no signs of their approach to the royal encampment, though more time had already elapsed than was originally allowed for reaching it. Shortly before entering Zaran, Pizarro had heard that a Peruvian garrison was established in a place called Caxas, lying among the hills, at no great distance from his present quarters. He immediately despatched a small party under Hernando de Soto in that direction to reconnoitre the ground and bring him intelligence of the actual state of things at Zaran, where he would halt until his officer's return.

Day after day passed on, and a week had elapsed before tidings were received of his companions, and Pizarro was becoming seriously alarmed for their fate, when on the eighth morning de Soto appeared bringing with him an envoy from the Inca himself. He was a person of rank and was attended by several followers of inferior condition. He had met the Spaniards at Caxas and now accompanied them on their return to deliver his sovereign's message, with a present to the Spanish commander. The present consisted of two fountains made of stone, in the form of fortresses; some fine stuffs of woollen embroidered with gold and silver; and a quantity of goose-flesh, dried and seasoned in a peculiar manner, and much used as a perfume, in a pulverized state, by the Peruvian nobles. The Indian ambassador came charged also with his master's greeting to the strangers, whom Atahuallpa welcomed to his country and invited to visit him in his camp among the mountains.

Pizarro well understood that the Inca's object in this diplomatic visit was less to do him courtesy than to inform himself of the strength and condition of the invaders. But he was well pleased with the embassy and dissembled his consciousness of its real purpose. He caused the Peruvian to be entertained in the best manner the camp could afford and paid him the respect, says one of the Conquerors, due to the ambassador of so great a monarch. Pizarro urged him to prolong his visit for some days, which the Indian envoy declined, but made the most of his time while there by gleaning all the information he could in respect to the uses of every strange article which he saw, as well as the object of the white men's visit to the land and the quarter whence they came.

The Spanish captain satisfied his curiosity in all these particulars. The intercourse with the natives, it may be here remarked, was maintained by means of two of the youths who had accompanied the Conquerors on their return home from their preceding voyage. They had been taken by Pizarro to Spain, and as much pains had been bestowed on teaching them the Castilian, they now filled the office of interpreters and opened an easy communication with their countrymen. It was of inestimable service; and well did the Spanish commander reap the fruits of his forecast.

On the departure of the Peruvian messenger, Pizarro presented him with a cap of crimson cloth, some cheap but showy ornaments of glass, and other toys, which he had brought for the purpose from Castile. He charged the envoy to tell his master that the Spaniards came from a powerful prince who dwelt far beyond the waters; that they had heard much of the fame of Atahuallpa's victories and were come to pay their respects to him and to offer their services by aiding him with their arms against his enemies; and he might be assured they would not halt on the road longer than was necessary before presenting themselves before him.

Pizarro now received from de Soto a full account of his late expedition. That chief, on entering Caxas, found the inhabitants mustered in hostile array, as if to dispute his passage. But the cavalier soon convinced them of his pacific intentions, and, laying aside their menacing attitude, they received the Spaniards with the same courtesy which had been shown them in most places on their march.

Here de Soto found one of the royal officers, employed in collecting the tribute for the government. From this functionary he learned that the Inca was quartered with a large army at Caxamalca, a place of considerable size on the other side of the Cordilleras, where he was enjoying the luxury of the warm baths, supplied by natural springs, for which it was then famous, as it is at the present day. The cavalier gathered, also, much important information in regard to the resources and the general policy of the government, the state maintained by the Inca, and the stern severity with which obedience to the law was everywhere enforced. He had some opportunity of observing this for himself, as, on entering the village, he saw several Indians hanging dead by their heels, having been executed for some violence offered to the Virgins of the Sun, of whom there was a convent in the neighborhood.

From Caxas, de Soto had passed to the adjacent town of Guancabamba, much larger, more populous, and better built than the preceding. The houses, instead of being made of clay baked in the sun, were many of them constructed of solid stone, so nicely put together that it was impossible to detect the line of junction. A river which passed through the town was traversed by a bridge, and the high road of the Incas, which crossed this district, was far superior to that which the Spaniards had seen on the seaboard. It was raised in many places, like a causeway, paved with heavy stone flags and bordered by trees that afforded a grateful shade to the passenger, while streams of water were conducted through aqueducts along the sides to slake his thirst. At certain distances, also, they noticed small houses, which, they were told, were for the accommodation of the traveller, who might thus pass without inconvenience from one end of the kingdom to the other. In another quarter they beheld one of those magazines destined for the army, filled with grain and with articles of clothing; and at the entrance of the town was a stone building, occupied by a public officer, whose business it was to collect the tolls or duties on various commodities brought into the place or carried out of it. These accounts of de Soto not only confirmed all that the Spaniards had heard of the Indian empire, but greatly raised their ideas of its resources and domestic policy. They might well have shaken the confidence of hearts less courageous.

Pizarro, before leaving his present quarters, despatched a messenger to San Miguel with particulars of his movements, sending at the same time the articles received from the Inca, as well as those obtained at different places on the route. The skill shown in the execution of some of these fabrics sent to Castile excited great admiration there. The fine woollen cloths, especially, with their rich embroidery, were pronounced equal to textures of silk, from which it was not easy to distinguish them. The material was probably the delicate wool of the vicuña, none of which had then been seen in Europe.

Pizarro, having now acquainted himself with the most direct route to Caxamalca—the Caxamarca of the present day—resumed his march, taking a direction nearly south. The first place of any size at which he halted was Motupe, pleasantly situated in a fruitful valley, among hills of no great elevation, which cluster round the base of the Cordilleras. The place was deserted by its *curaca*, who, with three hundred of its warriors, had gone to join the standard of their Inca. Here the general, notwithstanding his avowed purpose to push forward without delay, halted four days. The tardiness of his movements can be explained only by the hope which he may have still entertained of being joined by further reinforcements before crossing the Cordilleras. None such appeared, however; and advancing across a country in which tracts of sandy plain were occasionally relieved by a broad expanse of verdant meadow, watered by natural streams and still more abundantly by those brought through artificial channels, the troops at length arrived at the borders of a river. It was broad and deep, and the rapidity of the current opposed more than ordinary difficulty to the passage. Pizarro, apprehensive lest this might be disputed by the natives on the opposite bank, ordered his brother Hernando to cross over with a small detachment under cover of night and secure a safe landing for the rest of the troops. At break of day Pizarro made preparations for his own passage by hewing timber in the neighboring woods and constructing a sort of floating bridge, on which before nightfall the whole company passed in safety, the horses swimming, being led by the bridle. It was a day of severe labor, and Pizarro took his own share in it freely, like a common soldier, having ever a word of encouragement to say to his followers.

On reaching the opposite side, they learned from their comrades that the people of the country, instead of offering resistance, had fled in dismay. One of them, having been taken and brought before Hernando Pizarro, refused to answer the questions put to him respecting the Inca and his army; till, being put to the torture, he stated that Atahuallpa was encamped with his whole force, in three separate divisions, occupying the high ground and plains of Caxamalca. He further stated that the Inca was aware of the approach of the white men, and of their small number, and that he was purposely decoying them into his own quarters that he might have them more completely in his power.

This account, when reported by Hernando to his brother, caused the latter much anxiety. As the timidity of the peasantry, however, gradually wore off, some of them mingled with the troops, and among them the *curaca,* or principal person of the village. He had himself visited the royal camp, and he informed the general that Atahuallpa lay at the strong town of Huamachuco, twenty leagues south of Caxamalca, with a large army of at least fifty thousand men.

These contradictory statements greatly perplexed the chieftain; and he proposed to one of the Indians who had borne him company during a great part of the march to go as a spy into the Inca's quarters and bring him intelligence of his actual position and, as far as he could learn them, of his intentions towards the Spaniards. But the man positively declined this dangerous service, though he professed his willingness to go as an authorized messenger of the Spanish commander.

Pizarro acquiesced in this proposal and instructed his envoy to assure the Inca that he was advancing with all convenient speed to meet him. He was to acquaint the monarch with the uniformly considerate conduct of the Spaniards towards his subjects in their progress through the land and to assure him that they were now coming in full confidence of finding in him the same amicable feelings towards themselves. The emissary was particularly instructed to observe if the strong passes on the road were defended or if any preparations of a hostile character were to be discovered. This last intelligence he was to communicate to the general by means of two or three nimble-footed attendants, who were to accompany him on his mission.

Having taken this precaution, the wary commander again resumed his march and at the end of three days reached the base of the mountain rampart behind which lay the ancient town of Caxamalca. Before him rose the stupendous Andes, rock piled upon rock, their skirts below dark with evergreen forests, varied here and there by terraced patches of cultivated garden, with the peasant's cottage clinging to their shaggy sides and their crests of snow glittering high in the heavens—presenting altogether such a wild chaos of magnificence and beauty as no other mountain scenery in the world can show. Across this tremendous rampart, through a labyrinth of passes, easily capable of defence by a handful of men against an army, the troops were now to march. To the right ran a broad and level road, with its border of friendly shades, and wide enough for two carriages to pass abreast. It was one of the great routes leading to Cuzco and seemed by its pleasant and easy access to invite the wayworn soldier to choose it in preference to the dangerous mountain defiles. Many were accordingly of opinion that the army should take this course and abandon the original destination to Caxamalca. But such was not the decision of Pizarro.

The Spaniards had everywhere proclaimed their purpose, he said, to visit the Inca in his camp. This purpose had been communicated to the Inca himself. To take an opposite direction now would only be to draw on them the imputation of cowardice and to incur Atahuallpa's contempt. No alternative remained but to march straight across the sierra to his quarters. "Let every one of you," said the bold cavalier, "take heart and go forward like a good soldier, nothing daunted by the smallness of your numbers. For in the greatest extremity God ever fights for his own; and doubt not He will humble the pride of the heathen, and bring him to the knowledge of the true faith, the great end and object of the Conquest."

Pizarro, like Cortes, possessed a good share of that frank and manly eloquence which touches the heart of the soldier more than the parade of rhetoric or the finest flow of elocution. He was a soldier himself and partook in all the feelings of the soldier—his joys, his hopes, and his disappointments. He was not raised by rank and education above sympathy with the humblest of his followers. Every chord in their bosoms vibrated with the same pulsations as his own, and the conviction of this gave him a mastery over them. "Lead on," they shouted, as he finished his brief but animating address, "lead on wherever you think best. We will follow with good-will, and you shall see that we can do our duty in the cause of God and the King!" There was no longer hesitation. All thoughts were now bent on the instant passage of the Cordilleras.

*5. Massacre of the Indians and the Capture of the Inca**

[Pizarro's small force was allowed to pass on its way unmolested. They crossed through part of the Andes and approached Atahuallpa and his army of some 30,000 men on the plateau at Caxamalca. Pizarro's forces entered the city on 15 November, 1532. Their position was, needless to say, somewhat precarious. A desperate plan to seize the Inca by surprise and to massacre his troops was evolved, Pizarro being no doubt influenced in formulating it by the action of Cortes in seizing Montezuma in Tenochtitlan. The Inca Atahuallpa was invited to visit Pizarro in the town. There, both horse and foot soldiers had been concealed to effect an ambush on the giving of a signal.]

It was late in the day before any movement was visible in the Peruvian camp, where much preparation was making to approach the Christian quarters with due state and ceremony. A message was received from Atahuallpa, informing the Spanish commander that he should come with his warriors fully armed, in the same manner as the Spaniards had come to his quarters the night preceding. This was not an agreeable intimation to Pizarro, though he had no reason, probably, to expect the contrary. But to object might imply distrust or perhaps disclose, in some measure, his own designs. He expressed his satisfaction, therefore, at the intelligence, assuring the Inca that, come as he would, he would be received by him as a friend and brother.

* From *The Conquest of Peru,* Book III, chap. 5.

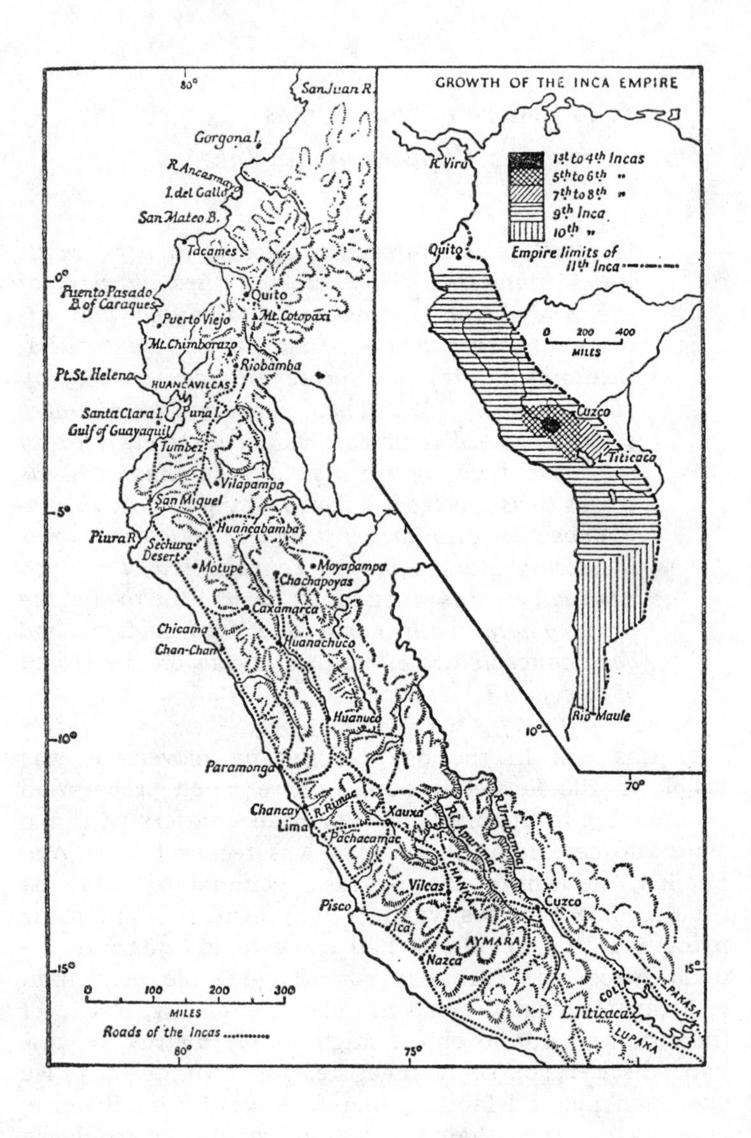
GROWTH OF THE INCA EMPIRE
1st to 4th Incas
5th to 6th
7th to 8th
9th Inca
10th
Empire limits of 11th Inca
MILES
R. Viru
Quito
Cuzco
L. Titicaca
Rio Maule
San Juan R.
Gorgona I.
R. Ancasmayo
I. del Gallo
San Mateo B.
Tacames
Puento Pasado
B. of Caraques
Quito
Puerto Viejo
Mt. Cotopaxi
Mt. Chimborazo
Riobamba
Pt. St. Helena
HUANCAVILCAS
Santa Clara I.
Puna I.
Gulf of Guayaquil
Tumbez
Vilapampa
San Miguel
Huancabamba
Piura R.
Sechura Desert
Motupe
Moyapampa
Chachapoyas
Caxamarca
Chicama
Chan-Chan
Huanachuco
Huanuco
Paramonga
Chancay
R. Rimac
Xauxa
Lima
Pachacamac
R. Apurimac
R. Urubamba
CHANKA
Vilcas
Pisco
Cuzco
Ica
AYMARA
Nazca
COLLA
PAKASA
L. Titicaca
LUPAKA
MILES
Roads of the Incas

It was noon before the Indian procession was on its march, when it was seen occupying the great causeway for a long extent. In front came a large body of attendants, whose office seemed to be to sweep away every particle of rubbish from the road. High above the crowd appeared the Inca, borne on the shoulders of his principal nobles, while others of the same rank marched by the sides of his litter, displaying such a dazzling show of ornaments on their persons that, in the language of one of the Conquerors, "they blazed like the sun." But the greater part of the Inca's forces mustered along the fields that lined the road, and were spread over the broad meadows as far as the eye could reach.

When the royal procession had arrived within half a mile of the city, it came to a halt; and Pizarro saw with surprise that Atahuallpa was preparing to pitch his tents, as if to encamp there. A messenger soon after arrived, informing the Spaniards that the Inca would occupy his present station the ensuing night and enter the city on the following morning.

This intelligence greatly disturbed Pizarro, who had shared in the general impatience of his men at the tardy movements of the Peruvians. The troops had been under arms since daylight, the cavalry mounted, and the infantry at their post, waiting in silence the coming of the Inca. A profound stillness reigned throughout the town, broken only at intervals by the cry of the sentinel from the summit of the fortress, as he proclaimed the movements of the Indian army. Nothing, Pizarro well knew, was so trying to the soldier as prolonged suspense in a critical situation like the present; and he feared lest his ardor might evaporate and be succeeded by that nervous feeling natural to the bravest soul at such a crisis, and which, if not fear, is near akin to it. He returned an answer, therefore, to Atahuallpa, deprecating his change of purpose; and adding that he had provided everything for his entertainment and expected him that night to sup with him.

This message turned the Inca from his purpose; and, striking his tents again, he resumed his march, first advising the general that he should leave the greater part of his warriors behind and enter the place with only a few of them, and without arms, as he preferred to pass the night at Caxamalca. At the same time he ordered accommodations to be provided for himself and his retinue in one of the large stone buildings, called, from a serpent sculptured on the walls, "the House of the Serpent." No tidings could have been more grateful to the Spaniards. It seemed as if the Indian monarch was eager to rush into the snare that had been spread for him! The fanatical cavalier could not fail to discern in it the immediate finger of Providence.

It is difficult to account for the wavering conduct of Atahuallpa, so different from the bold and decided character which history ascribes to him. There is no doubt that he made his visit to the white men in perfect good faith; though Pizarro was probably right in conjecturing that this amiable disposition stood on a very precarious footing. There is as little reason to suppose that he distrusted the sincerity of the strangers; or he would not thus unnecessarily have proposed to visit them unarmed. His original purpose of coming with all his force was doubtless to display his royal state and perhaps, also, to show greater respect for the Spaniards; but when he consented to accept their hospitality and pass the night in their quarters, he was willing to dispense with a great part of his armed soldiery and visit them in a manner that implied entire confidence in their good faith. He was too absolute in his own empire easily to suspect; and he probably could not comprehend the audacity with which a few men, like those now assembled in Caxamalca, meditated an assault on a powerful monarch in the midst of his victorious army. He did not know the character of the Spaniard.

It was not long before sunset when the van of the royal procession entered the gates of the city. First came some hundreds of the menials, employed to clear the path of every obstacle and singing songs of triumph as they came, "which, in our ears," says one of the Conquerors, "sounded like the songs of hell!" Then followed other bodies of different ranks and dressed in different liveries. Some wore a showy stuff, checkered white and red, like the squares of a chess-board. Others were clad in pure white, bearing hammers or maces of silver or copper; and the guards, together with those in immediate attendance on the prince, were distinguished by a rich azure livery and a profusion of gay ornaments, while the large pendants attached to the ears indicated the Peruvian noble.

Elevated high above his vassals came the Inca Atahuallpa, borne on a sedan, or open litter, on which was a sort of throne made of massive gold of inestimable value. The palanquin was lined with the richly colored plumes of tropical birds and studded with shining plates of gold and silver. The monarch's attire was much richer than on the preceding evening. Round his neck was suspended a collar of emeralds of uncommon size and brilliancy. His short hair was decorated with golden ornaments, and the imperial *borla*[1] encircled his temples. The bearing of the Inca was sedate and dignified; and from his lofty station he looked down on the multitudes below with an air of composure, like one accustomed to command.

As the landing files of the procession entered the great square, larger, says an old chronicler, than any square in Spain, they opened to the right and left for the royal retinue to pass. Everything was conducted with admirable order. The monarch was permitted to traverse the plaza in silence, and not a Spaniard was to be seen. When some five or six thousand of his people had entered the place, Atahuallpa halted and, turning round with an inquiring look, demanded, "Where are the strangers?"

At this moment Fray Vicente de Valverde, a Dominican friar, Pizarro's chaplain, and afterwards bishop of Cuzco, came forward with his breviary or, as other accounts say, a Bible, in one hand and a crucifix in the other, and, approaching the Inca, told him, that he came by order of his commander to expound to him the doctrines of the true faith, for which purpose the Span-

[1] Prescott here refers to the insignia of authority, the *mascapaicha,* a colored braid wound around the head.

iards had come from a great distance to his country. The friar then explained, as clearly as he could, the mysterious doctrine of the Trinity and, ascending high in his account began with the creation of man, thence passed to his fall, to his subsequent redemption by Jesus Christ, to the crucifixion, and the ascension, when the Savior left the Apostle Peter as his Viceregent upon earth. This power had been transmitted to the successors of the Apostle, good and wise men, who, under the title of Popes, held authority over all powers and potentates on earth. One of the last of these Popes had commissioned the Spanish emperor, the most mighty monarch in the world, to conquer and convert the natives of this Western Hemisphere; and his general, Francisco Pizarro, had now come to execute this important mission. The friar concluded with beseeching the Peruvian monarch to receive him kindly, to abjure the errors of his own faith, and embrace that of the Christians now proffered to him, the only one by which he could hope for salvation, and, furthermore, to acknowledge himself a tributary of the Emperor Charles the Fifth, who, in that event, would aid and protect him as his loyal vassal.

Whether Atahuallpa possessed himself of every link in the curious chain of argument by which the monk connected Pizarro with St. Peter may be doubted. It is certain, however, that he must have had very incorrect notions of the Trinity, if, as Garcilasso[1] states, the interpreter Felipillo explained it by saying that "the Christians believed in three Gods and one God, and that made four." But there is no doubt he perfectly comprehended that the drift of the discourse was to persuade him to resign his sceptre and acknowledge the supremacy of another.

The eyes of the Indian monarch flashed fire, and his dark brow grew darker as he replied, "I will be no man's tributary. I am greater than any prince upon earth. Your emperor may be a great prince; I do not doubt it,

---

[1] Garcilasso de la Vega (1540–1616), author of *The Royal Commentaries*, an important work on Peru. His father was a Spaniard, but his mother was of the Indian royal blood, being the niece of the Inca Huayna Capac.

when I see that he has sent his subjects so far across the waters; and I am willing to hold him as a brother. As for the Pope of whom you speak, he must be crazy to talk of giving away countries which do not belong to him. For my faith," he continued, "I will not change it. Your own God, as you say, was put to death by the very men whom he created. But mine," he concluded, pointing to his Deity—then, alas! sinking in glory behind the mountains—"my God still lives in the heavens and looks down on his children."

He then demanded of Valverde by what authority he had said these things. The friar pointed to the book which he held as his authority. Atahuallpa, taking it, turned over the pages a moment; then, as the insult he had received probably flashed across his mind, he threw it down with vehemence and exclaimed, "Tell your comrades that they shall give me an account of their doings in my land. I will not go from here till they have made me full satisfaction for all the wrongs they have committed."

The friar, greatly scandalized by the indignity offered to the sacred volume, stayed only to pick it up and, hastening to Pizarro, informed him of what had been done, exclaiming, at the same time, "Do you not see that while we stand here wasting our breath in talking with this dog, full of pride as he is, the fields are filling with Indians? Set on, at once; I absolve you." Pizarro saw that the hour had come. He waved a white scarf in the air, the appointed signal. The fatal gun was fired from the fortress. Then, springing into the square, the Spanish captain and his followers shouted the old war-cry of "St. Jago and at them." It was answered by the battle-cry of every Spaniard in the city, as, rushing from the avenues of the great halls in which they were concealed, they poured into the plaza, horse and foot, each in his own dark column, and threw themselves into the midst of the Indian crowd. The latter, taken by surprise, stunned by the report of artillery and muskets, the echoes of which reverberated like the thunder from the surrounding buildings, and blinded by the smoke which rolled in sulphurous volumes along the square, were seized with a panic. They knew not whither to fly for refuge from the coming ruin. Nobles and commoners—all were trampled down under the fierce charge of the cavalry, who dealt their blows, right and left, without sparing; while their swords, flashing through the thick gloom, carried dismay into the hearts of the wretched natives, who now for the first time saw the horse and his rider in all their terrors. They made no resistance, as, indeed, they had no weapons with which to make it. Every avenue to escape was closed, for the entrance to the square was choked up with the dead bodies of men who had perished in vain efforts to fly; and such was the agony of the survivors under the terrible pressure of their assailants that a large body of Indians, by their convulsive struggles, burst through the wall of stone and dried clay which formed part of the boundary of the plaza! It fell, leaving an opening of more than a hundred paces, through which multitudes now found their way into the country, still hotly pursued by the cavalry, who, leaping the fallen rubbish, hung on the rear of the fugitives, striking them down in all directions.

Meanwhile the fight, or rather massacre, continued hot around the Inca, whose person was the great object of the assault. His faithful nobles, rallying about him, threw themselves in the way of the assailants and strove, by tearing them from their saddles or at least by offering their own bosoms as a mark for their vengeance, to shield their beloved master. It is said by some authorities that they carried weapons concealed under their clothes. If so, it availed them little, as it is not pretended that they used them. But the most timid animal will defend itself when at bay. That the Indians did not do so in the present instance is proof that they had no weapons to use. Yet they still continued to force back the cavaliers, clinging to their horses with dying grasp, and, as one was cut down, another taking the place of his fallen comrade with a loyalty truly affecting.

The Indian monarch, stunned and bewildered, saw his faithful subjects falling around him without fully comprehending his situation. The litter on which he rode heaved to and fro, as the mighty press swayed backwards and forwards; and he gazed on the overwhelming ruin, like some forlorn mariner who, tossed about in his bark by the furious elements, sees the lightning's flash and hears the thunder bursting around him with the consciousness that he can do nothing to avert his fate. At length, weary with the work of destruction, the Spaniards, as the shades of evening grew deeper, felt afraid that the royal prize might, after all, elude them; and some of the cavaliers made a desperate attempt to end the affray at once by taking Atahuallpa's life. But Pizarro, who was nearest his person, called out with stentorian voice, "Let no one who values his life strike at the Inca"; and, stretching out his arm to shield him, received a wound on the hand from one of his own men—the only wound received by a Spaniard in the action.

The struggle now became fiercer than ever round the royal litter. It reeled more and more, and, at length, several of the nobles who supported it having been slain, it was overturned, and the Indian prince would have come with violence to the ground had not his fall been broken by the efforts of Pizarro and some other of the cavaliers, who caught him in their arms. The imperial *borla* was instantly snatched from his temples by a soldier named Estete, and the unhappy monarch, strongly secured, was removed to a neighboring building, where he was carefully guarded.

All attempts at resistance now ceased. The fate of the Inca soon spread over town and country. The charm which might have held the Peruvians together was dissolved. Every man thought only of his own safety. Even the soldiery encamped on the adjacent fields took the alarm and, learning the fatal tidings, were seen flying in every direction before their pursuers, who in the heat of triumph showed no touch of mercy. At length night, more pitiful than man, threw her friendly mantle over the fugitives, and the scattered troops of Pizarro rallied once more at the sound of the trumpet in the bloody square of Caxamalca.

*6. The Execution of Atahuallpa**

[*Atahuallpa was originally treated with some respect in his captivity. He was attended by both his nobles and his women. While the pacification of the country by the Spanish conquerors continued, the Inca attempted to buy his freedom by promising to fill the room in which he was kept with gold and silver to the height he could reach with his outstretched hand. This seemingly fantastic promise, which provided the Spaniards with so much of the material reward they had desired, was, in fact, fulfilled. In excess of 13,000 pounds of gold and 26,000 pounds of silver were turned over to the greedy conquerors. Yet when this was done, there remained the problem of what to do with the Inca who had now earned his release. The Spaniards, motivated more by expediency than by anything else, decided to remove him in the quickest possible fashion. The Inca was accused of a treasonous attempt to cause an uprising of the Indians to be led by his general Challcuchima.*]

The rumors of a rising among the natives pointed to Atahuallpa as the author of it. Challcuchima was examined on the subject, but avowed his entire ignorance of any such design, which he pronounced a malicious slander. Pizarro next laid the matter before the Inca himself, repeating to him the stories in circulation, with the air of one who believed them. "What treason is this," said the general, "that you have meditated against

* From *The Conquest of Peru*, Book III, chap. 7.

me—me, who have ever treated you with honor, confiding in your words, as in those of a brother?" "You jest," replied the Inca, who perhaps did not feel the weight of this confidence; "you are always jesting with me. How could I or my people think of conspiring against men so valiant as the Spaniards? Do not jest with me thus, I beseech you." "This," continues Pizarro's secretary, "he said in the most composed and natural manner, smiling all the while to dissemble his falsehood, so that we were all amazed to find such cunning in a barbarian."

But it was not with cunning but with the consciousness of innocence, as the event afterwards proved, that Atahuallpa thus spoke to Pizarro. He readily discerned, however, the causes, perhaps the consequences, of the accusation. He saw a dark gulf opening beneath his feet; and he was surrounded by strangers, on none of whom he could lean for counsel or protection. The life of the captive monarch is usually short; and Atahuallpa might have learned the truth of this, when he thought of Huascar.[1] Bitterly did he now lament the absence of Hernando Pizarro for, strange as it may seem, the haughty spirit of this cavalier had been touched by the condition of the royal prisoner, and he had treated him with a deference which won for him the peculiar regard and confidence of the Indian. Yet the latter lost no time in endeavoring to efface the general's suspicions and to establish his own innocence. "Am I not," said he to Pizarro, "a poor captive in your hands? How could I harbor the designs you impute to me, when I should be the first victim of the outbreak? And you little know my people, if you think that such a movement would be made without my orders; when the very birds in my dominions," said he, with somewhat of an hyperbole, "would scarcely venture to fly contrary to my will."

But these protestations of innocence had little effect on the troops, among whom the story of a general rising of the natives continued to gain credit every hour.

[1] Inca from 1525 to 1532, Huascar was overthrown by Atahuallpa and later killed by his successor's orders.

A large force, it was said, was already gathered at Huamachuco, not a hundred miles from the camp, and their assault might be hourly expected. The treasure which the Spaniards had acquired afforded a tempting prize, and their own alarm was increased by the apprehension of losing it. The patrols were doubled. The horses were kept saddled and bridled. The soldiers slept on their arms; Pizarro went the rounds regularly to see that every sentinel was on his post. The little army, in short, was in a state of preparation for instant attack.

Men suffering from fear are not likely to be too scrupulous as to the means of removing the cause of it. Murmurs, mingled with gloomy menaces, were now heard against the Inca, the author of these machinations. Many began to demand his life, as necessary to the safety of the army. Among these the most vehement were Almagro and his followers. They had not witnessed the seizure of Atahuallpa. They had no sympathy with him in his fallen state. They regarded him only as an encumbrance, and their desire now was to push their fortunes in the country, since they had got so little of the gold of Caxamalca. They were supported by Riquelme, the treasurer, and by the rest of the royal officers. These men had been left at San Miguel by Pizarro, who did not care to have such official spies on his movements. But they had come to the camp with Almagro, and they loudly demanded the Inca's death as indispensable to the tranquillity of the country and the interest of the Crown.

To these dark suggestions Pizarro turned—or seemed to turn—an unwilling ear, showing visible reluctance to proceed to extreme measures with his prisoner. There were some few, and among others Hernando de Soto, who supported him in these views and who regarded such measures as not at all justified by the evidence of Atahuallpa's guilt. In this state of things, the Spanish commander determined to send a small detachment to Huamachuco to reconnoitre the country and ascertain what ground there was for the rumors of an insurrection. De Soto was placed at the head of the expedition, which, as the distance was not great, would occupy but a few days.

After that cavalier's departure, the agitation among the soldiers, instead of diminishing, increased to such a degree that Pizarro, unable to resist their importunities, consented to bring Atahuallpa to instant trial. It was but decent, and certainly safer, to have the forms of a trial. A court was organized, over which the two captains, Pizarro and Almagro, were to preside as judges. An attorney-general was named to prosecute for the Crown, and counsel was assigned to the prisoner.

The charges preferred against the Inca, drawn up in the form of interrogatories, were twelve in number. The most important were: that he had usurped the crown and assassinated his brother Huascar; that he had squandered public revenues since the conquest of the country by the Spaniards and lavished them on his kindred and his minions; that he was guilty of idolatry and of adulterous practices, indulging openly in a plurality of wives; finally, that he had attempted to excite an insurrection against the Spaniards.

These charges, most of which had reference to national usages or to the personal relations of the Inca, over which the Spanish conquerors had clearly no jurisdiction, are so absurd that they might well provoke a smile, did they not excite a deeper feeling. The last of the charges was the only one of moment in such a trial; and the weakness of this may be inferred from the care taken to bolster it up with the others. The mere specification of the articles must have been sufficient to show that the doom of the Inca was already sealed.

A number of Indian witnesses were examined, and their testimony, filtrated through the interpretation of Felipillo, received, it is said, when necessary, a very different coloring from that of the original. The examination was soon ended, and "a warm discussion," as we are assured by one of Pizarro's own secretaries, "took place in respect to the probable good or evil that would result from the death of Atahuallpa." It was a question of expediency. He was found guilty—whether of all the crimes alleged we are not informed—and he was sentenced to be burnt alive in the great square of Caxamalca. The sentence was to be carried into execution that very night. They were not even to wait for the return of de Soto, when the information he would bring would go far to establish the truth or the falsehood of the reports respecting the insurrection of the natives. It was desirable to obtain the countenance of Father Valverde to these proceedings, and a copy of the judgment was submitted to the friar for his signature; which he gave without hesitation, declaring that, "in his opinion, the Inca, at all events, deserved death."

Yet there were some few in that martial conclave who resisted these high-handed measures. They considered them as a poor requital of all the favors bestowed on them by the Inca, who hitherto had received at their hands nothing but wrong. They objected to the evidence as wholly insufficient; and they denied the authority of such a tribunal to sit in judgment on a sovereign prince in the heart of his own dominions. If he were to be tried, he should be sent to Spain, and his cause brought before the Emperor, who alone had power to determine it.

But the great majority—and they were ten to one—overruled these objections by declaring there was no doubt of Atahuallpa's guilt, and they were willing to assume the responsibility of his punishment. A full account of the proceedings would be sent to Castile, and the Emperor should be informed who were the loyal servants of the Crown and who were its enemies. The dispute ran so high that for a time it menaced an open and violent rupture; till, at length, convinced that resistance was fruitless, the weaker party, silenced, but not satisfied, contented themselves with entering a written protest against these proceedings, which would leave an indelible stain on the names of all concerned in them.

When the sentence was communicated to the Inca, he was greatly overcome by it. He had, indeed, for some time, looked to such an issue as probable and had been heard to intimate as much to those about him. But the probability of such an event is very different from its certainty—and that, too, so sudden and speedy. For a moment, the overwhelming conviction of it unmanned him, and he exclaimed, with tears in his eyes, "What have I done, or my children, that I should meet such a fate? And from your hands, too," said he, addressing Pizarro; "you, who have met with friendship and kindness from my people, with whom I have shared my treasures, who have received nothing but benefits from my hands!" In the most piteous tones, he then implored that his life might be spared, promising any guaranty that might be required for the safety of every Spaniard in the army—promising double the ransom he had already paid, if time were only given him to obtain it.

An eyewitness assures us that Pizarro was visibly affected, as he turned away from the Inca, to whose appeal he had no power to listen, in opposition to the voice of the army and to his own sense of what was due to the security of the country. Atahuallpa, finding he had no power to turn his Conqueror from his purpose, recovered his habitual self-possession and from that moment submitted himself to his fate with the courage of an Indian warrior.

The doom of the Inca was proclaimed by sound of trumpet in the great square of Caxamalca; and, two hours after sunset, the Spanish soldiery assembled by torch-light in the plaza to witness the execution of the sentence. It was on the twenty-ninth of August, 1533. Atahuallpa was led out chained hand and foot—for he had been kept in irons ever since the great excitement had prevailed in the army respecting an assault. Father Vicente de Valverde was at his side, striving to administer consolation and, if possible, to persuade him at this last hour to abjure his superstition and embrace the religion of his Conquerors. He was willing to save the soul of his victim from the terrible expiation in the next world to which he had so cheerfully consigned his mortal part in this.

During Atahuallpa's confinement, the friar had repeatedly expounded to him the Christian doctrines, and the Indian monarch discovered much acuteness in apprehending the discourse of his teacher. But it had not carried conviction to his mind, and though he listened with patience, he had shown no disposition to renounce the faith of his fathers. The Dominican made a last appeal to him in this solemn hour; and, when Atahuallpa was bound to the stake, with the fagots that were to kindle his funeral pile lying around him, Valverde, holding up the cross, besought him to embrace it and be baptized, promising that, by so doing, the painful death to which he had been sentenced should be commuted for the milder form of the *garrote*—a mode of punishment by strangulation, used for criminals in Spain.

The unhappy monarch asked if this were really so, and, on its being confirmed by Pizarro, he consented to abjure his own religion and receive baptism. The ceremony was performed by Father Valverde, and the new convert received the name of Juan de Atahuallpa, the name of Juan being conferred in honor of John the Baptist, on whose day the event took place.

Atahuallpa expressed a desire that his remains might be transported to Quito, the place of his birth, to be preserved with those of his maternal ancestors. Then turning to Pizarro, as a last request, he implored him to take compassion on his young children and receive them under his protection. Was there no other one in that dark company who stood grimly around him to whom he could look for the protection of his offspring? Perhaps he thought there was no other so competent to afford it and that the wishes so solemnly expressed in that hour might meet with respect even from his Conqueror. Then, recovering his stoical bearing, which for a moment had been shaken, he submitted himself calmly to his fate—while the Spaniards, gathering around, muttered their *credos* for the salvation of his soul! Thus by the death of a vile malefactor perished the last of the Incas!

I have already spoken of the person and the qualities of Atahuallpa. He had a handsome countenance, though with an expression somewhat too fierce to be pleasing. His frame was muscular and well-proportioned; his air commanding; and his deportment in the Spanish quarters had a degree of refinement, the more interesting that it was touched with melancholy. He is accused of having been cruel in his wars and bloody in his revenge. It may be true, but the pencil of an enemy would be likely to overcharge the shadows of the portrait. He is allowed to have been bold, high-minded, and liberal. All agree that he showed singular penetration and quickness of perception. His exploits as a warrior had placed his valor beyond dispute. The best homage to it is the reluctance shown by the Spaniards to restore him to freedom. They dreaded him as an enemy, and they had done him too many wrongs to think that he could be their friend. Yet his conduct towards them from the first had been most friendly; and they repaid it with imprisonment, robbery, and death.

The body of the Inca remained on the place of execution through the night. The following morning it was removed to the church of San Francisco, where his funeral obsequies were performed with great solemnity. Pizarro and the principal cavaliers went into mourning, and the troops listened with devout attention to the service of the dead from the lips of Father Valverde. The ceremony was interrupted by the sound of loud cries and wailing, as of many voices at the doors of the church. These were suddenly thrown open, and a number of Indian women, the wives and sisters of the deceased, rushing up the great aisle, surrounded the corpse. This was not the way, they cried, to celebrate the funeral rites of an Inca; and they declared their intention to sacrifice themselves on his tomb and bear him company to the land of spirits. The audience, outraged by this frantic behavior, told the intruders that Atahuallpa had died in the faith of a Christian, and that the God of the Christians abhorred such sacrifices. They then caused the women to be excluded from the church, and several, retiring to their own quarters, laid violent hands on themselves, in the vain hope of accompanying their beloved lord to the bright mansions of the Sun.

Atahuallpa's remains, notwithstanding his request, were laid in the cemetery of San Francisco. But from thence, as is reported, after the Spaniards left Caxamalca, they were secretly removed, and carried, as he had desired, to Quito. The colonists of a later time supposed that some treasures might have been buried with the body. But, on excavating the ground, neither treasure nor remains were to be discovered.

A day or two after these tragic events, Hernando de Soto returned from his excursion. Great was his astonishment and indignation at learning what had been done in his absence. He sought out Pizarro at once and found him, says the chronicler, "with a great felt hat, by way of mourning, slouched over his eyes," and in his dress and demeanor exhibiting all the show of sorrow. "You have acted rashly," said de Soto to him bluntly; "Atahuallpa has been basely slandered. There was no enemy at Huamachuco; no rising among the natives. I have met with nothing on the road but demonstrations of good-will, and all is quiet. If it was necessary to bring the Inca to trial, he should have been taken to Castile and judged by the Emperor. I would have pledged myself to see him safe on board the vessel." Pizarro confessed that he had been precipitate and said that he had been deceived by Riquelme, Valverde, and the others. These charges soon reached the ears of the treasurer and the Dominican, who, in their turn, exculpated themselves and upbraided Pizarro to his face as the only one responsible for the deed. The dispute ran high; and the parties were heard by the by-standers to give one another the lie! This vulgar squabble among the leaders, so soon after the event, is the best commentary on the iniquity of their own proceedings and the innocence of the Inca.

The treatment of Atahuallpa, from the first to last, forms undoubtedly one of the darkest chapters in Spanish history. There may have been massacres perpetrated on a more extended scale and executions accompanied with a greater refinement of cruelty. But the blood-stained annals of the Conquest afford no such example of cold-hearted and systematic persecution, not of an enemy but of one whose whole deportment had been that of a friend and a benefactor.

From the hour that Pizarro and his followers had entered within the sphere of Atahuallpa's influence, the hand of friendship had been extended to them by the natives. Their first act, on crossing the mountains, was to kidnap the monarch and massacre his people. The seizure of his person might be vindicated by those who considered the end as justifying the means, on the ground that it was indispensable to secure the triumphs of the Cross. But no such apology can be urged for the massacre of the unarmed and helpless population—as wanton as it was wicked.

The long confinement of the Inca had been used by the Conquerors to wring from him his treasures with the hard grip of avarice. During the whole of this dismal period, he had conducted himself with singular generosity and good faith. He had opened a free passage to the Spaniards through every part of his empire and had furnished every facility for the execution of their plans. When these were accomplished, and he remained an encumbrance on their hands, notwithstanding their engagement, expressed or implied, to release him—and Pizarro, as we have seen, by a formal act acquitted his captive of any further obligation on the score of the ransom—he was arraigned before a mock tribunal and, under pretences equally false and frivolous, was condemned to an excruciating death. From first to last, the policy of the Spanish conquerors towards their unhappy victim is stamped with barbarity and fraud.

It is not easy to acquit Pizarro of being in a great degree responsible for this policy. His partisans have labored to show that it was forced on him by the necessity of the case and that in the death of the Inca, especially, he yielded reluctantly to the importunities of others. But, weak as is this apology, the historian who has the means of comparing the various testimony of the period will come to a different conclusion. To him it will appear that Pizarro had probably long felt the removal of Atahuallpa as essential to the success of his enterprise. He foresaw the odium that would be incurred by the death of his royal captive without sufficient grounds; while he labored to establish these, he still shrunk from the responsibility of the deed and preferred to perpetrate it in obedience to the suggestions of others, rather than his own. Like many an unprincipled politician, he wished to reap the benefit of a bad act and let others take the blame of it.

Almagro and his followers are reported by Pizarro's secretaries to have first insisted on the Inca's death. They were loudly supported by the treasurer and the royal officers, who considered it as indispensable to the interests of the Crown; and finally, the rumors of a conspiracy raised the same cry among the soldiers, and Pizarro, with all his tenderness for his prisoner, could not refuse to bring him to trial. The form of a trial was necessary to give an appearance of fairness to the proceedings. That it was only form is evident from the indecent haste with which it was conducted—the examination of evidence, the sentence, and the execution being all on the same day. The multiplication of the charges, designed to place the guilt of the accused on the strongest ground, had, from their very number, the opposite effect, proving only the determination to convict him. If Pizarro had felt the reluctance to his conviction which he pretended, why did he send de Soto, Atahuallpa's best friend, away when the inquiry was to be instituted? Why was the sentence so summarily executed as not to afford opportunity, by that cavalier's return, of disproving the truth of the principal charge—the only one, in fact, with which the Spaniards had any concern? The solemn farce of mourning and deep sorrow affected by Pizarro, who by these honors to the dead would intimate the sincere regard he had entertained for the living, was too thin a veil to impose on the most credulous.

It is not intended by these reflections to exculpate the rest of the army, and especially its officers, from their share in the infamy of the transaction. But Pizarro, as commander of the army, was mainly responsible for its measures. For he was not a man to allow his own authority to be wrested from his grasp, or to yield timidly to the impulses of others. He did not even yield to his own. His whole career shows him, whether for good or for evil, to have acted with a cool and calculating policy.

A story has been often repeated which refers the motives of Pizarro's conduct, in some degree at least, to personal resentment. The Inca had requested of the Spanish soldiers to write the name of God on his nail. This the monarch showed to several of his guards successively, and, as they read it, and each pronounced the same word, the sagacious mind of the barbarian was delighted with what seemed to him little short of a miracle—to which the science of his own nation afforded no analogy. On showing the writing to Pizarro, that chief remained silent; and the Inca, finding he could not read, conceived a contempt for the commander who was even less informed than his soldiers. This he did not wholly conceal, and Pizarro, aware of the cause of it, neither forgot nor forgave it. The anecdote is reported not on the highest authority. It may be true; but it is unnecessary to look for the motives of Pizarro's conduct in personal pique when so many proofs are to be discerned of a dark and deliberate policy.

Yet the arts of the Spanish chieftain failed to reconcile his countrymen to the atrocity of his proceedings. It is singular to observe the difference between the tone assumed by the first chroniclers of the transaction, while it was yet fresh, and that of those who wrote when the lapse of a few years had shown the tendency of public opinion. The first boldly avow the deed as demanded by expediency, if not necessity; while they deal in no measured terms of reproach with the character of their unfortunate victim. The latter, on the other hand, while they extenuate the errors of the Inca and do justice to his good faith, are unreserved in their condemnation of the Conquerors, on whose conduct, they say, Heaven set the seal of its own reprobation by bringing them all to an untimely and miserable end. The sentence of contemporaries has been fully ratified by that of posterity; and the persecution of Atahuallpa is regarded with justice as having left a stain, never to be effaced, on the Spanish arms in the New World.

*7. The Civil Wars of the Conquerors: The Murder of Pizarro**

[The aftermath of the conquest of Peru is a sordid tale. The Spanish conquerors, jealous of each other, ambitious, and ruthless, fell to bitter fighting and rivalry among themselves over the spoils of victory. Almagro, who had so often quarreled with Pizarro in the past, became openly estranged from his commander, and in 1538 was executed. His followers, however, remained embittered enemies of Pizarro. Pizarro seems to have ignored the danger of these "Men of Chili," as they were called, as he also seems to have ignored the bitter opposition being created to his own secretary, Picado, a clever and unscrupulous adventurer. The discontented element began to gather in the house of young Diego Almagro, the son of their former leader. They were heavily influenced by Juan de Rada, the adviser of the executed Almagro. The situation was made more dangerous by the news that the Emperor had appointed a judge, Vaca de Castro, to visit Peru and hold an inquiry.]

News now reached the colony of the appointment of a judge by the Crown to take cognizance of the affairs of Peru. Pizarro, although alarmed by the intelligence, sent orders to have him well entertained on his landing and suitable accommodations prepared for him on the route. The spirits of Almagro's followers were greatly raised by the tidings. They confidently looked to this

* From *The Conquest of Peru,* Book IV, chap. 5.

high functionary for the redress of their wrongs; and two of their body, clad in suits of mourning, were chosen to go to the north, where the judge was expected to land, and to lay their grievances before him.

But months elapsed, and no tidings came of his arrival, till, at length, a vessel coming into port announced that most of the squadron had foundered in the heavy storms on the coast and that the commissioner had probably perished with them. This was disheartening intelligence to the men of Chili, whose "miseries," to use the words of their young leader, "had become too grievous to be borne." Symptoms of disaffection had already begun openly to manifest themselves. The haughty cavaliers did not always doff their bonnets on meeting the governor in the street; and on one occasion three ropes were found suspended from the public gallows, with labels attached to them, bearing the names of Pizarro, Velasquez, the judge, and Picado, the governor's secretary. This last functionary was peculiarly odious to Almagro and his followers. As his master knew neither how to read nor write, all his communications passed through Picado's hands; and, as the latter was of a hard and arrogant nature, greatly elated by the consequence which his position gave him, he exercised a mischievous influence on the governor's measures. Almagro's poverty-stricken followers were the objects of his open ridicule, and he revenged the insult now offered him by riding before their young leader's residence, displaying a tawdry magnificence in his dress, sparkling with gold and silver, and with the inscription "For the Men of Chili" set in his bonnet. It was a foolish taunt; but the poor cavaliers who were the object of it, made morbidly sensitive by their sufferings, had not the philosophy to despise it.

At length, disheartened by the long-protracted coming of Vaca de Castro and still more by the recent reports of his loss, Almagro's faction, despairing of redress from a legitimate authority, determined to take it into their own hands. They came to the desperate resolution of assassinating Pizarro. The day named for this was Sunday, the twenty-sixth of June, 1541. The conspirators, eighteen or twenty in number, were to assemble in Almagro's house, which stood in the great square next to the cathedral, and when the governor was returning from mass they were to issue forth and fall on him in the street. A white flag, unfurled at the same time from an upper window in the house, was to be the signal for the rest of their comrades to move to the support of those immediately engaged in the execution of the deed.

These arrangements could hardly have been concealed from Almagro, since his own quarters were to be the place of rendezvous. Yet there is no good evidence of his having taken part in the conspiracy. He was, indeed, too young to make it probable that he took a leading part in it. He is represented by contemporary writers to have given promise of many good qualities, though, unhappily, he was not placed in a situation favorable for their development. He was the son of an Indian woman of Panama, but from early years had followed the troubled fortunes of his father, to whom he bore much resemblance in his free and generous nature, as well as in the violence of his passions. His youth and inexperience disqualified him from taking the lead in the perplexing circumstances in which he was placed, and made him little more than a puppet in the hands of others.

The most conspicuous of his advisers was Juan de Herrada, or Rada, as his name is more usually spelt—a cavalier of respectable family, who, having early enlisted as a common soldier, had gradually risen to the highest posts in the army by his military talents. At this time he was well advanced in years; but the fires of youth were not quenched in his bosom, and he burned with desire to avenge the wrongs done to his ancient commander. The attachment which he had ever felt for the elder Almagro he seems to have transferred in full measure to his son; and it was apparently with reference to him, even more than to himself, that he devised this audacious plot and prepared to take the lead in the execution of it.

There was one, however, in the band of conspirators who felt some compunctions of conscience at the part he was acting, and who relieved his bosom by revealing the whole plot to his confessor. The latter lost no time in reporting it to Picado, by whom in turn it was communicated to Pizarro. But, strange to say, it made little more impression on the governor's mind than the vague warnings he had so frequently received. "It is a device of the priest," said he; "he wants a mitre." Yet, he repeated the story to the judge Velasquez, who, instead of ordering the conspirators to be seized and the proper steps taken for learning the truth of the accusation, seemed to be possessed with the same infatuation as Pizarro; and he bade the governor be under no apprehension, "for no harm should come to him, while the rod of justice," not a metaphorical badge of authority in Castile, "was in his hands." Still, to obviate every possibility of danger, it was deemed prudent for Pizarro to abstain from going to mass on Sunday and to remain at home on pretence of illness.

On the day appointed, Rada and his companions met in Almagro's house and waited with anxiety for the hour when the governor should issue from the church. But great was their consternation when they learned that he was not there, but was detained at home, as currently reported, by illness. Little doubting that their design was discovered, they felt their own ruin to be the inevitable consequence, and that, too, without enjoying the melancholy consolation of having struck the blow for which they had incurred it. Greatly perplexed, some were for disbanding, in the hope that Pizarro might, after all, be ignorant of their design. But most were for carrying it into execution at once, by assaulting him in his own house. The question was summarily decided by one of the party, who felt that in this latter course lay their only chance of safety. Throwing open the doors, he rushed out, calling on his comrades "to follow him, or he would proclaim the purpose for which they had met." There was no longer hesitation, and the cavaliers issued forth, with Rada at their head, shouting, "Long live the king! Death to the tyrant!"

It was the hour of dinner, which, in this primitive age of the Spanish colonies, was at noon. Yet numbers, roused by the cries of the assailants, came out into the square to inquire the cause. "They are going to kill the marquis!" some said very coolly; others replied, "It is Picado." No one stirred in their defence. The power of Pizarro was not seated in the hearts of his people.

As the conspirators traversed the plaza, one of the party made a circuit to avoid a little pool of water that lay in their path. "What!" exclaimed Rada, "afraid of wetting your feet, when you are to wade up to your knees in blood!" And he ordered the man to give up the enterprise and go home to his quarters. The anecdote is characteristic.

The governor's palace stood on the opposite side of the square. It was approached by two court-yards. The entrance to the outer one was protected by a massive gate, capable of being made good against a hundred men or more. But it was left open, and the assailants, hurrying through to the inner court, still shouting their fearful battle-cry, were met by two domestics loitering in the yard. One of these they struck down. The other, flying in all haste towards the house, called out, "Help, help! The men of Chili are all coming to murder the marquis!"

Pizarro at this time was at dinner or, more probably, had just dined. He was surrounded by a party of friends, who had dropped in, it seems, after mass to inquire after the state of his health, some of whom had remained to partake of his repast. Among these was Don Martinez de Alcantara, Pizarro's half-brother by the mother's side, the judge Velasquez, the bishop elect of Quito, and several of the principal cavaliers in the place, to the number of fifteen or twenty. Some of them, alarmed by the uproar in the court-yard, left the saloon and, running down to the first landing on the stairway, inquired into the cause of the disturbance. No sooner were they informed of it by the cries of the servant than they retreated with precipitation into the house; and, as they had no mind to abide the storm unarmed, or at best imperfectly armed, as most of them were, they made their way to a corridor that overlooked the gardens, into which they easily let themselves down without injury. Velasquez, the judge, the better to have the use of his hands in the descent, held his rod of office in his mouth, thus taking care, says a caustic old chronicler, not to falsify his assurance that "no harm should come to Pizarro while the rod of justice was in his hands"!

Meanwhile, the marquis, learning the nature of the tumult, called out to Francisco de Chaves, an officer high in his confidence, and who was in the outer apartment opening on the staircase, to secure the door, while he and his brother Alcantara buckled on their armor. Had this order, coolly given, been as coolly obeyed, it would have saved them all, since the entrance could easily have been maintained against a much larger force, till the report of the cavaliers who had fled had brought support to Pizarro. But unfortunately, Chaves, disobeying his commander, half-opened the door and attempted to enter into a parley with the conspirators. The latter had now reached the head of the stairs and cut short the debate by running Chaves through the body and tumbling his corpse down into the area below. For a moment they were kept at bay by the attendants of the slaughtered cavalier, but these, too, were quickly despatched; and Rada and his companions, entering the apartment, hurried across it, shouting out, "Where is the marquis? Death to the tyrant!"

Martinez de Alcantara, who in the adjoining room was assisting his brother to buckle on his mail, no sooner saw that the entrance to the antechamber had been gained than he sprang to the doorway of the apartment and, assisted by two young men, pages of Pizarro, and by one or two cavaliers in attendance, endeavored to resist the approach of the assailants. A desperate struggle now ensued. Blows were given on both sides, some of which proved fatal, and two of the conspirators were slain, while Alcantara and his brave companions were repeatedly wounded.

At length, Pizarro, unable, in the hurry of the moment, to adjust the fastenings of his cuirass, threw it away and, enveloping one arm in his cloak, with the other seized his sword and sprang to his brother's assistance. It was too late; for Alcantara was already staggering under the loss of blood and soon fell to the ground. Pizarro threw himself on his invaders, like a lion roused in his lair, and dealt his blows with as much rapidity and force as if age had no power to stiffen his limbs. "What ho!" he cried, "traitors! Have you come to kill me in my own house?" The conspirators drew back for a moment, as two of their body fell under Pizarro's sword; but they quickly rallied and, from their superior numbers, fought at great advantage by relieving one another in the assault. Still the passage was narrow, and the struggle lasted for some minutes, till both of Pizarro's pages were stretched by his side, when Rada, impatient of the delay, called out, "Why are we so long about it? Down with the tyrant!" and taking one of his companions, Narvaez, in his arms, he thrust him against the marquis. Pizarro, instantly grappling with his opponent, ran him through with his sword. But at that moment he received a wound in the throat and, reeling, he sank on the floor, while the swords of Rada and several of the conspirators were plunged into his body. "Jesus!" exclaimed the dying man, and, tracing a cross with his finger on the bloody floor, he bent down his head to kiss it, when a stroke more friendly than the rest put an end to his existence.

The conspirators, having accomplished their bloody deed, rushed into the street and, brandishing their dripping weapons, shouted out, "The tyrant is dead! The laws are restored! Long live our master the emperor, and his governor, Almagro!" The men of Chili, roused by the cheering cry, now flocked in from every side to join the banner of Rada, who soon found himself at the head of nearly three hundred followers, all armed and prepared to support his authority. A guard was placed over the houses of the principal partisans of the late governor, and their persons were taken into custody. Pizarro's house, and that of his secretary Picado, were delivered up to pillage, and a large booty in gold and silver was found in the former. Picado himself took refuge in the dwelling of Riquelme, the treasurer; but his hiding-place was detected—betrayed, according to some accounts, by the looks, though not the words, of the treasurer himself—and he was dragged forth and committed to a secure prison. The whole city was thrown into consternation as armed bodies hurried to and fro on their several errands, and all who were not in the faction of Almagro trembled lest they should be involved in the proscription of their enemies. So great was the disorder that the Brothers of Mercy, turning out in a body, paraded the streets in solemn procession, with the host elevated in the air, in hopes by the presence of the sacred symbol to calm the passions of the multitude.

But no other violence was offered by Rada and his followers than to apprehend a few suspected persons and to seize upon horses and arms wherever they were to be found. The municipality was then summoned to recognize the authority of Almagro; the refractory were ejected without ceremony from their offices, and others, of the Chili faction, were substituted. The claims of the aspirant were fully recognized; and young Almagro, parading the streets on horseback and escorted by a well-armed body of cavaliers, was proclaimed by sound of trumpet governor and captain-general of Peru.

Meanwhile, the mangled bodies of Pizarro and his faithful adherents were left weltering in their blood. Some were for dragging forth the governor's corpse to the market-place and fixing his head upon a gibbet. But Almagro was secretly prevailed on to grant the entreaties of Pizarro's friends and allow his interment. This was stealthily and hastily performed, in the fear of momentary interruption. A faithful attendant and his wife, with a few black domestics, wrapped the body in a cotton cloth and removed it to the cathedral. A grave was hastily dug in an obscure corner, the services were hurried through, and, in secrecy and in darkness dispelled only by the feeble glimmering of a few tapers furnished by these humble menials, the remains of Pizarro, rolled in their bloody shroud, were consigned to their kindred dust. Such was the miserable end of the Conqueror of Peru—of the man who but a few hours before had lorded it over the land with as absolute a sway as was possessed by its hereditary Incas. Cut off in the broad light of day, in the heart of his own capital, in the very midst of those who had been his companions in arms and shared with him his triumphs and his spoils, he perished like a wretched outcast. "There was none, even," in the expressive language of the chronicler, "to say, God forgive him!"

A few years later, when tranquillity was restored to the country, Pizarro's remains were placed in a sumptuous coffin and deposited under a monument in a conspicuous part of the cathedral. And in 1607, when time had thrown its friendly mantle over the past, and the memory of his errors and his crimes was merged in the consideration of the great service he had rendered to the Crown by the extension of her colonial empire, his bones were removed to the new cathedral and allowed to repose side by side with those of Mendoza, the wise and good Viceroy of Peru.

Pizarro was, probably, not far from sixty-five years of age at the time of his death; though this, it must be added, is but loose conjecture, since there exists no authentic record of the date of his birth. He was never married, but by an Indian princess of the Inca blood, daughter of Atahuallpa and granddaughter of the great Huayna Capac, he had two children, a son and a daughter. Both survived him; but the son did not live to manhood. Their mother, after Pizarro's death, wed a Spanish cavalier named Ampuero and removed with him to Spain. Her daughter, Francisca, accompanied her and was there subsequently married to her uncle, Hernando Pizarro, then a prisoner in the Mota del Medina. Neither the title nor estates of the Marquis Francisco descended to his illegitimate offspring. But in the third generation, in the reign of Philip the Fourth, the title was revived in favor of Don Juan Hernando Pizarro, who, out of gratitude for the services of his ancestor, was created Marquis of the Conquest, *Marques de la Conquista,* with a liberal pension from government. His descendants, bearing the same title of nobility, are still to be found, it is said, at Truxillo, in the ancient province of Estremadura, the original birthplace of the Pizarros.

Pizarro's person has been already described. He was tall in stature, well-proportioned, and with a countenance not unpleasing. Bred in camps, with nothing of the polish of a court, he had a soldier-like bearing and the air of one accustomed to command. But, though not polished, there was no embarrassment or rusticity in his address, which, where it served his purposes, could be plausible and even insinuating. The proof of it is the favorable impression made by him on presenting himself, after his second expedition—stranger as he was to all its forms and usages—at the punctilious court of Castile.

Unlike many of his countrymen, he had no passion for ostentatious dress, which he regarded as an encumbrance. The costume which he most affected on public occasions was a black cloak, with a white hat and shoes of the same color; the last, it is said, being in imitation of the Great Captain, whose character he had early learned to admire in Italy, but to which his own certainly bore very faint resemblance.

He was temperate in eating, drank sparingly, and usually rose an hour before dawn. He was punctual in attendance to business and shrank from no toil. He had, indeed, great powers of patient endurance. Like most of his nation, he was fond of play and cared little for the quality of those with whom he played; though, when his antagonist could not afford to lose, he would allow himself, it is said, to be the loser—a mode of conferring an obligation much commended by a Castilian writer for its delicacy.

Though avaricious, it was in order to spend and not to hoard. His ample treasures, more ample than those, probably, that ever before fell to the lot of an adventurer, were mostly dissipated in his enterprises, his architectural works, and schemes of public improvement, which, in a country where gold and silver might be said to have lost their value from their abundance, absorbed an incredible amount of money. While he regarded the whole country in a manner as his own and distributed it freely among his captains, it is certain that the princely grant of a territory with twenty thousand vassals, made to him by the Crown, was never carried into effect; nor did his heirs ever reap the benefit of it.

To a man possessed of the active energies of Pizarro, sloth was the greatest evil. The excitement of play was in a manner necessary to a spirit accustomed to the habitual stimulants of war and adventure. His uneducated mind had no relish for more refined, intellectual recreation. The deserted foundling had neither been taught to read nor write. This has been disputed by some; but it is attested by unexceptionable authorities. Montesinos says, indeed, that Pizarro, on his first voyage, tried to learn to read, but the impatience of his temper prevented it, and he contented himself with learning to sign his name. But Montesinos was not a contemporary historian. Pedro Pizarro, his companion in arms, expressly tells us he could neither read nor write; and Zarate, another contemporary, well acquainted with the Conquerors, confirms this statement and adds that Pizarro could not so much as sign his name. This was done by his secretary—Picado, in his latter years—while the governor merely made the customary *rúbrica*, or flourish, at the sides of his name. This is the case with the instruments I have examined, in which his signature, written probably by his secretary, or his title of *Marques*, in later life substituted for his name, is garnished with a flourish at the ends, executed in as bungling a manner as if done by the hand of a ploughman. Yet we must not estimate this deficiency as we should in this period of general illumination—general, at least, in our own fortunate country. Reading and writing, so universal now, in the beginning of the sixteenth century might be regarded in the light of accomplishments; and all who have occasion to consult the autograph memorials of that time will find the execution of them, even by persons of the highest rank, too often such as would do little credit to a schoolboy of the present day.

Though bold in action and not easily turned from his purpose, Pizarro was slow in arriving at a decision. This gave him an appearance of irresolution foreign to his character. Perhaps the consciousness of this led him to adopt the custom of saying "No," at first, to applicants for favor and, afterwards, at leisure, to revise his judgment and grant what seemed to him expedient. He took the opposite course from his comrade Almagro, who, it was observed, generally said "Yes," but too often failed to keep his promise. This was characteristic of the careless and easy nature of the latter, governed by impulse rather than principle.

It is hardly necessary to speak of the courage of a man pledged to such a career as that of Pizarro. Courage, indeed, was a cheap quality among the Spanish adventurers, for danger was their element. But he possessed something higher than mere animal courage, in that constancy of purpose which was rooted too deeply in his nature to be shaken by the wildest storms of fortune. It was this inflexible constancy which formed the key to his character and constituted the secret of his success. A remarkable evidence of it was given in his first expedition, among the mangroves and dreary marshes of Choco. He saw his followers pining around him under the blighting malaria, wasting before an invisible enemy and unable to strike a stroke in their own defence. Yet his spirit did not yield, nor did he falter in his enterprise.

There is something oppressive to the imagination in this war against nature. In the struggle of man against man, the spirits are raised by a contest conducted on equal terms; but in a war with the elements we feel that, however bravely we may contend, we can have no power to control. Nor are we cheered on by the prospect of glory in such a contest; for, in the capricious estimate of human glory, the silent endurance of privations, however painful, is little in comparison with the ostentatious trophies of victory. The laurel of the hero—alas for humanity that it should be so!—grows best on the battlefield.

This inflexible spirit of Pizarro was shown still more strongly when, in the little island of Gallo, he drew the line on the sand which was to separate him and his handful of followers from their country and from civilized man. He trusted that his own constancy would give strength to the feeble and rally brave hearts around him for the prosecution of his enterprise. He looked with confidence to the future; and he did not miscalculate. This was heroic, and wanted only a nobler motive for its object to constitute the true moral sublime.

Yet the same feature in his character was displayed in a manner scarcely less remarkable when, landing on the coast and ascertaining the real strength and civilization of the Incas, he persisted in marching into the interior at the head of a force of less than two hundred men. In this he undoubtedly proposed to himself the example of Cortes, so contagious to the adventurous spirits of that day, and especially to Pizarro, engaged as he was in a similar enterprise. Yet the hazard assumed by Pizarro was far greater than that of the Conqueror of Mexico, whose force was nearly three times as large, while the terrors of the Inca name—however justified by the result—were as widely spread as those of the Aztecs.

It was doubtless in imitation of the same captivating model that Pizarro planned the seizure of Atahuallpa. But the situations of the two Spanish captains were as dissimilar as the manner in which their acts of violence were conducted. The wanton massacre of the Peruvians resembled that perpetrated by Alvarado in Mexico and might have been attended with consequences as disastrous if the Peruvian character had been as fierce as that of the Aztecs. But the blow which roused the latter to madness broke the tamer spirits of the Peruvians. It was a bold stroke, which left so much to chance that it scarcely merits the name of policy.

When Pizarro landed in the country, he found it distracted by a contest for the crown. It would seem to have been for his interest to play off one party against the other, throwing his own weight into the scale that suited him. Instead of this, he resorted to an act of audacious violence which crushed them both at a blow. His subsequent career afforded no scope for the profound policy displayed by Cortes when he gathered conflicting nations under his banner and directed them against a common foe. Still less did he have the opportunity of displaying the tactics and admirable strategy of his rival. Cortes conducted his military operations on the scientific principles of a great captain at the head of a powerful host. Pizarro appears only as an adventurer, a fortunate knight-errant. By one bold stroke he broke the spell which had so long held the land under the dominion of the Incas. The spell was broken, and the airy fabric of their empire, built on the superstition of ages, vanished. This was good fortune, rather than the result of policy.

Pizarro was eminently perfidious. Yet nothing is more opposed to sound policy. One act of perfidy fully established becomes the ruin of its author. The man who relinquishes confidence in his good faith gives up the best basis for future operations. Who will knowingly build on a quicksand? By his perfidious treatment of Almagro, Pizzaro alienated the minds of the Spaniards. By his perfidious treatment of Atahuallpa, and subsequently of the Inca Manco, he disgusted the Peruvians. The name of Pizarro became a by-word for perfidy. Almagro took his revenge in civil war; Manco in an insurrection which nearly cost Pizarro his dominion. The civil war terminated in a conspiracy which cost him his life. Such were the fruits of his policy. Pizarro may be regarded as a cunning man but not, as he has been often eulogized by his countrymen, as a politic one.

When Pizarro obtained possession of Cuzco, he found a country well advanced in the arts of civilization; institutions under which the people lived in tranquillity and personal safety; the mountains and the uplands whitened with flocks; the valleys teeming with the fruits of a scientific husbandry; the granaries and warehouses filled to overflowing; the whole land rejoicing in its abundance; and the character of the natives, softened under the influence of the mildest and most innocent form of superstition, well prepared for the reception of a higher and a Christian civilization. But, far from introducing this, Pizarro delivered up the conquered races to his brutal soldiery; the sacred cloisters were abandoned to their lust; the towns and villages were given up to pillage; the wretched natives were parcelled out like slaves, to toil for their conquerors in the mines; the flocks were scattered, and wantonly destroyed; the granaries were dissipated; the beautiful contrivances for the more perfect culture of the soil were suffered to fall into decay; the paradise was converted into a desert. Instead of profiting by the ancient forms of civilization, Pizarro preferred to efface every vestige of them from the land and on their ruin to erect the institutions of his own country. Yet these institutions did little for the poor Indian, held in iron bondage. It was little to him that the shores of the Pacific were studded with rising communities and cities, the marts of a flourishing commerce. He had no share in the goodly heritage. He was an alien in the land of his fathers.

The religion of the Peruvian, which directed him to the worship of that glorious luminary which is the best representative of the might and beneficence of the Creator, is perhaps the purest form of superstition that has existed among men. Yet it was much that, under the new order of things and through the benevolent zeal of the missionaries, some glimmerings of a nobler faith were permitted to dawn on his darkened soul. Pizarro, himself, cannot be charged with manifesting any overweening solicitude for the propagation of the Faith. He was no bigot, like Cortes. Bigotry is the perversion of the religious principle; but the principle itself was wanting in Pizarro. The conversion of the heathen was a predominant motive with Cortes in his expedition. It was not a vain boast. He would have sacrificed his life for it at any time; and more than once, by his indiscreet zeal, he actually did place his life and the success of his enterprise in jeopardy. It was his great purpose to purify the land from the brutish abominations of the Aztecs by substituting the religion of Jesus. This gave to his expedition the character of a crusade. It furnished the best apology for the Conquest and does more towards enlisting our sympathies on the side of the Conquerors.

But Pizarro's ruling motives, so far as they can be scanned by human judgment, were avarice and ambition. The good missionaries, indeed, followed in his train to scatter the seeds of spiritual truth, and the Spanish government, as usual, directed its beneficent legislation to the conversion of the natives. But the moving power with Pizarro and his followers was the lust of gold. This was the real stimulus to their toil, the price of perfidy, the true guerdon of their victories. This gave a base and mercenary character to their enterprise; and when we contrast the ferocious cupidity of the Conquerors with the mild and inoffensive manners of the conquered, our sympathies, the sympathies even of the Spaniard, are necessarily thrown into the scale of the Indian.

But as no picture is without its lights, we must not, in justice to Pizarro, dwell exclusively on the darker features of his portrait. There was no one of her sons to whom Spain was under larger obligations for extent of empire; for his hand won for her the richest of the Indian jewels that once sparkled in her imperial diadem. When we contemplate the perils he braved, the sufferings he patiently endured, the incredible obstacles he overcame, the magnificent results he effected with his single arm, as it were, unaided by the government—though neither a good, nor a great man in the highest sense of that term, it is impossible not to regard him as a very extraordinary one.

Nor can we fairly omit to notice, in extenuation of his errors, the circumstances of his early life; for, like Almagro, he was the son of sin and sorrow, early cast upon the world to seek his fortunes as he might. In his young and tender age he was to take the impression of those into whose society he was thrown. And when was it the lot of the needy outcast to fall into that of the wise and the virtuous? His lot was cast among the licentious inmates of a camp, the school of rapine, whose only law was the sword and who looked on the wretched Indian as their rightful spoil.

Who does not shudder at the thought of what his own fate might have been, trained in such a school? The amount of crime does not necessarily show the criminality of the agent. History, indeed, is concerned with the former, that it may be recorded as a warning to mankind; but it is He alone who knoweth the heart, the strength of the temptation, and the means of resisting it that can determine the measure of the guilt.

8. The Settlement of the Country: Pedro de la Gasca*

[There can be little doubt that Prescott was repelled by the history of Peru after the Conquest, with its bitter rivalry and low political struggles. Yet, as he noted in his journal, one character at the very end of the narrative relieved the general complexion of the picture. This was the "great and good" Viceroy Pedro de la Gasca, who gave to the end of Prescott's tale a sort of sublimity. In March, 1548, Gasca moved south toward Cuzco with 2,000 men to subdue Gonzalo Pizarro, the present source of confusion and strife in the conquered territories. He was able to overcome Gonzalo, who was captured and executed. Gasca then moved on into Cuzco and with rigorous justice succeeded in doing what no Spaniard had done before: He brought peace to the country. Following a stay in Cuzco, Gasca traveled on toward Lima.]

Meanwhile the president had continued his journey towards Lima, and on the way was everywhere received by the people with an enthusiasm the more grateful to his heart that he felt he had deserved it. As he drew near the capital, the loyal inhabitants prepared to give him a magnificent reception. The whole population came

* From *The Conquest of Peru*, Book V, chap. 4.

forth from the gates, led by the authorities of the city, with Aldana, as *corregidor,*[1] at their head. Gasca rode on a mule, dressed in his ecclesiastical robes. On his right, borne on a horse richly caparisoned, was the royal seal, in a box curiously chased and ornamented. A gorgeous canopy of brocade was supported above his robes of crimson velvet, walked bareheaded by his side. head by the officers of the municipality, who, in their Gay troops of dancers, clothed in fantastic dresses of gaudy-colored silk, followed the procession, strewing flowers and chanting verses as they went, in honor of the president. They were designed as emblematical of the different cities of the colony; and they bore legends or mottoes in rhyme on their caps, intimating their loyal devotion to the Crown and evincing much more loyalty in their composition, it may be added, than poetical merit. In this way, without beat of drum or noise of artillery or any of the rude accompaniments of war, the good president made his peaceful entry into the City of the Kings, while the air was rent with the acclamations of the people, who hailed him as their "Father and Deliverer, the Savior of their country!"

But, however grateful this homage to Gasca's heart, he was not a man to waste his time in idle vanities. He now thought only by what means he could eradicate the seeds of disorder which shot up so readily in this fruitful soil, and how he could place the authority of the government on a permanent basis. By virtue of his office, he presided over the Royal Audience, the great judicial and, indeed, executive tribunal of the colony; and he gave great despatch to the business, which had much accumulated during the late disturbances. In the unsettled state of property, there was abundant subject for litigation; but, fortunately, the new Audience was composed of able, upright judges, who labored diligently with their chief to correct the mischief caused by the misrule of their predecessors.

Neither was Gasca unmindful of the unfortunate natives; and he occupied himself earnestly with that diffi-

[1] Magistrate, corresponding to mayor.

cult problem—the best means practicable of ameliorating their condition. He sent a number of commissioners, as visitors, into different parts of the country, whose business it was to inspect the *encomiendas*[1] and ascertain the manner in which the Indians were treated by conversing not only with the proprietors but with the natives themselves. They were also to learn the nature and extent of the tributes paid in former times by the vassals of the Incas.

In this way a large amount of valuable information was obtained which enabled Gasca, with the aid of a council of ecclesiastics and jurists, to digest a uniform system of taxation for the natives, lighter even than that imposed on them by the Peruvian princes. The president would gladly have relieved the conquered races from the obligations of personal service; but, on mature consideration, this was judged impracticable in the present state of the country, since the colonists, more especially in the tropical regions, looked to the natives for the performance of labor, and the latter, it was found from experience, would not work at all unless compelled to do so. The president, however, limited the amount of service to be exacted with great precision, so that it was in the nature of a moderate personal tax. No Peruvian was to be required to change his place of residence, from the climate to which he had been accustomed to another—a fruitful source of discomfort, as well as of disease, in past times. By these various regulations, the condition of the natives, though not such as had been contemplated by the sanguine philanthropy of Las Casas, was improved far more than was compatible with the craving demands of the colonists; and all the firmness of the Audience was required to enforce provisions so unpalatable to the latter. Still, they were enforced. Slavery, in its most odious sense, was no longer tolerated in Peru. The term "slave" was not recognized as having relation to her institutions; and the historian of the Indies makes the proud boast—it should have

[1] A limited form of lordship, on a temporary and nonhereditary basis, over a certain number of Indians who were to perform labor service.

been qualified by the limitations I have noticed—that every Indian vassal might aspire to the rank of a freeman.

Besides these reforms, Gasca introduced several in the municipal government of the cities and others yet more important in the management of the finances and in the mode of keeping the accounts. By these and other changes in the internal economy of the colony he placed the administration on a new basis and greatly facilitated the way for a more sure and orderly government by his successors. As a final step, to secure the repose of the country after he was gone, he detached some of the more aspiring cavaliers on distant expeditions, trusting that they would draw off the light and restless spirits, who might otherwise gather together and disturb the public tranquillity; as we sometimes see the mists which have been scattered by the genial influence of the sun become condensed and settle into a storm on his departure.

Gasca had been now more than fifteen months in Lima, and nearly three years had elapsed since his first entrance into Peru. In that time he had accomplished the great objects of his mission. When he landed, he found the colony in a state of anarchy, or rather organized rebellion under a powerful and popular chief. He came without funds or forces to support him. The former he procured through the credit which he established in his good faith; the latter he won over by argument and persuasion from the very persons to whom they had been confided by his rival. Thus he turned the arms of that rival against himself. By a calm appeal to reason he wrought a change in the hearts of the people; and without costing a drop of blood to a single loyal subject he suppressed a rebellion which had menaced Spain with the loss of the wealthiest of her provinces. He had punished the guilty and in their spoils found the means to recompense the faithful. He had, moreover, so well husbanded the resources of the country that he was enabled to pay off the large loan he had negotiated with the merchants of the colony for the expenses of the war, exceeding nine hundred thousand *pesos de oro*. Nay, more, by his economy he had saved a million and a half ducats for the government, which for some years had received nothing from Peru; and he now proposed to carry back this acceptable treasure to swell the royal coffers. All this had been accomplished without the cost of outfit or salary, or any charge to the Crown except that of his own frugal expenditure. The country was now in a state of tranquillity. Gasca felt that his work was done and that he was free to gratify his natural longing to return to his native land.

Before his departure, he arranged a distribution of those *repartimientos* which had lapsed to the Crown during the past year by the death of the incumbents. Life was short in Peru; since those who lived by the sword, if they did not die by the sword, too often fell early victims to the hardships incident to their adventurous career. Many were the applicants for the new bounty of government; and, as among them were some of those who had been discontented with the former partition, Gasca was assailed by remonstrances and sometimes by reproaches couched in not very decorous or respectful language. But they had no power to disturb his equanimity; he patiently listened and replied to all in the mild tone of expostulation best calculated to turn away wrath; "by this victory over himself," says an old writer, "acquiring more real glory than by all his victories over his enemies."

An incident occurred on the eve of his departure, touching in itself and honorable to the parties concerned. The Indian caciques of the neighboring country, mindful of the great benefits he had rendered their people, presented him with a considerable quantity of plate in token of their gratitude. But Gasca refused to receive it, though in doing so he gave much concern to the Peruvians, who feared they had unwittingly fallen under his displeasure.

Many of the principal colonists, also, from the same wish to show their sense of his important services, sent to him, after he had embarked, a magnificent donative of fifty thousand gold *castellanos*. "As he had taken leave of Peru," they said, "there could be no longer any ground for declining it." But Gasca was as decided in his rejection of this present as he had been of the other. "He had come to the country," he remarked, "to serve the king and to secure the blessings of peace to the inhabitants; and now that, by the favor of Heaven, he had been permitted to accomplish this, he would not dishonor the cause by any act that might throw suspicion on the purity of his motives." Notwithstanding his refusal, the colonists contrived to secrete the sum of twenty thousand *castellanos* on board his vessel, with the idea that, once in his own country, with his mission concluded, the president's scruples would be removed. Gasca did, indeed, accept the donative, for he felt that it would be ungracious to send it back; but it was only till he could ascertain the relatives of the donors, when he distributed it among the most needy.

Having now settled all his affairs, the president committed the government, until the arrival of a viceroy, to his faithful partners of the Royal Audience, and in January, 1550, he embarked with the royal treasure on board of a squadron for Panama. He was accompanied to the shore by a numerous crowd of the inhabitants, cavaliers, and common people, persons of all ages and conditions, who followed to take their last look of their benefactor and watch with straining eyes the vessel that bore him away from their land.

His voyage was prosperous, and early in March the president reached his destined port. He stayed there only till he could muster horses and mules sufficient to carry the treasure across the mountains; for he knew that this part of the country abounded in wild, predatory spirits, who would be sorely tempted to some act of violence by a knowledge of the wealth which he had with him. Pushing forward, therefore, he crossed the rugged Isthmus and, after a painful march, arrived in safety at Nombre de Díos.

The event justified his apprehensions. He had been gone but three days when a ruffian horde, after murdering the bishop of Guatemala, broke into Panama with the design of inflicting the same fate on the president and of seizing the booty. No sooner were the tidings communicated to Gasca than, with his usual energy, he levied a force and prepared to march to the relief of the invaded capital. But Fortune—or, to speak more correctly, Providence—favored him here, as usual; and on the eve of his departure he learned that the marauders had been met by the citizens and discomfited with great slaughter. Disbanding his forces, therefore, he equipped a fleet of nineteen vessels to transport himself and the royal treasure to Spain, where he arrived in safety, entering the harbor of Seville after a little more than four years from the period when he had sailed from the same port.

Great was the sensation throughout the country caused by his arrival. Men could hardly believe that results so momentous had been accomplished in so short a time by a single individual—a poor ecclesiastic, who, unaided by the government, had by his own strength, as it were, put down a rebellion which had so long set the arms of Spain at defiance!

The emperor was absent in Flanders. He was overjoyed on learning the complete success of Gasca's mission and not less satisfied with the tidings of the treasure he had brought with him; for the exchequer, rarely filled to overflowing, had been exhausted by the recent troubles in Germany. Charles instantly wrote to the president requiring his presence at court, that he might learn from his own lips the particulars of his expedition. Gasca, accordingly, attended by a numerous retinue of nobles and cavaliers—for who does not pay homage to him whom the king delighteth to honor?—embarked at Barcelona and, after a favorable voyage, joined the Court in Flanders.

He was received by his royal master, who fully appreciated his services, in a manner most grateful to his feelings; and not long afterwards he was raised to the bishopric of Palencia—a mode of acknowledgment best suited to his character and deserts. Here he remained till 1561, when he was promoted to the vacant see of Siguenza. The rest of his days he passed peacefully in the discharge of his episcopal functions, honored by his sovereign and enjoying the admiration and respect of his countrymen.

In his retirement he was still consulted by the government in matters of importance relating to the Indies. The disturbances of that unhappy land were renewed, though on a much smaller scale than before, soon after the president's departure. They were chiefly caused by discontent with the *repartimientos* and with the constancy of the Audience in enforcing the benevolent restrictions as to the personal services of the natives. But these troubles subsided, after a very few years, under the wise rule of the Mendozas—two successive viceroys of that illustrious house which has given so many of its sons to the service of Spain. Under their rule the mild yet determined policy was pursued of which Gasca had set the example. The ancient distractions of the country were permanently healed. With peace, prosperity returned within the borders of Peru; and the consciousness of the beneficent results of his labors may have shed a ray of satisfaction, as it did of glory, over the evening of the president's life.

That life was brought to a close in November, 1567, at an age, probably, not far from the one fixed by the sacred writer as the term of human existence. He died at Valladolid and was buried in the church of Santa Maria Magdelena, in that city, which he had built and liberally endowed. His monument, surmounted by the sculptured effigy of a priest in his sacerdotal robes, is still to be seen there, attracting the admiration of the traveller by the beauty of its execution. The banners taken from Gonzalo Pizarro on the field of Xaquixaguana were suspended over his tomb as the trophies of his memorable mission to Peru. The banners have long since mouldered into dust, with the remains of him who slept beneath them; but the memory of his good deeds will endure for ever.

Gasca was plain in person, and his countenance was far from comely. He was awkward and ill-proportioned; for his limbs were too long for his body, so that when he rode he appeared to be much shorter than he really was. His dress was humble, his manners simple, and there was nothing imposing in his presence. But, on a nearer intercourse, there was a charm in his discourse that effaced every unfavorable impression produced by his exterior, and won the hearts of his hearers.

The president's character may be thought to have been sufficiently portrayed in the history already given of his life. It presented a combination of qualities which generally serve to neutralize each other, but which were mixed in such proportions in him as to give it additional strength. He was gentle, yet resolute; by nature intrepid, yet preferring to rely on the softer arts of policy. He was frugal in his personal expenditure and economical in the public, yet caring nothing for riches on his own account and never stinting his bounty when the public good required it. He was benevolent and placable, yet could deal sternly with the impenitent offender; lowly in his deportment, yet with a full measure of that self-respect which springs from conscious rectitude of purpose; modest and unpretending, yet not shrinking from the most difficult enterprises; deferring greatly to others, yet, in the last resort, relying mainly on himself; moving with deliberation—patiently waiting his time—but, when that came, bold, prompt, and decisive.

Gasca was not a man of genius, in the vulgar sense of that term. At least, no one of his intellectual powers seems to have received an extraordinary development, beyond what is found in others. He was not a great writer, nor a great orator, nor a great general. He did not affect to be either. He committed the care of his military matters to military men; of ecclesiastical to the clergy; and his civil and judicial concerns he reposed on the members of the Audience. He was not one of those little great men who aspire to do every thing themselves, under the conviction that nothing can be done so well by others. But the president was a keen judge of character. Whatever might be the office, he selected the best man for it. He did more. He assured himself of the fidelity of his agents, presided at their deliberations, dictated a general line of policy, and thus infused a spirit of unity into their plans which made all move in concert to the accomplishment of one grand result.

A distinguishing feature of his mind was his common sense—the best substitute for genius in a ruler who has the destinies of his fellow men at his disposal, and more indispensable than genius itself. In Gasca the different qualities were blended in such harmony that there was no room for excess. They seemed to regulate each other. While his sympathy with mankind taught him the nature of their wants, his reason suggested to what extent these were capable of relief, as well as the best mode of effecting it. He did not waste his strength on illusory schemes of benevolence, like Las Casas, on the one hand, nor did he countenance the selfish policy of the colonists, on the other. He aimed at the practicable—the greatest good practicable.

In accomplishing his objects, he disclaimed force equally with fraud. He trusted for success to his power over the convictions of his hearers; and the source of this power was the confidence he inspired in his own integrity. Amidst all the calumnies of faction, no imputation was ever cast on the integrity of Gasca. No wonder that a virtue so rare should be of high price in Peru.

There are some men whose characters have been so wonderfully adapted to the peculiar crisis in which they appeared that they seem to have been specially designed for it by Providence. Such was Washington in our own country, and Gasca in Peru. We can conceive of individuals with higher qualities, at least with higher intellectual qualities, than belonged to either of these great men. But it was the wonderful conformity of their characters to the exigencies of their situation, the perfect adaptation of the means to the end, that constituted the secret of their success—that enabled Gasca so gloriously to crush revolution and Washington still more gloriously to achieve it.

Gasca's conduct on his first coming to the colonies affords the best illustration of his character. Had he come backed by a military array, or even clothed in the paraphernalia of authority, every heart and hand would have been closed against him. But the humble ecclesiastic excited no apprehension; and his enemies were already disarmed before he had begun his approaches.

Had Gasca, impatient of Hinojosa's[1] tardiness, listened to the suggestions of those who advised his seizure, he would have brought his cause into jeopardy by this early display of violence. But he wisely chose to win over his enemy by operating on his conviction.

In like manner, he waited his time for making his entry into Peru. He suffered his communications to do their work in the minds of the people and was careful not to thrust in the sickle before the harvest was ripe. In this way, wherever he went, every thing was prepared for his coming; and when he set foot in Peru, the country was already his own.

After the dark and turbulent spirits with which we have been hitherto occupied, it is refreshing to dwell on a character like that of Gasca. In the long procession which has passed in review before us, we have seen only the mail-clad cavalier, brandishing his bloody lance and mounted on his war-horse, riding over the helpless natives or battling with his own friends and brothers; fierce, arrogant, and cruel, urged on by the lust of gold or the scarce more honorable love of a bastard glory. Mingled with these qualities, indeed, we have seen sparkles of the chivalrous and romantic temper which belongs to the heroic age of Spain. But, with some honorable exceptions, it was the scum of her chivalry that resorted to Peru and took service under the banner of the Pizarros. At the close of this long array of iron warriors we behold the poor and humble missionary coming into the land on an errand of mercy and everywhere proclaiming the glad tidings of peace. No warlike trumpet heralds his approach, nor is his course to be tracked by the groans of the wounded and the dying. The means he employs are in perfect harmony with his end. His weapons are argument and mild persuasion. It is the reason he would conquer, not the body. He wins his way by conviction, not violence. It is a moral victory to which he aspires, more potent, and happily more permanent, than that of the blood-stained conqueror. As he thus calm-

---

[1] A partisan of Gonzalo Pizarro who had command of Panama and the fleet in the Pacific. In November, 1546, he surrendered the fleet to Gasca.

ly and imperceptibly, as it were, comes to his great results, he may remind us of the slow, insensible manner in which Nature works out her great changes in the material world, that are to endure when the ravages of the hurricane are passed away and forgotten.

With the mission of Gasca terminates the history of the Conquest of Peru. The Conquest, indeed, strictly terminates with the suppression of the Peruvian revolt, when the strength, if not the spirit, of the Inca race was crushed for ever. The reader, however, might feel a natural curiosity to follow to its close the fate of the remarkable family who achieved the Conquest. Nor would the story of the invasion itself be complete without some account of the civil wars which grew out of it; which serve, moreover, as a moral commentary on preceding events by showing that the indulgence of fierce, unbridled passions is sure to recoil, sooner or later, even in this life, on the heads of the guilty.

It is true, indeed, that the troubles of the country were renewed on the departure of Gasca. The waters had been too fearfully agitated to be stilled at once into a calm; but they gradually subsided, under the temperate rule of his successors, who wisely profited by his policy and example. Thus the influence of the good president remained after he was withdrawn from the scene of his labors, and Peru, hitherto so distracted, continued to enjoy as large a share of repose as any portion of the colonial empire of Spain. With the benevolent mission of Gasca, then, the historian of the Conquest may be permitted to terminate his labors—with feelings not unlike those of the traveller who, having long journeyed among the dreary forests and dangerous defiles of the mountains, at length emerges on some pleasant landscape smiling in tranquillity and peace.

PART IV

History of the Reign of Philip II

1. *The Last Days of Charles V**

[Prescott had been thinking of writing on the reign of Philip II since the spring of 1838; in July, 1849, he began to write what was to prove to be his last work. In it he was able to incorporate some recently uncovered material on the latter days of the Emperor Charles V. In October, 1555, after a moving speech recounting his life's work, Charles V had abdicated the sovereignty of the Low Countries. In the following January, he abdicated all of his Spanish territories. In September, 1556, he sailed for Spain, and in February, 1557, he entered a monastery at Yuste, where he remained until his death in September, 1558. Prescott finished this chapter on the retirement of Charles V in 1851; before it was published, however, several other works appeared covering the same episode, notably Sir William Stirling-Maxwell's The Cloister Life of Charles V. *Until this time, the chief source of information on Charles V in English had been Robertson's history. It was now replaced and greatly modified by the material from the archives at Simancas incorporated in Stirling-Maxwell's book. Prescott had anticipated some of the arguments in his chapter; he was further able to revise his text in the light of the scholarship of Stirling-Maxwell and others. Commenting on this, Prescott noted: "The publication of these works has deprived my account of whatever novelty it might have possessed, since it rests on a similar basis with*

* **From *Philip II*, Book I, chap. 9.**

theirs, namely original documents in the Archives of Simancas. Yet the important influence which Charles exerted over the management of affairs, even in his monastic retreat, has made it impossible to dispense with the chapter."]

Charles, though borne across the mountains in a litter, had suffered greatly in his long and laborious journey from Valladolid. He passed some time in the neighboring village of Xarandilla, and thence, after taking leave of the greater part of his weeping retinue, he proceeded with the remainder to the monastery of Yuste. It was on the third of February, 1557, that he entered the abode which was to prove his final resting-place. The monks of Yuste had been much flattered by the circumstance of Charles having shown such a preference for their convent. As he entered the chapel, Te Deum was chanted by the whole brotherhood; and when the emperor had prostrated himself before the altar, the monks gathered round him anxious to pay him their respectful obeisance. Charles received them graciously and, after examining his quarters, professed himself well pleased with the accommodations prepared for him. His was not a fickle temper. Slow in forming his plans, he was slower in changing them. To the last day of his residence at Yuste—whatever may have been said to the contrary—he seems to have been well satisfied with the step he had taken and with the spot he had selected.

From the first, he prepared to conform, as far as his health would permit, to the religious observances of the monastery. Not that he proposed to limit himself to the narrow circumstances of an ordinary friar. The number of his retinue that still remained with him was at least fifty, mostly Flemings, a number not greater, certainly, than that maintained by many a private gentleman of the country. But among these we recognize those officers of state who belong more properly to a princely establishment than to the cell of the recluse. There was the major-domo, the almoner, the keeper of the wardrobe, the keeper of the jewels, the chamberlains, two watchmakers, several secretaries, the physician, the confessor, besides cooks, confectioners, bakers, brewers, game-keepers, and numerous valets. Some of these followers seem not to have been quite so content as their master with their secluded way of life, and to have cast many a longing look to the pomps and vanities of the world they had left behind them. At least such were the feelings of Quixada, the emperor's major-domo, in whom he placed the greatest confidence and who had the charge of his household. "His majesty's bedroom," writes the querulous functionary, "is good enough; but the view from it is poor: barren mountains, covered with rocks and stunted oaks; a garden of moderate size, with a few straggling orange-trees; the roads scarcely passable, so steep and stony; the only water, a torrent rushing from the mountains; a dreary solitude!" The low, cheerless rooms, he predicts, must necessarily be damp, boding no good to the emperor's infirmity. "As to the friars," observes the secretary, Gaztelu, in the same amiable mood, "please God that his majesty may be able to tolerate them—which will be no easy matter; for they are an importunate race." It is evident that Charles's followers would have been very willing to exchange the mortification of the monastic life for the good cheer and gayety of Brussels.

The worthy prior of the convent, in addressing Charles, greeted him with the title of *paternidad*,[1] till one of the fraternity suggested to him the propriety of substituting that of *magestad*.[2] Indeed, to this title Charles had good right, for he was still emperor. His resignation of the imperial crown, which, after a short delay, had followed that of the Spanish, had not taken effect, in consequence of the diet not being in session at the time when his envoy, the prince of Orange, was to have presented himself at Ratisbon, in the spring of 1557. The war with France made Philip desirous that his father should remain lord of Germany for some time longer. It was not, therefore, until more than a year after Charles's arrival at Yuste that the resignation was accepted by the diet,

[1] Father.
[2] Master.

at Frankfort, on the twenty-eighth of February, 1558. Charles was still emperor and continued to receive the imperial title in all his correspondence.

We have pretty full accounts of the manner in which the monarch employed his time. He attended mass every morning in the chapel when his health permitted. Mass was followed by dinner, which he took early and alone, preferring this to occupying a seat in the refectory of the convent. He was fond of carving for himself, though his gouty fingers were not always in the best condition for this exercise. His physician was usually in attendance during the repast and might, at least, observe how little his patient, who had not the virtue of abstinence, regarded his prescriptions. The Fleming Van Male, the emperor's favorite gentleman of the chamber, was also not infrequently present. He was a good scholar; and his discussions with the doctor served to beguile the tediousness of their master's solitary meal. The conversation frequently turned on some subject of natural history, of which the emperor was fond; and when the parties could not agree, the confessor, a man of learning, was called in to settle the dispute.

After dinner—an important meal, which occupied much time with Charles—he listened to some passages from a favorite theologian. In his worldly days, the reading he most affected was Comines's[1] account of King Louis the Eleventh—a prince whose maxim "Qui nescit dissimulare, nescit regnare"[2] was too well suited to the genius of the emperor. He now, however, sought a safer guide for his spiritual direction and would listen to a homily from the pages of St. Bernard, or more frequently St. Augustine, in whom he most delighted. Towards evening, he heard a sermon from one of his preachers. Three or four of the most eloquent of the Jeronymite order had been brought to Yuste for his especial benefit. When he was not in condition to be present at the discourse, he expected to hear a full report of it from the lips of his confessor, Father Juan de Regla. Charles was

---

1 Philippe de Comines (1445–1509), French historian.

2 "Who does not know how to dissemble does not know how to rule."

punctual in his attention to all the great fasts and festivals of the Church. His infirmities, indeed, excused him from fasting, but he made up for it by the severity of his flagellation. In Lent, in particular, he dealt with himself so sternly that the scourge was found stained with his blood; and this precious memorial of his piety was ever cherished, we are told, by Philip, and by him bequeathed as an heirloom to his son.

Increasing vigilance in his own spiritual concerns made him more vigilant as to those of others—as the weaker brethren sometimes found to their cost. Observing that some of the younger friars spent more time than was seemly in conversing with the women who came on business to the door of the convent, Charles procured an order to be passed that any woman who ventured to approach within two bowshots at the gate should receive a hundred stripes. On another occasion, his officious endeavor to quicken the diligence of one of the younger members of the fraternity is said to have provoked the latter testily to exclaim, "Cannot you be contented with having so long turned the world upside down, without coming here to disturb the quiet of a poor convent?"

He derived an additional pleasure, in his spiritual exercises, from his fondness for music, which enters so largely into those of the Romish Church. He sang well himself, and his clear, sonorous voice might often be heard through the open casement of his bedroom, accompanying the chant of the monks in the chapel. The choir was made up altogether of brethren of the order, and Charles would allow no intrusion from any other quarter. His ear was quick to distinguish any strange voice, as well as any false note in the performance—on which last occasion he would sometimes pause in his devotion and, in half-suppressed tones, give vent to his anger by one of those scurrilous epithets which, however they may have fallen in with the habits of the old campaigner, were but indifferently suited to his present way of life.

Such time as was not given to his religious exercises was divided among various occupations, for which he had always had a relish, though hitherto but little leisure to pursue them. Besides his employments in his garden, he had a decided turn for mechanical pursuits. Some years before, while in Germany, he had invented an ingenious kind of carriage for his own accommodation. He brought with him to Yuste an engineer named Torriano, famous for the great hydraulic works he constructed in Toledo. With the assistance of this man, a most skilful mechanician, Charles amused himself by making a variety of puppets representing soldiers, who went through military exercises. The historian draws largely on our faith by telling us also of little wooden birds which the ingenious pair contrived, so as to fly in and out of the window before the admiring monks! Both nothing excited their astonishment so much as a little handmill, used for grinding wheat, which turned out meal enough in a single day to support a man for a week or more. The good fathers thought this savored of downright necromancy; and it may have furnished an argument against the unfortunate engineer in the persecution which he afterwards underwent from the Inquisition.

Charles took, moreover, great interest in the mechanism of timepieces. He had a good number of clocks and watches ticking together in his apartments; and a story has obtained credit that the difficulty he found in making any two of them keep the same time drew from him an exclamation on the folly of attempting to bring a number of men to think alike in matters of religion, when he could not regulate any two of his timepieces so as to make them agree with each other—a philosophical reflection for which one will hardly give credit to the man who with his dying words could press on his son the maintenance of the Inquisition as the great bulwark of the Catholic faith. In the gardens of Yuste there is still, or was lately, to be seen a sun-dial constructed by Torriano to enable his master to measure more accurately the lapse of time as it glided away in the monotonous routine of the monastery.

Though averse to visits of curiosity or idle ceremony, Charles consented to admit some of the nobles whose estates lay in the surrounding country and who, with feelings of loyal attachment to their ancient master, were anxious to pay their respects to him in his retirement. But none who found their way into his retreat appear to have given him so much satisfaction as Francisco Borja, duke of Grandia, in later times placed on the roll of her saints by the Roman Catholic Church. Like Charles, he had occupied a brilliant eminence in the world, and like him found the glory of this world but vanity. In the prime of life he withdrew from the busy scenes in which he had acted and entered a college of Jesuits. By the emperor's invitation, Borja made more than one visit to Yuste; and Charles found much consolation in his society and in conversing with his early friend on topics of engrossing interest to both. The result of their conference was to confirm them both in the conviction that they had done wisely in abjuring the world and in dedicating themselves to the service of Heaven.

The emperor was also visited by his two sisters, the dowager queens of France and Hungary, who had accompanied their brother on his return to Spain. But the travelling was too rough, and the accommodations at Yuste too indifferent, to encourage the royal matrons to prolong their stay or, with one exception on the part of the queen of Hungary, to repeat their visit.

But an object of livelier interest to the emperor than either of his sisters was a boy, scarcely twelve years of age, who resided in the family of his major-domo, Quixada, in the neighboring village of Cuacos. This was Don John of Austria, as he was afterwards called, the future hero of Lepanto. He was the natural son of Charles, a fact known to no one during the father's lifetime except Quixada, who introduced the boy into the convent as his own page. The lad, at this early age, showed many gleams of that generous spirit by which he was afterwards distinguished—thus solacing the declining years of his parent and affording a hold for those affections which might have withered in the cold atmosphere of the cloister.

Strangers were sure to be well received who, coming

from the theatre of war, could furnish the information he so much desired respecting the condition of things abroad. Thus we find him in conference with an officer arrived from the Low Countries, named Spinosa, and putting a multitude of questions respecting the state of the army, the organization and equipment of the different corps, and other particulars, showing the lively interest taken by Charles in the conduct of the campaign.

It has been a common opinion that the emperor, after his retirement to Yuste, remained as one buried alive, totally cut off from intercourse with the world—"as completely withdrawn from the business of the kingdom and the concerns of government," says one of his biographers, "as if he had never taken part in them"; "so entirely abstracted in his solitude," says another contemporary, "that neither revolutions nor wars, nor gold arriving in heaps from the Indies, had any power to affect his tranquillity."

So far was this from being the case that not only did the emperor continue to show an interest in public affairs, but he took a prominent part, even from the depths of his retreat, in the management of them. Philip, who had the good sense to defer to the long experience and the wisdom of his father, consulted him constantly on great questions of public policy. And so far was he from the feeling of jealousy often imputed to him that we find him on one occasion, when the horizon looked particularly dark, imploring the emperor to leave his retreat and to aid him not only by his counsels but by his presence and authority. The emperor's daughter Joanna, regent of Castile, from her residence at Valladolid, only fifty leagues from Yuste, maintained a constant correspondence with her father, soliciting his advice in the conduct of the government. However much Charles may have felt himself relieved from responsibility for measures, he seems to have been as anxious for the success of Philip's administration as if it had been his own. "Write more fully," says one of his secretaries in a letter to the secretary of the regent's council; "the emperor is always eager to hear more particulars of events." He showed the deepest concern in the conduct of the Italian war. He betrayed none of the scruples manifested by Philip, but boldly declared that the war with the pope was a just war in the sight of both God and man. When letters came from abroad, he was even heard to express his regret that they brought no tidings of Paul's death, or Caraffa's![1] He was sorely displeased with the truce which Alva granted to the pontiff, intimating a regret that he had not the reins still in his own hand. He was yet more discontented with the peace, and the terms of it, both public and private; and when Alva talked of leaving Naples, his anger, as his secretary quaintly remarks, was "more than was good for his health."

The same interest he showed in the French war. The loss of Calais filled him with the deepest anxiety. But in his letters on the occasion, instead of wasting his time in idle lament, he seems intent only on devising in what way he can best serve Philip in his distress. In the same proportion he was elated by the tidings of the victory of St. Quentin. His thoughts turned upon Paris, and he was eager to learn what road his son had taken after the battle. According to Brantôme, on hearing the news, he abruptly asked, "Is Philip at Paris?" He judged of Philip's temper by his own.

At another time, we find him conducting negotiations with Navarre; and then again, carrying on a correspondence with his sister, the regent of Portugal, for the purpose of having his grandson, Carlos, recognized as heir to the crown in case of the death of the young king, his cousin. The scheme failed, for it would be as much as her life was worth, the regent said, to engage in it. But it was a bold one, that of bringing under the same sceptre these two nations, which, by community of race, language, and institutions, would seem by nature to have been designed for one. It was Charles's comprehensive idea; and it proves that even in the cloister the spirit of ambition had not become extinct in his bosom. How much would it have rejoiced that ambitious spirit

[1] Paul IV (Gian Pietro Caraffa), anti-Spanish Pope, 1555–1559. He allied with France but was defeated by the Duke of Alva.

could he have foreseen that the consummation so much desired by him would be attained under Philip!

But the department which especially engaged Charles's attention in his retirement, singularly enough, was the financial. "It has been my constant care," he writes to Philip, "in all my letters to your sister, to urge the necessity of providing you with funds—since I can be of little service to you in any other way." His interposition, indeed, seems to have been constantly invoked to raise supplies for carrying on the war. This fact may be thought to show that those writers are mistaken who accuse Philip of withholding from his father the means of maintaining a suitable establishment at Yuste. Charles, in truth, settled the amount of his own income; and in one of his letters we find him fixing this at twenty thousand ducats, instead of sixteen thousand, as before, to be paid quarterly and in advance. That the payments were not always punctually made may well be believed, in a country where punctuality would have been a miracle.

Charles had more cause for irritation in the conduct of some of those functionaries with whom he had to deal in his financial capacity. Nothing appears to have stirred his bile so much at Yuste as the proceedings of some members of the board of trade at Seville. "I have deferred sending to you," he writes to his daughter, the regent, "in order to see if, with time, my wrath would not subside. But, far from it, it increases, and will go on increasing till I learn that those who have done wrong have atoned for it. Were it not for my infirmities," he adds, "I would go to Seville myself, and find out the authors of this villainy and bring them to a summary reckoning." "The emperor orders me," writes his secretary, Gaztelu, "to command that the offenders be put in irons and in order to mortify them the more, that they be carried in broad daylight to Simancas and there lodged, not in towers or chambers but in a dungeon. Indeed, such is his indignation, and such are the violent and bloodthirsty expressions he commands me to use, that you will pardon me if my language is not so temperate as it might be." It had been customary for the board of trade to receive the gold imported from the Indies, whether on public or private account, and hold it for the use of the government, paying to the merchants interested an equivalent in government bonds. The merchants, naturally enough, not relishing this kind of security so well as the gold, by a collusion with some of the members of the board of trade, had been secretly allowed to remove their own property. In this way the government was defrauded—as the emperor regarded it—of a large sum on which it calculated. This, it would seem, was the offence which had roused the royal indignation to such a pitch. Charles's phlegmatic temperament had ever been liable to be ruffled by these sudden gusts of passion; and his conventual life does not seem to have had any very sedative influence on him in this particular.

For the first ten months after his arrival at Yuste, the emperor's health, under the influence of a temperate climate, the quiet of monastic life, and more than all, probably, his exemption from the cares of state, had generally improved. His attacks of gout had been less frequent and less severe than before. But in the spring of 1558 the old malady returned with renewed violence. "I was not in a condition," he writes to Philip, "to listen to a single sermon during Lent." For months he was scarcely able to write a line with his own hand. His spirits felt the pressure of bodily suffering and were still further depressed by the death of his sister Eleanor, the queen-dowager of France and Portugal, which took place in February, 1558.

A strong attachment seems to have subsided between the emperor and his two sisters. Queen Eleanor's sweetness of disposition had particularly endeared her to her brother, who now felt her loss almost as keenly as that of one of his own children. "She was a good Christian," he said to his secretary, Gaztelu; and, as the tears rolled down his cheeks, he added, "We have always loved each other. She was my elder by fifteen months; and before that period has passed I shall probably be with her." Before half that period, the sad augury was fulfilled.

At this period the attention of the government was

called to the Lutheran heresy, which had already begun to disclose itself in various quarters of the country. Charles was possessed of a full share of the spirit of bigotry which belonged to the royal line of Castile, from which he was descended. While on the throne, this feeling was held somewhat in check by a regard for his political interests. But in the seclusion of the monastery he had no interests to consult but those of religion; and he gave free scope to the spirit of intolerance which belonged to his nature. In a letter addressed, the third of May, 1558, to his daughter Joanna, he says: "Tell the grand-inquisitor from me to be at his post, and lay the axe at the root of the evil before it spreads further. I rely on your zeal for bringing the guilty to punishment and for having them punished, without favor to any one, with all the severity which their crimes demand." In another letter to his daughter, three weeks later, he writes: "If I had not entire confidence that you would do your duty and arrest the evil at once by chastising the guilty in good earnest, I know not how I could help leaving the monastery and taking the remedy into my own hands." Thus did Charles make his voice heard from his retreat among the mountains, and by his efforts and influence render himself largely responsible for the fiery persecution which brought woe upon the land after he himself had gone to his account.

About the middle of August the emperor's old enemy, the gout, returned on him with uncommon force. It was attended with symptoms of an alarming kind, intimating, indeed, that his strong constitution was giving way. These were attributed to a cold which he had taken, though it seems there was good reason for imputing them to his intemperate living; for he still continued to indulge his appetite for the most dangerous dishes as freely as in the days when a more active way of life had better enabled him to digest them. It is true, the physician stood by his side, as prompt as Sancho Panza's[1] doctor, in his island domain, to remonstrate

[1] Sancho Panza, the peasant taken as squire by Don Quixote in Cervantes' novel.

against his master's proceedings. But, unhappily, he was not armed with the authority of that functionary; and an eel-pie, a well-spiced capon, or any other savory abomination offered too great a fascination for Charles to heed the warnings of his physician.

The declining state of the emperor's health may have inspired him with a presentiment of his approaching end, to which, we have seen, he gave utterance some time before this, in his conversation with Gaztelu. It may have been sober reflections which such a feeling would naturally suggest that led him, at the close of the month of August, to conceive the extraordinary idea of preparing for the final scene by rehearsing his own funeral. He consulted his confessor on the subject and was encouraged by the accommodating father to consider it as a meritorious act. The chapel was accordingly hung in black, and the blaze of hundreds of waxlights was not sufficient to dispel the darkness. The monks in their conventual dresses, and all the emperor's household, clad in deep mourning, gathered round a huge catafalque, shrouded also in black, which had been raised in the centre of the chapel. The service for the burial of the dead was then performed; and, amidst the dismal wail of the monks, the prayers ascended for the departed spirit, that it might be received into the mansions of the blessed. The sorrowful attendants were melted to tears as the image of their master's death was presented to their minds, or they were touched, it may be, with compassion for this pitiable display of his weakness. Charles, muffled in a dark mantle and bearing a lighted candle in his hand, mingled with his household, the spectator of his own obsequies; and the doleful ceremony was concluded by his placing the taper in the hands of the priest, in sign of his surrendering up his soul to the Almighty.

Such is the account of this melancholy farce given us by the Jeronymite chroniclers of the cloister life of Charles the Fifth, and which has since been repeated—losing nothing in the repetition—by every succeeding historian to the present time. Nor does there seem to have been any distrust of its correctness till the historical skepticism of our own day had subjected the narrative to a more critical scrutiny. It was then discovered that no mention of the affair was to be discerned in the letters of any one of the emperor's household residing at Yuste, although there are letters extant written by Charles's physician, his major-domo, and his secretary, both on the thirty-first of August, the day of the funeral, and on the first of September. With so extraordinary an event fresh in their minds, their silence is inexplicable.

One fact is certain, that, if the funeral did take place, it could not have been on the date assigned to it; for on the thirty-first the emperor was laboring under an attack of fever, of which his physician has given full particulars and from which he was destined never to recover. That the writers, therefore, should have been silent in respect to a ceremony which must have had so bad an effect on the nerves of the patient is altogether incredible.

Yet the story of the obsequies comes from one of the Jeronymite brethren then living at Yuste, who speaks of the emotions which he felt, in common with the rest of the convent, at seeing a man thus bury himself alive, as it were, and perform his funeral rites before his death. It is repeated by another of the fraternity, the prior of Escorial, who had ample means of conversing with eyewitnesses. And finally, it is confirmed by more than one writer near enough to the period to be able to assure himself of the truth. Indeed, the parties from whom the account is originally derived were so situated that if the story be without foundation it is impossible to explain its existence by misapprehension on their part. It must be wholly charged on a wilful misstatement of facts. It is true, the monkish chronicler is not always quite so scrupulous in this particular as would be desirable—especially where the honor of his order is implicated. But what interest could the Jeronymite fathers have had in so foolish a fabrication as this? The supposition is at variance with the respectable character of the parties, and with the air of simplicity and good faith that belongs to their narratives.

We may well be staggered, it is true, by the fact that no allusion to the obsequies appears in any of the letters from Yuste; while the date assigned for them, moreover, is positively disproved. Yet we may consider that the misstatement of a date is a very different thing from the invention of a story and that chronological accuracy, as I have more than once had occasion to remark, was not the virtue of the monkish or indeed of any other historian of the sixteenth century. It would not be a miracle if the obsequies should have taken place some days before the period assigned to them. It so happens that we have no letters from Yuste between the eighteenth and twenty-eighth of August. At least, I have none myself and have seen none cited by others. If any should hereafter come to light, written during that interval, they may be found possibly to contain some allusion to the funeral. Should no letters have been written during the period, the silence of the parties who wrote at the end of August and the beginning of September may be explained by the fact that too long a time had elapsed since the performance of the emperor's obsequies for them to suppose it could have any connection with his illness, which formed the subject of their correspondence. Difficulties will present themselves, whichever view we take of the matter. But the reader may think it quite reasonable to explain those difficulties by the supposition of involuntary error as by that of sheer invention.

Nor is the former supposition rendered less probable by the character of Charles the Fifth. There was a taint of insanity in the royal blood of Castile, which was most fully displayed in the emperor's mother, Joanna. Some traces of it, however faint, may be discerned in his own conduct before he took refuge in the cloisters of Yuste. And though we may not agree with Paul the Fourth in regarding this step as sufficient evidence of his madness, we may yet find something in his conduct, on more than one occasion, while there, which is near akin to it. Such, for example, was the morbid relish which he discovered for performing the obsequies not merely of his kindred but of any one whose position seemed to him to furnish an apology for it. Not a member of the *toison*[1] died but he was prepared to commemorate the event with solemn funeral rites. These, in short, seemed to be the festivities of Charles's cloister life. These lugubrious ceremonies had a fascination for him that may remind one of the tenacity with which his mother, Joanna, clung to the dead body of her husband, taking it with her wherever she went. It was after celebrating the obsequies of his parents and his wife, which occupied several successive days, that he conceived, as we are told, the idea of rehearsing his own funeral—a piece of extravagance which becomes more credible when we reflect on the state of morbid excitement to which his mind may have been brought by dwelling so long on the dreary apparatus of death.

But, whatever be thought of the account of the mock funeral of Charles, it appears that on the thirtieth of August he was affected by an indisposition which on the following day was attended wth most alarming symptoms. Here also we have some particulars from his Jeronymite biographers which we do not find in the letters. On the evening of the thirty-first, according to their account, Charles ordered a portrait of the empress, his wife, of whom he had more than one in his collection, to be brought to him. He dwelt a long while on its beautiful features, "as if," says the chronicler, "he were imploring her to prepare a place for him in the celestial mansions to which she had gone." He then passed to the contemplation of another picture, Titian's "Agony in the Garden," and from this to that immortal production of his pencil, the "Gloria," as it is called, which is said to have hung over the high altar at Yuste and which, after the emperor's death, followed his remains to the Escorial. He gazed so long and with such rapt attention on the picture as to cause apprehension in his physician, who, in the emperor's debilitated state, feared the effects of such excitement on his nerves. There was good reason for apprehension; for Charles, at length, rousing from his reverie, turned to the doctor and complained that

[1] The Golden Fleece, the highest order of Spanish knighthood.

he was ill. His pulse showed him to be in a high fever. As the symptoms become more unfavorable, his physician bled him, but without any good effect. The Regent Joanna, on learning her father's danger, instantly despatched her own physician from Valladolid to his assistance. But no earthly remedies could avail. It soon became evident that the end was approaching.

Charles received the intelligence not merely with composure but with cheerfulness. It was what he had long desired, he said. His first care was to complete some few arrangements respecting his affairs. On the ninth of September, he executed a codicil to his will. This will, made a few years previous, was of great length, and the codicil had not the merit of brevity. Its principal object was to make provision for those who had followed him to Yuste. No mention is made in the codicil of his son Don John of Austria. He seems to have communicated his views in regard to him to his major-domo, Quixada, who had a private interview of some length with his master a few days before his death. Charles's directions on the subject appear to have been scrupulously regarded by Philip.

One clause in the codicil deserves to be noticed. The emperor conjures his son most earnestly, by the obedience he owes him, to follow up and bring to justice every heretic in his dominions, and this without exception and without favor or mercy to any one. He conjures Philip to cherish the Holy Inquisitions as the best instrument for accomplishing this good work. "So," he concludes, "shall you have my blessing, and the Lord shall prosper all your undertakings." Such were the last words of the dying monarch to his son. They did not fall on a deaf ear; and the parting admonition of his father served to give a keener edge to the sword of persecution which Philip had already begun to wield.

On the nineteenth of September, Charles's strength had declined so much that it was thought proper to administer extreme unction to him. He preferred to have it in the form adopted by the friars, which, comprehending a litany, the seven penitential psalms, and sundry other passages of Scripture, was much longer and more exhausting than the rite used by the laity. His strength did not fail under it, however; and the following day he desired to take the communion, as he had frequently done during his illness. On his confessor's representing that, after the sacrament of extreme unction, this was unnecessary, he answered, "Perhaps so, but it is good provision for the long journey I am to set out upon." Exhausted as he was, he knelt a full quarter of an hour in his bed during the ceremony, offering thanks to God for his mercies and expressing the deepest contrition for his sins, with an earnestness of manner that touched the hearts of all present.

Throughout his illness he had found consolation in having passages of Scripture, especially the Psalms, read to him. Quixada, careful that his master should not be disquieted in his last moments, would allow very few persons to be present in his chamber. Among the number was Bartolomé de Carranza, who had lately been raised to the archiepiscopal see of Toledo. He had taken a prominent part in the persecution in England under Mary. For the remainder of his life he was to be the victim of persecution himself, from a stronger arm than his—that of the Inquisition. Even the words of consolation which he uttered in this chamber of death were carefully treasured up by Charles's confessor and made one of the charges against him in his impeachment for heresy.

On the twenty-first of September, St. Matthew's day, about two hours after midnight, the emperor, who had remained long without speaking, feeling that his hour had come, exclaimed, "Now it is time!" The holy taper was placed lighted in his right hand as he sat up leaning on the shoulder of the faithful Quixada. With his left he endeavored to clasp a silver crucifix. It had comforted the empress, his wife, in her dying hour; and Charles had ordered Quixada to hold it in readiness for him on the like occasion. It had lain for some time on his breast; and as it was now held up before his glazing eye by the archbishop of Toledo, Charles fixed his gaze long and earnestly on the sacred symbol—to him the memento of earthly love as well as heavenly. The archbishop was repeating the psalm *De Profundis*—"Out of the adjoining room, "*Ay Jesus!*" and sinking back on dying man, making a feeble effort to embrace the crucifix, exclaimed, in tones so audible as to be heard in the adjoining room, "*Ay Jesus!*" and sinking back on the pillow, expired without a struggle. He had always prayed—perhaps fearing the hereditary taint of insanity—that he might die in possession of his faculties. His prayer was granted.

*2. The Revolt of the Netherlands: The Gueux**

[*In writing his account of Philip II, Prescott devoted attention to a subject which has become associated with his contemporary Motley, the revolt of the Netherlands. The complex series of factors which led the Netherlands to rebel against Spain were not fully analyzed by Prescott, and, as a general history of the Dutch revolt, his work would be found lacking. Still, he composed several spirited accounts of major events. One such is his account of the origin of Gueux, as the rebels came to be known. What had originally been a nobles' revolt spread to the townsmen and lesser nobility, and these latter took the leadership of resistance to Spain from the prominent figures Count Egmont and the Prince of Orange. They formed a league, or "Compromise," indicating that their chief object was to resist the Inquisition. In April, 1566, they came to Brussels to present a petition to the regent, Margaret of Parma, an illegitimate daughter of Charles V.*]

*** From *Philip II*, Book II, chap. 10.**

The party of the malcontents in the Netherlands comprehended persons of very different opinions, who were by no means uniformly satisfied with the reasonable objects proposed by the Compromise. Some demanded entire liberty of conscience. Others would not have stopped short of a revolution that would enable the country to shake off the Spanish yoke. And another class of men without principle of any kind—such as are too often thrown up in strong political fermentations—looked to these intestine troubles as offering the means of repairing their own fortunes out of the wreck of their country's. Yet, with the exception of the last, there were few who would not have been content to accept the Compromise as the basis of their demands.

The winter had passed away, however, and the confederacy had wrought no change in the conduct of the government. Indeed, the existence of the confederacy would not appear to have been known to the regent till the latter part of February, 1566. It was not till the close of the following month that it was formally disclosed to her by some of the great lords. If it was known to her before, Margaret must have thought it prudent to affect ignorance till some overt action on the part of the league called for her notice.

It became, then, a question with the members of the league what was next to be done. It was finally resolved to present a petition in the name of the whole body to the regent, a measure which received the assent, if not the approbation, of the Prince of Orange. The paper was prepared, as it would seem, in William's own house at Brussels, by his brother Louis, and was submitted, we are told, to the revision of the prince, who thus had it in his power to mitigate, in more than one instance, the vehemence, or rather violence, of the expressions.

To give greater effect to the petition, it was determined that a large deputation from the league should accompany its presentation to the regent. Notice was given to four hundred of the confederates to assemble at the beginning of April. They were to come well-mounted and armed, prepared at once to proceed to Brussels. Among the number thus enrolled we find three gentlemen of Margaret's own household, as well as some members of the companies of *ordonnance* commanded by the prince and by the Counts Egmont and Hoorne and other great lords.

The duchess, informed of these proceedings, called a meeting of the council of state and the knights of the Golden Fleece to determine the course to be pursued. The discussion was animated, as there was much difference of opinion. Some agreed with Count Barlaimont in regarding the measure in the light of a menace. Such a military array could have no other object than to overawe the government, and was an insult to the regent. In the present excited state of the people, it would be attended with the greatest danger to allow their entrance into the capital.

The Prince of Orange, who had yielded to Margaret's earnest entreaties that he would attend this meeting, took a different view of the matter. The number of the delegates, he said, only proved the interest taken in the petition. They were men of rank, some of them kinsmen or personal friends of those present. Their characters and position in the country were sufficient sureties that they meditated no violence to the state. They were the representatives of an ancient order of nobility; and it would be strange indeed if they were to be excluded from the right of petition, enjoyed by the humblest individual.

In the course of the debate, William made some personal allusions to his own situation, delivering himself with great warmth. His enemies, he said, had the royal ear and would persuade the king to kill him and confiscate his property. He was even looked upon as the head of the confederacy. It was of no use for him to give his opinion in the council, where it was sure to be misinterpreted. All that remained for him was to ask leave to resign his offices and withdraw to his estates. Count Hoorne followed in much the same key, inveighing bitterly against the ingratitude of Philip. The two nobles yielded, at length, so far to Margaret's remonstrances as to give their opinions on the course to be pursued. But when she endeavored to recall them to their duty by reminding them of their oaths to the king, they boldly replied they would willingly lay down their lives for their country, but would never draw sword for the edicts or the Inquisition. William's views in regard to the admission of the confederates into Brussels were supported by much the greater part of the assembly and finally prevailed with the regent.

On the third of April, 1566, two hundred of the confederates entered the gates of Brussels. They were on horseback, and each man was furnished with a brace of pistols in his holster, wearing in other respects only the usual arms of a private gentleman. The Viscount Brederode and Louis of Nassau rode at their head. They prudently conformed to William's advice not to bring any foreigners in their train and to enter the city quietly, without attempting to stir the populace by any military display or the report of fire-arms. Their coming was welcomed with general joy by the inhabitants, who greeted them as a band of patriots ready to do battle for the liberties of the country. They easily found quarters in the houses of the principal citizens; and Louis and Brederode were lodged in the mansion of the Prince of Orange.

On the following day a meeting of the confederates was held at the hotel of Count Culemborg, where they listened to a letter which Brederode had just received from Spain, informing him of the death of Morone, a Flemish nobleman well known to them all, who had perished in the flames of the Inquisition. With feelings exasperated by this gloomy recital, they renewed, in the most solemn manner, their oaths of fidelity to the league. An application was then made to Margaret for leave to lay their petition before her. The day following was assigned for the act; and at noon, on the fifth of April, the whole company walked in solemn procession through the streets of Brussels to the palace of the regent. She received them, surrounded by the lords, in the great hall adjoining the council-chamber. As they defiled before her, the confederates ranged themselves along the sides of the apartment. Margaret seems to have been somewhat disconcerted by the presence of so martial an array within the walls of her palace. But she soon recovered herself and received them graciously.

Brederode was selected to present the petition, and he prefaced it by a short address. They had come in such numbers, he said, the better to show their respect to the regent and the deep interest they took in the cause. They had been accused of opening a correspondence with foreign princes, which he affirmed to be a malicious slander, and boldly demanded to be confronted with the authors of it. Notwithstanding this stout denial, it is very possible the audience did not place implicit confidence in the assertions of the speaker. He then presented the petition to the regent, expressing the hope that she would approve of it, as dictated only by their desire to promote the glory of the king and the good of the country. If this was its object, Margaret replied, she doubted not she should be content with it. The following day was named for them again to wait on her and receive her answer.

The instrument began with a general statement of the distresses of the land, much like that in the Compromise, but couched in more respectful language. The petitioners had hoped that the action of the great lords, or of the states-general, would have led to some reform. But finding these had not moved in the matter, while the evil went on increasing from day to day until ruin was at the gate, they had come to beseech her highness to lay the subject herself before the king and implore his majesty to save the country from perdition by the instant abolition of both the Inquisition and the edicts. Far from wishing to dictate laws to their sovereign, they humbly besought her to urge on him the necessity of convoking the states-general and devising with them some effectual remedy for the existing evils. Meanwhile they begged of her to suspend the further execution of the laws in regard to religion until his majesty's pleasure could be known. If their prayer were not granted, they at least were absolved from all responsibility as to the consequences, now that they had done their duty as true and loyal subjects. The business-like character of this document forms a contrast to the declamatory style of the Compromise; and in its temperate tone, particularly, we may fancy we recognize the touches of the more prudent hand of the Prince of Orange.

On the sixth, the confederates again assembled in the palace of the regent, to receive her answer. They were in greater force than before, having been joined by a hundred and fifty of their brethren, who had entered the city the night previous under the command of Counts Culemborg and Berg. They were received by Margaret in the same courteous manner as on the preceding day, and her answer was made to them in writing, being endorsed on their own petition.

She announced in it her purpose of using all her influence with her royal brother to persuade him to accede to their wishes. They might rely on his doing all that was conformable to his *natural and accustomed benignity*. She had herself, with the advice of her council and the knights of the Golden Fleece, prepared a scheme for moderating the edicts, to be laid before his majesty, which she trusted would satisfy the nation. They must, however, be aware that she herself had no power to suspend the execution of the laws. But she would send instructions to the inquisitors to proceed with all discretion in the exercise of their functions, until they should learn the king's pleasure. She trusted that the confederates would so demean themselves as not to make it necessary to give different orders. All this she had done with the greater readiness, from her conviction that they had no design to make any innovation in the established religion of the country, but desired rather to uphold it in all its vigor.

To this reply, as gracious in its expressions and as favorable in its import as the league could possibly have expected, they made a formal answer in writing, which they presented in a body to the duchess on the eighth of the month. They humbly thanked her for the prompt attention she had given to their petition, but would have been still more contented if her answer had been more full and explicit. They knew the embarrassments under which she labored, and they thanked her for the assurance she had given—which, it may be remarked, she never did give—that all proceedings connected with the Inquisition and the edicts should be stayed until his majesty's pleasure should be ascertained. They were most anxious to conform to whatever the king, *with the advice and consent of the states-general,* duly assembled, should determine in matters of religion; and they would show their obedience by taking such order for their own conduct as should give entire satisfaction to her highness.

To this the duchess briefly replied that if there were any cause for offence hereafter it would be chargeable not on her but on them. She prayed the confederates henceforth to desist from their secret practices and to invite no new member to join their body.

This brief and admonitory reply seems not to have been to the taste of the petitioners, who would willingly have drawn from Margaret some expression that might be construed into a sanction of their proceedings. After a short deliberation among themselves, they again addressed her by the mouth of one of their own number, the lord of Kerdes. The speaker, after again humbly thanking the regent for her favorable answer, said that it would have given still greater satisfaction to his associates if she would but have declared, in the presence of the great lords assembled, that she took the union of the confederates in good part and for the service of the king; and he concluded with promising that they would henceforth do all in their power to give contentment to her highness.

To all this the duchess simply replied she had no doubt of it. When again pressed by the persevering deputy to express her opinion of this assembly, she bluntly answered she could form no judgment in the matter. She gave pretty clear evidence, however, of her real opinion, soon after, by dismissing the three gentlemen of her household whom we have mentioned as having joined the league.

As Margaret found that the confederates were not altogether satisfied with her response to their petition, she allowed Count Hoogstraten, one of her councillors, to inform some of them, privately, that she had already written to the provinces to have all processes in affairs of religion stayed until Philip's decision should be known. To leave no room for distrust, the count was allowed to show them copies of the letters.

The week spent by the league in Brussels was a season of general jubilee. At one of the banquets given at Culemborg House, where three hundred confederates were present, Brederode presided. During the repast he related to some of the company, who had arrived on the day after the petition was delivered, the manner in which it had been received by the duchess. She seemed at first disconcerted, he said, by the number of the confederates, but was reassured by Barlaimont, who told her "they were nothing but a crowd of beggars." This greatly incensed some of the company—with whom, probably, it was too true for a jest. But Brederode, taking it more good-humoredly, said that he and his friends had no objection to the name, since they were ready at any time to become beggars for the service of their king and country. This sally was received with great applause by the guests, who, as they drank to one another, shouted forth, "*Vivent les Gueux!*"—"Long live the beggars!"

Brederode, finding the jest took so well—an event, indeed, for which he seems to have been prepared—left the room and soon returned with a beggar's wallet and a wooden bowl such as was used by the mendicant fraternity in the Netherlands. Then, pledging the company in a bumper, he swore to devote his life and fortune to the cause. The wallet and the bowl went round the table; and, as each of the merry guests drank in turn to his confederates, the shout arose of "*Vivent les Gueux!*" until the hall rang with the mirth of the revellers.

It happened that at the time the Prince of Orange and the Counts Egmont and Hoorne were passing by on their way to the council. Their attention was attracted by the noise, and they paused a moment, when William, who knew well the temper of the jovial company, proposed that they should go in and endeavor to break up their revels. "We may have some business of the council to transact with these men this evening," he said, "and at this rate they will hardly be in a condition for it." The appearance of the three nobles gave a fresh impulse to the boisterous merriment of the company; and as the new-comers pledged their friends in the wine-cup, it was received with the same thundering acclamation of *"Vivent les Gueux!"* This incident, of so little importance in itself, was afterwards made of consequence by the turn that was given to it in the prosecution of the two unfortunate noblemen who accompanied the Prince of Orange.

Every one knows the importance of a popular name to a faction—a *nom de guerre,* under which its members may rally and make head together as an independent party. Such the name of *"Gueux"* now became to the confederates. It soon was understood to signify those who were opposed to the government and, in a wider sense, to the Roman Catholic religion. In every language in which the history of these acts has been recorded—the Latin, German, Spanish, or English—the French term *Gueux* is ever employed to designate this party of malcontents in the Netherlands.

It now became common to follow out the original idea by imitations of the different articles used by mendicants. Staffs were procured, after the fashion of those in the hands of the pilgrims, but more elaborately carved. Wooden bowls, spoons, and knives became in great request, though richly inlaid with silver, according to the fancy or wealth of the possessor. Medals resembling those stuck by the beggars in their bonnets were worn as a badge; and the "Gueux penny," as it was called—a gold or silver coin—was hung from the neck, bearing on one side the effigy of Philip, with the inscription *"Fideles au roi"*; and on the other, two hands grasping a beggar's wallet, with further legend, *"Jusques à porter las besace"*— "Faithful to the king, even to carrying the wallet." Even the garments of the mendicant were affected by the confederates, who used them as a substitute for their family liveries; and troops of their retainers, clad in the ash-grey habiliments of the begging friars, might be seen in the streets of Brussels and the other cities of the Netherlands.

On the tenth of April, the confederates quit Brussels, in the orderly manner in which they had entered it; except that, on issuing from the gate, they announced their departure by firing a salute in honor of the city which had given them so hospitable a welcome. Their visit to Brussels had not only created a great sensation in the capital itself but throughout the country. Hitherto the league had worked in darkness, as it were, like a band of secret conspirators. But they had now come forward into the light of day, boldly presenting themselves before the regent and demanding redress of the wrongs under which the nation was groaning. The people took heart as they saw this broad aegis extended over them to ward off the assaults of arbitrary power. Their hopes grew stronger as they became assured of the interposition of the regent and the great lords in their favor; and they could hardly doubt that the voice of the country, backed as it was by that of the government, would make itself heard at Madrid and that Philip would at length be compelled to abandon a policy which menaced him with the loss of the fairest of his provinces. They had yet to learn the character of their sovereign.

3. The Revolt of the Netherlands: The Iconoclasts*

[The Low Countries were by now in a state of extreme confusion. Something approaching anarchy swept over the land, and, although the Calvinists did not form a majority of the population, the authorities did little to curb them. Preachings took place openly, and the furor of the mob was turned against the images and other

* From *Philip II*, Book II, chap. 12.

relics of Catholicism which filled the churches of the country.]

While Philip was thus tardily coming to concessions which even then were not sincere, an important crisis had arrived in the affairs of the Netherlands. In the earlier stages of the troubles, all orders the nobles, the commons, even the regent had united in the desire to obtain the removal of certain abuses, especially the Inquisition and the edicts. But this movement, in which the Catholic joined with the Protestant, had far less reference to the interests of religion than to the personal rights of the individual. Under the protection thus afforded, however, the Reformation struck deep root in the soil. It flourished still more under the favor shown to it by the confederates, who did not scruple to guaranty security of religious worship to some of the sectaries who demanded it.

But the element which contributed most to the success of the new religion was the public preachings. These in the Netherlands were what the Jacobin clubs were in France, or the secret societies in Germany and Italy —an obvious means for bringing together such as were pledged to a common hostility to existing institutions, and thus affording them an opportunity for consulting on their grievances and for concerting the best means of redress. The direct object of these meetings, it is true, was to listen to the teachings of the minister. But that functionary, far from confining himself to spiritual exercises, usually wandered to more exciting themes, as the corruptions of the Church and the condition of the land. He rarely failed to descant on the forlorn circumstances of himself and his flock, condemned thus stealthily to herd together like a band of outlaws, with ropes, as it were, about their necks, and to seek out some solitary spot in which to glorify the Lord, while their enemies, in all the pride of a dominant religion, could offer up their devotions openly and without fear, in magnificent temples. The preacher inveighed bitterly against the richly beneficed clergy of the rival Church, whose lives of pampered ease too often furnished an indifferent commentary on the doctrines they inculcated. His wrath was kindled by the pompous ceremonial of the Church of Rome, so dazzling and attractive to its votaries, but which the Reformer sourly contrasted with the naked simplicity of the Protestant service. Of all abominations, however, the greatest in his eyes was the worship of images, which he compared to the idolatry that in ancient times had so often brought down the vengeance of Jehovah on the nations of Palestine; and he called on his hearers not merely to remove idolatry from their hearts but the idols from their sight. It was not wonderful that, thus stimulated by their spiritual leaders, the people should be prepared for scenes similar to those enacted by the Reformers in France and in Scotland, or that Margaret, aware of the popular feeling, should have predicted such an outbreak. At length it came, and on a scale and with a degree of violence not surpassed either by the Huguenots or the disciples of Knox.

On the fourteenth of August, the day before the festival of the Assumption of the Virgin, a mob some three hundred in number, armed with clubs, axes, and other implements of destruction, broke into the churches around St. Omer, in the province of Flanders, overturned the images, defaced the ornaments, and in a short time demolished whatever had any value or beauty in the buildings. Growing bolder from the impunity which attended their movements, they next proceeded to Ypres and had the audacity to break into the cathedral and deal with it in the same ruthless manner. Strengthened by the accession of other miscreants from the various towns, they proceeded along the banks of the Lys and fell upon the churches of Menin, Comines, and other places on its borders. The excitement now spread over the country. Everywhere the populace was in arms. Churches, chapels, and convents were involved in indiscriminate ruin. The storm, after sweeping over Flanders and desolating the flourishing cities of Valenciennes and Tournay, descended on Brabant. Antwerp, the great commercial capital of the country, was its first mark.

The usual population of the town happened to be swelled at this time by an influx of strangers from the neighboring country, who had come up to celebrate the great festival of the Assumption of the Virgin. Fortunately, the prince of Orange was in the place and by his presence prevented any molestation to the procession, except what arose from the occasional groans and hisses of the more zealous spectators among the Protestants. The priests, however, on their return, had the discretion to deposit the image in the chapel instead of the conspicuous station usually assigned to it in the cathedral, to receive there during the coming week the adoration of the faithful.

On the following day, unluckily, the prince was recalled to Brussels. In the evening some boys, who had found their way into the church, called out to the Virgin, demanding "why little Mary had gone so early to her nest, and whether she were afraid to show her face in public." This was followed by one of the party mounting into the pulpit and there mimicking the tones and gestures of the Catholic preacher. An honest waterman who was present, a zealous son of the Church, scandalized by this insult to his religion, sprang into the pulpit and endeavored to dislodge the usurper. The lad resisted. His comrades came to his rescue; and a struggle ensued, which ended in both the parties being expelled from the building by the officers. This scandalous proceeding, it may be thought, should have put the magistrates of the city on their guard and warned them to take some measures of defence for the cathedral. But the admonition was not heeded.

On the following day a considerable number of the reformed party entered the building and were allowed to continue there after vespers, when the rest of the congregation had withdrawn. Left in possession, their first act was to break forth into one of the Psalms of David. The sound of their own voices seemed to rouse them to fury. Before the chant had died away, they rushed forward as by a common impulse, broke open the doors of the chapel, and dragged forth the image of the Virgin. Some called on her to cry, "*Vivent les Gueux!*" while others tore off her embroidered robes and rolled the dumb idol in the dust, amidst the shouts of the spectators.

This was the signal for havoc. The rioters dispersed in all directions on the work of destruction. Nothing escaped their rage. High above the great altar was an image of the Savior, curiously carved in wood and placed between the effigies of the two thieves crucified with him. The mob contrived to get a rope round the neck of the statue of Christ and dragged it to the ground. They then fell upon it with hatchets and hammers, and it was soon broken into a hundred fragments. The two thieves, it was remarked, were spared, as if to preside over the work of rapine below.

Their fury now turned against the other statues, which were quickly overthrown from their pedestals. The paintings that lined the walls of the cathedral were cut into shreds. Many of these were the choicest specimens of Flemish art, even then, in its dawn, giving promise of the glorious day which was to shed a lustre over the land.

But the pride of the cathedral, and of Antwerp, was the great organ, renowned throughout the Netherlands, not more for its dimensions than its perfect workmanship. With their ladders the rioters scaled the lofty fabric, and with their implements soon converted it, like all else they laid their hands on, into a heap of rubbish.

The ruin was now universal. Nothing beautiful, nothing holy was spared. The altars—and there were no less than seventy in the vast edifice—were overthrown one after another; their richly embroidered coverings rudely rent away; their gold and silver vessels appropriated by the plunderers. The sacramental bread was trodden under foot; the wine was quaffed by the miscreants, in golden chalices, to the health of one another, or of the Gueux; and the holy oil was profanely used to anoint their shoes and sandals. The sculptured tracery on the walls, the costly offerings that enriched the shrines, the screens of gilded bronze, the delicately carved wood-work of the pulpit, the marble and alabaster ornaments—all went down under the fierce blows of the iconoclasts. The pavement was strewed with the ruined splendors of a church which in size and magnificence was perhaps second only to St. Peter's among the churches of Christendom.

As the light of day faded, the assailants supplied its place with such light as they could obtain from the candles which they snatched from the altars. It was midnight before the work of destruction was completed. Thus toiling in darkness, feebly dispelled by tapers the rays of which could scarcely penetrate the vaulted distances of the cathedral, it is a curious circumstance—if true—that no one was injured by the heavy masses of timber, stone, and metal that were everywhere falling around them. The whole number engaged in this work is said not to have exceeded a hundred men, women, and boys—women of the lowest description, dressed in men's attire.

When their task was completed, they sallied forth in a body from the doors of the cathedral, some singing the Psalms of David, others roaring out the fanatical war-cry of *"Vivent les Gueux!"* Flushed with success, and joined on the way by stragglers like themselves, they burst open the doors of one church after another; and by the time morning broke, the principal temples in the city had been dealt with in the same ruthless manner as the cathedral.

No attempt all this time was made to stop these proceedings, on the part of magistrates or citizens. As they beheld from their windows the bodies of armed men hurrying to and fro by the gleam of their torches, and listened to the sounds of violence in the distance, they seem to have been struck with a panic. The Catholics remained within-doors, fearing a general rising of the Protestants. The Protestants feared to move abroad, lest they should be confounded with the rioters. Some imagined their own turn might come next and appeared in arms at the entrances of their houses, prepared to defend them against the enemy.

When gorged with the plunder of the city, the insurgents poured out at the gates and fell with the same violence on the churches, convents, and other religious edifices in the suburbs. For three days these dismal scenes continued, without resistance on the part of the inhabitants. Amidst the ruin in the cathedral, the mob had alone spared the royal arms and the escutcheons of the knights of the Golden Fleece, emblazoned on the walls. Calling this to mind, they now returned into the city to complete the work. But some of the knights, who were at Antwerp, collected a handful of their followers and, with a few of the citizens, forced their way into the cathedral, arrested ten or twelve of the rioters, and easily dispersed the remainder; while a gallows erected on an eminence admonished the offenders of the fate that awaited them. The facility with which the disorders were repressed by a few resolute men naturally suggests the inference that many of the citizens had too much sympathy with the authors of the outrages to care to check them, still less to bring the culprits to punishment. An orthodox chronicler of the time vents his indignation against a people who were so much more ready to stand by their hearths than by their altars.

The fate of Antwerp had its effect on the country. The flames of fanaticism, burning fiercer than ever, quickly spread over the northern as they had done over the western provinces. In Holland, Utrecht, Friesland—everywhere, in short, with a few exceptions on the southern borders—mobs rose against the churches. In some places, as Rotterdam, Dort, Haarlem, the magistrates were wary enough to avert the storm by delivering up the images, or at least by removing them from the buildings. It was rarely that any attempt was made at resistance. Yet on one or two occasions this so far succeeded that a handful of troops sufficed to rout the iconoclasts. At Anchyn, four hundred of the rabble were left dead on the field. But the soldiers had no relish for their duty, and on other occasions, when called on to perform it, refused to bear arms against their countrymen. The leaven of heresy was too widely spread among the people.

Thus the work of plunder and devastation went on vigorously throughout the land. Cathedral and chapel, monastery and nunnery, religious houses of every description, even hospitals were delivered up to the tender mercies of the Reformers. The monks fled, leaving behind them treasures of manuscripts and well-stored cellars, which latter the invaders soon emptied of their contents, while they consigned the former to the flames. The terrified nuns, escaping half naked, at dead of night from their convents were too happy to find a retreat among their friends and kinsmen in the city. Neither monk nor nun ventured to go abroad in the conventual garb. Priests might be sometimes seen hurrying away with some relic or sacred treasure under their robes, which they were eager to save from the spoilers. In the general sack not even the abode of the dead was respected; and the sepulchres of the counts of Flanders were violated and laid open to the public gaze!

The deeds of violence perpetrated by the iconoclasts were accompanied by such indignities as might express their contempt for the ancient faith. They snatched the wafer, says an eyewitness, from the altar and put it into the mouth of a parrot. Some huddled the images of the saints together and set them on fire, or covered them with bits of armor and, shouting *"Vivent les Gueux!"*, tilted rudely against them. Some put on the vestments stolen from the churches and ran about the streets with them in mockery. Some basted the books with butter, that they might burn the more briskly. By the scholar, this last enormity will not be held light among their transgressions. It answered their purpose, to judge by the number of volumes that were consumed. Among the rest, the great library of Vicogne, one of the noblest collections in the Netherlands, perished in the flames kindled by these fanatics.

*4. The Revolt of the Netherlands: The Duke of Alva and the Council of Blood**

[The excesses of the iconoclasts disgusted many in the Netherlands, and because of this it became possible to establish a shaky religious peace in the Low Countries. The Spanish government seemed once more to be in the ascendancy. But in August, 1567, Philip II despatched the Duke of Alva to the Netherlands. Alva had already established an impressive record as a tough-minded royal servant. His attitude toward the situation in the Netherlands is well indicated in his comment, "I have tamed men of iron, and I shall soon have done with these men of butter." Alva was not welcomed by the regent; when she resigned, he took her place under the titles of Regent and Governor-General. His policy proved to be as harsh as his words indicated; one of his major steps was the creation of a new council, officially termed the Council of Troubles, but soon known as the Council of Blood.]

"Thank God," writes the duke of Alva to his sovereign, on the twenty-fourth of October, "all is tranquil in the Low Countries." It was the same sentiment he had uttered a few weeks before. All was indeed tranquil. Silence reigned throughout the land. Yet it might have spoken more eloquently to the heart than the murmurs of discontent or the loudest tumult of insurrection. "They say many are leaving the country," he writes in another despatch. "It is hardly worth while to arrest them.

* From *Philip II*, Book III, chap. 2.

The repose of the nation is not to be brought about by cutting off the heads of those who are led astray by others."

Yet in less than a week after this we find a royal ordinance declaring that "whereas his majesty is averse to use rigor towards those who have taken part in the late rebellion, and would rather deal with them in all gentleness and mercy, it is forbidden to any one to leave the land, or to send off his effects, without obtaining a license from the authorities, under pain of being regarded as having taken part in the late troubles, and of being dealt with accordingly. All masters and owners of vessels who shall aid such persons in their flight shall incur the same penalties." The penalties denounced in this spirit of "gentleness and mercy" were death and confiscation of property.

That the law was not a dead letter was soon shown by the arrest of ten of the principal merchants of Tournay as they were preparing to fly to foreign parts, and by the immediate confiscation of their estates. Yet Alva would have persuaded the world that he, as well as his master, was influenced only by sentiments of humanity. To the Spanish ambassador at Rome he wrote, soon after the seizure of the Flemish lords: "I might have arrested more; but the king is averse to shedding the blood of his people. I have the same disposition myself. I am pained to the bottom of my soul by the necessity of the measure."

But now that the great nobles had come into the snare, it was hardly necessary to keep up the affectation of lenity; and it was not long before he threw away the mask altogether. The arm of justice—of vengeance—was openly raised to strike down all who had offended by taking part in the late disturbances.

The existing tribunals were not considered as competent to this work. The regular forms of procedure were too dilatory, and the judges themselves would hardly be found subservient enough to the will of Alva. He created, therefore, a new tribunal with extraordinary powers for the sole purpose of investigating the causes of the late disorders and for bringing the authors to punishment. It was called originally the "Council of his Excellency." The name was soon changed to that of the "Council of Tumults." But the tribunal is better known in history by the terrible name it received from the people, of the "Council of Blood."

It was composed of twelve judges, "the most learned, upright men, and of the purest lives"—if we may take the duke's word for it—that were to be found in the country. Among them were Noicarmes and Barlaimont, both members of the council of state. The latter was a proud noble, of one of the most ancient families in the land, inflexible in his character and staunch in his devotion to the Crown. Besides these there were the presidents of the councils of Artois and Flanders, the chancellor of Gueldres, and several jurists of repute in the country. But the persons of most consideration in the body were two lawyers who had come in the duke's train from Castile. One of these, the doctor Del Rio, though born in Bruges, was of Spanish extraction. His most prominent trait seems to have been unlimited subserviency to the will of his employer. The other, Juan de Vargas, was to play the most conspicuous part in the bloody drama that followed. He was a Spaniard and had held a place in the council of the Indies. His character was infamous; and he was said to have defrauded an orphan ward of her patrimony. When he left Spain, two criminal prosecutions were reported to have been hanging over him. This only made him the more dependent on Alva's protection. He was a man of great energy of character, unwearied in application to business, unscrupulous in the service of his employer, ready at any price to sacrifice to his own interest not only every generous impulse but the common feelings of humanity. Such, at least, are the dark colors in which he is portrayed by the writers of a nation which held him in detestation. Yet his very vices made him so convenient to the duke that the latter soon bestowed on him more of his confidence than on any other of his followers; and in his correspondence with Philip we find him commending Vargas to the monarch's favor and contrasting his "activity, altogether juvenile," with the apathy of others of the council. As Vargas was unacquainted with Flemish, the proceedings of the court were conducted, for his benefit, in Latin. Yet he was such a bungler even in this language that his blunders furnished infinite merriment to the people of Flanders, who took some revenge for their wrongs in the ridicule of their oppressor.

As the new court had cognizance of all cases, civil as well as criminal, that grew out of the late disorders, the amount of business soon pressed on them so heavily that it was found expedient to distribute it into several departments among the different members. Two of the body had especial charge of the processes of the Prince of Orange, his brother Louis, Hoogstraten, Culemborg, and the rest of William's noble companions in exile. To Vargas and Del Rio was intrusted the trial of the Counts Egmont and Hoorne. And two others, Blasere and Hessels, had the most burdensome and important charge of all such causes from the provinces.

The latter of these two worthies was destined to occupy a place second only to that of Vargas on the bloody roll of persecution. He was a native of Ghent, of sufficient eminence in his profession to fill the office of attorney-general of his province under Charles the Fifth. In that capacity he enforced the edicts with so much rigor as to make himself odious to his countrymen. In the new career now opened to him he found a still wider field for his mischievous talents, and he entered on the duties of his office with such hearty zeal as soon roused general indignation in the people, who at a later day took terrible vengeance on their oppressor.

As soon as the Council of Troubles was organized, commissioners were despatched into the provinces to hunt out the suspected parties. All who had officiated as preachers, or had harbored or aided them, who had joined the consistories, who had assisted in defacing or destroying the Catholic churches or in building the Protestant, who had subscribed the Compromise, or who, in short, had taken an active part in the late disorders were to be arrested as guilty of treason. In the hunt after victims, informations were invited from every source.

Wives were encouraged to depose against husbands, children against parents. The prisons were soon full to overflowing, and the provincial and the local magistrates were busy in filing informations of the different cases, which were forwarded to the court at Brussels. When deemed of sufficient importance, the further examination of a case was reserved for the council itself. But for the most part the local authorities, or a commission sent expressly for the purpose, were authorized to try the case, proceeding even to a definitive sentence, which, with the grounds of it, they were to lay before the Council of Troubles. The process was then revised by the committee for the provinces, who submitted the result of their examination to Vargas and Del Rio. The latter were alone empowered to vote in the matter, and their sentence, prepared in writing, was laid before the duke, who reserved to himself the right of final decision. This he did, as he wrote to Philip, that he might not come too much under the direction of the council. "Your majesty well knows," he concludes, "that the gentlemen of the law are unwilling to decide anything except upon evidence, while measures of state policy are not to be regulated by the laws."

It might be supposed that the different judges to whom the prisoner's case was thus separately submitted for examination would have afforded an additional guaranty for his security. But quite the contrary: It only multiplied the chances of his conviction. When the provincial committee presented their report to Vargas and Del Rio—to whom a Spanish jurist, auditor of the chancery of Valladolid, named Roda, was afterwards added—if it proposed sentence of death, these judges declared it "was right, and that there was no necessity of reviewing the process." If, on the contrary, a lower penalty was recommended, the worthy ministers of the law were in the habit of returning the process, ordering the committee, with bitter imprecations, to revise it more carefully!

As confiscation was one of the most frequent as well as momentous penalties adjudged by the Council of Blood, it necessarily involved a large number of civil actions; for the estate thus forfeited was often burdened with heavy claims on it by other parties. These were all to be established before the council. One may readily comprehend how small was the chance of justice before such a tribunal, where the creditor was one of the parties and the Crown the other. Even if the suit was decided in favor of the creditor, it was usually so long protracted, and attended with such ruinous expense, that it would have been better for him never to have urged it.

The jurisdiction of the court, within the limits assigned to it, wholly superseded that of the great court of Mechlin, as well as of every other tribunal, provincial or municipal, in the country. Its decisions were final. By the law of the land, established by repeated royal charters in the provinces, no man in the Netherlands could be tried by any but a native judge. But of the present court, one member was a native of Burgundy, and two were Spaniards.

It might be supposed that a tribunal with such enormous powers, which involved so gross an outrage on the constitutional rights and long-established usages of the nation, would at least have been sanctioned by some warrant from the Crown. It could pretend to nothing of the kind—not even a written commission from the duke of Alva, the man who created it. By his voice alone he gave it an existence. The ceremony of induction into office was performed by the new member placing his hands between those of the duke and swearing to remain true to the faith, to decide in all cases according to his sincere conviction, finally, to keep secret all the doings of the council, and to denounce any one who disclosed them. A tribunal clothed with such unbounded power, and conducted on a plan so repugnant to all principles of justice, fell nothing short, in its atrocity, of that Inquisition so much dreaded in the Netherlands.

Alva, in order to be the better able to attend the council, appointed his own palace for the place of meeting. At first the sittings were held morning and afternoon, lasting sometimes seven hours in a day. There was a general attendance of the members, the duke presiding in person. After a few months, as he was drawn to a distance by more pressing affairs, he resigned his place to Vargas. Barlaimont and Noircarmes, disgusted with the atrocious character of the proceedings, soon absented themselves from the meetings. The more respectable of the members imitated their example. One of the body, a Burgundian, a follower of Granvelle,[1] having criticized the proceedings somewhat too freely, had leave to withdraw to his own province; till at length only three or four councillors remained—Vargas, Del Rio, Hessels, and his colleague—on whom the despatch of the momentous business wholly devolved. To some of the processes we find not more than three names subscribed. The duke was as indifferent to forms as he was to the rights of the nation.

It soon became apparent that, as in most proscriptions, wealth was the mark at which persecution was mainly directed. At least, if it did not actually form a ground of accusation, it greatly enhanced the chances of a conviction. The commissioners sent to the provinces received written instructions to ascertain the exact amount of property belonging to the suspected parties. The expense incident to the maintenance of so many officials, as well as of a large military force, pressed heavily on the government; and Alva soon found it necessary to ask for support from Madrid. It was in vain he attempted to obtain a loan from the merchants. "They refuse," he writes, "to advance a *real*[2] on the security of the confiscations, till they see how the game we have begun is likely to prosper!"

In another letter to Philip, dated on the twenty-fourth of October, Alva, expressing his regret at the necessity of demanding supplies, says that the Low Countries ought to maintain themselves and be no tax upon Spain. He is constantly thwarted by the duchess and by the council of finance in his appropriation of the confiscated property. Could he only manage things in his own way, he would answer for it that the Flemish cities, un-

---

[1] Antoine Perrenot de Granvelle (1517–1586), cardinal-minister of Charles V and Philip II.

[2] Castilian coin equivalent to thirty-four *maravedis.*

certain and anxious as to their fate, would readily acquiesce in the fair means of raising a revenue proposed by the king. The ambitious general, eager to secure the sole authority to himself, artfully touched on the topic which would be most likely to operate with his master. In a note on this passage, in his own handwriting, Philip remarked that this was but just, but, as he feared that supplies would never be raised with the consent of the states, Alva must devise some expedient by which their consent in the matter might be dispensed with, and communicate it privately to him. This pregnant thought he soon after develops more fully in a letter to the duke. It is edifying to observe the cool manner in which the king and his general discuss the best means for filching a revenue from the pockets of the good people of the Netherlands.

5. *The Revolt of the Alpujarras**

[The problems of Philip II were not confined to the Low Countries. The Morisco communities that remained in Spain posed a double threat. They were far from assimilated into the population; moreover, they were closely associated with Spain's traditional enemy, the Turk. An uneasy peace had been maintained since the first revolt of the Alpujarras in 1499. However, a royal order for the reform of Morisco customs was published by Philip II in January, 1567. This led directly to the second revolt of the Alpujarras in 1568-1570. Troops had to be summoned back from Italy to crush the rebels, whose movement as-

* From *Philip II*, Book V, chap. 8.

sumed serious proportions. After a particularly brutal campaign, the king's half-brother Don John of Austria broke the back of the resistance. As a final blow to the Moriscoes, Philip II ordered their deportation from the province of Granada.]

On the twenty-eighth of October Don John received advices of a final edict of Philip, commanding that all the Moriscoes in the kingdom of Granada should be at once removed into the interior of the country. None were to be excepted from this decree, not even the *Moriscoes de la Paz,* as those were called who had loyally refused to take part in the rebellion. The arrangements for this important and difficult step were made with singular prudence and, under the general direction of Don John of Austria, the Grand Commander Requesens, and the dukes of Sesa and Arcos, were carried into effect with promptness and energy.

By the terms of the edict, the lands and houses of the exiles were to be forfeited to the Crown. But their personal effects—their flocks, their herds, and their grain —would be taken, if they desired it, at a fixed valuation by the government. Every regard was to be paid to their personal convenience and security; and it was forbidden, in the removal, to separate parents from children, husbands from wives, in short, to divide the members of a family from one another—"an act of clemency," says a humane chronicler, "which they little deserved; but his majesty was willing in this to content them."

The country was divided into districts, the inhabitants of which were to be conducted, under the protection of a strong military escort, to their several places of destination. These seem to have been the territory of La Mancha, the northern borders of Andalusia, the Castiles, Estremadura, and even the remote provinces of Galicia. Care was taken that no settlement should be made near the borders of Murcia or Valencia, where large numbers of the Moriscoes were living in comparative quiet on the estates of the great nobles, who were exceedingly jealous of any interference with their vassals.

The first of November, All Saints' Day, was appointed for the removal of the Moriscoes throughout Granada. On that day they were gathered in the principal churches of their districts and, after being formed into their respective divisions, began their march. The grand commander had occupied the passes of the Alpujarras with strong detachments of the military. The different columns of emigrants were placed under the direction of persons of authority and character. The whole movement was conducted with singular order—resistance being attempted in one or two places only, where the blame, it may be added, as intimated by a Castilian chronicler, was to be charged on the brutality of the soldiers. Still, the removal of the Moriscoes, on the present occasion, was attended with fewer acts of violence and rapacity than the former removal, from Granada. At least this would seem to be inferred by the silence of the chroniclers; though it is true such silence is far from being conclusive, as the chroniclers, for the most part, felt too little interest in the sufferings of the Moriscoes to make a notice of them indispensable. However this may be, it cannot be doubted that, whatever precautions may have been taken to spare the exiles any unnecessary suffering, the simple fact of their being expelled from their native soil is one that suggests an amount of misery not to be estimated. For what could be more dreadful than to be thus torn from their pleasant homes, the scenes of their childhood, where every mountain, valley, and stream were as familiar friends—a part of their own existence—to be rudely thrust into a land of strangers, of a race different from themselves in faith, language, and institutions, with no sentiment in common but that of a deadly hatred! That the removal of a whole nation should have been so quietly accomplished proves how entirely the strength and spirit of the Moriscoes must have been broken by their reverses.

The war thus terminated, there seemed no reason for John of Austria to prolong his stay in the province. For some time he had been desirous to obtain the king's consent to his return. His ambitious spirit, impatient of playing a part on what now seemed to him an obscure field of action, pent up within the mountain barrier of the Alpujarras, longed to display itself on a bolder theatre before the world. He aspired, too, to a more independent command. He addressed repeated letters to the king's ministers—to the Cardinal Espinosa and Ruy Gomez de Silva in particular—to solicit their influence in his behalf. "I should be glad," he wrote to the latter, "to serve his majesty, if I might be allowed, on some business of importance. I wish he may understand that I am no longer a boy. Thank God, I can begin to fly without the aid of other's wings, and it is full time, as I believe, that I was out of swaddling-clothes." In another letter he expresses his desire to have some place more fitting the brother of such a monarch as Philip and the son of such a father as Charles the Fifth. On more than one occasion he alludes to the command against the Turk as the great object of his ambition.

His importunity to be allowed to resign his present office had continued from the beginning of summer, some months before the proper close of the campaign. It may be thought to argue an instability of character, of which a more memorable example was afforded by him at a later period of life. At length he was rejoiced by obtaining the royal consent to resign his command and return to court.

On the eleventh of November, Don John repaired to Granada. Till the close of the month he was occupied with making the necessary arrangements preparatory to his departure. The greater part of the army was paid off and disbanded. A sufficient number was reserved to garrison the fortresses and to furnish detachments which were to scour the country and hunt down such Moriscoes as still held out in the mountains. As Requesens was to take part in the expedition against the Ottomans, the office of captain-general was placed in the hands of the valiant duke of Arcos. On the twenty-ninth of November, Don John, having completed his preparations, quit Granada and set forth on his journey to Madrid, where the popular chieftain was welcomed with enthusiasm by the citizens as a conqueror returned from a victorious campaign. By Philip and his newly-married bride, Anne of Austria, he was no less kindly greeted; and it was not long before the king gave a substantial proof of his contentment with his brother by placing in his hands the baton offered by the allies of the generalissimo in the war against the Turks.

There was still one Morisco insurgent who refused to submit and who had hitherto eluded every attempt to capture him, but whose capture was of more importance than that of any other of his nation. This was Aben-Aboo, the "little king" of the Alpujarras. His force of five thousand men had dwindled to scarcely more than four hundred. But they were men devoted to his person and seemed prepared to endure every extremity rather than surrender. Like the rest of his nation, the Morisco chief took refuge in the mountain caves, in such remote and inaccessible districts as had hitherto baffled every attempt to detect his retreat. In March, 1571, an opportunity presented itself for making the discovery.

Granada was at this time the scene of almost daily executions. As the miserable insurgents were taken, they were brought before Deza's tribunal, where they were at once sentenced by the inexorable president to the galleys or the gibbet, or the more horrible doom of being torn in pieces with red-hot pincers. Among the prisoners sentenced to death was one Zatahari, who was so fortunate as to obtain a respite of his punishment at the intercession of a goldsmith named Barredo, a person of much consideration in Granada. From gratitude for this service, or perhaps as the price of it, Zatahari made some important revelations to his benefactor respecting Aben-Aboo. He disclosed the place of his retirement and the number of his followers, adding that the two persons on whom he most relied were his secretary, Abou-Amer, and a Moorish captain named El Senix. The former of these persons was known to Barredo, who in the course of his business had frequent occasion to make journeys into the Alpujarras. He resolved to open a correspondence with the secretary and, if possible, win him over to the Spanish interests. Zatahari consented to bear the letter, on condition of a pardon. This was readily granted by the president, who approved the plan and who authorized the most liberal promises to Abou-Amer in case of his co-operation with Barredo.

Unfortunately—or, rather fortunately for Zatahari, as it proved—he was intercepted by El Senix, who, getting possession of the letter, carried it to Abou-Amer. The loyal secretary was outraged by this attempt to corrupt him. He would have put the messenger to death, had not El Senix represented that the poor wretch had undertaken the mission only to save his life.

Privately the Moorish captain assured the messenger that Barredo should have sought a conference with him, as he was ready to enter into negotiations with the Christians. In fact, El Senix had a grudge against his master and had already made an attempt to leave his service and escape to Barbary.

A place of meeting was accordingly appointed in the Alpujarras, to which Barredo secretly repaired. El Senix was furnished with an assurance, under the president's own hand, of a pardon for himself and his friends, and of an annual pension of a hundred thousand *maravedis*, in case he should bring Aben-Aboo, dead or alive, to Granada.

The interview could not be conducted so secretly but that an intimation of it reached the ears of Aben-Aboo, who resolved to repair at once to the quarters of El Senix and ascertain the truth for himself. That chief had secreted himself in a cavern in the neighborhood. Aben-Aboo took with him his faithful secretary and a small body of soldiers. On reaching the cave, he left his followers without, and placing two men at the entrance, he, with less prudence than was usual with him, passed alone into the interior.

There he found El Senix, surrounded by several of his friends and kinsmen. Aben-Aboo, in a peremptory tone, charged him with having held a secret correspondence with the enemy, and demanded the object of his late interview with Barredo. Senix did not attempt to deny the charge, but explained his motives by saying that he had been prompted only by a desire to serve his master. He had succeeded so well, he said, as to obtain from the president an assurance that if the Morisco would lay down his arms, he should receive an amnesty for the past and a liberal provision for the future.

Aben-Aboo listened scornfully to this explanation; then, muttering the word "Treachery!" he turned on his heel and moved towards the mouth of the cave, where he had left his soldiers, intending probably to command the arrest of his perfidious officer. But he had not given them, it appears, any intimation of the hostile object of his visit to El Senix; and the men, supposing it to be on some matter of ordinary business, had left the spot to see some of their friends in the neighborhood. El Senix saw that no time was to be lost. On a signal which he gave, his followers attacked the two guards at the door, one of whom was killed on the spot, while the other made his escape. They then all fell upon the unfortunate Aben-Aboo. He made a desperate defence. But though the struggle was fierce, the odds were too great for it to be long. It was soon terminated by the dastard Senix coming behind his master and with the butt-end of his musket dealing him a blow on the back of his head that brought him to the ground, where he was quickly despatched by a multitude of wounds.

The corpse was thrown out of the cavern. His followers, soon learning their master's fate, dispersed in different directions. The faithful secretary fell shortly after into the hands of the Spaniards, who, with their usual humanity in this war, caused him to be drawn and quartered.

The body of Aben-Aboo was transported to the neighborhood of Granada, where preparations were made for giving the dead chief a public entrance into the city, as if he had been still alive. The corpse was set astride on a mule and supported erect in the saddle by a wooden frame, which was concealed beneath ample robes. On one side of the body rode Barredo; on the other, El Senix, bearing the scimitar and arquebuse of his murdered master. Then followed the kinsmen and friends of the Morisco prince, with their arms by their side. A regiment of Castilian infantry and a troop of horse brought up the rear. As the procession defiled along the street of Zacatin, it was saluted by salvoes of musketry, accompanied by peals of artillery from the ancient towers of the Alhambra, while the population of Granada, with eager though silent curiosity, hurried out to gaze on the strange and ghastly spectacle.

In this way the company reached the great square of Vivarambla, where were assembled the president, the duke of Arcos, and the principal cavaliers and magistrates of the city. On coming into their presence, El Senix dismounted and, kneeling before Deza, delivered to him the arms of Aben-Aboo. He was graciously received by the president, who confirmed the assurances which had been given him of the royal favor. The miserable ceremony of a public execution was then gone through with. The head of the dead man was struck off. His body was given to the boys of the city, who, after dragging it through the streets with scoffs and imprecations, committed it to the flames. Such was one of the lessons by which the Spaniards early stamped on the minds of their children an indelible hatred of the Morisco.

The head of Aben-Aboo, enclosed in a cage, was set up over the gate which opened on the Alpujarras. There, with the face turned towards his native hills, which he had loved so well and which had witnessed his brief and disastrous reign, it remained for many a year. None ventured, by removing it, to incur the doom which an inscription on the cage denounced on the offender: "This is the head of the traitor, Aben-Aboo. Let no one take it down, under penalty of death."

Such was the sad fate of Aben-Aboo, the last of the royal line of the Omeyades who ever ruled in the Peninsula. Had he lived in the peaceful and prosperous times of the Arabian empire in Spain, he might have swayed the sceptre with as much renown as the best of his dynasty. Though the blood of the Moor flowed in his veins, he seems to have been remarkably free from some of the greatest defects in the Moorish character. He was temperate in his appetites, presenting in this respect a contrast to the gross sensuality of his predecessor. He had a lofty spirit, was cool and circumspect in his judgments, and, if he could not boast that fiery energy of character which belonged to some of his house, he had a firmness of purpose not to be intimidated by suffering or danger. Of this he gave signal proof when the most inhuman tortures could not extort from him the disclosure of the lurking-place of his friends. His qualities, as I have intimated, were such as peculiarly adapted him to a time of prosperity and peace. Unhappily, he had fallen upon evil times, when his country lay a wreck at his feet; when the people, depressed by long servitude, were broken down by the recent calamities of war; when, in short, it would not have been possible for the wisest and most warlike of his predecessors to animate them to a successful resistance against odds so overwhelming as those presented by the Spanish monarchy in the zenith of its power.

The Castilian chroniclers have endeavored to fix a deep stain on his memory by charging him with the murder of El Habaqui[1] and the refusal to execute the treaty to which he had given his sanction. But in criticizing the conduct of Aben-Aboo we must not forget the race from which he sprung, or the nature of its institutions. He was a despot, and a despot of the Oriental type. He was placed in a situation—much against his will, it may be added—which gave him absolute control over the lives and fortunes of his people. His word was their law. He passed the sentence and enforced its execution. El Habaqui he adjudged to be a traitor; and in sentencing him to the bowstring he inflicted on him only a traitor's doom.

With regard to the treaty, he spoke of himself as betrayed, saying that its provisions were not such as he had intended. And when we consider that the instrument was written in the Spanish tongue, that it was drafted by a Spaniard, finally, that the principal Morisco agent who subscribed the treaty was altogether in the Spanish interest, as the favors heaped on him without measure too plainly prove, it can hardly be doubted

[1] El Habaqui, Morisco chief who negotiated terms of surrender with Don John and was executed by Aben-Aboo.

that there were good grounds for the assertion of Aben-Aboo. From the hour of his accession he seems to have devoted himself to the great work of securing the independence of his people. He could scarcely have agreed to a treaty which was to leave the people in even a worse state than before the rebellion. From what we know of his character, we may more reasonably conclude that he was sincere when he told the Spanish envoy Palacios, who had come to press the execution of the treaty and to remind him of the royal promise of grace, that "his people might do as they listed, but, for himself, he would rather live and die a Mussulman than possess all the favors which the king of Spain could heap on him." His deeds corresponded with his words; and, desperate as was his condition, he still continued to bid defiance to the Spanish government, until he was cut off by the hand of a traitor.

The death of Aben-Aboo severed the last bond which held the remnant of the Moriscoes together. In a few years the sword, famine, and the gallows had exterminated the outcasts who still lurked in the fastnesses of the mountains. Their places were gradually occupied by Christians, drawn thither by the favorable terms which the government offered to settlers. But it was long before the wasted and famine-stricken territory could make a suitable return to the labors of the colonists. They were ignorant of the country and were altogether deficient in the agricultural skill necessary for turning its unpromising places to the best account. The Spaniard, adventurous as he was, and reckless of danger and difficulty in the pursuit of gain, was impatient of the humble drudgery required for the tillage of the soil; and many a valley and hill-side, which under the Moriscoes had bloomed with all the rich embroidery of cultivation, now relapsed into its primitive barrenness.

The exiles carried their superior skill and industry into the various provinces where they were sent. Scattered as they are, and wide apart, the presence of the Moriscoes was sure to be revealed by the more minute and elaborate culture of the soil—as the secret course of the mountain-stream is betrayed by the brighter green of the meadow. With their skill in husbandry they combined a familiarity with various kinds of handicraft, especially those requiring dexterity and fineness of execution, that was unknown to the Spaniards. As the natural result of this superiority, the products of their labor were more abundant and could be afforded at a cheaper rate than those of their neighbors. Yet this industry was exerted under every disadvantage which a most cruel legislation could impose on it. It would be hard to find in the pages of history a more flagrant example of the oppression of a conquered race than that afforded by the laws of this period in reference to the Moriscoes. The odious law of 1566, which led to the insurrection, was put in full force. By this the national songs and dances, the peculiar baths of the Moriscoes, the *fêtes* and ceremonies which had come down to them from their ancestors were interdicted under heavy penalties. By another ordinance, dated October 6th, 1572, still more cruel and absurd, they were forbidden to speak or write the Arabic, under penalty of thirty days' imprisonment in irons for the first offence, double that term for the second, and for the third a hundred lashes and four years' confinement in the galleys. By another monstrous provision in the same edict, whoever read, or even had in his possession, a work written or printed in the Arabic was to be punished with a hundred stripes and four years in the galleys. Any contract or public instrument made in that tongue was to be void, and the parties to it were condemned to receive two hundred lashes and to tug at the oar for six years.

But the most oppressive part of this terrible ordinance related to the residence of the Moriscoes. No one was allowed to change his abode, or to leave the parish or district assigned to him, without permission from the regular authorities. Whoever did so, and was apprehended beyond these limits, was to be punished with a hundred lashes and four years' imprisonment in the galleys. Should he be found within ten leagues of Granada, he was condemned, if between ten and seventeen years of age, to toil as a galley-slave the rest of his days; if above seventeen, he was sentenced to death!

On the escape of a Morisco from his limits, the hue and cry was to be raised as for the pursuit of a criminal. Even his own family were required to report his absence to the magistrate; and in case of their failure to do this, although it should be his wife or his children, says the law, they incurred the penalty of a whipping and a month's imprisonment in the common jail.

Yet in the face of these atrocious enactments we find the Moriscoes occasionally making their escape into the province of Valencia, where numbers of their countrymen were living as serfs on the estates of the great nobles, under whose powerful protection they enjoyed a degree of comfort, if not of independence, unknown to their race in other parts of the country. Some few also, finding their way to the coast, succeeded in crossing the sea to Barbary. The very severity of the law served in some measure to defeat its execution. Indeed, Philip, in more than one instance in which he deemed that the edicts pressed too heavily on his Moorish vassals, judged it expedient to mitigate the penalty, or even to dispense with it altogether—an act of leniency which seems to have found little favor with his Castilian subjects.

Yet, strange to say, under this iron system the spirits of the Moriscoes, which had been crushed by their long sufferings in the war of the rebellion, gradually rose again as they found a shelter in their new homes and resumed their former habits of quiet industry. Though deprived of their customary amusements, their *fêtes*, their songs, and their dances, though debarred from the use of the language, which they had lisped from the cradle, which embodied their national traditions and was associated with their fondest recollections—they were found to be cheerful, and even gay. They lived to a good age, and examples of longevity were found among them to which it was not easy to find a parallel among the Spaniards. The Moorish stock, like the Jewish, seems to have thriven under persecution.

One would be glad to find any authentic data for an account of the actual population at the time of their expulsion from Granada. But I have met with none. They must have been sorely thinned by the war of the insurrection and the countless woes it brought upon the country. One fact is mentioned by the chroniclers which shows that the number of the exiles must have been very considerable. The small remnant still left in Granada, with its lovely vega and the valley of Lecrin, alone furnished, we are told, over six thousand. In the places to which they were transported they continued to multiply to such an extent that the cortes of Castile, in the latter part of the century, petitioned the king not to allow the census to be taken, lest it might disclose to the Moriscoes the alarming secret of their increase of numbers. Such a petition shows, as strongly as language can show, the terror in which the Spaniards still stood of this persecuted race.

Yet the Moriscoes were scattered over the country in small and isolated masses, hemmed in all around by the Spaniards. They were transplanted to the interior, where, at a distance from the coast, they had no means of communicating with their brethren of Africa. They were without weapons of any kind; and, confined to their several districts, they had not the power of acting in concert together. There would seem to have been little to fear from a people so situated. But the weakest individual, who feels that his wrongs are too great to be forgiven, may well become an object of dread to the person who has wronged him.

The course of the government in reference to the Moriscoes was clearly a failure. It was as impolitic as it was barbarous. Nothing but the blindest fanaticism could have prevented the Spaniards from perceiving this. The object of the government had been to destroy every vestige of nationality in the conquered race. They were compelled to repudiate their ancient usage, their festivals, their religion, their language—all that gave them a separate existence as a nation. But this served only to strengthen in secret the sentiment of nationality. They were to be divorced for ever from the past. But it was the mistake of the government that it opened to them no future. Having destroyed their independence as a nation, it should have offered them the rights of citizenship and raised them to an equality with the rest of the community. Such was the policy of ancient Rome towards the nations which she conquered; and such has been that of our own country towards the countless emigrants who have thronged to our shores from so many distant lands. The Moriscoes, on the contrary, under the policy of Spain, were condemned to exist as foreigners in the country—as enemies in the midst of the community in which they were thrown. Experience had taught them prudence and dissimulation; and in all outward observances they conformed to the exactions of the law. But in secret they were as much attached to their national institutions as were their ancestors when the caliphs of Cordova ruled over half the Peninsula. The Inquisition rarely gleaned an apostate from among them to swell the horrors of an *auto da fé;*[1] but whoever recalls the facility with which, in the late rebellion, the whole population had relapsed into their ancient faith will hardly doubt that they must have still continued to be Mahometans at heart.

Thus the gulf which separated the two races grew wider and wider every day. The Moriscoes hated the Spaniards for the wrongs which they had received from them. The Spaniards hated the Moriscoes the more that they had themselves inflicted these wrongs. Their hatred was further embittered by the feeling of jealousy caused by the successful competition of their rivals in the various pursuits of gain—a circumstance which forms a fruitful theme of complaint in the petition of the cortes above noticed. The feeling of hate became in time mingled with that of fear, as the Moriscoes increased in opulence and numbers; and men are not apt to be overscrupulous in their policy towards those whom they both hate and fear.

With these evil passions rankling in their bosoms, the Spaniards were gradually prepared for the consummation of their long train of persecutions by that last act, reserved for the reign of the imbecile Philip the Third—the expulsion of the Moriscoes from the Peninsula—an

[1] Sentence given by the Inquisition.

act which deprived Spain of the most industrious and ingenious portion of her population and which must be regarded as one of the principal causes of the subsequent decline of the monarchy.

6. *Spain and the Turks: The Battle of Lepanto**

[The situation of the Moriscos in Granada was a single aspect of a larger problem, the threat of the Turks to Christendom. The Turks, in fact, were very much on the offensive. In the year of Philip II's accession, they had seized Tripoli from the Knights of St. John. In 1559 a naval force of over 12,000 Spaniards, Germans, and Italians had been surprised and destroyed by the Turks. In 1570 the Pope had appealed to Philip II to join a Holy League with Rome and Venice to assail the Turks, who were then attacking Cyprus. Philip agreed and sent Don John of Austria as commander-in-chief of the combined operation. By the time the fleet reached the eastern Mediterranean, the Turks had taken Cyprus and lay in the Bay of Lepanto near Corinth. It was there that battle was joined. This, the last great battle piece that Prescott wrote, shows that his powers of description were still great at the end of his career. In his diary he noted on 16 June, 1857: "Finished Battle of Lepanto. I hope it will smell of the ocean."]

On the third of October, Don John, without waiting longer for the missing vessels, again put to sea and

* From *Philip II*, Book V, chap. 10.

stood for the gulf of Lepanto. As the fleet swept down the Ionian Sea, it passed many a spot famous in ancient story. None, we may imagine, would be so likely to excite an interest at this time as Actium, on whose waters was fought the great naval battle of antiquity.[1] But the mariner, probably, gave little thought to the past, as he dwelt on the conflict that awaited him at Lepanto. On the fifth, a thick fog enveloped the armada and shut out every object from sight. Fortunately, the vessels met with no injury, and passing by Ithaca, the ancient home of Ulysses, they safely anchored off the eastern coast of Cephalonia. For two days their progress was thwarted by head-winds. But on the seventh, Don John, impatient of delay, again put to sea, though wind and weather were still unfavorable.

While lying off Cephalonia he had received tidings that Famagosta, the second city of Cyprus, had fallen into the hands of the enemy, and this under circumstances of unparalleled perfidy and cruelty. The place, after a defence that had cost hecatombs of lives to the besiegers, was allowed to capitulate on honorable terms. Mustapha, the Moslem commander, the same fierce chief who had conducted the siege of Malta, requested an interview at his quarters with four of the principal Venetian captains. After a short and angry conference, he ordered them all to execution. Three were beheaded. The other, a noble named Bragadino who had held the supreme command, he caused to be flayed alive in the market-place of the city. The skin of the wretched victim was then stuffed; and with this ghastly trophy dangling from the yard-arm of his galley, the brutal monster sailed back to Constantinople to receive the reward of his services from Selim. These services were great. The fall of Famagosta secured the fall of Cyprus, which thus became permanently incorporated in the Ottoman empire.

The tidings of these shocking events filled the breast of every Venetian with an inextinguishable thirst for

---

[1] A battle in 31 B.C. in which Octavian defeated Antony and Cleopatra.

vengeance. The confederates entered heartily into these feelings; and all on board of the armada were impatient for the hour that was to bring them hand to hand with the enemies of the Faith.

It was two hours before dawn, on Sunday, the memorable seventh of October, when the fleet weighed anchor. The wind had become lighter; but it was still contrary, and the galleys were indebted for their progress much more to their oars than their sails. By sunrise they were abreast of the Curzolari, a cluster of huge rocks, or rocky islets, which on the north defends the entrance of the gulf of Lepanto. The fleet moved laboriously along, while every eye was strained to catch the first glimpse of the hostile navy. At length the watch on the foretop of the *Real* called out "A sail!" and soon after declared that the whole Ottoman fleet was in sight. Several others, climbing up the rigging, confirmed his report; and in a few moments more, word was sent to the same effect by Andrew Doria, who commanded on the right. There was no longer any doubt; and Don John, ordering his pennon to be displayed at the mizzen-peak, unfurled the great standard of the League, given by the pope, and directed a gun to be fired, the signal for battle. The report, as it ran along the rocky shores, fell cheerily on the ears of the confederates, who, raising their eyes towards the consecrated banner, filled the air with their shouts.

The principal captains now came on board the *Real* to receive the last orders of the commander-in-chief. Even at this late hour there were some who ventured to intimate their doubts of the expediency of engaging the enemy in a position where he had a decided advantage. But Don John cut short the discussion. "Gentlemen," he said, "this is the time for combat, not for counsel." He then continued the dispositions he was making for the attack.

He had already given to each commander of a galley written instructions as to the manner in which the line of battle was to be formed in case of meeting the enemy. The armada was now disposed in that order. It extended on a front of three miles. Far on the right, a squadron of sixty-four galleys was commanded by the Genoese admiral, Andrew Doria—a name of terror to the Moslems. The centre, or battle, as it was called, consisting of sixty-three galleys, was led by John of Austria, who was supported on the one side by Colonna, the captain-general of the pope, and on the other by the Venetian captain-general, Veniero. Immediately in the rear was the galley of the Grand Commander Requesens, who still remained near the person of his former pupil; though a difference which arose between them on the voyage, fortunately now healed, showed that the young commander-in-chief was wholly independent of his teacher in the art of war.

The left wing was commanded by the noble Venetian Barbarigo, whose vessels stretched along the Aetolian shore, to which he approached as near as, in his ignorance of the coast, he dared to venture, so as to prevent his being turned by the enemy. Finally, the reserve, consisting of thirty-five galleys, was given to the brave marquis of Santa Cruz, with directions to act in any quarter where he thought his presence most needed. The smaller craft, some of which had now arrived, seem to have taken little part in the action, which was thus left to the galleys.

Each commander was to occupy so much space with his galley as to allow room for manoeuvring it to advantage, and yet not enough to allow the enemy to break the line. He was directed to single out his adversary, to close with him at once, and board as soon as possible. The beaks of the galleys were pronounced to be a hindrance rather than a help in the action. They were rarely strong enough to resist a shock from an antagonist, and they much interfered with the working and firing of the guns. Don John had the beak of his vessel cut away. The example was followed throughout the fleet and, as it is said, with eminently good effect. It may seem strange that this discovery should have been reserved for the crisis of a battle.

When the officers had received their last instructions, they returned to their respective vessels; and Don John, going on board of a light frigate, passed rapidly through the part of the armada lying on his right, while he commanded Requesens to do the same with the vessels on his left. His object was to feel the temper of his men and to rouse their mettle by a few words of encouragement. The Venetians he reminded of their recent injuries. The hour for vengeance, he told them, had arrived. To the Spaniards and other confederates he said: "You have come to fight the battle of the Cross; to conquer or to die. But whether you are to die or conquer, do your duty this day, and you will secure a glorious immortality." His words were received with a burst of enthusiasm which went to the heart of the commander and assured him that he could rely on his men in the hour of trial. On returning to his vessel, he saw Veniero on his quarterdeck; and they exchanged salutations in as friendly a manner as if no difference had existed between them. At this solemn hour both these brave men were willing to forget all personal animosity in a common feeling of devotion to the great cause in which they were engaged.

The Ottoman fleet came on slowly and with difficulty. For, strange to say, the wind, which had hitherto been adverse to the Christians, after lulling for a time, suddenly shifted to the opposite quarter and blew in the face of the enemy. As the day advanced, moreover, the sun, which had shone in the eyes of the confederates, gradually shot its rays into those of the Moslems. Both circumstances were of good omen to the Christians, and the first was regarded as nothing short of a direct interposition of Heaven. Thus ploughing its way along, the Turkish armament, as it came more into view, showed itself in greater strength than had been anticipated by the allies. It consisted of nearly two hundred and fifty royal galleys, most of them of the largest class, besides a number of smaller vessels in the rear, which, like those of the allies, appear scarcely to have come into action. The men on board, of every description, were computed at not less than a hundred and twenty thousand. The galleys spread out, as usual with the Turks, in the form of a regular half-moon, covering a wider extent of surface than the combined fleets, which they somewhat exceeded in number. They presented, indeed, as they drew nearer, a magnificent array, with their gilded and gaudily-painted prows and their myriads of pennons and streamers fluttering gaily in the breeze; while the rays of the morning sun glanced on the polished scimitars of Damascus and on the superb aigrettes of jewels which sparkled in the turbans of the Ottoman chiefs.

In the centre of the extended line, and directly opposite to the station occupied by the captain-general of the League, was the huge galley of Ali Pasha. The right of the armada was commanded by Mahomet Sirocco, viceroy of Egypt, a circumspect as well as courageous leader; the left, by Uluch Ali, dey of Algiers, the redoubtable corsair of the Mediterranean. Ali Pasha had experienced a difficulty like that of Don John, as several of his officers had strongly urged the inexpediency of engaging so formidable an armament as that of the allies. But Ali, like his rival, was young and ambitious. He had been sent by his master to fight the enemy; and no remonstrances, not even those of Mahomet Sirocco, for whom he had great respect, could turn him from his purpose.

He had, moreover, received intelligence that the allied fleet was much inferior in strength to what it proved. In this error he was fortified by the first appearance of the Christians; for the extremity of their left wing, commanded by Barbarigo, stretching behind the Aetolian shore, was hidden from his view. As he drew nearer and saw the whole extent of the Christian lines, it is said his countenance fell. If so, he still did not abate one jot of his resolution. He spoke to those around him, with the same confidence as before, of the result of the battle. He urged his rowers to strain every nerve. Ali was a man of more humanity in his nature than often belonged to his nation. His galley-slaves were all, or nearly all, Christian captives; and he addressed them in this brief and pithy manner: "If your countrymen are to win this day, Allah give you the benefit of it: yet, if I win it, you shall certainly have your freedom. If you feel that I do well by you, do then the like by me."

As the Turkish admiral drew nearer, he made a change

in his order of battle, by separating his wings farther from his centre, thus conforming to the dispositions of the allies. Before he had come within cannon-shot, he fired a gun by way of challenge to his enemy. It was answered by another from the galley of John of Austria. A second gun discharged by Ali was promptly replied to by the Christian commander. The distance between the two fleets was now rapidly diminishing. At this solemn moment a death-like silence reigned throughout the armament of the confederates. Men seemed to hold their breath, as if absorbed in the expectation of some great catastrophe. The day was magnificent. A light breeze, still adverse to the Turks, played on the waters, somewhat fretted by the contrary winds. It was nearly noon; and as the sun, mounting through a cloudless sky, rose to the zenith, he seemed to pause, as if to look down on the beautiful scene, where the multitude of galleys, moving over the water, showed like a holiday spectacle rather than a preparation for mortal combat.

The illusion was soon dispelled by the fierce yells which rose on the air from the Turkish armada. It was the customary war-cry with which the Moslems entered into battle. Very different was the scene on board of the Christian galleys. Don John might be there seen, armed *cap-à-pie*, standing on the prow of the *Real*, anxiously awaiting the conflict. In this conspicuous position, kneeling down, he raised his eyes to heaven and humbly prayed that the Almighty would be with his people on that day. His example was followed by the whole fleet. Officers and men, all prostrating themselves on their knees and turning their eyes to the consecrated banner which floated from the *Real*, put up a petition like that of their commander. They then received absolution from the priests, of whom there were some in every vessel; and each man, as he rose to his feet, gathered new strength, as he felt assured that the Lord of Hosts would fight on his side.

When the foremost vessels of the Turks had come within cannon-shot, they opened their fire on the Christians. The firing soon ran along the whole of the Turkish line and was kept up without interruption as it advanced. Don John gave orders for trumpet and atabal to sound the signal for action; which was followed by the simultaneous discharge of such of the guns in the combined fleet as could be brought to bear on the enemy. The Spanish commander had caused the *galeazzas*, those mammoth war-ships, to be towed half a mile ahead of the fleet, where they might intercept the advance of the Turks. As the latter came abreast of them, the huge galleys delivered their broadsides right and left, and their heavy ordnance produced a startling effect. Ali Pasha gave orders for his galleys to open their line and pass on either side, without engaging these monsters of the deep, of which he had had no experience. Even so their heavy guns did considerable damage to several of the nearest vessels and created some confusion in the pacha's line of battle. They were, however, but unwieldy craft, and having accomplished their object, seem to have taken no further part in the combat.

The action began on the left wing of the allies, which Mahomet Sirocco was desirous of turning. This had been anticipated by Barbarigo, the Venetian admiral, who commanded in that quarter. To prevent it, as we have seen, he lay with his vessels as near the coast as he dared. Sirocco, better acquainted with the soundings, saw there was space enough for him to pass, and darting by with all the speed that oars could give him, he succeeded in doubling on his enemy. Thus placed between two fires, the extreme of the Christian left fought at terrible disadvantage. No less than eight galleys went to the bottom, and several others were captured. The brave Barbarigo, throwing himself into the heat of the fight, without availing himself of his defensive armor, was pierced in the eye by an arrow and, reluctant to leave the glory of the field to another, was borne to his cabin. The combat still continued with unabated fury on the part of the Venetians. They fought like men who felt that the war was theirs and who were animated not only by the thirst for glory but for revenge.

Far on the Christian right a manoeuvre similar to that so successfully executed by Sirocco was attempted by Uluch Ali, the dey of Algiers. Profiting by his superiority in numbers, he endeavored to turn the right wing of the confederates. It was in this quarter that Andrew Doria commanded. He had foreseen this movement of his enemy, and he succeeded in foiling it. It was a trial of skill between the two most accomplished seamen in the Mediterranean. Doria extended his line so far to the right, indeed, to prevent being surrounded that Don John was obliged to remind him that he left the centre too much exposed. His dispositions were so far unfortunate for himself that his own line was thus weakened and afforded some vulnerable points to his assailant. These were soon detected by the eagle eye of Uluch Ali; and, like the king of birds swooping on his prey, he fell on some galleys separated by a considerable interval from their companions and, sinking more than one, carried off the great *Capitana* of Malta in triumph as his prize.

While the combat opened thus disastrously to the allies both on the right and on the left, in the centre they may be said to have fought with doubtful fortune. Don John had led his division gallantly forward. But the object on which he was intent was an encounter with Ali Pasha, the foe most worthy of his sword. The Turkish commander had the same combat no less at heart. The galleys of both were easily recognized, not only from their position but from their superior size and richer decoration. The one, moreover, displayed the holy banner of the League; the other, the great Ottoman standard. This, like the ancient standard of the caliphs, was held sacred in its character. It was covered with texts from the Koran, emblazoned in letters of gold, and had the name of Allah inscribed upon it no less than twenty-eight thousand nine hundred times. It was the banner of the sultan, having passed from father to son since the foundation of the imperial dynasty, and was never seen in the field unless the grand seigneur or his lieutenant was there in person.

Both the chiefs urged on their rowers to the top of their speed. Their galleys soon shot ahead of the rest of the line, driven through the boiling surges as by the force of a tornado, and closed with a shock that made every timber crack and the two vessels to quiver to their very keels. So powerful, indeed, was the impetus they received that the pasha's galley, which was considerably the larger and loftier of the two, was thrown so far upon its opponent that the prow reached the fourth bench of rowers. As soon as the vessels were disengaged from each other, and those on board had recovered from the shock, the work of death began. Don John's chief strength consisted in some three hundred Spanish arquebusiers, culled from the flower of his infantry. Ali, on the other hand, was provided with an equal number of janizaries.[1] He was followed by a smaller vessel, in which two hundred more were stationed as a *corps de réserve*. He had, moreover, a hundred archers on board. The bow was still as much in use with the Turks as with the other Moslems.

The pacha opened at once on his enemy a terrible fire of cannon and musketry. It was returned with equal spirit and much more effect; for the Turks were observed to shoot over the heads of the adversaries. The Moslem galley was unprovided with the defences which protected the sides of the Spanish vessels; and the troops crowded together on the lofty prow presented an easy mark to their enemy's balls. But, though numbers of them fell at every discharge, their places were soon supplied by those in reserve. They were enabled, therefore, to keep up an incessant fire, which wasted the strength of the Spaniards; and, as both Christians and Mussulman fought with indomitable spirit, it seemed doubtful to which side victory would incline.

The affair was made more complicated by the entrance of other parties into the conflict. Both Ali and Don John were supported by some of the most valiant captains in their fleets. Next to the Spanish commander, as we have seen, were Colonna and the veteran Veniero, who, at the age of seventy-six, performed feats of arms worthy of a paladin of romance. In this way a little squadron of combatants gathered round the principal leaders, who sometimes found themselves assailed by several enemies

[1] Soldiers of the Turkish foot-guards.

at the same time. Still the chiefs did not lose sight of one another; but, beating off their inferior foes as well as they could, each, refusing to loosen his hold, clung with mortal grasp to his antagonist.

Thus the fight raged along the whole extent of the entrance to the gulf of Lepanto. The volumes of vapor rolling heavily over the waters effectually shut out from sight whatever was passing at any considerable distance, unless when a fresher breeze dispelled the smoke for a moment, or the flashes of the heavy guns threw a transient gleam on the dark canopy of battle. If the eye of the spectator could have penetrated the cloud of smoke that enveloped the combatants and have embraced the whole scene at a glance, he would have perceived them broken up into small detachments, separately engaged one with another, independently of the rest, and indeed ignorant of all that was doing in other quarters. The contest exhibited few of those large combinations and skilful manoeuvres to be expected in a great naval encounter. It was rather an assemblage of petty actions, resembling those on land. The galleys' grappling together presented a level arena, on which soldier and galley-slave fought hand to hand, and the fate of the engagement was generally decided by boarding. As in most hand-to-hand contests, there was an enormous waste of life. The decks were loaded with corpses, Christian and Moslem lying promiscuously together in the embrace of death. Instances are recorded where every man on board was slain or wounded. It was a ghastly spectacle, where blood flowed in rivulets down the sides of the vessels, staining the waters of the gulf for miles around.

It seemed as if a hurricane had swept over the sea and covered it with the wreck of the noble armaments which a moment before were so proudly riding on its bosom. Little had they now to remind one of their late magnificent array, with their hulls battered, their masts and spars gone or splintered by the shot, their canvas cut into shreds and floating wildly on the breeze, while thousands of wounded and drowning men were clinging to the floating fragments and calling piteously for help. Such was the wild uproar which succeeded the Sabbath-like stillness that two hours before had reigned over these beautiful solitudes.

The left wing of the confederates, commanded by Barbarigo, had been sorely pressed by the Turks, as we have seen, at the beginning of the fight. Barbarigo himself had been mortally wounded. His line had been turned. Several of his galleys had been sunk. But the Venetians gathered courage from despair. By incredible efforts they succeeded in beating off their enemies. They became the assailants in their turn. Sword in hand, they carried one vessel after another. The Capuchin was seen in the thickest of the fight, waving aloft his crucifix and leading the boarders to the assault. The Christian galley-slaves, in some instances, broke their fetters and joined their countrymen against their masters. Fortunately, the vessel of Mahomet Sirocco, the Moslem admiral, was sunk; and though extricated from the water himself, it was only to perish by the sword of his conqueror, Giovanni Contarini. The Venetian could find in his heart no mercy for the Turk.

The fall of their commander gave the final blow to his followers. Without further attempt to prolong the fight, they fled before the avenging swords of the Venetians. Those nearest the land endeavored to escape by running their vessels ashore, where they abandoned them as prizes to the Christians. Yet many of the fugitives, before gaining the land, perished miserably in the waves. Barbarigo, the Venetian admiral, who was still lingering in agony, heard the tidings of the enemy's defeat, and, uttering a few words expressive of his gratitude to Heaven, which had permitted him to see this hour, he breathed his last.

During this time the combat had been going forward in the centre between the two commanders-in-chief, Don John and Ali Pasha, whose galleys blazed with an incessant fire of artillery and musketry that enveloped them like "a martyr's robe of flames." The parties fought with equal spirit though not with equal fortune. Twice the Spaniards had boarded their enemy, and both times they had been repulsed with loss. Still, their superiority in the use of fire-arms would have given them a decided advantage over their opponents if the loss they had inflicted had not been speedily repaired by fresh reinforcements. More than once the contest between the two chieftains was interrupted by the arrival of others to take part in the fray. They soon, however, returned to each other, as if unwilling to waste their strength on a meaner enemy. Through the whole engagement both commanders exposed themselves to danger as freely as any common soldier. In such a contest even Philip must have admitted that it would be difficult for his brother to find, with honor, a place of safety. Don John received a wound in the foot. It was a slight one, however, and he would not allow it to be dressed till the action was over.

Again his men were mustered, and a third time the trumpets sounded to the attack. It was more successful than the preceding. The Spaniards threw themselves boldly into the Turkish galley. They were met with the same spirit as before by the janizaries. Ali Pasha led them on. Unfortunately, at this moment he was struck in the head by a musket-ball and stretched senseless in the gangway. His men fought worthily of their ancient renown. But they missed the accustomed voice of their commander. After a short but ineffectual struggle against the fiery impetuosity of the Spaniards, they were overpowered and threw down their arms. The decks were loaded with the bodies of the dead and the dying. Beneath those was discovered the Turkish commander-in-chief, severely wounded, but perhaps not mortally. He was drawn forth by some Castillian soldiers, who, recognizing his person, would at once have despatched him. But the disabled chief, having rallied from the first effects of his wound, had sufficient presence of mind to divert them from their purpose by pointing out the place below where he had deposited his money and jewels; and they hastened to profit by the disclosure before the treasure should fall into the hands of their comrades.

Ali was not so successful with another soldier, who came up soon after, brandishing his sword and preparing to plunge it into the body of the prostrate commander. It was in vain that the latter endeavored to turn the ruffian from his purpose. He was a convict, one of those galley-slaves whom Don John had caused to be unchained from the oar and furnished with arms. He could not believe that any treasure would be worth so much as the head of the pacha. Without further hesitation, he dealt him a blow which severed it from his shoulders. Then, returning to his galley, he laid the bloody-trophy before Don John. But he had miscalculated on his recompense. His commander gazed on it with a look of pity mingled with horror. He may have thought of the generous conduct of Ali to his Christian captives, and have felt that he deserved a better fate. He coldly inquired "of what use such a present could be to him"; and then ordered it to be thrown into the sea. Far from the order being obeyed, it is said the head was stuck on a pike and raised aloft on board of the captured galley. At the same time the banner of the Crescent was pulled down; while that of the Cross, run up in its place, proclaimed the downfall of the pacha.

The sight of the sacred ensign was welcomed by the Christians with a shout of "Victory!" which rose high above the din of battle. The tidings of the death of Ali soon passed from mouth to mouth, giving fresh heart to the confederates, but falling like a knell on the ears of the Moslems. Their confidence was gone. Their fire slackened. Their efforts grew weaker and weaker. They were too far from shore to seek an asylum there, like their comrades on the right. They had no resource but to prolong the combat or to surrender. Most preferred the latter. Many vessels were carried by boarding, others were sunk by the victorious Christians. Ere four hours had elapsed, the centre, like the right wing, of the Moslems might be said to be annihilated.

Still the fight was lingering on the right of the confederates, where, it will be remembered, Uluch Ali, the Algerine chief, had profited by Doria's error in extending his line so far as to greatly weaken it. Uluch Ali, attacking it on its most vulnerable quarter, had succeeded, as we have seen, in capturing and destroying several vessels, and would have inflicted still heavier losses on his enemy had it not been for the seasonable succor received from the marquis of Santa Cruz. This brave officer, who commanded the reserve, had already been of much service to Don John when the *Real* was assailed by several Turkish galleys at once during his combat with Ali Pasha; for at this juncture the marquis of Santa Cruz arriving and beating off the assailants, one of whom he afterwards captured, enabled the commander-in-chief to resume his engagement with the rebels.

No sooner did Santa Cruz learn the critical situation of Doria than, supported by Cardona, "general" of the Sicilian squadron, he pushed forward to his relief. Dashing into the midst of the *mêlée*, the two commanders fell like a thunderbolt on the Algerine galleys. Few attempted to withstand the shock. But in their haste to avoid it they were encountered by Doria and his Genoese galleys. Thus beset on all sides, Uluch Ali was compelled to abandon his prizes and provide for his own safety by flight. He cut adrift the Maltese *Capitana*, which he had lashed to his stern and on which three hundred corpses attested the desperate character of her defence. As tidings reached him of the discomfiture of the centre and of the death of Ali Pasha, he felt that nothing remained but to make the best of his way from the fatal scene of action and save as many of his own ships as he could. And there were no ships in the Turkish fleet superior to his, or manned by men under more perfect discipline. For they were the famous corsairs of the Mediterranean, who had been rocked from infancy on its waters.

Throwing out his signals for retreat, the Algerine was soon to be seen, at the head of his squadron, standing towards the north, under as much canvas as remained to him after the battle and urged forward through the deep by the whole strength of his oarsmen. Doria and Santa Cruz followed quickly in his wake. But he was borne on the wings of the wind and soon distanced his pursuers. Don John, having disposed of his own assailant, was coming to the support of Doria and now joined in the pursuit of the viceroy. A rocky headland, stretching far into the sea, lay in the path of the fugitive; and his enemies hoped to intercept him there. Some few of his vessels were stranded on the rocks. But the rest, near forty in number, standing more boldly out to sea, safely doubled the promontory. Then, quickening their flight, they gradually faded from the horizon, their white sails, the last thing visible, showing in the distance like a flock of Arctic sea-fowl on their way to their native homes. The confederates explained the inferior sailing of their own galleys on this occasion by the circumstance of their rowers, who had been allowed to bear arms in the fight, being crippled by their wounds.

The battle had lasted more than four hours. The sky, which had been almost without a cloud through the day, began now to be overcast and showed signs of a coming storm. Before seeking a place of shelter for himself and his prizes, Don John reconnoitred the scene of action. He met with several vessels too much damaged for further service. These, mostly belonging to the enemy, after saving what was of any value on board, he ordered to be burnt. He selected the neighboring port of Petala, as affording the most secure and accessible harbor for the night. Before he had arrived there, the tempest began to mutter and darkness was on the water. Yet the darkness rendered only more visible the blazing wrecks, which, sending up streams of fire mingled with showers of spark, looked like volcanoes on the deep.

*7. The Administration of Philip II**

[*Although Prescott was never to complete* Philip II, *he left in it a careful and interesting picture of the monarch at work. The character of the Spanish monarch seemed to him a dominant principle of the history of sixteenth-century Spain, and he pictured in his mind the king, "the master spirit," buried deep in the Escorial, unseen by his subjects but watching over the lines of communication running out from his capital to the furthest quarters of the earth. Philip was called by contemporaries the king of paper because of his immense and laborious paper work. In this excerpt, Prescott gives an account of the monarch and of his approach to government.*]

Philip, unlike most of his predecessors, rarely took his seat in the council of state. It was his maxim that his ministers would more freely discuss measures in the absence of their master than when he was there to overawe them. The course he adopted was for a *consulta*, or a committee of two or three members, to wait on him in his cabinet and report to him the proceedings of the council. He more commonly, especially in the later years of his reign, preferred to receive a full report of the discussion, written so as to leave an ample margin for his own commentaries. These were eminently characteristic of the man and were so minute as usually to cover several sheets of paper. Philip had a reserved and unsocial temper. He preferred to work alone, in the seclusion of his closet, rather than in the presence of

* From *Philip II*, Book VI, chap. 1.

others. This may explain the reason, in part, why he seemed so much to prefer writing to talking. Even with his private secretaries, who were always near at hand, he chose to communicate by writing; and they had as large a mass of his autograph notes in their possession as if the correspondence had been carried on from different parts of the kingdom. His thoughts too—at any rate his words—came slowly; and by writing he gained time for the utterance of them.

Philip has been accused of indolence. As far as the body was concerned, such an accusation was well founded. Even when young, he had no fondness for the robust and chivalrous sports of the age. He never, like his father, conducted military expeditions in person. He thought it wiser to follow the example of his great-grandfather, Ferdinand the Catholic, who stayed at home and sent his generals to command his armies. As little did he like to travel—forming too in this respect a great contrast to the emperor. He had been years on the throne before he made a visit to his great southern capital, Seville. It was a matter of complaint in cortes that he thus withdrew himself from the eyes of his subjects. The only sport he cared for—not by any means to excess—was shooting with his gun or his crossbow such game as he could find in his own grounds at the Wood of Segovia, or Aranjuez, or some other of his pleasant country seats, none of them at a great distance from Madrid.

On a visit to such places he would take with him as large a heap of papers as if he were a poor clerk earning his bread; and after the fatigues of the chase he would retire to his cabinet and refresh himself with his despatches. It would indeed be a great mistake to charge him with sluggishness of mind. He was content to toil for hours, and long into the night, at his solitary labors. No expression of weariness or of impatience was known to escape him. A characteristic anecdote is told of him in regard to this. Having written a despatch, late at night, to be sent on the following morning, he handed it to his secretary to throw some sand over it. This functionary, who happened to be dozing, suddenly roused himself and, snatching up the inkstand, emptied it on the paper. The king, coolly remarking that "it would have been better to use the sand," set himself down, without any complaint, to rewrite the whole of the letter. A prince so much addicted to the pen, we may well believe, must have left a large amount of autograph materials behind him. Few monarchs, in point of fact, have done so much in this way to illustrate the history of their reigns. Fortunate would it have been for the historian who was to profit by it, if the royal composition had been somewhat less diffuse and the handwriting somewhat more legible.

Philip was an economist of time and regulated the distribution of it with great precision. In the morning he gave audience to foreign ambassadors. He afterwards heard mass. After mass came dinner, in his father's fashion. But dinner was not an affair with Philip of so much moment as it was with Charles. He was exceedingly temperate both in eating and drinking, and not infrequently had his physician at his side to warn him against any provocative of the gout—the hereditary disease which at a very early period had begun to affect his health. After a light repast, he gave audience to such of his subjects as desired to present their memorials. He received the petitioners graciously and listened to all they had to say with patience—for that was his virtue. But his countenance was exceedingly grave—which, in truth, was its natural expression; and there was a reserve in his deportment which made the boldest feel ill at ease in his presence. On such occasions he would say, "Compose yourself," a recommendation that had not always the tranquillizing effect intended. Once when a papal nuncio forgot, in his confusion, the address he had prepared, the king coolly remarked, "If you will bring it in writing, I will read it myself, and expedite your business." It was natural that men of even the highest rank should be overawed in the presence of a monarch who held the destinies of many millions in his hands and who surrounded himself with a veil of mystery which the most cunning politician could not penetrate.

The reserve so noticeable in his youth increased with age. He became more difficult to access. His public audiences were much less frequent. In the summer he would escape from them altogether by taking refuge in some one of his country-places. His favorite retreat was his palace-monastery of the Escorial, then slowly rising under his patronage and affording him an occupation congenial with his taste. He seems, however, to have sought the country not so much from the love of its beauties as for the retreat it afforded him from the town. When in the latter, he rarely showed himself to the public eye, going abroad chiefly in a closed carriage and driving late so as to return to the city after dark.

Thus he lived in solitude even in the heart of the capital, knowing much less of men from his own observation than from the reports that were made to him. In availing himself of these sources of information he was indefatigable. He caused a statistical survey of Spain to be prepared for his own use. It was a work of immense labor, embracing a vast amount of curious details, such as were rarely brought together in those days. He kept his spies at the principal European courts, who furnished him with intelligence; and he was as well acquainted with what was passing in England and in France as if he had resided on the spot. We have seen how well he knew the smallest details of the proceedings in the Netherlands, sometimes even better than Margaret herself. He employed similar means to procure information that might be of service in making appointments to ecclesiastical and civil office.

In his eagerness for information, his ear was ever open to accusations against his ministers, which, as they were sure to be locked up in his own bosom, were not slow in coming to him. This filled his mind with suspicions. He waited till time had proved their truth, treating the object of them with particular favor till the hour of vengeance had arrived. The reader will not have forgotten the terrible saying of Philip's own historian, "His dagger followed close upon his smile."

Even to the ministers in whom Philip appeared most

to confide he often gave but half his confidence. Instead of frankly furnishing them with a full statement of facts, he sometimes made so imperfect a disclosure that, when his measures came to be taken, his counsellors were surprised to find of how much they had been kept in ignorance. When he communicated to them any foreign despatches, he would not scruple to alter the original, striking out some passages and inserting others, so as best to serve his purpose. The copy, in this garbled form, was given to the council. Such was the case with a letter of Don John of Austria, containing an account of the troubles of Genoa, the original of which, with its numerous alterations in the royal handwriting, still exists in the Archives of Simancas.

But, though Philip's suspicious nature prevented him from entirely trusting his ministers—though with chilling reserve he kept at a distance even those who approached him nearest—he was kind, even liberal, to his servants, was not capricious in his humors, and seldom, if ever, gave way to those sallies of passion so common in princes clothed with absolute power. He was patient to the last degree and rarely changed his ministers without good cause. Ruy Gomez was not the only courtier who continued in the royal service to the end of his days.

Philip was of a careful or, to say the truth, of a frugal disposition, which he may well have inherited from his father; though this did not, as with his father in later life, degenerate into parsimony. The beginning of his reign, indeed, was distinguished by some acts of uncommon liberality. One of these occurred at the close of Alva's campaigns in Italy, when the king presented that commander with a hundred and fifty thousand ducats, greatly to the discontent of the emperor. This was contrary to his usual policy. As he grew older, and the expenses of government pressed more heavily on him, he became more economical. Yet those who served him had no reason, like the emperor's servants, to complain of their master's madness. It was observed, however, that he was slow to recompense those who served him until they had proved themselves worthy of it. Still, it was a man's own fault, says a contemporary, if he was not well paid for his services in the end.

In one particular he indulged in a most lavish expenditure. This was his household. It was formed on the Burgundian model—the most stately and magnificent in Europe. Its peculiarity consisted in the number and quality of the members who composed it. The principal officers were nobles of the highest rank, who frequently held posts of great consideration in the state. Thus, the duke of Alva was chief major-domo; the prince of Eboli was first gentlemen of the bedchamber; the duke of Feria was captain of the Spanish guard. There was the grand equerry, the grand huntsman, the chief muleteer, and a host of officers, some of whom were designated by menial titles, though nobles and cavaliers of family. There were forty pages, sons of the most illustrious houses in Castile. The whole household amounted to no less than fifteen hundred persons. The king's guard consisted of three hundred men, one-third of whom were Spaniards, one-third Flemings, and the remainder Germans.

The queen had also her establishment on the same scale. She had twenty-six ladies-in-waiting and, among other functionaries, no less than four physicians to watch over her health.

The annual cost of the royal establishment amounted to fully two hundred thousand florins. The cortes earnestly remonstrated against this useless prodigality, beseeching the king to place his household on the modest scale to which the monarchs of Castile had been accustomed. And it seems singular that one usually so averse to extravagance and pomp should have so recklessly indulged in them here. It was one of those inconsistencies which we sometimes meet with in private life, when a man habitually careful of his expenses indulges himself in some which taste or, as in this case, early habits have made him regard as indispensable. The emperor had been careful to form the household of his son, when very young, on the Burgundian model; and Philip, thus early trained, probably regarded it as essential to the royal dignity.

The king did not affect an ostentation in his dress corresponding with that of his household. This seemed to be suited to the sober-colored livery of his own feelings, and was almost always of black velvet or satin with shoes of the former material. He wore a cap, garnished with plumes after the Spanish fashion. He used few ornaments, scarce any but the rich jewel of the Golden Fleece, which hung from his neck. But in his attire he was scrupulously neat, says the Venetian diplomatist who tells these particulars; and he changed his dress for a new one every month, giving away his cast-off suits to his attendants.

It was a capital defect in Philip's administration that his love of power and his distrust of others made him desire to do everything himself—even those things which could be done much better by his ministers. As he was slow in making up his own opinions, and seldom acted without first ascertaining those of his council, we may well understand the mischievous consequences of such delay. Loud were the complaints of private suitors, who saw month after month pass away without an answer to their petitions. The state suffered no less, as the wheels of government seemed actually to stand still under the accummulated pressure of the public business. Even when a decision did come, it often came too late to be of service; for the circumstances which led to it had wholly changed. Of this the reader has seen more than one example in the Netherlands. The favorite saying of Philip, that "time and he were a match for any other two," was a sad mistake. The time he demanded was his ruin. It was in vain that Granvelle, who, at a later day, came to Castile to assume the direction of affairs endeavored, in his courtly language, to convince the king of his error, telling him that no man could bear up under such a load of business, which sooner or later must destroy his health, perhaps his life.

A letter addressed to the king by his grand almoner, Don Luis Manrique, told the truth in plainer terms, such as had not often reached the royal ear. "Your majesty's subjects everywhere complain," he says, "of your manner of doing business—sitting all day long over your papers, from your desire, as they intimate, to seclude yourself from the world, and from a want of confidence in your ministers. Hence such interminable delays as fill the soul of every suitor with despair. Your subjects are discontented that you refuse to take your seat in the council of state. The Almighty," he adds, "did not send kings into the world to spend their days in reading or writing, or even in meditation and prayer"—in which Philip was understood to pass much of his time—"but to serve as public oracles, to which all may resort for answers. If any sovereign have received this grace, it is your majesty; and the greater sin, therefore, if you do not give free access to all." One may be surprised to find that language such as this was addressed to a prince like Philip the Second, and that he should have borne it so patiently. But in this the king resembled his father. Churchmen and jesters—of which latter he had usually one or two in attendance—were privileged persons at his court. In point of fact, the homilies of the one had as little effect as the jests of the other.

ABOUT THE EDITORS

Hugh R. Trevor-Roper, general editor of *The Great Histories Series,* is the distinguished Regius Professor of Modern History at Oxford University. He is probably most well known to American readers for his book *The Last Days of Hitler,* which is a classic in the field of modern German history and was the result of official investigations carried out by Professor Trevor-Roper at the behest of British Intelligence in an attempt to unshroud the mystery surrounding the dictator's fate. The book has already been translated into twenty languages. Professor Trevor-Roper is a specialist in sixteenth- and seventeenth-century history and has published several other notable works: *Archbishop Laud, Man and Events.* He has contributed numerous articles on political and historical subjects to the journals and is familiar to American readers of *The New York Times Magazine* and *Horizon.*

Roger Howell, the editor of this volume, is currently Assistant Professor of History at Bowdoin College, where he specializes in Early Modern History. He holds the degree of Doctor of Philosophy from St. John's College, Oxford University, which he attended as a Rhodes scholar. His published articles include "The World of the Aztecs and the Incas" and "The Spaniards and the Conflict of Ideas," as well as numerous articles on the religious and intellectual history of the sixteenth and seventeenth centuries.

Index

Index

INDEX